Memorial Book of Shebreshin
(Szczebrzeszyn, Poland)

Translation of
Sefer zikaron le-kehilat Shebreshin

Memorial Book to the Community of Shebreshin

Original Yizkor Book Edited by: Dov Shuval,
Association of Former Inhabitants
of Shebreshin in Israel and the Diaspora
Published in Haifa, 1984

Published by JewishGen

**An Affiliate of the Museum of Jewish Heritage—A Living Memorial to the Holocaust
New York**

Memorial Book of Shebreshin
(Szczebrzeszyn, Poland)
Translation of: *Sefer Shebreshin:*
Sefer zikaron le-kehilat Shebreshin
Memorial Book to the Community of Shebreshin

Copyright © 2020 by JewishGen, Inc.
All rights reserved.
First Printing: November 2020, Heshvan 5781

Editor of the original Yizkor Book: Dov Shuval
Association of Former Inhabitants of Shebreshin in Israel and the Diaspora
Published in Haifa, 1984
Layout: Jonathan Wind
Cover Design: Jan R. Fine
Name Indexing: Bena Shklyanoy

Published by JewishGen, Inc.
An Affiliate of the Museum of Jewish Heritage
A Living Memorial to the Holocaust
36 Battery Place, New York, NY 10280

JewishGen, Inc. is not responsible for inaccuracies or omissions in the original work and makes no representations regarding the accuracy of this translation. Digital images of the original book's contents can be seen online at the New York Public Library website.

The mission of the JewishGen organization is to produce a translation of the original work, and we cannot verify the accuracy of statements or alter facts cited.

Printed in the United States of America by Lightning Source, Inc.

Library of Congress Control Number (LCCN): 2020947613
ISBN: 978-1-939561-95-4 (hard cover: 542 pages, alk. paper)

Cover Credits:

Front Cover: Drawing is from page 142 in the original Yizkor Book

Back Cover: Photograph of synagogue is from page 109 in original Yizkor Book.

JewishGen and the Yizkor Books in Print Project

This book has been published by the **Yizkor Books in Print Project**, as part of the **Yizkor Book Project** of JewishGen, Inc.

JewishGen, Inc. is a non-profit organization founded in 1987 as a resource for Jewish genealogy. Its website [www.jewishgen.org] serves as an international clearinghouse and resource center to assist individuals who are researching the history of their Jewish families and the places where they lived. JewishGen provides databases, facilitates discussion groups, and coordinates projects relating to Jewish genealogy and the history of the Jewish people. In 2003, JewishGen became an affiliate of the **Museum of Jewish Heritage — A Living Memorial to the Holocaust** in New York.

The **JewishGen Yizkor Book Project** was organized to make more widely known the existence of Yizkor (Memorial) Books written by survivors and former residents of various Jewish communities throughout the world. Later, volunteers connected to the different destroyed communities began cooperating to have these books translated from the original language — usually Hebrew or Yiddish — into English, thus enabling a wider audience to have access to the valuable information contained within them. As each chapter of these books was translated, it was posted on the JewishGen website and made available to the general public.

The **Yizkor Books in Print Project** began in 2011 as an initiative to print and publish Yizkor Books that had been fully translated, so that hard copies would be available for purchase by the descendants of these communities and also by scholars, universities, synagogues, libraries, and museums.

These Yizkor books have been produced almost entirely through the volunteer effort of researchers from around the world, assisted by donations from private individuals. The books are printed and sold at near cost, so as to make them as affordable as possible. Our goal is to make this important genre of Jewish literature and history available in English in book form, so that people can have the personal histories of their ancestral towns on their bookshelves for themselves and for their children and grandchildren.

A list of all published translated Yizkor Books in the project with prices and ordering information can be found at:
http://www.jewishgen.org/Yizkor/ybip.html

Lance Ackerfeld, Yizkor Book Project Manager
Joel Alpert, Yizkor-Book-in-Print Project Coordinator
Susan Rosin, Yizkor-Book-in-Print Project Associate Coordinator

JewishGen
Yizkor Book Project

This book is presented by the
Yizkor-Books-In-Print Project
Project Coordinator: Joel Alpert

Part of the Yizkor Books Project of JewishGen. Inc.
Project Manager: Lance Ackerfeld

These books have been produced solely through efforts of volunteers
from around the world. The books are printed using the Print-on-Demand technology and sold at
near cost, to make them as affordable as possible.

Our goal is to make this intimate history of the destroyed Jewish shtetls
of Eastern Europe available in book form in English, so that people can
experience the near-personal histories of their ancestral town on their
bookshelves and those of their children and grandchildren.

All donations to the Yizkor Books Project, which translated the books,
are sincerely appreciated.

Please send donations to:

Yizkor Book Project
JewishGen, Inc.
36 Battery Place
New York, NY, 10280

JewishGen, Inc. is an affiliate of the
Museum of Jewish Heritage
A Living Memorial to the Holocaust

Notes to the Reader:

We apologize ahead of time for the poor quality of images in the book. Often these images had been scanned from the original Yizkor books which were of poor quality to begin with, being copies of old photographs. Each transfer results in loss of quality. We have done the best we could, given the original material and the resources and technology at hand. Even though images often appear of higher quality on computer screens, that does not transfer to high quality images in print. A reader can view the original scans on the web sites listed below.

Within the text the reader will note "{34}" standing ahead of a paragraph. This indicates that the material translated below was on page 34 of the original book. However, when a paragraph was split between two pages in the original book, the marker is placed in this book after the end of the paragraph for ease of reading.

Also please note that all references within the text of the book to page numbers, refer to the page numbers of the original Yizkor Book.

The original book can be seen online at the New York Public Library site:

https://digitalcollections.nypl.org/search/index?utf8=%E2%9C%93&keywords=shebreshin

or at the Yiddish Book Center web site:

https://www.yiddishbookcenter.org/collections/yizkor-books/yzk-nybc314035/shuval-dov-sefer-zikaron-li-kehilat-shebreshin

In order to obtain a list of all Shoah victims from Shebreshin, the reader should access the Yad Vashem web site listed below; one can also search for specific family names using family name option. These lists are continually updated by Yad Vashem, so it is worthwhile to periodically search these lists.

There is much valuable information available on this web site, including the Pages of Testimony, etc.
http://yvng.yadvashem.org

A list of this book and all books available in the Yizkor-Book-In-Print Project along with prices is available at:
http://www.jewishgen.org/Yizkor/ybip.html

In loving memory of Riva (Sonia) Manes (née Dym), z'l, Mendel (Mike) Dym, z'l, brother and sister Partisans, their parents, Raizel and Yankel Dym, and the Dym family members of Szczebrzeszyn who perished in the Holocaust.

Geopolitical Information:

Szczebrzeszyn, Poland
The town is located at 50°42' N 22°58' E 137 miles SE of Warszawa

Period	Town	District	Province	Country
Before WWI (c. 1900):	Szczebrzeszyn	Zamość	Lublin	Russian Empire
Between the wars (c. 1930):	Szczebrzeszyn	Zamość	Lublin	Poland
After WWII (c. 1950):	Szczebrzeszyn			Poland
Today (c. 2000):	Szczebrzeszyn			Poland

Alternate names for the town: Szczebrzeszyn [Polish], Shebreshin [Yiddish], Shchebreshin [Russian], Shevershin, Szebrzeszyn, Shabeshin

Nearby Jewish Communities:

- Zwierzyniec 7 miles S
- Chłaniów 10 miles NNW
- Zamość 12 miles E
- Goraj 13 miles W
- Frampol 13 miles W
- Turobin 14 miles NW
- Krasnobród 15 miles SE
- Tarnogóra 15 miles NNE
- Żółkiewka 15 miles NNW
- Izbica 15 miles NE
- Biłgoraj 16 miles SW
- Chrzanów 16 miles WNW
- Józefów 16 miles S
- Gorzków 17 miles N
- Wysokie 20 miles NW
- Skierbieszów 20 miles ENE
- Zdziłowice 21 miles WNW
- Krasnystaw 22 miles NNE
- Komarów 23 miles ESE
- Łukowa 23 miles S
- Kraśniczyn 24 miles NE
- Janów Lubelski 24 miles W
- Łopiennik Górny 24 miles N
- Tarnogród 25 miles SSW
- Tomaszów Lubelski 26 miles SE
- Grabowiec 28 miles ENE
- Modliborzyce 28 miles W
- Narol 29 miles SSE
- Bychawa 29 miles NW
- Lipsko 29 miles SE
- Wojsławice 30 miles ENE
- Rejowiec 30 miles NNE
- Biskupice 30 miles N
- Trawniki 30 miles N
- Ułazów 30 miles S
- Bełżec 30 miles SE
- Zakrzówek 30 miles NW
- Piaski Luterskie 30 miles N

Jewish Population: 2,518 (in 1897), 2,644 (in 1921)

BALTIC SEA

LITHUANIA

RUSSIA

Vilnius ●

POLAND

BELARUS

Ostrów Mazowieka ●

GERMANY

● Poznan

Warsaw ●

● Lodz

Szczebrzeszyn
(Shebreshin) ●

● Prague

Krakow ●

UKRAINE

CZECH REPUBLIC

SLOVAKIA

250 miles
0

0
250 Km
500 Km

OSTRÓW MAZOWIECKA
POLAND - Current Borders

Map of Poland with Szczbrzeszyn (Shebreshin)

Hebrew Title Page of Original Hebrew/Yiddish Book

ספר זכרון
לקהילת שֶׁבְּרְשִׁין

יצא לאור על־ידי ארגון יוצאי שברשין בישראל ובתפוצות

חיפה, תשמ״ד — 1984

Translation of the Title Page of the Original Hebrew Book

Memorial Book
Of the Shebreshin Community

Published by the Former Residents of Shebreshin in Israel and the Diaspora

Haifa 1984 - 5744

העורך : דב שובל

כתובת המערכת :

אפרים פרבר, רח' ז'בוטינסקי 8א', קריות-ים 000 29

**Book of Memory
to the Jewish Community of Shebreshin**

"אותי", דפוס קואופרטיבי בע"מ, חיפה

Translation of previous page

Editor: Dov Shuval

Editorial Board Address:
Ephraim Farber, Jabotinsky 8A, Kiryat Yam 29000

Printed by "OT" Cooperative Printing House Ltd. Haifa

Table of Contents

Figures in our town

Old Szczebreszyn

The History of R' Yakov Reifman

The Book of Memory to the
Jewish Community of Shebreshin

(Szczebrzeszyn, Poland)

50°42' / 22°58'

Translation of Sefer zikaron le-kehilat Shebreshin

Editors: Dov Shuval, Association of Former Inhabitants of Shebreshin in Israel and the Diaspora

Published in Haifa, 1984

This is a translation of: Sefer zikaron le-kehilat Shebreshin (Book of memory to the Jewish community of Shebreshin)

Editors: Dov Shuval, Haifa, Association of Former Inhabitants of Shebreshin in Israel and the Diaspora, 1984 (Y, H, E, 518 pages)

Note: The original book can be seen online at the NY Public Library site: Szczebrzeszyn

ספר זכרון
לקהילת שֶׁבְּרְשִׁין

Friends of the Book committee
Moshe Weinstock, Afroim Preber, Abraham Wolfson, Shimon Sher, Zvi Traeger
Sitting: Tanuch Becher, Chaia Schissel

The organization committee in Israel
Efraim Farber, Chaia Schissel, Moshe Weinstock, Shimon Scher

[Page 11 - Hebrew] [Page 15 - Yiddish]

Forward

by the Editors

Translated by Moses Milstein

This Yizkor book of the Shebreshiner community, one of the more than one thousand Jewish communities in Poland destroyed, is published 42 years after the massacres in the shtetl, and 39 years after the defeat of the Nazi regime and the end of the Second World War. Is it not too late? Is it not in the sense of too little, too late? Has not everything already been written about the destruction of Jewish life in Poland? Has the material not already been exhausted?

Of course this sad chapter in the history of our people has not been forgotten, but everything which has been written up to now has not emphasized enough the extent of the loss: the tragic end of the life-giving, thousand year old Jewish existence in Poland.

Many yizkor books of the devastated communities have been published, but it is not sufficient. Every one of the survivors wants to cherish the memories of the past, everyone wants to see his own city and story in the book, wants to immortalize that which is most intimate to him. Every city and shtetl was a little world of its own, a Jewish world with social institutions, political parties, organizations, schools, and synagogues, and a shared tradition. It is all unforgettable and demands expression.

Such was also Shebreshin, a shtetl in the Zamosc area, Lublin province, which was populated by 8,000 people before the war, 3,000 of whom were Jews.

Since that time, not only have many years passed; an upheaval in life has also occurred. Changes have occurred in society and in politics, ideas have changed, the landscape has changed, new alliances have been made, the state of Israel has been founded. Nevertheless, there is still, to some extent, a longing for that era, when there was a full Jewish life, a communal life, a feeling of togetherness in suffering and hope.

*

There were no lack of problems in editing this book.

Most of the material was written by the survivors of the catastrophe, the sharit haplita, in the early years after the war. Some was written abroad near the time when the events occurred, when memories were still fresh. Most of the articles were written in Yiddish, before aliyah to Israel or soon after aliyah. Few were written in Hebrew in the original version.

In order for the younger generation–children of the survivors born in Israel for whom Yiddish is not their first language–to be able to read the book, so they will not be estranged from the work but will be able to share in the experiences and feelings of their parents and recognize the history that that generation endured , that went through hell, we have translated part of the material into Hebrew.

This book was not written by historians or practiced writers. The contributors have presented the details of what they lived through–persecution, humiliation, repression, torture, mass murder, and also by contrast–personal life during peaceful times, deep, colorful, lively, the passion for life, the struggle to survive and prevail.

As a result, there are a few problems such as a lack of consistency about dates of occurrences. Understandably, in the heat of the horrible events, it was not possible, nor did it occur to most, to concern themselves with chronological issues. Only a few with a historical bent had the notion of writing memoirs in order to document the horrifying events for future generations.

Not everything dealt with in the book is the height of artistic creation, and not every poem pretends to be the best. Ordinary people, not authors or poets, tried to describe their feelings and what they lived through in that catastrophic era, with the skills they had. But it is precisely because of these authentic descriptions, personal events, and intimate experiences, that a documentary value is brought to the work.

In collecting the material at the beginning, no attention was given to assigning topics. Unfortunately, no direction was given at the time, and every contributor wrote according to his understanding. As a result, many contributors wrote about "everything"–a few sentences about the way of life in shtetl, a few about the Holocaust, about flight and wandering, about suffering and death, at times about certain personalities, and all of it mixed together.

Since any one topic was only touched upon, and everything was mixed together as one, no one point was completely elaborated. Such a treatment could not serve any one theme. Furthermore there were many duplications and repetitions which made the material unsuitable. It was not easy to sift through the material and choose what was appropriate to publish, and to supplement what was missing.

In contrast, it is worth pointing out that there were other contributors who intuitively described their memories in a specific form and at the appropriate level.

As time went by, the editors underwent personal changes which impeded the work and delayed publication. As well, the difficulty of collecting this unusual material took much time.

The contributors are widely dispersed in Israel and abroad. Every revision or edit was therefore difficult.

Nevertheless, in spite of the difficulties and constraints, we did all we could to achieve completeness. We overcame the difficulties through strict selection of material, careful editing and efforts to supplement what was lacking. Hopefully, we brought the book to a worthy level.

The editors took no political position. If somewhere a sympathetic tone to a particular political position is perceived, it arises from the legitimate and natural inclinations of the writer, and it is his responsibility.

*

The editors took care that the material was true to the original, accurate, without obvious changes, and as far as possible, in the language of the writer.

We tried to improve the style but not to make it too lofty; correct it, but not embellish it or make it overly literary, or fit a prescribed form. We tried to avoid confusion, and to sort through, pick out and make the material clear and pertinent.

*

In the Yiddish section, we struggled with various expressions: Polish, Russian, German as well as Hebrew, and local words and idioms. We wanted to bring out the particular characteristics of the language of the writers, not to omit the local argot, but without inaccuracies, or illiteracies, or foreign designations. Sometimes it was not easy to decide.

*

The residents of the town were usually not known by their family names. Almost everyone had a nickname–sometimes after the name of the father or mother, sometimes according to a trade or business, and sometimes by external appearance, after a given event, or a humorous trait. These nicknames were so popular that omitting them would have made people hard to identify.

*

We thank all those who have helped us in this holy effort–the contributors as well as the sponsors without whose financial contribution it would not have been possible to publish this yizkor book.

A special heartfelt thanks goes to our comrade Mendl Boim, who spent years collecting the material in Israel and from abroad. He was the address for contacts from Israel, Poland, the United States, Canada, Argentina, and motivated them to write. He did all this voluntarily. The five journals he published–with contributions from our shtetl folk–were the predecessors that laid the foundation for the publication of our book.

Now, so long after the destruction of our shtetl, the former residents are ready to forgive it all its flaws and still long for it. People yearn for their childhood home, and look to it for the roots of their origins. But no, they do not want to return there, not even for a quick visit. They have no one there to visit. There, after all, was where their dear ones were murdered, and slaughtered, and the few survivors fled wherever their feet took them. That place will bring them no pleasure, only pain and grief.

The shtetl has probably changed in appearance with the passage of time. There are probably new houses built on the graves and ruins. But they, the former residents, carry its memory in their hearts as it once was, before the terrible events. The fabled town has become a symbol which draws them together as one family.

The landsleit are now spread far and wide, separated by continents, their souls split asunder. They are putting down roots in new homes spending their days and nights among family, at work, business, but they feel a greater bond with their childhood friends with whom they can share memories, their feelings, and hopes for the future, with whom they can discuss any subject better than with anyone else. The shared spiritual heritage is their common bond. Someone from New York, Montreal, Buenos Aires, Sao Paulo, feels closer to his landsman from Haifa, Tel Aviv and Jerusalem than to his present neighbor.

It is natural for the yizkor book to be published in Israel. It is not only because it is the center of the Jewish people, but also because here reside the greatest number of the sherit haplita of our shtetl.

May this book be a symbol and a witness to our shared fate and shared thoughts. Here the contributors brought their thoughts, their energy, their neshome yese'yre[1], in order to bring out their sense of community, the shared feelings that transcend geographical borders. It seems that in spite of the contradictions, the conflicts and struggles of the past, they find themselves again together, arm in arm, united in thought and feeling.

The Editors

Translator's Footnote
1. Sabbath soul/joy

[Page 23 - Hebrew] [Page 29 - Yiddish]

Everyday life

The Desire to Acquire Knowledge
by Moshe Messinger
Translated by Moses Milstein

During my childhood, as far as I can remember, the shtetl was economically and culturally quite backward. Very few people could read or write, or possessed worldly knowledge. Nevertheless, there were some young people who strived to acquire any ray of knowledge which managed to come their way, often in secret, against the wishes of their parents.

Some of the Jewish youth-I among them-began to conduct educational activities such as teaching others to read and write. The circle was composed mostly of "shtibl[1]" youth. There was no one from the trades. On any street in shtetl there might be one person who could write an address in Russian.

We worked hard to find instructional books on reading and writing. These were the so-called "brivnshteller".[2]

I studied in the Russian school, before the First World War, with another Jewish friend and six Jewish girls. We were very envied.

The desire to acquire knowledge was just beginning. I remember that several shtiblboys began to be interested in what and how we studied. We would often pass on to them our lectures from the Russian school.

It went so far that some went out "in the wider world", to the big cities, to acquire an education. Preparation for the journey took place in secret. No one was supposed to know, especially not the parents. Not until the person crossed the Russian-Austrian border did we reveal the secret.

For the parents of that era, it constituted a great shame. The family was embarrassed to let anyone know. That's how it was until the First World War.

Secretly organized

The first ones to begin to actively help in the cultural development of Jewish youth were: Baruch Bibel, Abraham Itzhak Becher, Nechamia Feiler, and I. We had received some brochures from the Zionist movement, and we decided to organize the first lecture. We hid the brochures with Shaul Yosef Feiler. During the Czarist years, fear was great. The lecture, therefore, took place in great secrecy.

We had decided to found a Zionist organization, but the plan did not come to fruition because World War I broke out. My friends and I went off to war, and all plans were postponed.

On my return from the war, I found things had changed. Youth were striving for something without knowing what that something was. We got together again, this time in larger numbers. Among the assembled were: Mordechai Behagen, Baruch Bibel, Hersh Geld, David Hersh Messinger, Yosel Springer, Ephraim Boim and many others.

Founding a library

Our first task was to establish a city library. Others who helped were: Henik Bronstein, Ruzhe Bronstein, and the Schnitser family. We went from house to house, and everyone greeted our endeavors enthusiastically. A large number of books and journals were donated by Yosel Schnitser, Mordechai Behagen, Nechemiah Feiler, and Yechiel Weinberg.

In order to enrich the library with more books, much money was needed. To that end, we established a drama club which consisted of the following people: Yosef Schnitser, H. Bronstein, Leib Schnitser, Ruzhe Bronstein, A. Y. Becher, and Maleh Oberferscht. The registrar was Moshe Messinger, prompter-Abraham Itzhak Weinrib, set design-Niche Schnitser and Chaia Boim.

Thanks to the drama presentation we were able to raise the required sums of money. Thus, we were able to create a significant contribution to education and knowledge-the library named for Mendele Mocher Sforim, in Shebreshin.

Founding of the Zionist organization

At the same time, we founded the Zionist organization located at Chaim Moishe Vasser's. Then the most interesting work began: awakening the consciousness of Jewish youth in the shtetl.

With the passage of time, the youth evolved and ideas crystallized-opinions on world problems, especially about Jewish national-social questions.

Coming to our circle were: Yosel Merzel, Shmuel Klieger, Abraham Bernstein, (who came from "the outside world," Warsaw), Henech Becher, and David Merzel. The new members helped greatly with our work, and thanks to their intellectual efforts, we advanced hugely and expanded our reach.

Worker-Zionist thinking entered for the first time. Up to then, youth were affiliated with the General Zionist organizations. Later, in larger numbers in the Worker-Zionist circle-Polae Zion, Tzeirei Zion.

Rise of the Bund

Then Epharaim Boim, and Yosel Nar arrived (Laizer Papieroshnik's son and Gretzker's son). Both had been yeshive boys, very spiritually evolved, with a broad understanding of the world, people, nation and class. They began to conduct special educational work and founded a Leftist, for its time, workers union, the Bund. The union consolidated, and with time, attracted a large part of the working class in S. The leaders were: Ephraim Boim, Abraham Itzhak Weinrib, Yosel Springer, Leib Springer, David Weiss, Itzhak Gall, Esther Tulkop and others.

Thus, Jewish youth was split in its way of thinking and understanding into two camps. One camp-Worker-Zionist. The other, a larger part-under the leadership of the Bund.

The general cultural endeavors, especially with regard to the library, were carried out by the two workers parties-Poalei Zion-Tzeirei Zion and the Bund. The management were-librarian, Moshe Messinger-chairman, Yosef Schnitser-secretaries, Henik Bronstein, Mordechai Behagen, Abraham Bernstein-board of directors, Abraham Itche Becher, Yosel Springer, Hersh Geld, Abraham Itche Weinrib.

The Mendele Mocher Sforim library grew from day to day. Every month saw new arrivals of books in Polish, Hebrew and, above all, in Yiddish.

Intensive cultural activities

A broad educational work was carried out by the two yeshive boys, Ephraim Boim and Yosel Nar. They paid special attention to the boys studying at the Radziner shtibl. One of the boys, Yacov Gerstenblit (today in America) helped us secretly, until the day when the Chasidim found out about the clandestine educational activities carried out in the shtibl.

It led to an open strike. Due to the intense educational work of the library directors on one side, and the open strike which broke out in the Radziner shtibl on the other, the cultural corpus of S. was enriched by the fruitful, new, cultural talents of: Moishe Bub, Moishe Tzvi Berger, Pesach Berger, Hersh Getsl Hochboim, and his two brothers Abraham and Nachum Hochboim, and Yankel Honigman.

At that time, the two Zionist-socialist parties united-Poalei Zion and Tzeirei Zionand blossomed into the large Zionist-socialist movement Pielei Zion.

In spite of the growth of the library, and the even greater growth of the enlightened youth, cultural activities did not solve all the problems and needs of the previously backward youth who had so yearned for knowledge. The courses in reading and writing through the Poalei Zion party were not sufficient.

Thanks to the work of the Bund leadership, a second, splendid, cultural organization, the[3]א ש י צ school, was established which took in the illiterate among the older youth, and also, to a greater degree, the poorer children of the worker class who did not have the means to pay fees for cheder.

The א ש י צ school was established with the help of the members of Poalei Zionwho emphasized Yiddish, such as Shmuel Klieger and Yankel Honigman. Later, the school went entirely under the aegis of the Bund.

Parallel to this, the two drama circles developed and expanded. One was from Poalei Zion under the direction of Moshe Messinger; the second, under the management of Berl Koil, Zanvl Ashenberg, and Yehuda Kelner. Both filled , to a great extent, the cultural needs of both workers parties.

The "gang"

We mustn't forget the bet hamidrash youth who served as a reservoir for intellectual talent in cultural social, political endeavors, above all for the Poalei Zion camp. But the Bund did not ignore the well of intellectual yeshive boys.

Thus, we later attracted, and dragged out of the bet hamidrash, Asher Shapiro, and Shmuel Ber Klieger, Abraham Chaim Nus and Mendl Boim. Both parties fought over Mendl Boim. He had an "open mind." Providing books in secret for the boys in the bet hamidrash, just as we had done in the Radziner shtible, we noticed that Mendl did not study at the same time as the others. We followed him once, and discovered that he got up at three in the morning, and he and Shmuel Ber Klieger went to the bet hamidrash where each sat in a different corner and studied his Gemorrah.

One evening, one of the older members, Leibl Sheiner, who still studied in the bet hamidrash and was a secret "underground member", spent the night there. At three am, when Mendl Boim and his friend Klieger arrived, he noticed that instead of opening the Gemorrah, Mendl pulled out a forbidden object from his bosom-Marx's "Kapital."

We smuggled Borochov's "Platform", and "Class Interests and the National Question" to him. He became, along with others, followers of the Worker-Zionist ideology, and founder of the HeChalutz and HeChalutz Hatzair in S.

Before the "gang" from the bet hamidrash took over the management of party work, there was another group who faithfully helped us spread socialist-Zionist ideas. Mendl Messinger, Yehoshua Zisbrenner, Yerachmiel Ginzberg, and Yankel Lam. Most responsible for bringing the "gang" into the movement were Mendl Messinger who founded Hashomer, and later, Yehoshua Zisbrenner, Henech Becher and Shmuel Ber Klieger.

    *

A group of members from both parties were successful in taking the helm of "dozor" and "parnes."[4] The Jewish population was given the right to elect their representatives in municipal elections. For years, the group fought for the social-political interests of the laboring masses in the shtetl. In certain cases, it was with the help of progressive representatives like Moishe Hersh Berger and Hersh Getzl Hochboim.

The struggle in city hall was mostly carried out by the chaverim: Yosel Springer, Abraham Itche Weinrib, Itzhak Gall, and Abraham Springer-from the Bund, Moshe Messinger and others, and from Poalei Zion, and from other representatives of other affiliations like Leibl Licht and Shia Lerner.

Social Aid

Aside from the cultural activities of the broadly developed workers unions, there were also wide-ranging and intensive social aid projects, especially at the beginning of winter to provide the needy poor with clothing. Before Pesach, when Jews could not obtain matzohs, "collective bakeries" were established where volunteer members contributed two to three days of work. These "collective bakeries", also called "laden", were run by both parties.

There were also public kitchens with hot mid-day meals, for the poor, and especially for children, financed by American Jewry. Besides this, there was a committee for social aid that I had the honor of heading. For years, it was supported by our expatriate brothers in America.

In later years, before World War II, the "Tropen Milch"[5], institution arose under the leadership of Devorah Fleischer, Hindele Briks, Sheva Macharovski and others. This was one of the most magnificent institutions in the social realm. The two workers parties helped out by getting subsidies from city hall.

Translator's Footnotes

1. Hasidic house of prayer

2. Handbook of sample letters.

3. Possibly the Zionistishe Yiddishe Shule Organizatzieh. MM

4 Synagogue and community councils

5. Milk Drops

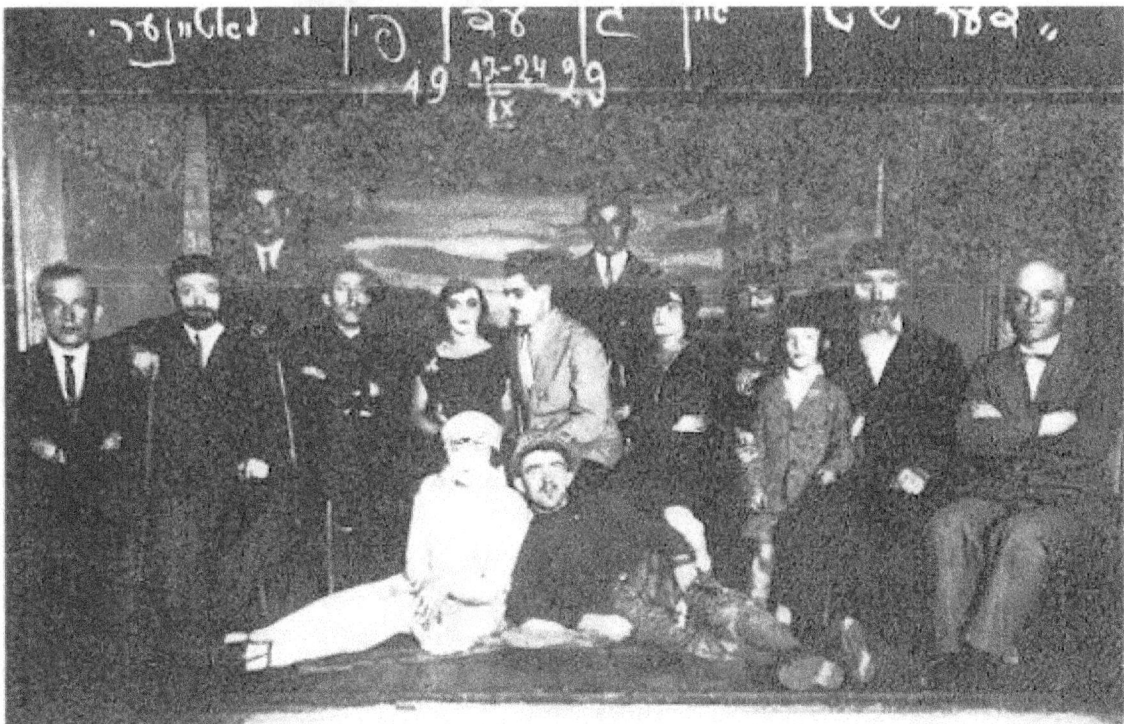

[Page 36 - Hebrew] [Page 39 - Yiddish]

How the Young Generation Flourished
by David Fuks
Translated by Moses Milstein

In 1926, as a 12 year old boy, I began to learn the trade of tailor at Mordechai Leib Lerner's, where I met an older worker, Chaim Berger. He immediately took me up to the trade union and registered me in the youth section.

It was located at Yosel Kulpe's. There was a library in the union named for Esther Tolkop. The librarian was Shlomo Bendler ("Der Langer Shloime"). I was given books to read.

A little while later, I became a member of the youth wing of the Bund-"Tzukunft". Young people would gather there. The youth section, "Yugent Bund Tzukunft", grew steadily. The lecturers at the time were: Abraham Itche Weinreib, Yosel Springer, Yechiel Borenstein, Zanvl Ashenberg, Itzhak Gall, Moishe Leib Mitlpunkt, and others.

The older members, seeing how the youth flocked to us, constantly looked for ways to broaden the frame of our work. They established the "Yiddishe Shul Organizatzieh" for which they found another location at Wolf Gedacht's. A drama circle was established which included: Ettl Litvak, Abraham Springer, Chaia Berger, Balche Blei, Aharon Frieling, Berl Koil, and others. Young people became activists.

The youth coming to us were from the poorer class, lacking in elementary education, some illiterate, their poverty preventing them from acquiring an education. As a result, our representatives established night courses where the young tailors, shoemakers, and domestics learned to read and write. They also taught Jewish history, natural history and other subjects. In that way, the impoverished Jewish youth educated themselves until they we able to take part in the social-political life of the shtetl.

Our trade union carried out a very active social-economic agenda. In the early days, a worker in the shtetl had to work twelve to fourteen hours a day. Thanks to the intensive work of the union, the work day was shortened, at first to ten hours and, later, after a short strike of all the trade workers, to eight hours.

Gathering of "Young Bund Tzukunft", in the middle, the author

Workers achieved better working conditions and higher wages. Thanks to the trade union, the oppressive burden of the workers was lightened. A big role in this was played by the leaders of the Bund.

During that period, the Yiddishe Folks Shule was established aided greatly by the work of the Poalei Zion party especially: Shmuel Klieger, Yosef Merzel, Henich Becher and others. But later, for a variety of reasons, the work was carried out almost exclusively by the Bund leadership. Noteworthy in the development of Jewish education were the members Yankel Honigman, and Isaac Weisfeld.

The school was hard to maintain. But thanks to the help of almost the entire Jewish population, including the religious Jews, and our brethren in America, the school flourished. The school consisted of five grades. The teachers came from the Jewish seminary in Vilna. From time to time, the pupils put on plays attended by the whole Jewish population.

Thus, our Jewish youth flourished and became an integral part of social and political life without distinction as to political orientation be it the Bund, HeChalutz, Betar or the Communist movement.

Drama club

With the coming of May, on a Saturday morning, you could see young Jewish people, flushed, breathless, excited, running through the streets of town in various directions-marching in formation or in groups. Coming to the "Vigon"[1], or the Frampol road, you could see groups of youngsters sitting on the grass, listening to one of their own holding forth on existing social questions.

Our youth lived a free and beautiful life. They were seen everywhere-in organizational locales, at Groise Shloime's budke, on the new promenade. They gathered everywhere and talked about the Bund, Zionism, pioneering.

I remember when we, the youth wing ,"Zukunft", were leading a recruitment drive and organized a youth meeting to that effect. Moishe Tenenboim and I took part. Moishele Zisbrenner (who fell in battle in Eretz Israel), Shmuel Zilberlicht, and other pioneers came to debate with us.

In general, Jewish youth was politically and socially very evolved.

Kibutzei   hachshara[2] from HeChalutz and Betar were   established   in   S. The kibbutzniks were seen in every corner of the shtetl going out to chop wood. I remember how the Betar youth would march out from Mordechai Fleischer's street under the leadership of Yosel Boim.

After the youth of the Bund grew, and with the rise of the Jewish school, a location was rented at the Grules. Across from there, the Poalei Zion had their locale and songs of the striving for life and struggle, started by one group and picked up by the other, continued on.

> There once were youths like blossoming oaks.
> I see them before me sharp and clear.
> Flowing and bubbling from poor Jewish streets.
> exuberant youth, once bloomed long ago.
>
> I still hear the music of the hora
> hands intertwined along the happy way. Boys and girls dancing together
> dreaming of the future, and a happier day...
>
> I hear the song of the Shvuah[3],
> sung by the "Tzukunft[4]" youth of the Bund,
> from impoverished streets, and good Jewish homes,
> fighters for tomorrow, the young working men.

Montreal, Canada

———

Translator's Footnotes

1. A park-like area in S.
2. Preparatory training for prospective agricultural immigrants to Israel. Weinreich
3. "The Oath," anthem of the Bund
4. "The Future," youth wing of the Bund

———

[Pages 43-44]

The Struggle for Cultural Progress
by Yehoshua Zisbrenner
Translated by Moses Milstein

In 1915-1916, during the opposition to Czarist oppression in Poland, Jewish youth were captivated and inspired by the burning currents of "Geyn Zum Folk".

The beginning was very difficult. Many had to endure a hard battle at home with their Hasidic parents. In spite of this, we pursued our struggle even in the Radziner shtibl[1]. It was a battle whose purpose was to show that the tradition of waiting for the meshiach was unrealistic: We had to find our own way to free the Jewish people, and that was through Zionism.

A large segment of Jewish youth did, in fact, come over to us. The work of organizing for Zionist parties, and the joint committees of the Keren Kayemet and Keren Hayesod, was undertaken. In a short time, we managed to draw the majority of the youth, who had belonged to the General Zionists, to the Worker Zionist parties.

Educational work in shtetl was undertaken by: Abraham Itche Becher, Moshe Messinger, Baruch Bibel, and others. Secret activities in the Radziner shtibl were conducted by some older chaverim: David Merzel, Abraham Bernstein, and Shmulke Gerenreich.

Among the above-named were the founders of the Mendele Mocher Sforim library. Every evening found chaverim studying to learn to read and write in the library.

In 1920, the new Polish government accused us of Communist sympathies and confiscated the library. The entire inventory of several thousand books was in jeopardy. Several chaverim were arrested.

A few years later, permission to reopen the library was granted, and we got to work again. Some of the books were damaged, a large number were missing.

A struggle for control of the library was waged between both workers parties-Poalei Zion and the Bund. The Poalei Zion party fought to keep it a city library, non-party, freely available to everyone, so that everyone could benefit from Jewish literature. After long and hard work, the library was transformed into a cultural institution for the entire Jewish population.

The library had an active drama club which successfully put on plays from "Moshe Chait" to Ansky's "The Dybbuk." The plays were put on in the fire-hall.

The drama club consisted of the following people: Esther Stern, Nechama Lerner, Shia Zisbrenner, Isrulke Lerner, Mendl Boim, Mordechai Mintz, Rivke Weinstock, Yacov Lam, Yosef Lerner, Sarah and Chaia Boim, Peshe Hochgelernter, Leah Groiser, Tile Schwarzberg, and others. The "Dybbuk" was replayed at the reopening of the library. It was a colossal hit.

People came from the surrounding shtetlach and from Zamosc to see the play. It resulted in significant income which was dedicated for the library, and helped to acquire newly published books of Jewish literature.

The cultural activities gave our shtetl much inspiration and a big push forward. Many young people joined the activities, and we progressed in social and political domains.

Translator's Footnote

1. A park-like area in S.

Friends of Zze'irei Zion, May 1, 1922

[Pages 45-46]

How we have thrown away the long Kapotas[1]

by Yehuda Kelner

Translated by Moses Milstein

A new wind began to blow in the shtetl. In 1914, with the beginning of World War I, a new society was beginning. Parties were founded, workers organizations and trade unions arose. Calls for equality, brotherhood and national revival were heard.

An uprising occurred among the youth. Seeing a new way of life in the shtetl, the youth abandoned the bet hamidrash and the shtibl,[2] threw off the long kapote and the "Yiddish hitl"[3], and put on a suit and hat.

At first, there was opposition from the parents, mostly expressed on Shabes in the bet hamidrash. One could hear the arguments, "Where is it heard that girls and boys should get together, light lamps on Shabes, play the comedian in theatre? There will, God forbid, come a punishment on the shtetl for its sins."Shebreshiner youth, with its social and political work, acquired a reputation in the whole Lublin area. At the Zionist, or Bundist, or Communist gatherings, if you said you were from S., you were immediately given a seat of honor.

A group from "Tzukunft" Bund

I remember that, every Saturday, when we went out for a walk, the Bundists walked in one group singing the "Shvueh"[4], and the Zionists, in another group singing Zionist songs. When the two groups encountered each other, they quickly separated, as if they were enemy armies.

About making a living, the youth did not concern themselves. Their mothers and fathers fed them, and there were few opportunities for work. Jews worked as tailors, shoemakers, carpenters. The city had no heavy industry. In Graf Zamoisky's sugar factory, only Polish workers were employed. Jews were not allowed.

*

That is how Jewish youth lived and acted. Parents could not accept the new spirit of the times and rejected the new directions.

Nevertheless, disregarding all that, I still miss those times, those battles, and I can't believe that it is all in the irretrievable past.

Buenos Aires

———

Translator's Footnotes

1. Hasidic garment

2. Hasidic prayer house

3. A characteristically Jewish hat

4. "The Oath." Anthem of the Bund

———

[Pages 47-48]

You Need to See a Psychiatrist

by Baruch Bibel

Translated by Moses Milstein

A terrible darkness pervaded S. when I arrived there from studying in the Brikser yeshiva in Chelm. Young people knew nothing and wanted to know nothing other than how to get out of being conscripted into the Czar's army.

I felt suffocated by the Chasidic society I found myself in. I yearned for a ray, just one ray of light. Today, in San Francisco, among the assimilated, I can feel better and appreciate better the sanctity of our Jewish people in general, and Chasidism in particular, and I miss it.

I became acquainted with Wolf Klotser, a bit of a Maskil[1], in those days. The first thing I discussed with him was the idea of founding a Jewish library in S. I still see before my eyes the sharp look he gave me when I uttered the word, library, and he suggested I should see a psychiatrist, because my thoughts were disordered.

1933, before the immigration of Messinger to Israel

But when I repeated the idea again and again, he said, "Maybe?" and we sent off a request for permission.

Yes, the truth is that it came to nothing, but even to dare it was a great achievement in those days. One can truthfully say that I planted a seed from which, years later, a Shebreshiner library grew.

I became aqauainted with Abraham Itche Becher, a man full of energy and strength whose like is hard to find. I truly loved him. I also became acquainted with Nechemiah Feiler, Yechiel Weinrib, Mordechai Behagen, and Itzhak Hersh, my neighbor. With each one, I argued that it was a big crime not to do something for Zionism. I succeeded, during a holiday, to bring them together in the Gorajec mountains, and there Weinberg delivered a talk from a paper about Zionism that he had almost certainly sweated over for weeks.

There, we founded the first Shebreshiner Zionist organization. We determined to establish Zionist memberships and National Fund "pushkes." But we had a problem: what do we do with this paper so that it shouldn't fall into the hands of some Jew. We decided to bury it. When the paper was lying in its grave, someone suggested we should burn it, and we did so. The poor paper suffered such an end.

The First World War broke out. The Austrians brought a more cultured approach to Poland, and something of it, also to S. I brought together the youth at Yosel Springer's house, and there it was determined that we would found a Jewish library.

San Francisco

———

Translator's Footnote

1. Proponent of the Haskalah, the Jewish Enlightenment

———

[Pages 49-55]

Memories of a Non-Shebreshiner
by Luba Gall
Translated by Moses Milstein

1927/28 כיתה I .ג'

1929

Do you wonder why I, a non Shebreshiner, write about S and not about other shtetlach? The reason: as a non-observant Jew, I felt free from my first day in S. I quickly felt at home, a part of her. The people became my brothers. my best years and fondest dreams are bound up with her. S was dear and beloved by me, and that is why I claim the right, together with you others, to lament the destruction of this shtetl, so holy to me.

Without personal enemies

A shtetl like any other in the Lublin region, you might think, the courthouse in the middle of the muddy market, surrounded by rows of shops, and tables with various goods. Women, preoccupied men, grimy, hurrying in the morning to the kloiz[1] and later to work. Like any other place, only not the same.

S in my time had this characteristic-that anyone could freely live according to his convictions. There were pious Jews, honest, sincere, who completely believed, but did not want to force anyone to believe as they did. Or, perhaps, in their naove honest way they thought that no one could believe in any other way. Above all, the two camps of religious and free[2] did not wage open war. Everyone lived their own life, went their own way. This was the uniqueness of S.

There were all sorts of parties. On the extreme Right and extreme Left, there wee strikes along party lines-often heated strikes. There were even instances of violence and fighting. But although the Shebreshiner people were faithful to their party struggle, they did not carry any personal bitterness against each other. After the most heated conflict in the library, or after an election, or a city council meeting (because there were always differences of opinions) you could see, strolling together in the street, cordially talking, Moishe Hersh Berger (Zionist) and Yosel Springer (Bundist) and in like manner others. Shebreshiners always displayed the greatest care for their fellow-man, even if he was from an opposing party.

Fruitful activities of the Bund

There has been much written already about Shebreshin and Shebreshiners. I, however, as someone from a different direction, would like, in my modest way, and with my modest skills, to write a few words about the Bund, in particular about certain Bundists.

When I arrived in S in 1921, I encountered a good number of Bundists, who carried out some modest programs: an illegal trade union, evening classes for workers, and party related discussions. Yet these modest works developed deep roots in the poorest social classes. Later, when the union was legalized, and in the city elections, the strength of the Bund was seen among the workers and masses.

Of the total of 24 aldermen (Jews and Christians), we received eight mandates (out of 11 Jewish). On paper, that is, because the Polish reactionary powers had only provided four places (the remainder were invalidated) and it was here that the Bund first began its activities. The battle in city hall was twofold-as Jews and as socialists. There was no question, God forbid, of overthrowing the powers.

The issues were ordinary ones, mostly economic. Onerous taxes were imposed on Jewish artisans and businessmen. Incidentally, even the big merchants were not such big capitalists. With the exception of a small group, most of the shtetl struggled to make a living. There were worries about taxes, various ordinances, and social aid which consisted of a free hospital bed (if there was place), a doctor's house-call and medicine (up to two Zl) for those who couldn't pay and mostly suffered.

To a certain extent, the activities were political: bringing protests and resolutions against the savage anti-Semitic provocations in the country and in our shtetl. The Bundist work in city council went on from the beginning until Hitler ended it all.

And here, I would like to mention two aldermen-Yosel Springer and Abraham Itche Weinrib (Now in Brazil, he was a city councilman). Not only did they have to wage the battle in city hall (along with others, but perhaps more so), but they gave much time and energy when elections neared preparing our candidates for the examinations. According to Polish law, a candidate had to be able to read Polish, and sign his name in Polish, and had to have a certain number of signatures to be eligible.

Polish harassment

But the situation of Jewish candidates in general, and the Bund in particular, was different. No matter how many times a candidate was elected, he still had to take the exam, and a hard one it was. Not only were they not ashamed to examine certain council men, among them Yosel Springer and Abraham Itche Weinrib (a trade school teacher), but they were even not ashamed to examine Yosel Blei, a student in the faculty of law. So a working man, after a hard day of work, had to set himself to learn Polish grammar and history. The group of potential candidates had to be ever larger because one never knew who would be invalidated. So they, Yosel Springer and A.I. Weinrib, had to, after their own work day, work again, without payment, teaching grown men, most of whom had not attended school. But they did it.

Our group of alderman consisted almost always of: Yosel Springer, A.Y. Weinrib, Itzhak Gall, Leb Springer, Abraham Springer, Yosel Blei, Yakov Yehoshua Feder, and my humble self. I was elected three times in a period of eleven years. And that is why I am acquainted more or less with the details of the persecutions undergone by the council men, especially me.

In spite of the presence at every session of the police chief and his staff who could arrest us for any wrong word, our aldermen, with the help of other Jewish aldermen, repelled the dirtiest attacks, delved into all the corners of municipal life, examined, searched, scrutinized, and prevented misappropriation of municipal funds. (Yosel Springer was exceptionally effective at this) We showed that, in a time when funds for social aid were so limited, the money for balls and banquets and church renovations were unlimited. As a woman, I was always given the honor of reading the political resolutions, for which I was often "sent to Russia."

We couldn't always achieve our goals, because the Poles held power. But it was not easy for them, because they were wary of the Bund. That's why they never failed to take revenge on our people where and when they could: creating protocols for sins that had not occurred, sentencing to jail, or paying fines which was worse than sitting in jail. We were, however, not deterred.

Not for personal goals

For Shebreshiner people in general and for Bundists in particular, ideals were more important than life. A few examples:

Yosel Springer's father-in-law was a shochet and Yosel was a dozor[3] in the Jewish community. The shochets were paid by the Jewish community and paid well. The community had to impose taxes on meat, so that the poor could not afford meat even for Shabes. When the pressure became too great, a resolution was brought in-to divorce the shochets from the community. Let them be paid by those who use their services. They didn't like it, they protested, but when it came to a vote, Yosel was the first to vote for it. Nu? Afterwards at home, a scene: His wife cried for her father's livelihood. But Yosel paid no attention.

A second example: The Bund decided to open a secular school. So, among the initiators of the school committee we find three names whose families are again at stake: again Sprnger, Weinrib, Gall. They had to choose: themselves or the ideals. Springer and Weinrib were Jewish teachers in a trade school, and Gall was the son of a Jewish religion teacher. The families asked: "A Jewish school? And what will happen to you? How will you make a living?" (They could not be teachers in the school). Shloime Gall asked, "A school that's anti-cheder? Is that how you treat a father in his old age?" Itzhak was a good son, he loved his father, but.It was decided to open the school. Personal interests were not considered-the principle, that the masses should not suffer, mattered.

The Bund accomplished a lot in the area of educating the poorest youngsters whose parents could not afford to pay. For years they led classes, organized lectures, and from this work an educated youth grew up. When I was in Montreal, Canda, an erstwhile Zukunfunftist, now a grown man with children, no longer a Bundist, explained to me with the greatest respect, that were it not for the Bund he would not know the little he now knows. And this man knows quite a lot.

A talented working-class intellectual

Of all the youth growing up in our shtetl, I want to highlight one: Berl Koil. His father, Batchmak was a treger[4]. He was a simple, uneducated, honest and poverty-stricken man. Not only were his parents unable to provide an education for him, but struggled even to keep him properly nourished. As a result, he had to learn a trade from his earliest years-shoemaker.

At the time, the youth organization, Zukunft, was already in existence. Berl, along with Yosel Blei, Zainvel Ashenberg, Moishe Leib Mitlpunkt and others joined Zukunft, and there, began receiving their first education. Berl lapped it up like a man dying of thirst. He learned to read and write, especially to read. He read voraciously, he had a wonderful memory, and exceptional receptiveness. In a very short time he developed into a wonderful debater, a shining public-speaker with an extraordinary understanding of art and literature, a gifted actor on the stage, an occasional song writer. Berl "Bantchmak", became Berl Koil, a working class intellectual, a conscientious party worker, but remained a very naove and honest man.

He married and had two children whom he loved more than his own life. But when the Second World War broke out, he was the first to enlist to fight against Hitler. He knew he could not accomplish much, but he wanted, he said, to at least direct a few bullets into the fascist beasts. He fell into German captivity where he underwent the worst agonies. In March, 1940, Hitler decided to liquidate the Jewish prisoners of war, and they were sent to Lublin where I also found myself at this time. They arrived half-naked. The Jewish community received an order: If any of the prisoners wanted to be liberated,, he must be claimed by a someone near to him within two days. They must also provide clothing. If not, they would be shot. Those not liberated were, in fact, all shot.

On one of those days, Mirl Zeidl, (Gershon Shuster's) came to see me to tell me that Berl Koil was among the prisoners. We immediately went to the camp, and after a whole day's efforts, we were able to bring Berl out. With him was Ephraim Farber, (Mendl Kliske's son). Berl was sick and swollen from starvation, in a state that I can never forget. I took them both to my place where they washed and changed clothes. Berl took to bed and a doctor was called. He was given medication, but he suffered a lot. He said, "Luba, I don't know if I will survive this war, but Hitler will be defeated, and I am lucky to have participated in the war. Oy, did I shoot at them!" And he smiled in such a childlike way. I will never forget that smile. He got a little better and he left for S. What happened to him? The same as to all the other dear, holy Jews.

Never forget

And so, writing this, I would like these lines to be inscribed on the hearts of all Shebreshiner, their children and grandchildren. And in the days of our greatest joy, of the rise of the Jewish state, our great tragedy must not be forgotten, the fate of a third of our people, and our dear shtetl Shebreshin. And may we, like in days of old at the rivers of Babylon say, "May my tongue cleave to my mouth and my right hand wither," at every simcha, if we forget this, because the world wants to and has already forgotten.

Jewish blood is again ignored. If an injustice is committed against a state, the whole world is upset and it is remembered. But our holy victims are being forgotten even among Jews. The survivors of hell want to forget in order not to awaken their wounds: too much have they suffered. Our brothers who were lucky to have lived far from the tragedy do not want to bring the darkness into their lives. Conscience is appeased with a few dollars. We perform acts of ablution and we are certain our sins will be forgiven.

But no matter how strong the pain is, we must not forget. It is the greatest holocaust and we must write about it with the very blood of our hearts for the coming generations, etched into the hearts of our children and grandchildren so that such a time will never come again.

Winnipeg, Canada

———

Translator's Footnotes

1. Small synagogue whose worshippers were often from the same trade

non-observant Jew

2. Member of the Jewsih community council

3. Porter

———

[Pages 56-58]

A Street in Szczebrzeszyn
by Emanuel Chmielash
Translated by Moses Milstein

On the street where we lived, Green Street, there were many Jewish tradesmen: shoemakers, shtepers, tailors, carpenters, bakers, water-carriers, gardeners, carriage drivers, shochets. There were all kinds of stores including food stores. There were merchants handling wheat, animals, fruit from the orchards, dairy products, etc. There was even a factory for cigarette products.

The nicest house in S. was on Green Street, and belonged to Mordechai Fleischer the richest man in S. His cellars were used to store apples from the sadovnickes[1] in winter. In the house there was a closet which opened to a set of stairs leading to a water well.

At one end of the house stood a permanent succah, beautifully decorated inside with paintings of Jewish holy images, and passages of scripture.

On one side of Green Street, there was a door with concrete stairs leading to the house of Estherishe, Mordechai Fleischer's daughter. Upstairs, the daughters and their husbands and children lived. The husband of his daughter, Feigele, was R' Yermiah Rabinovitch, a son of the Bialobrzeg rabbinical dynasty. Feigele and her sister, Matche, had a large shared kitchen.

In another dwelling lived Chanake and her husband Reuben Minzberg and their children. Below, with windows facing Green Street, lived Mordechai Fleischer's only son, Dantshe, and his wife, Dvoirele, and young son, Siomek.

Mordechai Fleischer's "imperium."

All the sons-in-law and daughters-in-law stemmed from important families. As long as Mordechai Fleischer was alive, all his sons-in-law were employed in his "imperium"his mill and sawmill.

Summer, Friday evening, his children sat outside on the front stairs, and neighbors came over to chat. Mordechai himself sat in the entrance on a feather-stool, and rested until candle lighting. He handed out money to his grandchildren who ran to Shimon Goldman's candy store to buy nashvarg.

The Fleischers also established a little bet hamidrash, and he and his sons-in-law and some neighbors prayed there. Every shabos they celebrated sholesh sides there sponsored by the Fleischers. R' Yermiah Rabinovitch read Torah and sang zmires.

His son-in-law, Yankele Minzberg, lived in Lublin and often came to S. On shaboshe davened for the congregation. The prayers took on a special flavor as he had a beautiful voice. Friday evening or Saturday morning, many people gathered at the windows and listened to his singing.

After Mordeschai's death his businesses suffered. His "imperium" fell apart and finances deteriorated. After a while, R' Yermiah Rabinovitch left S. It was said that he went to Belz to ask the rabbi for advice as to whether he should become a rabbi. The Belzer rabbi gave him his blessing, and he returned to his family as a rabbi. After a short while, he moved to Warsaw and established his rabbinate there.

When I went to Warsaw to look for work, he helped me find my first job at a halvah factory.

The good-hearted carriage driver[2]

In Mordecahi Fleischer's courtyard there was a grain elevator where my father, a wheat merchant, used to store his wheat. Afterwards, it became home to Chana Balagule. He lived there with his wife, Menuche, and his children. Nearby was the stall for his horse.

He furnished the loft of the stall with straw, and provided a place for the poor of other towns to spend the night, when they came to S. to seek alms,.

Jews from surrounding villages who came to town would stable their horses and wagons in the large courtyard.

The rabbi's prescription

In a new, wooden, one story building lived Israel David Shochet and his family. He was a Gerer Chasid known as "the Vonvonitser shochet". One of his children, Binyimale, fell ill with encephalitis. Three doctor's "attended"Klukowski, Kozicki, and a doctor from Zamosc. A prescription from the Sokolover rabbi, R' Zelig Morgenstern, arrived. The doctors were astonishedthe child was cured.

Montreal, Canada 1980

———

Translator's Footnotes

1. A sadovnick was the term for someone who rented orchards from a landowner in order to grow and sell the fruit.

2. Ba'al agala, in Hebrew, Bal a gule in Yiddish

[Page 59]

On the Shore of the River Wieprz

by Rivkah Shmali Translated by Moses Milstein

It is impossible to speak about the shtetl, Shebreshin, without mentioning the river Wieprz which has existed since time immemorial. The area around the river was densely settled by Jewish homes, especially of the poorer sort.

The river was the scene of lovers' secret meetings which lasted long, and sometimes created surprise and consternation when they were revealed... There, under the boughs of the willow trees, ideas, some legal some illegal, were spun like webs. The river was the greatest attraction for the young of both genders.

But the river was also witness to bitter disappointments, and personal heartbreaking tragedies.

*

In the deep grass near the river, families rested after a week's work. They found an oasis there among the thick groves of willow trees.

Women bathed modestly in shifts feeling at home and comfortable. Fridays, Jews arrived en masse with towels around their necks. Your people, the Jews, demonstrated with skill and bravado how to do the swimmer's crawl. They wanted, for at least 24 hours in the week, to forget the storm which was gathering at the gates of the yishuv.

Girls would come here to wash dishes. Winter, when the river was frozen, boys would come with sleds and skates to horse around. More than once they fell into a hole that someone had created to wash clothing.

Business in town was done by the women who threw themselves into work to help their families, each according to her talent and ability. Their entire fortune consisted of a few Zlotys. Their lot was a hard one. Winter, they protected themselves against the cold with a pot of glowing coals which my father, Zalman, donated to them.

Their nutrition was meager and pitiful. Their daily food consisted of potatoes. But they ate them with a hearty appetite, their faces glowing with satisfaction. Someone once asked Chaiah–Libl, "What is the secret to the great taste of your potatoes?" She answered sarcastically, " You have to cook them well." In truth, S. knew the secret of how to cook potatoes. It was the favorite food of the poor.

Meat was a rare guest at the table of most of the population. Shabes was the day when meat appeared on the table accompanied by singing and zmires. The holy Sabbath reigned in every house in S.

*

In spite of the hard economic conditions people grew up in, there was no crime. Zionist pride and honor bloomed among the young. One helped the other. Social activities blossomed. With their last pennies, they subscribed to newspapers, founded libraries, reading rooms, created drama groups, and so on. There was a strong drive to raise the cultural level. Educated and knowledgeable comrades contributed freely to the social endeavors.

One of them was Leibel Licht, z"l. He established groups, one of which I joined. He taught us Hebrew, awakened Zionist pride in us. Those were hours of rich emotion for us.

Leibel Licht evolved from a yeshive bocher to an energetic leader of Herut in S. He was full of talent. He gave his free time to organizing the youth and raising them to a higher level. And he succeeded.

Jewish national holidays were celebrated by our group in our house. Thus, at Chanukah, 1934, our choir, named after Sarah Chizik, led by Leibel Licht, came to our house. A holiday atmosphere reigned. Our faces were aglow even though the streets were frosty. We sat around the table, and Leibel Licht spoke masterfully about the time of the Hasmonaim, their struggle and their tragic end. We were all electrified by his words. We were transported into that long–ago era, with the heroic warriors. Tears fell from our young faces. When he ended, we sat entranced, reluctant to leave the story.

Spontaneously, we stood up and threw ourselves into a hora dance which brought us back to the real world. The last attraction were the hot latkes which we had prepared ourselves, their magical aroma calling us. Roosters were already crowing in the street and still we danced.

Szczebrzeszyn (Ziemia Lubelska) — Straż ogniowa

In Russia, even in great hunger and need, we did not forget our home. It was impossible to forget our beloved Jews who had slaved so hard their entire lives without losing hope or pride.

I see before me as on a movie screen the hard working families, engaged in various trades–carpenters, shoemakers, tailors, rope makers, water carriers, accompanying their work with song. My ears ring with the sweet nigunim of different shuls. I hear the prayers from the houses, the maleve malkahs with their tunes accompanied by the clapping of hands. I hear it now as I write these lines.

Kiryat Gat

[Pages 62-66]

The Competition

by Aharon Shrift

Translated by Moses Milstein

Family Sreibt, the author, Ahron-below left

Shia Poitek was a man of average-size. He had a black beard, longer at the sides and shorter in the middle. He wore a dirty kapote, boots with many patches, and a Yiddish hitl on his head.

He was supposedly a timber seller, but as I understood it, he was only a broker. He would wander around the villages buying wood from the goyim, and give them a down payment. The rest would be paid by the buyer to whom he would quickly sell the wood. The next day he would run back to the village. He never had the money to pay for the timber himself. That's how he wheeled-and-dealed.

He had a wife and children. His wife, Iteh, was a good wife and a good mother. Because she was tall, much taller than her husband, she was given the nickname, "Hosh". I used to visit them because their son went to cheder with me.

Iteh Hosh was very nearsighted. I noticed that everything she picked up, she held up close to her eyes. I would laugh seeing how, on Fridays, when she was chopping the fish for Shabes, she would bring the chopping board and the chopping blade so close to her face that she sometimes struck her nose. There was a story going around that, once, when she was preparing cholent for Shabes, and stuffing the kishke, one of the children began crying. She stopped to quiet the child. When she returned she continued to sew up the kishke not noticing that a cat had got into it, until the kishke began to dance...I myself did not see this.

Every couple of years a new baby arrived and Iteh gave each child no fewer than three names. I accompanied my father to one bris. Pinchas Shochet was the mohl. And I heard how he called him no less than four names-Israel Abraham Yacov Laizer. My father, Reuben, told Shia that he shouldn't scatter so many names about lest he run out of names.

Shia Poitek was always ready to help someone out. Whenever something happened, he was ready with advice. But, his advice wasn't always followed.

I remember when the bailiff came to take some things-and he was a frequent guest at our place-someone threw a dirty sack on his head from the attic, and he was almost blinded. He took us to court. We needed a witness to say that the sack "fell out of the attic by itself."

So who do you think was the witness? Shia Poitek. When he received the summons to go to court, he came to ask us what he should say. My father discussed it with him, and his testimony turned out successfully.

The bailiff came to Shia often demanding money, but Shia had more important uses for his money. But how do you get rid of this goy? Shia had an idea. He closed off the damper from the oven and smoke filled the house. The bailiff could not withstand the smoke. His eyes burned and his nose ran. He left with nothing. He would try again with Shia, from time to time, but he never managed to accomplish anything.

A game on Shabes

At that time, the Zionist movement was very popular in S, and Jews tried to find ways to leave for Israel. The antisemites were aroused and frequently you heard, "Zhidi, do Palestini!" We enrolled in various organizations: Betar, Ha'chalutz, Bund, from a young age. And we were filled with all kinds of ideologies.

But the young people were more interested in sport. Teams were established: football, swimming. We would march around town singing. Little children would run after us, parents were filled with pride.

The best football players were chosen and a team was established headed by Shimon Diamant. I was also on the team. Uniforms like today, we couldn't afford, because they cost a lot of money. My father used to say that, for one shirt, nine people could have a good meal. So, what's more important? We had no choice, and everyone played with what he had. We tried for an effect that was more or less acceptable.

No one should know

We competed against all the teams in S., and always won. We received invitations from other shtetlach and succeeded there as well. It went so far that our captain, Shimon Ariks accepted a challenge to play against a Christian team from Bilgoraj, thirty kilometers from S. The game was to take place on a Shabes. "This is impossible! we all cried, "It will cause a riot in the shtetl!"

But to no avail. The temptation was too great, and we decided to play. How can we make it so no one will find out? We chose four teammates to hire two wagons with high sides filled with straw, and arranged for them to be waiting for us Shabes after noon, about two km outside town.

We reasoned that, after prayers, after lunch, after zmires, it would be 12:30. Then a half hour to get there, and we would meet at 1:00 o'clock at the wagons. The thinking was that, every Shabes, winter or summer, kids would always leave the house, the parents would be left alone, and we wouldn't return until after dark.

All the players, and the fans, arrived punctually. There were about forty youngsters. We got into the wagons and the horses, like eagles, pulled away. The excitement was high. It was a beautiful day, the sky was blue, the fields covered in yellow corn stalks being harvested by the farmers. Green orchards full of juicy apples, pears and plums stretched along both sides of the road. The air was full of the scent of flowers.

We were enchanted by the whole scene and so overwhelmed we started singing Hebrew songs. Our voices carried far. In this way we covered eight kilometers.

Suddenly, I saw a Jew on the road. Who was it? Shia Poitek! He hid behind a fence and saw everyone traveling in the wagons. I quickly understood that this would not end well.

We lost the game. Almost everyone came back with black and blue eyes, swollen feet, bruised ribs, and worst of all, a heavy heart. We realized that this would not be the only problem. Back home we would have to answer for it, and this is what actually happened.

Shia Poitek, upon seeing the two wagons stuffed with kids, most of whom he knew, quickly returned to town and went straight to the bet hamidrash. There were already people there come to study pirkei avot, to daven minche-maariv and to celebrate sholes sides. He went straight to the shulchan, banged on it, and cried out with a tearful voice, "Yidden, a terrible tragedy, heaven help us, will befall the shtetl! I saw with my own eyes two wagons full of youngsters traveling on Shabes, desecrating the Sabbath. I can swear by my peyes and beard that what I say is true!" And he proceeded to name all those he recognized.

The mood among the parents was very dark. Each felt the burden of guilt for their sinning sons. They decided that the boys must be punished. Every father was to do as he saw fit.

A riot in shtetl

We arrived back in town in the dark. From a distance, we could see the shtetl was bubbling. We descended from the wagons and approached the crowd. Some people were shouting, others were crying. The town was in an uproar. Some of the mothers also came because they didn't trust their husbands not to punish the boys too severely. When one of the fathers grabbed his son and was about to beat him, his mother leapt into the fray to protect him. Finally, everyone took his son and went home.

Nobody was waiting for me. I knew my father would punish me without mercy. And that's how it was. But in the meantime, I went to spend the night at my friend, Ephraim Farber's (Kliski) house. They had a loft filled with hay cut in their fields. It was a pleasure to sleep there in ordinary times, but not now, when I knew what was hanging over me. I also had to worry about food, because I had an appetite like a wolf.

In the morning, I went out to see what the situation was, and also to grab a bite. I waited until my father left the house, and then I went in. While my mother fed me she said, "Is that how one behaves, desecrating the Sabbath? How are you going to end up? I, your mother, won't do anything to you, but your father will not let you get away with it."

I stayed in Ephraim's loft for three nights coming home in the morning to eat. My father knew that this cat and mouse game would not last long. He knew that I was hiding behind the wall waiting for him to leave. On the third day, I watched him leave, and soon after, I went into the house. I didn't have time to look around before I heard the door shut. I turned around and saw my father standing by the door, slowly removing his belt. He said to me cold-bloodedly, "Lie down on the bench."

Nothing helped. My father laid into me with the belt until my backside was black and blue. I couldn't sit down for days. My screams carried to the farthest streets. My mother fled from the house unable to withstand the sight of her husband beating her son. Her heart was breaking. She is a mother, after all. And that was how the competition ended.

Until today I can not understand what Shia Poitek was doing eight kilometers from town.

It didn't occur to anyone to ask him-What he was he looking for on Shabes, after lunch, in a village outside the techum[1] Shabbat?

Translator's Footnote

1. The boundary line outside of which it is not permitted to walk on Shabbat.

[Pages 67-71]

Episodes of Heroism
by Yankel Lam
Translated by Moses Milstein

There were some tough, strong men in Shebreshin. They did not stand idly by when Polish hooligans attacked the Jews. They were ready to fight back to defend their honor.

*

This took place a few years before the Second World War. One night, a number of wagon-loads of Polish recruits arrived from Zamosc. They rushed wildly out of the train, scaring everyone, and creating a commotion. Jewish taverns closed. People hurried to get off the streets and into their homes.

A group of Jewish porters assembled at Groisse Shloime's budke, wooden clubs in hand...

The first of those running riot saw them and gave a signal to the others—and, straight-away, the recruits left town.

1930, young people of "Tzukunft"

Reb Rokeach from Bilgoraj (from the Belz court) came to visit the Belzer Chasidim for Shabes. Friday evening, leaving Shloime Maimon's house on the way to the Great Shul, accompanied by about twenty Chasidim, the group was attacked, without warning, by a bunch of Polish hooligans. The Jews energetically repulsed them accompanied by angry oaths from R. Menashe Katzenelboigen, and R. Berish Katzenelboigen, and Shimon Nickselberg. The hooligans took off.

*

Hertz, a Pole from Zwierzyniec, used to come to town on Tuesdays, after the horse market closed, to get drunk. Immediately, the Jewish beer stores would close up shop.

One evening, he was strolling along the sidewalk surround by a gang of shkootzim. In front of Shloime's budke he was greeted in a hearty manner by the porters, Aaron Yankel, Moshke Milstein, and Shimshon Garfinkel. They got him into a conversation about horse trading, and distracted him skillfully while they dispersed the gang of shkootzim. The bus from Zamosc to Zwierzyniec arrived and they put the drunk on the bus.

*

Summer, 1937. Several days before the "Khage"[1] was to take place, the Jewish community received a letter from the magistrat[2] that no Jews should dare to show themselves on the streets during the procession.

The community decided: Not to go out. But the youth decided against. And, like any other time, they went out in the streets, the procession went on, and nothing, thank goodness, happened.

*

Shabes, summer, 1937, ten am. I go out. Near the well, on the trottoir, a group of young people are gathered directing angry looks at the Rathaus. They point to the wall in front of the Rathaus which is covered with anti-Semitic posters decorated with art work.

I call out, "Let's go and tear them down." I don't wait for a response but start to tear down the rows from right to left. I finish and manage to get away without injury.

*

Yom Kippur, 1937, about 1:00 pm. Jewish youth are strolling on the trottoir. The well-known Polish hooligan of the town, Shustak, appears in the company of a Polish corporal, and both are trying to start fights with the Jews.

Moshke Milstein is standing near Shloime's budke. The two heroes are drawing close to him. He stands his ground, unafraid. The corporal asks Shustak, "So, this is a Jew?" Shustak throws a glance at Moshke, and begins to drag the corporal away.

The corporal is insulted by the "chutzpah of the Jew", and attacks Moshke. Moshke rains blows on both, and beats them up good and proper...A bunch of guys grab Shustak to keep him from running away, and rough him up some more. Shustak is not seen in town for a good while after.

*

1938. Berish Katzenelboigen's wife travels, like most Wednesdays, to the Zwierzyniec market with some goods. There, Polish pickets are preventing customers from shopping at the Jewish stalls. The secretary of the "sond grochki" is standing watch in front of her store. She musters her courage and pushes him away.

The patriots lodge a complaint against her according to the generally accepted style of the time: calling a Pole "parszywy" [vile]. The Jewish community paid for a lawyer, and she was sentenced to six months in jail. They appealed and, it seems, that the appeal was still pending at the start of the war.

*

Yom Kippur, 1939, 4:00 pm. The Germans are retreating. Slowly, Jewish youth are reappearing in the streets. A group of Poles break into Leml Hochgelernter's cellar and steal about ten barrels of herring belonging to Chana Reiz.

At that moment, I find myself on the trottoir across from Heni Yorpest's house. I observe from a distance the Goyishe chutzpah. They get to the well, rolling the barrels with laughter and bravado.

My patience explodes. I call out to the group of young people near-by. "Let's stop the robbery!" We fall on them and tear the stolen goods from them. We quickly bring them to the "potchene"[3] , and roll them into Azriel Zirer's house.

A German military truck stands in the corner near Nicklesberg's house while one of its tires is being repaired. Some of the Poles try to salvage the situation by running to the Germans for help. Luckily, the soldiers did not want to mix in.

Brooklyn, New York.

Translator's Footnotes

1. Christian holiday
2. City hall
3. he "potchene" was the area opposite the market marked by a raised sidewalk with stairs leading up from the road. Many shops were located there.

[Pages 71-74]

Poland

by Pinchas Bibel
Translated by Yocheved Klausner

Poland, my homeland,
You are like our health:
Only those who have lost it
Can realize your value
And understand what they
have lost.
No, I shall not sing to you
One of the odes of the poet
Mickiewicz,
Although not less than he
I have longed for you.
It was on your own soil
That I made my very first
steps,
I saw your skies, I ate your
bread,
I felt my first love.

Your vast pine–woods,

Your red poppy fields,

The beautiful boulevards,

The village roads and modern
highways

That extend into the great
world –

Are deeply etched in my
memory.

The words of my school–
teacher

Are stridently resounding in
my ears:

"Jews are parasites, Jews are
leeches

On the healthy Polish body.

We must get rid of the Jews."

[Page 72]

My home was part of the
Lublin Circle,

A house with a garden, large
and warm,

At the edge of town.

The door was open, the table
set –

By day and by night

Could wanderers and
peasants

Receive a free meal

And a free place to sleep.

My grandfather and six blond
uncles

Were simple and honest
carpenters,

Making beds, tables, chests

for future brides.

One of the uncles, his name was Meir,

Decorated the furniture with a steady hand:

He made roses, daffodils and tulips –

They were artistic and looked so real

That bees would come to gather the nectar.

Every summer, from Monday morning to Sabbath eve,

Until Friday at dusk

My uncles made the peasants' homes

Beautiful and pleasant.

And before the Sabbath candles were lit

They brought their earnings to their father.

It was a warm–hearted home.

My grandmother, small and round,

Would sit by the oven

And fill jars of goose–fat and preserves.

The grandchildren, like the little chicks

Would play joyfully in the courtyard.

[Page 73]

Beyond the town lay the cemetery

Waiting calmly, like a warm bed,

For the tired Jews.

An old cemetery,

Tombstones barely legible,

Six, seven, eight hundred years old.

And one stone, a tall stone,

On the grave of a good, long–forgotten Jew,

Kept growing and growing,

Taller and taller from year to year,

Guarding the cemetery like a watchman.

The synagogue was old, with the thick walls

Its foundations set deep in the earth,

Not to irritate Christian eyes.

Although Cazimir the Great had permitted to build it,

The Jews, with concern for the future,

Have built it as a fortress,

With splendor inside and modest on the outside.

The days and the nights

In light steps paced over the town.

But in the back of town,

In the darkness of the night,

Animal hands sharpened the axes

And prepared the warm Polish soil

To be a grave

For my entire past.

San Francisco

1932 Beitar group

1930 Beitar group

[Pages 75-77]

Economic sources

by Moshe Messinger

Translated by Moses Milstein

In economic terms, Shebreshin was backward. People made do with little.

Tradesmen [ba'alei meluches] played a large role in economic life, especially tailors, shoemakers, and wood-workers. All week, the Jewish and Christian artisans employed workers to prepare clothing and shoes for the farmers of the surrounding area who came once a week on Tuesday, market day, to sell their produce, and to buy the necessities for their families.

The Jewish artisans sold their handiwork to the farmers. The farmers sold their produce, and the Jewish businessmen distributed it to the whole country.

A lot of Jews pinned their hopes on a big Tuesday. They would lay out their poor wares on almost empty shelves. The markets did not lead to great expectations. They earned pennies, and almost every one failed to earn enough for shabes. There were many who had to be helped, or who helped themselves, by visiting homes and asking for alms. In the years before the First World War, there was always a great need among both the middle classes and the craftsmen.

In those days, there was a priest, Jan Grobowski, who helped many, particularly the poor Jewish population. He knew who was poor and helped them provide for shabes. He would employ many Jewish artisans and help them make a living. In summer, he would lend money to the sadovnikes [orchard keepers] to help them lease the orchards.

If a Jew had to marry off a child and had no money, he would go to the priest, and he would receive a nice wedding present which covered the wedding expenses.

His sister, who was called "Pani Treletzka", was an eye doctor. She would treat Jewish children for free and would also not charge for prescriptions.

The entire Jewish community attended his funeral and brought a bouquet of flowers to his grave.

A large role in economic life was played by the Jewish sadovnikes who leased orchards from the farmers of the surrounding area before the growing season. Dozens of Jewish families depended on it.

Economic life was especially enriched by the timber trade. The first pioneer in the field was R. Mordechai Fleischer and his family. It later passed to many Jewish hands. This Jewish enterprising ability allowed for respectable employment.

*

There were also a few factories in S. which helped ameliorate the economic problems for Jews and Christians.

Most prominent was the sugar factory which belonged to Hrabia Zamoyski. In recent times, before the outbreak of W.W.II, business conditions were disrupted by the anti-Semitic organizations such as N.D. and H.D., which took away the livelihoods of many Jewish businessmen.

A second was Tsebrik's factory which manufactured various wood products which were distributed by Jews throughout Poland. The Messinger family, especially their sons, Yosel, and Moishe profited from this.

The third factory, built just before the Second World War, was the turpentine factory, "Alpha". The Groiser family was mostly involved with it.

But this very factory left sorrowful memories for the survivors of Hitler's devastation. The turpentine factory served as a concentration point for those taken from the villages, and mostly from S., and transported to Belzec and Majdanek. They spent the night in the fortified factory and waited for the death-trains.

So life went on until the shtetl tore itself out of its economic straitjacket. Youth began to learn trades. After the First World War, Jewish youth enrolled in government schools in great numbers. Many dared to openly study in the "wider world"—in Zamosc, Lublin and Warsaw. In the last years, Jewish students began to attend teacher seminaries. A Hebrew and a Yiddish school were founded where Jewish students studied in the afternoons.

Israelka the water carrier

[Pages 78-79 - Yiddish] [Pages 80-81 - Hebrew]

Making a Living Was Very Hard
by Zvi Treger (Tal)
Translated by Moses Milstein

More than anything, I remember how my mother, Chana-Tshele, z"l, struggled hard and bitterly to support the family. She ran our tailor business, traveled to markets, bought goods in Warsaw, and did the cutting herself for the workers that worked for us in our house. And she still managed the house-hold. Later, following bankruptcy, things became harder. We were forced to try everything to support our family.

Father, Mordechai, was a fisher-sadovnick, and was always away in the villages. Summer, he would bring fish, which we would sell in large tubs near the market hall. Winter, when there were few fish, he would bring geese and ducks. But the main business was in renting orchards. At the beginning of summer, we would lock up the house and move to the orchards to tend the fruit trees and bring the fruit to town to sell. The winter fruit, we would bring back home, store it in the cellar, and select some from time to time for sale. We tried to make it last as long as possible in order to get higher prices.

From all these businesses, we barely made a living. As it is said: a lot of work and few rewards.[1] Nevertheless, we managed quite well. Erev shabos, the neighbors would bring us pots of cholent and bottles of milk-coffee. My mother would consider it a mitzvah to put the pots in the oven, and the coffee with milk in the wall-oven. All the neighbors were very grateful to my mother and wished her many blessings.

I can't forget the chaos in our house when we were getting ready for the "lad", that is, to bake matzes. The whole family worked long and hard, because everything had to be done in the two weeks before yom tov. Erev yom tov, everything had to be ready to bring Pesach into the home. Mother worked harder than anyone. Nothing was too hard for her so that no one would go hungry in our house.

My mother was blessed with good-looking children, one better-looking than the other. We were proud of our oldest brother, Eli-Moishe, who did not live at home but studied in the yeshives.

During the examination[2] in shul, there was a competition between him and the rabbi's son, Meier. Each wanted to show that he knew more pages of Gemorrah off by heart. The examination stimulated a lot of interest. All the participants were dressed in their best and listened attentively to the competition. My mother and father, sitting in their places, thought themselves the luckiest in the world to have such a son. Many people were envious of them for having raised such a Torah-bucher.

Being young, I didn't understand this. I just remember my mother's beaming face and her tears when she spoke of her children and especially of her oldest son.

Eli-Moishe was a rabbi in Tomaszow-Mazowiecki until the war. I never visited him. He had five beautiful girls. He perished with his family early on in the occupation of Poland.

*

Since we lived on the shul street, I used to hear the singing of the yeshiva boys every Saturday and holiday as they danced their Chasidic dances. Their ecstatic voices would echo through the streets.

I remember the Friday evenings when every youngster would go somewhere-to Zionist or Bundist meetings where lectures, and discussions were held. Others gathered in private houses to enjoy cultural events.

Similar evenings were held in our house due to the initiative of my brothers and sisters. I also remember my neighbor, Berl Koil, who took part in the evenings. He was very talented and full of ideas. He used to read and act out the characters from Sholom Aleichem, from the "Dybbuk", and from other authors and works. He did much for the cultural life of the working youth. There were many like Berl Koil in our shtetl. Shebreshin could be proud of their cultural activities.

Tel-Chanan

Translator's Footnotes

1. A sach parnuses un veinik bruches.

2. Farher

[Page 82]

Respectful Behavior, Honest Trading

by Emanuel Chmielash

Translated by Moses Milstein

I am now 69 years old, 43 years after Shebreshin, and I still see before me Shebreshin, its streets, its houses, the Jewish homes and the Jews there. I see before me the poor, but honorable, Jewish lives.

The interpersonal relations between Shebreshiner Jews were at a high level. We did not live for ourselves alone. Neighbors, or any other Jew, aside from family, were an important component of our lives. Each helped the other in word and deed.

I have been in America now for 32 years. I know life here, and I can see who and what we have lost. All the shtetlach were similar to S., and American Jews, who, after all, came from there, often came to visit, not only to see their relatives, but also to receive spiritual strength in order to carry on a Jewish life in the new world, America.

When I lived and worked in Warsaw, I would return every year to S. on vacation. I did not travel to Kazimierz or other resorts, but only to S. Home, to my father and mother, sister, brothers, and to spend at least two weeks in Shebreshiner society. Then, being only in my twenties, I could have maybe had more fun in the resorts, but I chose my little shtetl for my two weeks of vacation.

Today, not a day goes by when I don't see before me, or think about, my old home, about S. and all her Jews, with all her streets and lanes.

Our shtetl had a true Jewish life in the traditional sense, in the highly moral sense. Family life was pure and honest. One Jew was ready to help another. There was great love between them.

In the synagogue and the shtiblach[1], no matter how many strangers came on a Friday evening or Saturday morning, no one was left without a shabes meal. The shames of the shul made sure that the men were provided with a guest at the shabes table. No matter how great the worries were over earning a living during the week, the needy were still helped with money. There was also anonymous giving.

Gemilut Chasadim

My father, Berish, was a nervous man, but a very good man, honest, with an open heart. As a child, I saw events in our house that stemmed from Jewish customs that I do not see today.

I remember that, once, R' Yermiah Rabinovitch came to my father, and said that we needed to take a young woman to the hospital in Lublin, and we needed 100 Zl for it. So R' Yermiah and my father set off on a short walk to see some people who could and would help. Even some Christian priests who were in town contributed, and in the space of an hour, the sum was obtained.

One Saturday morning, after the meal, Baruch Shisl, and someone else, went into the room where my father had his shabes nap. My father woke up and Baruch said, "Berish, we have come for a donation." My father replied, "If you are here on a shabes, then it must be urgent." He pointed to the credenza and said, "There are the keys. Open it up and take what you need." Baruch did that and said, "Berish, I took 10 Zlotys."

One winter evening, a Shebreshiner was visiting with us. He had a wife and two young children, but as for money, he was destitute. They lived on packages from America. My father said, "Take my horse and wagon. The horse sits in the stable anyway and eats, and drive out to the country and buy wheat for me from the farmers. Bring it back to town. You can either sell it to the mill, or, if not, I will buy it from you."

And another fact. One day a wheat merchant came to see my father. He was a scholar, a ba'al pilpul. Chatting with my father, he proposed a deal. My father called him by his name, and said to him, "Mah yomru habrios?"[2]...In business there were also "barriers", moral ones, where you could reject remuneration so as not to transgress human, Jewish principles.

In our old home, in the small shtetlach, we Jews conducted business without contracts or lawyers, relying on a person's word.

I have been in America more than 32 years, involved in the world of small business. I see the difference between our old ways and today. I don't want to minimize or deny Jewish life in this rich world. But it should only be noted that we, the sherit haplita, have lost the old, beloved world where we were raised.

Montreal, Canada, 1982

Translator's Footnotes

1. House used for prayers

2. What will people say?

[Page 84]

Breaking Windows – Winning the Strike
by Yankel Itche Treger and Leibl Akerflug
Translated by Moses Milstein

Yankel Yitze Traeger and Leib Akerflug, from those days...

We lived in a shtetl without electricity, running water, or in-door bathrooms, with no future for our youth, sometimes with little to eat, or without a shirt to cover our backs. A piece of cloth to sew clothes for children was considered a "big fortune."

We could become tailors, shoemakers, carpenters, barbers, or engage in other trades. But, to go on to study in a gymnasium or university was, for the Jewish youth, a utopian dream, an impossibility. The Poles did not permit it.

We worked under masters who exploited us, although among them were "capitalists" who didn't have enough for shabes themselves. However, there were other masters who could afford to pay their workers, but were only concerned for themselves. So we, the executive committee members of the trade union, had to send a few tough comrades to the masters, and only then did they find the money to pay the impoverished workers three to four weeks of back pay.

On one occasion, the trade union had to fight for its very existence. A strike was declared against a wealthy tailor, Kalman Kalfeld, who had a prosperous shop. He vowed that he would break the union, and one of his workers was a strike-breaker. It was a difficult time: either we win, or we lose and the union breaks up.

We agonized over the issue along with the head of the Bund, Yosel Springer. What should we do? There was a proposal to destroy Kalman's goods with vitriol. Another proposal was to smash his fine, big shop window. We, the activist youth, immediately took it on and carried it out. In short order, the strike was won.

After this the union committee had a meeting. Yosel Springer, the leader of the Bund, said, "Blessed are the hands that did this."

One must ask: How did we have the courage to carry this out? The answer is: our strong belief in a better tomorrow, and the loyalty of our comrades. (They were later murdered by the Nazis with the help of the Poles and Ukrainians.)

We, the authors, enthusiastically fought for this idea of a better future for mankind, and were ready to sacrifice our young lives. Unfortunately, we were disappointed by our experiences in Russia during the war where we witnessed the anti-Semitic policies of Russians against Jews in general, and, later, towards Israel.

Shebreshiner youth were among the most progressive in the area. When we met with comrades from neighboring shtetlach and even from larger places, we found ourselves to be among the most conscious of our cause. Not only the socialists and the Zionists, but even the religious youth were activists.

We remember a shabes, or a yom tov, or the beautiful days of May, when our young fit people went out for walks, talking about, and hoping for, a better tomorrow. We would walk together to the bloine and the mountains, enjoying the fine Polish climate.

But the society around us was antagonistic and hateful towards us. We were afraid to walk in the Christian streets. We were often attacked going to the bloine, to the "vigon."

We lived with our Polish neighbors for hundreds of years, but, in truth, they were always distant from us. Nevertheless, we hoped that we would achieve a better life.

Montreal, Canada. 13.10.1960

[Pages 87-88]

On Weekdays and on Holidays
by Yankel Frost
Translated by Moses Milstein

In the shul court-yard, near the large bet hamidrash, among the jumble of dwellings, stood half-sunken "huts", their windows close to the ground, twisted like a joker's smile. The stench from the large "Optrit"[1] could be smelled from afar. The road to the city cemetery passed by the court-yard, and funerals went by this shambles and the big bet hamidrash.

In the huts, lived honest, hard-working Jews and their families. Among them were the families of Binyamin Frost and David Frost. Both extended families worked hard to make a living.

Binyamin Frost, with thick ropes bound around him, carried heavy sacks of flour from the wagons of the ba'al hagoles[2]. He was lucky if there were enough sacks for him to unload. More than once, he waited entire, fruitless, days without anything to unload from the wagons. On many of those days he dragged himself around without earning a groschen for his purse.

He never complained to anyone. He always had a smile on his gentle face. He was happy with his lot, a Lamed Vovnik[3]. For his hard work, the bosses paid him pennies. He never bargained for his fee. A "Bontche Schweig."[4]

And when the holy Sabbath comes, Jews with reddened faces, wet beards and payes, come from the mikvah, Binyamin Frost among them. They hurry to the shul in order to welcome the revered guest, Shabes, with shining, holy fervor, dressed in Shabes robes and Shabes hats, the children with hair washed clean. The Sabbath queen presides over the Sabbath table. Pleasing songs and hymns release us from our daily worries.

Binyamin liked people and people liked him. He was esteemed by everyone because of his simplicity, friendliness and manner. He shone with a special Jewish charm.

*

The years flew by until the great sorrow of the devastation of the Jews and Yiddishkeit. Satan the Destroyer got the upper hand and his demons, the Nazis, destroyed the thousand-year existence of the Jews in Poland. With beastly cruelty they killed and annihilated with all kinds of incomprehensible methods. And these two extended families were also wiped from the earth through the hands of the German murderers.

May these words serve as a memorial, for there is no gravestone to mark their deaths.

Haifa, June, 1982

Translator's Footnotes

1. Public lavatory

2. Carriage drivers

3. One of the 36 Righteous Men

4. "Bontche Schweig", "Bontche the Silent", is a story by Y.L. Peretz about a meek unassuming soul.

[Pages 89-91]

Night Work in a Bakery

by Avigdor Rieder

Translated by Moses Milstein

My father was a baker. We had our own bakery, not mechanized of course. We worked with primitive methods, everything was done by hand. We worked day and night, mostly at night, by the light of a flickering naphtha lamp. We looked forward to Pesach so we could finally get some sleep, and rest our weary bones.

My father stood with tired, sticky eyes at the flour bin, sleeves rolled up, his fingers in the dough. At first the wet dough sticks to the fingers and it seems like you will never get rid of it. You keep kneading the dough and slowly the moisture disappears and the dough becomes smoother. Little pockets of air form and whistle until the dough is ready.

During the holidays, the smell of cinnamon and raisins carried for kilometers. The baked goods were not only tasty but esthetically appealing. The braided challahs, glistened on the table and were beautifully symmetrical. They were not just challahs, they were beautiful jewelry.

In our small, crowded house dwelt our whole family, father, mother, and twelve children-four sons, and eight daughters.

After I finished cheder, I was forced, at the age of fifteen, to begin working. I traveled to Lublin to look for work. I found work at a bakery. But the wages were so small that I couldn't afford to buy a pair of shoes or a suit of clothing. I worked there for two years for a piece of bread and sometimes, not even that.

My landsleit Yehoshua Waks, and Shalom Walwish's son found me there, tattered and poverty stricken. They immediately found me a better job at a pastry bakery. I think about them on Shabes, and still today, I am grateful for their good heartedness in my time of need.

In 1914, after my father died, I returned home to work.

In 1926, I opened a bakery in Ephraim Shtil's house. He was Shimon Geld's son-in-law. But things were made difficult for me by the sanitation commission on one side, and Zalman Stern, the landlord, on the other. One Friday, while I was in Zamosc to buy flour, the commission came to shut me down. So my wife, z"l, ran to Koszel, a Christian, to beg him to rent us a rooms for a bakery. She paid him 1,500 Zl without signing a contract.

When I returned from Zamosc, I went to see Koszel in order to conclude the contract. He told me to come back Saturday night. When I returned, he presented me with a ready contract and asked me to sign. When I read the contract, I was stunned, because the terms were so awful. I demanded that he return my money, but he laughed at me.

So I went to Zamosc to see Yehoshua Peretz (Y.L. Peretz's brother[1]), and he wrote a request for me to the komornik[2] for the return of my money. When the komornik came to the landlord, he argued that he would not return the money. So I sued him in court, hired a lawyer, and gave Zelig Berger as a witness. On the first occasion, I lost. So Yosel Lerner (Yehoshua Lerner's son) advised me to appeal to the court in Lublin and attach a poverty certificate from the magistrat.[3] Abraham Itche Weinreib procured the certificate for me with the signature of the mayor. I won the appeal and some additional costs as well.

Then the landlord sold the house and my debt became part of the mortgage. Isaac Weisfeld and his son-in-law bought the house, paid me the amount owing, and I was saved from goyishe hands.

*

But one does not live by bread alone. There was also interest in quality of life and neshome yese'yre.[4]

*

But, in time, new winds began to blow. The younger generation began to frequent various organizations where we learned to read, and take part in lectures, discussions, and cultural evenings.

Understandably, the older generation looked askance at all these things. They were very pious and believed deeply. We inherited the ardor and beliefs of our parents, but replaced the Meshiach Ben David with a socialist redeemer, and waited for a brighter tomorrow, or for a national home in "Palestine."

*

I pray God to carry me and my longing soul to my shtetl, to my old home with its good and bad characters, to the working man and the rich man, to the water carrier and the scholar, to the bet hamidrash and the old organizations and life-sustaining institutions, to the close relatives and the warm neighbors.

Akko

Translator's Footnotes

1. Well-known Jewish author
2. Bailiff
3. city hall
4. The additional soul which is said to possess a Jew on the Sabbath: hence, Sabbath festiveness. Weinreich.

[Pages 92-95]

Do Not Miss the Train!

by Abraham Becher

Translated by Moses Milstein

We were still young after the First World War. Just finished cheder. Shaul Zisbrenner and I went to study at the Radziner shtibl.

Every evening our older friends would get out of studying and leave the shtibl. We never knew where they disappeared to, and this interested us greatly. We looked into it and were amazed and excited to discover that they were engaging in clandestine activities and attending Poalei Zion party meetings.

One night, my friend, Shaul Zisbrenner, and I, quietly followed them to their destination. To our chagrin, we were not allowed to enter the place. On the way back, we met Abraham Chaim Nus, and Shmuel Ber Klieger. We walked ahead for a little and then they called us back. We noticed that earlier they had been whispering to each other. Shmuel Ber Klieger ("Der Veisser Kop") suddenly asked us, "Where are you coming from, chevreh?" We told them that we were prevented from getting into the Poalei Zion club. They looked at each other and said, "They won't let us in either."

Conspiracy

The four of us went to the center of town where we met Lutshe Kandel. He shared some seeds with us-and we waited. For what?-I didn't know myself. But it turned out that Kandel and Klieger did know, because a short time later, when I asked, "What are we waiting for?" one of them replied, "Wait a while, what are you afraid of?"

It didn't take long, and Mendl Boim appeared. We called him "the Belzer dreilock", because he had long peyes. He looked us over and said, "Come, but one at a time!" It was a time when youth organizations like Hashomer, Football Youth, were founded in our shtetl, and we were also eager to join an organization like our older classmates in the shtibl.

We followed him quietly, one at a time, almost at a run. we got as far as "Lame Shmuel's" and went into Pinchas Bibel's. "The Belzer dreilock" took a brochure out of his coat and read to us about Joseph Trumpledor. That same evening we founded HeChalutz.

We would meet every evening. I remember one night Abraham Chaim Nus asked, "Nu, Belzer Dreilock, where are we going today?" And so Belzer Dreilock would lead us out-sometimes to Pinchas Bibel, in Shoshele's shtibl where an oren kodesh stood against a wall, sometimes to Asher Shapira in a multistory house, sometimes to Shaul Moishe Pinieh in a small alcove. We followed him everywhere.

Founding the HeChalutz

We were almost eighteen years old. Mendl Boim is at the head of HeChalutz, HeChalutz HaTzair. New male and female members join. We enroll a large part of the youth from the shtetl. Mendl Boim organizes lectures on political and economic topics, on Bogdanov, Borochov's class interests, and the nationalist "question." Most of the time we held the lectures in nature's lap, among the beautiful mountains.

No matter how big HeChalutz became, the six of us remained together. Lutshe Kandel was always elected treasurer, and Mendl Boim as secretary along with Shmuel Ber Klieger. We four friends named them "the couple." At each event, either Mendl Boim spoke or Shmuel Ber. Even after marriage-and I was the first-my house was always open to "the six."

As fate would have it, Shmuel Ber Krieger, Abraham Chaim Nus, and Shaul Zisbrenner, perished at Hitler's hand.

If you want to stay alive

The economic situation in Poland deteriorated. Existence became difficult.

Once, sitting in our house discussing solutions, Mendl remarked, "Whoever builds a life in Poland will come to a bad end." This was after an evening when we had selected members of the HeChalutz to make aliyah. Coming to us tired and wrung out, he, like a prophet, laid out the prospects of Polish Jewry.

Then Lutshe said, "Everyone else you provide for, but us you don't consider and provide us with a certificate." We sat for a long time in silence. Then Mendl said, "There are only three of us friends left. Shmuel Ber got married and left. Abrham Chaim got married and went away. The same with Shaul Zisbrenner. They strived for a dowry and as a result got closer to death. My friends, for ten years we have worked for one thing, for the idea. I have had enough. I am leaving for Eretz Israel, and if you want to stay alive, come with me!"

In our hearts, we felt he was right. We kept silent. I remember, as if it were yesterday, Mendl and his manner, how he began to speak loudly. The children were sleeping in another room. Rivke, my wife, was serving tea. We listened attentively to Mendl's prognosis on the political situation in Poland and on the Jewish minority in Poland.

He was silent again. My wife broke the silence and said, " You've been leaving for Eretz Israel for the last ten years and you're never going to go!"

A little while later he stood up and said, "Listen my friends, Lutshe and Abraham! I am leaving at the end of 1932 or the beginning of 1933. If you want, I will organize passes for you and you can come with me. If you don't come now, you will-whether you want to or not-perish . But remember, take care you do not miss the train!"

At the beginning of February 1933, Mendl and Rechtshe Alerhand left for Eretz-Israel.

Haifa

[Pages 96-102]

The Devil was out of Work

by Pinchas Bibel

Translated by Moses Milstein

R' Shmuel Yakov, the fine Jew and Ba'al Teke'ye[1] in the shul, used to begin practicing blowing the shofar, a few days before Rosh Hashana. One day, while practicing, he noticed that the devil was standing beside him. So he directed a curse at him in his mind. "May he go to hell, he has already sniffed out the shofar!" But only in his mind, because with the devil, you don't fool around. God forbid what he would do if he got mad.

So R'Shmuel forced a cheerful expression on his face. He extended his arm to the devil and asked, "How are you, R' Devil."

"Oy, R'Shmuel, I don't feel so good."

"Probably over worked yourself, R' Devil, because it's very hard now to make Jews sin. It's no small matter. It is, after all, before Yom HaDin, and Jews are afraid."

Hearing the words of R' Shmuel Yakov, the devil laughed, and his laughter was heard in all the worlds.

"Ay, R' Shmuel Yakov, I thought you were a smart Jew, because all the Jews in town think so. What do you think, R'Shmuel Yakov, that it is like it used to be, when I used to have to work so hard to bring a Jew to sinfulness?"

"You surely remember that Friday before dawn when they caught R'Shmuel Asher, the shochet, in the bath house with the shikse Zuzge who heats the bath. Do you think it was so easy for me to get this Jew who guards every mitzvah like the eyes in his head and runs from sin like from a fire, to get him together with the shikse Zzuzge? Ay, ay, how much work I had to put into this job! Night after night, I brought Zuzgeh to him and she took off all her clothes until she was naked, and I would say to him, 'R'Shmuel Asher, take a good look at those legs, how pretty and pink they are! How the blood pulses in them.' But R' Shmuel shut his eyes and shouted, 'What does the devil want from me. Go to hell!' But on the third night, he half–opened his eyes and peeked at Zuzge's pink legs. Little by little, he was unable to tear his eyes away from her legs.

"When I saw that I had him a little, I went further. 'R' Shmuel Asher, take a look at Zuzge's breasts. Ach, how nice and graceful they protrude from her chest.' And again the same scene was repeated. First, he shut his eyes and threw curses at me. After, he couldn't tear his eyes away from them. And so the thing went on until last Thursday night when R' Shmuel Asher, the shochet, did not only not shut his eyes at Zuzge's naked body, but he climbed onto her naked body with both hands so that I allowed myself a little joke with him. 'You see, R' Shmuel Asher, this right breast of Zuzgeh is Moshe, and the left one is Aharon. ' The joke appealed to him very much. He burst out laughing and said, 'That's all we need, a funny devil. Go to hell!'

"At two in the morning, I said to him, ' R' Shmuel Asher, let Zuzge go, already. She has to go light the oven for the baths to heat up the mikveh for the women for shabes." But R' Shmuel Asher no longer had control over himself. A terrible pain gripped him and he would not let Zuzge out of his hands. Nu, I thought, now I can talk business with R' Shmuel. 'Listen, R' Shmuel Asher, Zuzge has to go, work is work. But how long can you go on arousing yourselves and not finding consummation? My advice is the following: Let Zuzge go now and do her work. She'll be done in about an hour. So get dressed and go to her and put a little money in her hand. I promise you, she will give herself completely to you, and you will still your suffering.' And R' Shmuel did just that...

But don't think for a minute that the sin came so easily to R' Shmuel Asher. That's why I am a devil, in order to do evil as much as I am able.

The same night, I sent to David Zvi, a gentle young man, my helper, a passionate girl, (also a devil) she should work him over...And what and how to do it, I didn't have to tell her. She knew this better than me...

David Zvi, the gentle young man, was oblivious to everything. He was just interested in sitting and studying and making babies. About money, he didn't have to worry. His father–in–law took care of it. Six weeks had already passed since his wife had given birth to a girl, and he was so removed from her that he would not even hand her the keys, but would throw them on the table, and six weeks would have to go by before he could come in contact with her.

It was to this gentle young man that that very night I sent the girl–devil to work him over...When David Zvi woke up at daybreak, he felt that his night–shirt was very wet in a certain area... A cold sweat broke out on his head, and quick as a cat, he jumped out of bed, poured water over his hands, stood in a corner and said, "Reboinu–shel–oilem, you are my witness that the whole time I could not have contact with my wife, I allowed no evil thoughts to enter my head, and when evil thoughts threatened, I threw myself into study and did not permit these thoughts to overtake me. How could this have happened to me today? But since your ways are full of righteousness and mercy, so the ways of the devil are crooked and full of hatred. I will undertake a fast of two weeks and will only eat a morsel at night in order to have the strength to serve you, mighty God."

And although David Zvi knew that on a really cold night the mikveh is not yet warmed, and a thin patina of ice still covers the mikveh water, nevertheless, he hastened there. God in heaven, what David Zvi's eyes saw once he got to the bath!

R' Shmuel Asher's kapote was lying spread out on the floor, near the oven which was full of burning wood, and R' Shmuel was lying there with his arms wrapped around Zuzge's half naked body. The long front end of the tsitsis of his talis–katan were entwined around her body. The fire in the oven was blazing. From the ends of the wood which the fire had not yet reached, water blisters hissed. The water blisters were the tears of the wood...The tears and the hissing and the crackling were an expression of protest that light and warmth were now involved in works of sin instead of works of goodness, instead of warming the mikveh for Jews in honor of the Sabbath.

Upon seeing this horrible picture, David Zvi shouted, " Evil one, what are you doing? " and jumped into the mikveh. R' Shmuel Asher, pale and frightened, wanted to get up and flee the bath. But Zuzge embraced him with her strong arms. "Hey you, filthy Jew, what do you think? My blood is water? You inflamed it, now cool it off." Nu, what choice did R' Shmuel have?

R' Shmuel, after the events on Friday at dawn, ran through the streets pale and frightened, and I, the devil, blocked his way and said to him, "Hey, you fine Jew, was this nasty shikse, may she go to hell, worth it, to lose both worlds?!"

And how it ended you know well. That same shabes he had to flee the shtetl for the forest where he hung himself with his gartl.[2]

Yes, that's how hard I had to work in the old days in order to get a fine Jew to sin. But not today! Today, when I think up a nice little sin for a fine Jew, by the time I get to him, he has already done it himself. Yes my friend, it's really tough! I'm in danger of not only losing my livelihood, but to be completely liquidated. Don't forget that the Reboinu–shel–oilem is very old and when you reach that stage you tend to become nervous and cranky. Yes, nothing will do but that I must bring the fine Jews to sinfulness.

I recently met with the Reboinu–shel–oilem's servants and asked that they beg him to make me a yeytser tov[3], so I could have better work bringing Jews to perform worthwhile mitsves.[4] But they replied that when the Reboinu–shel–oilem makes someone a devil, he remains a devil until he drops dead...

Yes, my friend, I've gotten fat from doing nothing. So I come to you to see if your shofar is big enough so that when you get to lamnazeach, and you get yourself worked up and begin to blow, I can crawl into your shofar so that you will, with great difficulty, squeeze out nothing but a croak... Don't think I like this. But what won't a person do to keep the wolf from the door?

A group of members of He'Chaluts

Translator's Footnotes

1. Shofar blower
2. Cloth belt
3. Personification of good
4. Good deeds

[Page 101]

The Religious Life

A view of the synagogue of S. after the renovation by the Polish government

The Synagogue in Szczebrzeszyn, a Work of Art
Modest on the Outside, Richly Adorned Inside
by Eng. David Davidowitz
Translated by Yocheved Klausner

The Halacha[1] in Maimonides (RAMBAM: Hilchot Tefilla [Laws of Prayer], chapter 11, paragraph 2) states: "One builds a synagogue on the elevated part of the town, and the structure should be taller than any other structure in town." This law has been strictly and beautifully observed in Jewish Shebreshin. The picturesque synagogue, with its two–level roof, stood out among the buildings of the town and rightly symbolized its important function in the old and deep–rooted community, of a noble historical past. The community is first mentioned in the 17th century.

The Shebreshin rabbis, delegates at the Council of the Four Lands, served in famous communities in Europe and their names are deeply involved with the history of the Polish Jewry, until the days of its destruction (see Pinkas Vaad Arba Aratzot,[2] a collection of regulations, articles and records, ed. Israel Halperin, Jerusalem 1945, pp. 32, 35, 37, 40, 63, 67, 78, 120, 143, 169, 182, 209, 214, 267, 274, 287, 289, 307, 333, 453, 456, 516). We shall mention in particular the name of R'Meir the son of R'Shmuel, one of the respected members of the Shebreshin community in the first half of the 17th century, who fled to Krakow after the invasion by the Kozacks. He authored the book Mizmor Shir Leyom Hashabbat[3] (Venice 1639) and the well-known chronicle about the 1648–49 pogroms Tzok Ha'itim[4] (Krakow 1650; Venice 1656). This book is very rare today and only a small number of copies of the second edition (Venice 1656) are kept in the Bodleian Library, the British Museum. Before the war there were copies in the Jewish Community Library in Vienna and in the library of the Rabbinical Seminary in Breslau.

This old synagogue of the Shebreshin Community is worthy of special mention among the square–structured synagogues built in the Renaissance style, which in the past adorned the Jewish communities of Congress–Poland. It was built by the end of the 16th century, about the same time that the Renaissance– style square synagogue was built in the neighboring community Zamosc.[5] Indeed, these two synagogues resembled each other in style (see D. Davidowitz: The synagogue in the old city, the Zamosc Community, in the memorial book: "Zamosc in its Glory and its Ruin," Tel Aviv 1953).

Among the synagogues in the Zamosc district, the synagogue in Shebreshin had the richest ornaments. The dome of the main praying area (21.35 m. x 23.48 m.) was of a monastery style,

[Page 104]

with six lunettes and six openings to the women's gallery. As was the custom, the women's gallery was on the upper floor next to the west wall, while the first floor of that area was occupied by the Poolish [entry room, passageway] and the assembly room (community room). Attached to the women's gallery were several small rooms, at the north and south walls.

All those building additions were modest and had no architectural ornaments. The façade was modest as well: the walls were divided by pilasters and the tall mansard roof was the only outside ornament of the building. However, the inside was marked by relatively rich ornamentation.

Geometrical paintings were on the rim of the dome, their outlines similar to those in the Shebreshin churches, probably from the time the Zamosc Collegiate was built. On part of the dome – the spaces between the lunettes and above the Torah Ark, along the axes of the walls and above the entrance – the ornaments were richer and extended on the line below the windows. The Holy Ark, built of stone, was in local late Renaissance style, although quite simply executed. The gate of the Holy Ark, of carved wood, was more delicate, of a distinct oriental shape. The interior polychromy, which accentuated parts of the dome, was mainly light blue.

(A. Szyszko–Bohusz: Materjaly do architektury boznikw Polsce – Krakow 1926, p. 23)

The bimah,[6] made of forged iron, was built much later, probably in the 19th century. Its modern style was noticeable on the background and general character of the interior of the old synagogue. A special piece of furniture was standing on the bimah, perhaps one of the most interesting and unique in the synagogue furniture in those times, which enlivened the center of the place: "Eliyahu's Chair,"[7] made of wood, its shape reminding a canopy. The chair adjoined the western side of the bimah's beautiful banister that was supported by two poles. The contours were made in the spirit of the heraldry of the smaller Arks, found in private synagogues or Hassidic shtiblech.[8]

While the general architecture and interior ornaments of the synagogue were not much different from those of the Zamosc synagogue (the dome, the square shape of the praying area), the wall ornaments of the Shebreshin synagogue showed great advancement. A beautiful ornament, which can be defined as a classical "blind arcade" appears on the walls, on the areas between the windows and between the openings to the women's gallery. This ornament will be found later as well, in the interior of the synagogues of the baroque and "fortress" types. The blind arcade is actually a line of flat recesses topped with arcs and set between pilasters. The flat areas of the arcade were sometimes used to post various prayers or announcements (see Davidowitz: The Hebrew Letter as an Ornamentation Element in Synagogues, Part III, Hed Hadefus, booklet 1953).

[Page 105]

There was a distinct and interesting difference between the two synagogues in the structure of the roof as well. While the roof of the Zamosc synagogue was quite simple and did not add any special beauty to its rich architecture, the double–roof structure of the Shebreshin synagogue was a strong reminder of the picturesque roofs of most of the wooden synagogues in Poland. This feature enlivened the exterior of the synagogue. It can be assumed, that this mansard roof was not built at the beginning, but it replaced the original roof – as was the case with most of the square and fortress–like synagogues, after a fire or other predicament that necessitated rebuilding.

Among the ritual objects of artistic value, which in the past adorned the interior of the synagogue, we shall mention the brass chandeliers (the "spiders" – nine–branched chandeliers decorated with an eagle mounted on a spring, characteristic of the old Polish synagogues), little trays, "Torah Crowns," reflectors, many Torah Scrolls, Ark Coverings, etc.

The Shebreshin synagogue was destroyed by the Nazi murderers during the first days of the terrible war, sharing the bitter fate of the other synagogues in Poland, as well as the fate of its members, its visitors and its admirers.

Tel Aviv

Professional terms in the area of architecture used in this article

Lunette – a crescent–shaped window in a dome roof, to let in light

Pilaster – a square pillar, having a base and a capital (a specially constructed top)

Mansard – a sloped roof with a flat top

Collegiate – a group of churches

Translator's Notes

1. Jewish law. [translator's note]

2. Register of the Council of the Four Lands. [translator's note]

3. "A poem for the Sabbath Day", see Psalms 92:1. [translator's note]

4. Stress of the Times. [translator's note]

5. Contrary to Eng. D. Davidowitz's statement, which seems well–founded and correct, another, traditional, version circulated in Shebreshin – that the synagogue was 900 (or more) years old – and this is the version adopted by all other authors in this book. Because of this deep–rooted opinion, we have not changed the statements of the authors, even when they differ from the scientific assertion. n

6. The elevated part in the center of the synagogue, where the Torah is being read. [translator's note]

7. The chair where the sandek is sitting, holding the baby during circumcision. [translator's note]

8. Hassidic small synagogues. [translator's note]

[Page 107]

One of the famous Synagogues

by Meir Balaban

Translated by Moses Milstein

Extract from the book: Zabtyki Historyczne Zydow w Polsce

The Shebreshiner shul is included among the famous shuls–like the Vilna shul, and the Kracow, Lemberg, Lublin, and Poznan shuls.

Almost all the shuls in Eastern Poland are built in the form of a quadrangle. The first thing you notice on entering such a shul is that the prayer hall is below street level. You descend the stairs to go in. The educated explain it in a religious way based on the passage from T'hilim, "Mi'ma'amkim karaticha Adonai[1]."

The reality was different. In order to comply with the requirement of depth (Mi'ma'amkim), the chazzan's spot was lowered a little. But the general lowering of the building was due to an old church ruling, "The unbelieving Jews are not to build synagogues of great splendor, or richness, but of moderation and moderate size." In order to get permission to build a shul, in spite of the bishops and the government, the area had to be reduced.

To the right of the chazzan, in most shuls, on both sides of the oren kodesh, stood a stone table in the form of a mizbe'ach[2]. The Yizkor candles burned there on Yom Kippur. A nine-armed candelabra, in the form of the seven candled menorah seen on Titus' gate in Rome, sat on the table. Similar menorahs, small and large, were found in many shuls. Examples of the larger ones are found in Pogrebiszcz, S., and Zamosc. Some have smooth arms, some have arms covered with brass buttons, flowers, etc.

The name of the donor can sometimes be seen on the foot of the candelabra.

The ceiling in the Shebreshiner and the Zamosc shul is built over the center. The prayer hall is a regular and moderately sized quadrangle.

Translator's Notes

1. Psalm 130 "Out of the depths I have called you, Lord."

2. Altar

[Page 109]

Little Angels Sing a Song of Praise
by Menachem Messinger
Translated by Moses Milstein

Going down the broad stone stairs into the shul a dazzling light would strike you. You stood inspired and in wonder. Your eyes closed involuntarily.

At the entrance, seven rows of tall pews symbolizing the days of the week. Saturdays, the cheder teachers would bring all their little students, seat them in the tall benches, and like a choir of birds at dawn, their voices would echo out in resonse to the ba'al tefilah, "Baruch shemo," and "Amen."

They sat clustered together like little angels, dressed in their shabes best. In each little hand, an apple or a cookie that their mothers prepared in honor of shabes. They listened to the ba'al tefilah with awe, and their responses echoed louder–"Baruch shemo, amen"

The gaze of the assembled was drawn to the little heavenly angels who sang a song of praise to the creator of the world.

*

In the middle of the shul, rose the tall, elaborate, engraved and decorated balemer[1]. On both sides, seven wooden stairs. On the wide wooden table with many drawers, there lay several sefer torahs, graced with beautiful colored velevet cloaks, through which were woven golden threads, with magnificent artistically engraved crowns–"keter Israel", tiny gold bells which sang out musically with every movement. The sound evokes in our childish breasts the memory of the splendid past about which we learned every day in cheder and awaken in us the strong belief that we will live to see the rebuilding of our ancient homeland. How many of the cheder children survived to see the rebuilding and return to our beautiful, sunny, colorful land!

Lifting our childish eyes to the high painted ceiling, our eyes were dazzled and drawn to the play of the sun in the high tower–like windows. We followed the reflections of the passage of the sun over the various artful drawings made by Jewish artists with fascination.

Then we saw the four brass plates in the high colored relief, arranged in a square, from which extended thick, woven, twisted, flax ropes ending in brass chains from which hung beautifully engraved chandeliers with branches holding white candles.

Slowly and solemnly we chidren lit our little candles that shone together with the light from the chandlelier on all four sides of the balemer in honor of seder hakafot.

The tall chazzan, R' Moishe, with his wide, long white beard, with his strong, appealing voice, carries in his strong arms a shein covered with a red velvet mantle, a sefer torah with a double crown set on the every–day knobs, and graced with pealing musical bells.

He descends the wooden stairs followed by worthy men carrying torahs in their arms, snaking their way with measured steps, and begins to sing with his echoing, strong voice, "Ana adonai, hoshia na, ana donai, hatslicha na!"

The dancing and singing becomes more energetic after each of the seven hakafot and we children sing along.

Suddenly, the tall wide wooden cupboards which are locked throughout the year are opened by R' Moishe Farber who calls out solemnly the names and grants everyone a sefer torah inscribed hundreds of years ago, and considered to be one of the greatest honors and which were donated at certain times accompanied with dancing and music into the shul.

1939, synagogue after the fire

1939, synagogue after the fire

At the end of 1905, major social struggles took place during the election of a new dozor[2]. The newly elected dozor, Nicklesberg, applied himself energetically to the renovation of the fire damaged shul, with the help of Mordechai Fleischer, the large extended Sher family that dominated the takse[3] of the shtetl in those days, and also the business men and trades–men and even some of the Christian population.

World famous artists were brought in. The centuries–old chandeliers were converted to gas lamps. The ancient balemer was refurbished, new stairs were constructed. The ornaments of the oren kodesh were refurbished and the amod, where the old chazzan and shochet, R' Moishe Hersh, used to daven, was rebuilt in the previous style. And so too was the Eastern wall where old Reb Simchaleh, the father of R' Fishele Goldberg, used to sit.

At the ehtrance of the shul, tall benches were built for the little children so they could say, "Baruch hu uvaruch shemo" and "Amen." And the arcades, on which were written almost all the prayers in black letters, were redone with great skill and talent by the worthy R' Abraham Morechai Boim, the son of Leizer Papieroshnik.

That was how the old, fire–damaged shul was given its historic and artistic appearance in the year 1905.

Haifa

Translator's Notes

1. Table where the torah is read

2. A community leader

3. Tax on kosher meat

[Page 113]

Crown of Gold and Diamonds
by Mendl Farber
Translated by Moses Milstein

The Shebreshin shul, which was as old as Jewish Poland, was very beautiful. Inside, it was high and round with beautiful cornices. The walls were painted with phrases from the prayers. There were also carvings symbolizing episodes of Jewish history beginning from the destruction of the Second Temple.

Two wooden chains hung over the oren kodesh and between them a grape vine. A date was visible between the boughs of grapes indicating the age of the work—900 years it is believed.[1] The oren kodesh held 310 torahs. One sefer contained only the haftorahs. The parchment was made of deerskin.

The shul's siddur was full of piyutim from all the holidays, slichot for the yamim norim, as well as slichot for the yohrzeit days of the many tragic epochs suffered by the Jews of Poland in general, and the Jews of S. in particular. The siddur's date indicated 910 years.

The shul contained many crowns for the sefer-torahs, mostly made of gold, diamonds and other precious gems, inscribed with dates of 300, 500 and 900 years ago. There were also silver crowns used on shabes and holidays. But for the Days of Awe, only the golden crowns were used.

There were also costly curtains over the ark from various eras. One of the curtains was adorned with the "yizkor" and "El Maleh Rachamim" sewn in gold thread. It was donated by R' Yuzil ben Chaiah and was 300 years old. The torah covers were 300 to 500 years old. Every fringe was of silver.

The vessels for hand washing for the kohanim also received special attention. They were made of silver, and there was a jug made of gold donated by R' Naphtali.

Lighting was provided by 12 golden lamps, 600 years old, donated by pious women. One of the lamps was dated 140 years ago. Inscribed on it was the name Bat Tovah Shper. A two-meter tall, 8 branched menorah hung over the balemer[2], and above it a golden bird. The menorah was only lit on Chanukah.

In 1906, the shul was renovated using only old Jewish tradesmen under the supervision of Abraham Mordechai Boim, z"l, a great scholar who was also talented in painting and carving. At the entrance of the shul, he created a painting and signed it.

In a corner of the shul's attic, a small room for one person was walled off. It was popularly believed that the room was used to imprison those, for a short period of time, who had sinned against the kehila, or had committed a crime. There were also old clothes in the attic. Since it was the custom to put only old books in the attics of shuls and not clothing, it was believed that they stemmed from the victims of Chmielnicki.

Many old books were also found in the attic.

Kiryat Yam

Curtain from the year 1733-1823

Translator's Notes

1. As opposed to the contention by the engineer, David Davidowitz, which appears to be well founded and accurate, that the shul was built in the 1600s. The popular and deeply held version in shtetl was that the shul was 900 years old, and even though this version does not conform with the scientific facts, the editors have decided not to alter this version.

2. Torah reading table

[Page 116]

Superb Holiness

by Chava Sapian

Translated by Moses Milstein

When you came into the shul, you were overcome with awe, just as if you had entered the Temple. I can scarcely believe that I saw it with my own eyes. The colors and shades held the light of the sun, and the moon, and the rainbow.

It is said that, hundreds of years ago, a Jew whom no one knew, arrived in town. He undertook the building of the shul, which took several years. After the work was completed, he disappeared.

The following day, all the money he had been paid by the community for his work was found in a corner of the shul.

It was said that it was no other than Eliyahu Hanavi who had been the master builder, because no ordinary person could have made such superb holiness, and especially not without payment.

As I write these words and realize that the shul has been destroyed, tears fall, and my heart is sore.

The entrance gate, top, for the women's section

[Page 119]

Resemblance to the Portuguese
Synagogue in Amsterdam
by Aharon Lass
Translated by Yocheved Klausner

Our synagogue was one of the oldest and most beautiful synagogues in Poland. The exact date of its construction is not known, but according to the tradition of the Elders of the town in was built 900 years ago. When I visited the Portuguese Synagogue in Amsterdam, I found a striking similarity between the shapes of the windows of both synagogues.

I remember well the weekdays Shahrit prayer [Morning Prayer] in the synagogue. One Monday – a day when the Portion of the Torah is recited – it was an autumn day, at the time when Poland achieved its independence. Bad news had arrived about the pogroms of Petliura's soldiers in the Ukraine and utter sadness was felt all over town.

At about that time, R'Nachum'che Twerski, of the dynasty of the Trisk ADMORs, arrived in Shebreshin. R'Nachum'che was a handsome Jew, a Talmid Chacham [Torah scholar], had a pleasant voice and was an excellent cantor. Although my father was not a Trisk Hassid, he had a special affection for this ADMOR. One morning R'Nachum'che was cantor, and when, in the prayer Tachnun [supplication] he came to the part Shomer Israel [the guardian of Israel] he left his place, circled the bimah and begged with his pleasant voice: "The Guardian of Israel, protect the Children of Israel, who recite Shema Israel, so that we do not lose Israel." At that moment I felt that in this combination – the synagogue and the people praying, led by R'Nachum'che – a huge treasure of confidence and security is stored, which gives hope to overcome the bad times.

In the Tractate Megillah it is written: "What is called a great city? The city that has ten batlanim" – and Rashi explains: ten people who are always present in the synagogue at the morning and evening prayers.

In our synagogue we had a group of Omrei Tehillim [reciters of Psalms], headed by R'Hersh Neta's. Our house was not far from the synagogue and every Sabbath at an early hour I would hear R'Hersh's strong and clear voice repeating the Psalms. It was said that R'Hersh knew by heart the entire Book of Psalms – not only from beginning to end, but also from the end to the beginning.

Rechovot, 1981

[Page 120]

Sabbath in my Town

by Emanuel Chmielash

Translated by Moses Milstein

You could say that our shtetele was poor. But it is we who are poor today. From that little shtetl of yesteryear shone greatness and spiritual richness. It is of little use to compare the small satisfactions of life in little Shebreshin to the wealthier life in the outside world. Those of us who still dream can be forgiven if we still dream of the past in S., and not of something else.

We had a colorful and meaningful life. All sorts of images of the past come quickly to mind, but to transcribe them to paper is harder.

*

Shabes. Every Shabes has an Erev Shabes

A hot, summer Friday, about 3:00 or 4:00 in the afternoon. I lived with my parents, sister and brother, HY"D,[1] on Green Street (R' Mordechai Fleischer's street).

My Shabes clothes are prepared with great attention. Having finished work, I leave the house by the "front", near Geshichter's pharmacy warehouse. Years before, it had belonged to Shnitser.)

On the stairs of the warehouse sit R' Zelig Getzl, and R' Shaul Moshe Pinye HY"D. At the wall, in front of Mordechai Fleischer's house stand, like soldiers at a fortress,

Zelig Getzl's sons. Now, they aren't looking for a farmer and a sack of wheat, they are just out for a breath of air after a week of hard work. During the week, they were oppressed by the stress of making a living: Friday night, the air was free.

On Friday night, the cement stairs in front of Estherishe Fleischer's , HY"D, closed front door are also occupied.

The merchants on and around the street are still busily engaged in getting ready for Shabes. Some carry cholents, and following them come small girls carrying little pieces of wood to contribute to the oven. The mitzvah of keeping the ovens going for the neighborhood cholents belonged to Chaiele, Moishe Pinye's, and Menuche Chana the ba'al hagule's daughter-in-law, HY"D. Merchants run to Shimon Goldman and Feigele Gedalia's, HY"D, food stores to buy chicory with coffee they had forgotten to add to Thursday's shopping list.

There is still smoke coming out of the chimney of the wooden house belonging to Mordechai Fleischer and where his daughter Nechama Gernreich lives. In other homes, floors are still being washed. Other men carry the milchedik borscht and the food for sholes sudes down into the cellars where they each have a locker. At Laizer Shtifim's, half the floor is washed while, on the other half, the father and sons still sit at their sewing machines, hurriedly finishing a bit of work. It needs to be ready for early Sunday morning for a customer in Cukrownia.

Closer to Shabes, the children of R' Mordechai Fleischer come out of the house, a Sabbath glow spread over their faces. Dressed already in their Shabes clothes, they sit around the stairs. From time to time, you can see the grandchildren come running from their zayde's house and straight to Shimon Oldman's store to buy treats.

From afar comes the sound of R' Moishe Shemesh's hammer calling out the time for candle lighting. Then follow the sounds of doors closing and keys jingling as Jews close their stores for Shabes. The streets thin out. Soon the windows begin to display the red flames of the Shabes candles. Shabes!

*

With the coming of Shabes, the appearance of the street changes. The stores are shut behind iron bars. Locks, serious and determined, hang on the bars as if to say, "We are having Shabes!" The sidewalk is cleared of the weekly dust and dirt, the gutters whitewashed. The stones of the sidewalk arrogantly say to the bricks, "The wheels of the farmer's heavy wagons will no longer batter our backs." And the bricks answer, "And, over us, will walk Shabesdike Yidden."

And indeed, the wheels fall silent, and young, Jewish girls, full of charm, come out to go walking after a long hard Friday at work. Jews in satin and cloth kapotes with sidurim under their arms hurry to the synagogues for Kaballat Shabbat.

Prayers in R' Mordechai Fleischer's small beit hamidrash, in his courtyard, were attended by himself, his sons-in-law, his son Dan, HY"D, all the neighbors, the carpenters from the courtyard next door, and others. The Gabai was Zelig Blachazh, HY"D, fanatically religious, but an honest Jew. In the seat of honor sat Mordechai Fleischer. His sons-in-law occupied the Eastern wall. In the first row, sat R' Yermiyahu Rabinovitch (Later rabbi for Bialobrzeg, from Czepla Street in Warsaw). His presence truly graced the little bet hamidrash and the shtetl. The west wall was occupied by the ordinary citizens with Dantsche Fleisher at the head. He didn't, it seems, want to sit next to his brothers-in-law.

Even before Kabbales Shabes, the prayers take on a cheerful tone. Faces, shed of the gloom of the work week, the stresses of making a living, of hard toil, take on a Shabes appearance. Some are already looking for someone to play a joke on. They arrange for a real ba'al menagn[2] to lead the prayers. The initiative usually comes from the west wall group. In the middle of "lechu neranena" they mischievously lead him to the tones of the Days of Awe to the pleasure of the audience. But R' Yermiahu turns his face from the ark to the west, and with one look, they are serious again.

As the worshippers return home, the young people end their walks, and the street is deserted. From the open doors and windows, you can hear the sounds of dishes clattering, intermingled with the songs of Shabes

Saturday morning, and singing is heard. Familiar words, heimische melodies. The closer it gets, the clearer. They are in Hebrew. Curiosity takes you out of your house. In the distance–columns of soldiers. As they near, you can make out a brown reflection–the Betar youth, returning from their military muster.

There are already a few youngsters out walking on the "trottoir"–one in new shoes, another in a new suit. A new suit, on the first Shabes, means the young man has to undergo a public exam. His friends circle him, appraise him from all angles, ask who the tailor was, and of course, give their opinions.

The barber shops are busy. Stubble-faced boys go in and come out with clean shaven faces.

The new sidewalk becomes steadily livelier. Some stand in groups hotly engaged in conversation. Others walk along companionably, softly singing a workers song. Coming from Gershon Cooper's house are the strains of a newly composed march, "El Adon." That would be the Gerrer Chasidim davening Shachris. Their Shachris always began earlier so that they could take a break before Musaf to study Talmud.

Fathers and their children, talissim under their arms, are streaming, either towards the shul, or to the large beit hamidrash. And in that beit hamidrash, daven together Chasidim without a shtibl, Chasidim quarreling with their shtibl, Zionist business men, non-Zionist business men, and plain, simple people. The left half of the eastern wall was Zionist. Seated in that pew were Moishe Hersh Berger, Abraham Finkel, Yerachmiel Ginzberg, Benjamin Chmielash, Shia Wertman, and Moishe Mantile.

Prayers from the Zionist pew only begin to get going at the Kriat shema. After the first shmone esrei, the eastern half becomes livelier. Important issues are thrashed out, taken from the news in "Heint", or "Moment". With great relish, they repeat words of Yeushson, argue about an article by Itshak Greenboim, remark favorably on an essay by Hillel Zeitlin, or criticize a statement by Zev Jabotinsky. Neither banging on the table or hisses of "sha..." from the congregation can subdue their heated discussions. An excited participant can only be silenced when the Gabai honors him with an oleh torah. It isn't until "katar" that they realize the davening is coming to an end, and they take off their talissim. Slowly, some just ending their "vikoach," people make their way home.

Walking back from the beit hamidrash, you run into girls and boys coming out from the beit hamidrash and getting in a walk while their fathers are still davening at the shtibls. They usually end later. Slowly the strolling groups leave, and the street empties. The air carries the sharp smell of cholent being carried by the mothers.

After the meal, we go out to the benches near the houses. We eat fruit and chat amicably with neighbors. A little later, the older people retire for a nap, and the young take the afternoon to leave the city. In town, it is blazingly hot. Hezkel's soda water factory is packed with people. There they slake their thirst caused by the salty, fatty cholent they have eaten, with bubbly, cold soda water.

Some people avoid the heat and play chess in the shade of the half-open candy stores of Yankel Yar, or Yosele Warman.. Many of the young go to the "plazhe," others to the Bloiner orchards, and others to the valleys between the hills around the cemetery.

Young girls and boys, half dressed, take the sun lying on the lawns of the "plazhe". They smear cream on their faces, put leaves on their noses to avoid sunburn. Boys splash in the water, teaching others how to swim. Swimmers show off their skills.

In the orchards, ex-shtibl boys and girls gather, and eat the fresh fruit. On blankets spread close to one another on the ground, or on suit jackets, couples lie, and declare their love.

The valleys between the mountains were used by the various organizations, Zionists, Bundists, HeChalutz. There the Yudenshtats Partei arose and held several meetings. This was after the putsch by the revisionist party in 1933. The leaders were Yankel Gewertz, Chaim Ber Bach. I was a member of the committee.

Many youthful secrets were left in the valleys, expressions of affection, words of love. More than once, their sweet dreams were interrupted by a goy running after them swinging a scythe or a sickle.

*

Around 5:00 o'clock, they all begin to stream back to town. At 6:00 o'clock, the promenading begins in and around the shtetl. Girls dressed elegantly. Boys in presentable suits, striped shirts with stiff shiny collars–like at an exhibition.

The new promenade, the Zamosc Road, the Roslop Road, and Fleischer's sawmill, are filled with people–newlyweds, boys and girls walking side by side, or girls in a group, with boys eagerly following. Flirting is the order of the day. From time to time a girl's embarrassed giggle can be heard, and a blushing face can be seen. The strolling goes on until late in the night.

With the appearance of stars in the sky, you hear the shop doors opening with a weekday clang. "Have a good week," they call out.

Business partners get together for their weekly accounting. Many of the strollers leave to begin their work week. Couples tarry as late as possible until the girl says," It's time to go home." The boy takes her home silently, and waits by the door, unwilling to part, until she says," Yes, it's late," and steals into the house so as not to wake anyone.

Montreal, Canada

Translator's Notes

הי"ד "May the lord avenge his blood"
Someone proficient in music

[Page 125]

Illegal activity in the shtibl

by Moshe Zisser

Translated by Moses Milstein

My father, Laizer Zalman, was a Radziner Chasid. He would study all year in the Radziner shtibl . His entire livelihood came from selling Passover salt. He was the only one in town who was occupied in this business.

In 1904, when I was eight years old, my father took me to the Radziner shtibl to study. The older boys studied separately from the younger boys.

Mornings and evenings were for studying and davening, but the rest of the day was given over to the clandestine work of Zionism which was illegal under the Tsar.

At first the older boys kept their activities from us, driving us away with blows when we approached their desks. But later, they took us gradually into the "work." We would stand guard, stationed 20 meters apart, and when we saw the police or the watchman approach, we would give the signal, "Lecha dodi," "Barach dodi ch'tsevi", and the one closest to the shtibl would shout, "Tchivchak is coming."

While we kept guard outside, the older boys were inside reading various Hebrew newspapers, mostly, HaTsfira , whose editor was R' Nachum Sokolow. There was always a fire going in the stove when they were reading the newspapers and books, so they could, in the worst case, burn the material.

Illegal even among our own

One Friday, we were visited by several prominent young people, among them, the Talmud chochem, R' Abraham Mordechai–Laizer Papieroshnik's son, Leibish Kretchish, David Groiser, Yankel Gershtenblit–Israel Milchiker's son, Leibish Kiro, Abraham Itche Becher, Todros Nickelsberg, and others. They had brought a sack, and from it they distributed Keren Kayemet pushkes to the boys. The pushkes were considered traif by the frume Jews of the shtetl. When they found out about the "great transgression," they threw the boys out of the shtibl. It was a big disgrace for the parents.

I remember that once, before I began going to the Radziner shtibl, I went to call my brother to come home for dinner. I saw none of the older students there, except for R' Moshe Honigman who told me. "Go tell your father that Yosel is also now with the "learned ones."

And so, nationalist enlightenment gradually spread throughout our shtetl.

Haifa

[Page 127]

The Blue-White Boxes of Herzl

by Feige Ethel Boim

Translated by Moses Milstein

With great secrecy, we brought 15 blue-white boxes with a Star of David in the middle, into our shtetl. My husband, a Chasid in the Belz court, in spite of being very pious, and a renowned Talmudist, was greatly interested in the keren kayemet boxes.

One Friday evening, he came running home, perspiring, red-faced, and said, " Feigele, look, this is the pushke from R' 'Dr. Herzl. He is a great leader of our generation and, without fail, every Friday evening, before candle lighting, you must deposit a few groschen in the box, and should you be faced with the dilemma of either buying wine for the Kiddush or putting it into the pushke, you must not buy the wine because Kiddush you can say over the chales. The mitzvah of building Eretz-Israel in our time is greater than wine for Kiddush."

Of course, I obeyed my honest husband, z"l, and immediately began throwing our last few couple of groschen in the pushke, and didn't buy the wine, and my husband made Kiddush over the chales. But the Kiddush rang differently in my ears than at any other time, because tears of joy ran from my husband's eyes, because we two were participants in the mitzvah of the building of Eretz Israel. And this very Shabes was the happiest one.

But here began our troubles thanks to the blue-white pushke of R' Dr. Herzl.

The whole shtetl became aware of this. My husband, along with other young men was thrown out of all the shtiblach by the fanatics and had nowhere to daven. These were: Todros Nicklesberg, Yehoshua Waldman, Simcha Reifman, Yakov Honigman,

Ephraim Yehoshua Stern, Naphtali Hop, and others. They were the first members of the Zionist movement in the shtetl. Their wives were also prevented from praying in the women's shul.

My husband died very young. He was among the first of the youth in our town to accept the blue-white pushkes. I believe that as a result of the pushkes, God helped me, and I was saved from Hitler's hands, and together with my children, may they be healthy and strong, we arrived at different times in Israel, and we are all here today.

[Page 128]

Memories from the Heder and from the Shtibl

by Aharon Lass

Translated by Yocheved Klausner

Every time I hear about Shebreshin, my childhood years appear in my memory, although I lived in that town only a few years. When I was 11, I went to live with my grandmother in Chelm, and returned to Shebreshin only for the holidays of Pesach [Passover] and Sukkot.

My parents, Sara Ita and David Lass, were religious, Hassidic, and the mitzvot [commandments] were strictly observed in our home. Thanks to my mother, our home was always clean and beautiful, and the children were always neat and dressed in good taste. In addition to raising her seven children, my mother excelled in embroidery, especially tablecloths for Sabbath and holidays. It was not in vain that my father, every Friday night before the Sabbath meal, sang the Eshet Chayil song ["a woman of valor" (Proverbs 31:10)] with a special emphasis.

My father, R'David the son of Zev Hakohen Lass, was born in Chelm. He was a learned Jew, one of the important Radzin Hassidim in Shebreshin. Twice a week, he would wake me and my brother Lipman at 5 in the morning, before we got ready to go to the Heder, and teach us the Tractate Sanhedrin. To this day I remember his clear explanations of the Talmud's various subjects.

Joy and cheerfulness was always present in our home, in particular during the evening meals of Shabbath and holidays, when all members of the family – my parents, my brothers, Lipman and Mordechai, and my sisters, Yenta, Zlata, Tova and Chana (and sometimes a guest as well) – were sitting at the beautifully set table, and singing together the Sabbath songs. All this remains etched in my memory to this day.

Wrapped in the prayer-shawl – to the Heder

My first memories are from the day I heard my father's voice calling me to leave the children that I played with and come into the house. Inside, my parents waited for me and happily announced that on that day I would begin heder. My mother dressed me in my Sabbath clothes, and my father wrapped me in his prayer-shawl, took me in his arms, and carried me to my first melamed, Shlomo Belfer.

In the heder, I met many children my age, three and four, and some older children as well. Two long tables stood in the middle of the room and along the wall were low benches for the children. The melamed, Shlomo, sat on a chair at one of the tables – he was the teacher of the older children. His son Yitzhak sat at the other table with the young children. Here I learned the Alef-Bet and continued until I began Chumash (the five books of the Torah). I remember one Saturday, a crowd of people gathered in our house. I was standing on a table, "decorated" with my new gold watch, uneasy and apprehensive – but I "passed the exam:" I translated the entire first sedra [Torah portion] of the book of Leviticus from Hebrew, the "holy language" to Yiddish.

[Page 129]

After I "graduated" from Shlomo Belfer's heder I went to the heder of Avreime'le Binyomin's. With him I continued studying Chumash, with Rashi, the known and beloved commentator. The room was small and not many children were in this class. The rabbi would eat his meager meals at the pupils' table. He would recite silently the blessing after meals, but when he reached the verse "And He shall lead us upright to our Land" he would raise his voice and recite the passage with a special melody. I can truly say that this kindled in me the first sparks of Zionist education.

My third place of study was the heder of Yankel Shloimele's. This heder was more orderly and methodical, and the explanations were much clearer. Here I began to study Talmud. R'Yankel Shloimele's was a good teacher, he gave us not only meaningful explanations of the "weekly portion" [sedra] but he did it with special, heartfelt melodies. I remember well the sweet and moving tune of Jacob's "confession" facing his son Yosef, [Va'ani Bevo'i] in the last portion of the Book of Genesis. The period of time we studied with him was interesting from another aspect as well: besides the regular study we were very interested in the news from the various fronts of the First World War.

Iron bars supporting the walls

[Page 130]

After Yankel's heder I qualified for Pinchas Groebard's heder. The melamed's nickname was "the blind Pinchas." The study in this heder was advanced. Every Thursday we studied the Weekly Portion [parashat hashavu'a] with Rashi commentary. R'Pinchas was very learned in Torah and Talmud and we enjoyed his beautiful comments and explanations.

The Radzin Shtibl

Among the Hassidim in town, the Radzin Hassidim were the most remarkable and the most numerous. They owned their shtibl and were not forced to wander from place to place. Shelves loaded with books were placed along the walls of the shtibl and the Hassidim would study Mishna, Eyn Yaakov, Talmud and Midrash. I remember R'Daniel Becher, grandfather of the Bechers, always sitting by the table and studying the Yalkut Shimoni Midrash.

The shtibl was open day and night and was always filled with people, in particular during the winter, thanks to the hot stove in the room. On Saturdays, they had a common lesson of Gemara [Talmud], with the participation of R'Moshe David, R'David Elboim, Pinyele Suessberger the "reader" of the text, my father z"l and others. It was nice to listen to the Gemara "music" coming from these fine people.

I would like to mention a few of these "shtibl–goers" that I always met there.

R'Mote'le Binyamin, a relative of the Maimon family of Shebreshin. He was a widower or a divorced man, always alone, moved to our shtetl as an adult man. He was a scholar, erudite in Talmud and Poskim, always studying. From him I learned the Tractate Bechorot with the commentary of R'Yom–Tov Elgazi from Izmir. Studying with R'Motele was very enlightening.

R'Moshe Honigman, a short man, a widower, with protruding eyes from so much reading without glasses. He never participated in the discussions. Always reading the "Zohar" book or another book on Kabala, bent over the book. Always sitting or standing in the same place at the table.

R'Meir Pinye, a widower, did not have a fixed place. He would move from wall to wall. He would always join the discussion and argue for his opinions. I remember a discussion on a winter day, in the shtibl near the warm stove, on the subject of the Christians' relation to Jews. All participants mentioned the negative attitude of the "goyim." Suddenly R'Meir Pinye sprung up and cried: – "Not true! There are good goyim too!" and he told us a story, something that happened to him.

Once on a winter day, he was walking to the village. It was almost dark and he was freezing. One of the Christians took him into his house, asked his son to bring firewood and lit the stove to warm him up. I remember how he repeated the Christian's call to his son, in Polish: "Pal, Pal!" (light the fire!).

Rechovot, 1981

[Page 131]

On the Chair of the Rabbinate

by Yankel Lam

Translated by Moses Milstein

In the Shebreshiner cemetery, there was a tombstone of the gaon, author of the book, Nodah Beyehuda, in two volumes containing 855 questions and answers, divided into four parts of the Shulchan Aruch: Orach Chaim, Yoreh De'ah, Even Ha'ezer, Choshen Mishpat.

In the "Encyclopedia Klalit," published by Masada, Tel Aviv, we find the following comments about him.

Yechezkel Halevi Landau—born in 1713. Died—1793. One of the foremost torah scholars and rabbis of his time. He was a Rav, a Rosh Yeshiva, and a Pusk[1] in Brodi, Yampoli, and Prague. He founded a large yeshivah, and graduated thousands of students. Was an authority on Halacha. He was recognized by the authorities and lobbied on behalf of the Jews on occasion. He opposed Frankism[2], Chasidism and Haskala. Came out strongly against Mendelssohn's commentary on the Tanach. His books: Nodah Beyehuda, Zion Lenefesh Chaiah, Ahavat Zion. (He wanted to immigrate to Israel).

*

The chair of the rabbinate in the 70s and 80s was occupied by the Biyaler R' Shmuel Levi, a great gaon, famous for his modesty. It was said that he was a stranger to monetary matters. He was known for hosting others at his table.

Later, when he was taken to Biale, the chair was occupied by Simchele Goldberg from Lublin. After his term, around 1909-1910, his son, R' Fishele Goldberg, took over. He was sickly and died in middle age, around 1920-1921.

His place was taken by R' Yechiel Blankman, a young 30 year old. He differed from all the others in that he was not only preoccupied with Halacha, but also with economic and cultural issues, as well as the needs of the community. He was also fluent in other languages, especially Polish. He appeared in open meetings and intervened when the need arose.

In contrast to the strict R' Hershele Shenker, he offered lenient interpretations of the law. I remember, when a poor woman came to R' Hershele to ask about a defect in a chicken. His decision: treif. The woman was despondent. It was Erev-shabes. Malkah, Pinchas the shochet's wife, calmed her down and suggested she go see R' Yechiel. She left R' Yechoel's happy, the hen was kosher. R' Yechiel would search and search until he found an appropriate interpretation.

*

The so-called "Koziner Rabiner", R' Abraham Bronstein, arrived in the shtetl in the 90s. He was, at the time, the official representative of the Czarist government. He was fluent in Russian and Polish.

He was one of the founding members, at the beginning of the 1900s, of the savings-and-loan bank, a Jewish and Christian society, which provided much aid to the Jewish community, merchants and tradesmen. The last two decades, he was occupied with writing petitions, and was an advisor on government affairs.

Times were hard during the period of Poland's emerging independence. The White Cross sent food and clothing aid. He was put in charge of distributing it. He needed helpers and the Zionist organizations came to his aid. They created a children's kitchen and a distribution center in the old poorhouse.

Brooklyn, New York

Translator's Notes

1. Jurist, decisive commentator on Jewish law from 11th century onward.

2. Jacob Frank, 18th century messiah claimant

[Page 133]

The Rabbi Passed Away
by Yosef Boim
Translated by Yocheved Klausner

On that Saturday morning, bitter, heartbreaking screams broke out from the throats of hundreds, or thousands in the shtetl. The cries of the women could be heard from all alleys and corners of the town, in particular the cries of the pious women, whose husbands were spending most of their time in the Bet Midrash, studying Torah with the rabbi R'Fishele Goldberg z"l.

Our world was darkened at midday! – cried one woman to her neighbor.

The crown of our head has fallen! – cried another.

Woe to us, for we have become orphans! – a bitter cry was heard from an alley.

The bitter mourning and cries soon penetrated the closed doors and shutters. Frightened people ran out into the street, some dressed hastily and some in their underwear: – what happened?

Hearing the terrible news, that the rabbi had died, even the men cried bitterly and silently. Soon they disappeared into their houses and came out dressed in their Sabbath clothes, and began walking toward the house of the Rav. It was freezing outside. The fresh snow that had fallen during the night squeaked under their boots. Rivers of hot tears streamed from their eyes, melting in the cold snow below.

Some of the people kept repeating the customary phrase on such occasions: Baruch Dayan Emet [Blessed be the True Judge], and others sighed and said: because of our sins God is punishing the righteous. We are the sinners and the great men of the generation are paying with their lives. The town is full of non–believers, young men have left the Bet Midrash and the study of the Torah, women go without head-covering and do not observe the law...

The crowd reached the apartment of the rabbi, who lived in the house of R'Shalom Maimon z"l – and we, the children followed them. From all parts of town people – men, women and children – streamed toward the house of R'Shalom Maimon.

Silently, the details of the tragedy passed from person to person: the rabbi R'Fishe'le was studying with his two pupils, one was his first–born son Yankele, the other was his good friend Leibele, the son of Binyamin Kamashenshtepper.

[Page 134]

The rabbi had decided to teach Leibele together with his son because of his intelligence and sharp mind. He loved him as he loved his own son Yankele, and he taught them until his soul rose to Heaven in holiness and purity.

It was the night of the Holy Sabbath. The family had gone to bed, and only the rabbi and his two pupils were still studying. At midnight the pupils became tired and the rabbi sent them to bed as well – Leibele slept in the house of the rabbi with his own children. The rabbi continued to study the Gemara, alling asleep now and then, until finally he closed the volume, kissed it and went to bed. He had an internal hemorrhage, and returned his pure and righteous soul to his Maker.

Since R'Shalom Maimon was one of the Belz Hassidim and their shtibl was in my grandfather's house, and since R'Shalom Maimon knew all the details about the tragedy of the rabbi's death, for many days I was the hero of all the children of my age, because I was the source of the news about the tragedy, in all details – I was the "primary source", as the saying goes.

Although it is forbidden to mourn on the Sabbath day, on that Sabbath no songs were heard in our shtetl....

In the evening, as the Sabbath ended, the snow stopped, but it was still freezing. Midnight came. The full moon was shining gloriously in the sky, exactly above the center of the town, over the roof of the City Hall, as if it was sent to lead the Tzadik to the other world. No one, young or old, remained at home that night. Everyone was outside, waiting for the funeral. Some managed to get into the synagogue. I don't remember how, but I was among them – suddenly I found myself inside the synagogue. What I saw and heard there became engraved in my memory for the rest of my life...

At midnight the rabbis from the neighboring villages arrived. The coffin was placed on the bimah. During the eulogies, weeping was heard from all sides, especially from the women's rooms, which intensified the feeling of mourning. This weeping, which penetrated the depth of my soul, I shall never forget.

*

It was said in the shtetl, that if the two pupils of the rabbi had been of the right age, one of them would have taken the rabbi's place and served as the town's rabbi; but they were not yet Bar–Mitzva.

However, when these two pupils reached adulthood, they were among the founders of the Hechalutz Hamizrachi organization. Leibele, the son of Binyamin Kamashenshtepper, is Leibl Licht, a leader in town, who headed the Hechalutz Hamizrachi and the library in the name of Mendele Mocher Sefarim and was one of the founders of BEITAR. He was also a member of the Town Council. He made Aliya in 1933.

Binyamina

[Page 135]

Legends and Mystery Stories

[Page 137 - Yiddish] [Page 138 - Hebrew]

Why Shebreshin?

by Moshe Messinger

Translated by Moses Milstein

Why is our shtetl called Shebreshin?

When the enemy of Israel, Chmielnicki, entered our shtetl with military forces, it was a Saturday long ago. Since there lived in our town many pious Jews, all the stores were shut.

Chmielnicki and his Cossacks had no idea where they were and what the name of the town was. Everything was closed. People were afraid to be seen in the street.

Suddenly, the Cossacks spotted an old Jew, a pious businessman, who was on his way to shul. They stopped him and asked him the name of the town. The Jew, not wanting to speak about secular matters, was silent. One of the soldiers became enraged and hit him on the face with his Cossack fist and broke his teeth. Even then the Jew did not want to desecrate the Sabbath, but from great pain he screamed, "Shavar shen!"[1]

The Cossacks then happily replied, "Now we know the name of the town, Shebreshin." Since then our shtetl has been called Shebreshin.

*

When I was a small child, a very old man told me all kinds of stories. He liked to gather the children around him and tell them stories. This was one of his anecdotes.

Translator's Footnote

1. "Broken tooth!"

———

[Page 139]

The Jewish School

by Feige Ethel Boim

Translated by Moses Milstein

After the Jews were expelled from Spain, a number of them settled in Shebreshin. At the time, the authorities forbade the Jews to study.

So the Jews, early in the morning, on a secret signal, stole out of town far into the countryside. In a village, Kovencik, there were tall mountains and deep valleys and even deeper hidden caves. In one of these caves, the Jews gathered and studied Talmud and the laws. When they finished a tractate, they carved the name of the tractate on a tree so that they would know which portion they had done, and what remained to do.

The goyim, on more than one occasion, would tell them when the authorities, who persecuted them, were coming.

The spot was holy to the goyim, especially the mountain, under which, in the deep cave, the Jews studied Torah. They called it, "Zhidovske Szkole."[1]

*

When I married R' Abraham Mordechai Boim, z"l, and moved to S., my mother-in-law, Rachel Leahle, told me this story of the old Shebreshin.

———

Translator's Footnote

1. Jewish school

————

[Page 140]

About the Spanish Exiles in Poland

by Menashe Unger

Translated by Moses Milstein

In the New York newspaper, "Der Tog," a fragment of the serial, "Fun Eibekn Kvall", by Menashe Unger, was published. It referred to the book, "Chutim Meshulshim," by Abraham Stern, published in Montreal, Canada. We cite below the following excerpt.

Among the old people of Shebreshin it was said that in the middle of the forest there was an empty spot, where no snow ever persisted, and the local peasants called, "Zhidovske Szkole." (Jewish school), and that on some of the old trees there were words carved in Hebrew, "Here we ended the tractate Shabbat," and so on.

This oral tradition says that these words were carved by a contingent of Spanish exiles that ended up in Poland and founded the nine communities of which S. was one.

Among the exiles, great mystics were to be found. In the deep caves and cellars found in those forests, these mystics used holy words to create a pathway so that those who are worthy can, via the cave, come quickly and easily to Eretz-Israel.

————

[Page 143 - Yiddish] [Page 141 - Hebrew]

Bringing Salvation Before its Time

by Ephraim Farber

Translated by Moses Milstein

It is winter. The whole town is covered with a blanket of snow. Near the bridge over the Wiepz, sits the old wooden Radziner shtibl, holes in its shingled roof. Some of its windows are sunken close to the earth from old age. But now it is winter and the shtibl has a holiday air, the snow covering it with a white coat.

Glimmers of light from the burned out candles can be seen through the sunken window. The voice of someone late to prayer carries over the shtetl.

The winter would have passed like all other winters in Shebreshin had not a shleper, or just a buffon, showed up in town claiming to be a Radziner Chasid. He stayed in the Radziner shtibl and said that he had heard of the cave in Kovencik that leads to Eretz-Israel, and he intends to make his way there.

Upon hearing such a story, we became very interested in the honored guest. Everyone wanted to have this remarkable guest at his table. It's no small thing! A Jew is ready to attempt the hidden Kovencik cave! And if he were successful and arrived in Israel? The very thought that he might make it, meant salvation could be so near: Kovencik—Eretz Isael. Every Jew in the Diaspora held, deep in his heart, a secret longing.

Evey cheder boy, hearing such bizarre, secretive words from the adults, began to fantasize. We imagined the cave full of snakes and evildoers. Legends about the cave were widespread among the residents of Kovencik. The farmers in the surrounding region used to say that at the time of "Bozhe Tshialo" you could hear the muffled sound of church bells. They said, that at other Christian holidays, you could hear the secret church bells.

The whole area was hidden in mystery. There were names of scholarly books carved in the bark of the trees in the forest around the cave by wandering Jews. In the caves of the mountain in Kovencik, the Jews from the time of the expulsion from Germany, found a hiding place not daring to settle yet in the occupied settlements. In all probability, most of the Shebreshiner Jews came from these harried and persecuted Jews. A fog of legend surrounded the cave that the Chasid was ready to descend into in order to reach Eretz-Israel.

One frosty morning, the visitor got himself ready. He put on a pair of big boots with double leggings, wrapped straw around his boots, then sprayed water over them in order to form an icy barrier. He put a fur cap with ear flaps on his head. He stuffed his nostrils with cotton so as not to lose any body heat. Over his Chasidic mantle he pulled a farmer's sheepskin coat, and bound it all tightly with his Shabes gartle. No small thing! He was going to discover the way to the land of our fathers.

Of course, they made a lechaim. He took his leave of everyone, except for those who were to accompany him to the cave. Horses and wag,ons were harnessed and a mass of people and children accompanied the bizarre visitor. The Shebreshiner gentiles, observing the commotion before the departure, wondered at the celebration of the "zhidkes." Are they accompanying a rabbi, or a messenger going to greet the Messiah? The Shebreshiner gentiles already had seen how the Chasidim hosted a rabbi visiting the shtetl. That the rabbi was not wearing a shtreml, they did not understand. So they stood and gaped at the unusual Jewish celebration.

After mutual good wishes, the wagon moved out. The wagon was accompanied a good distance out of town to the mill. The wagon moved further away on the road leading to Bloine , until it was lost to view in the orchards of the village.

The shtetl held its breath waiting for the good news to arrive. The accompanying men returned. Days and weeks passed and no news came. Those who went with him did not look each other in the eyes when they met. All were dazzled as if by a solar eclipse. According to all calculations the Chasid should have already returned from Eretz-Israel and announced: "Yidden, pack your things and set forth!

But the Kovencik goyim brought bad tidings to the shtetl. They had seen a Jew, a shleper, stumbling around in the snowy mountains of the village. Winter passed and the mountains were covered in green, and the messenger had not returned. The shtetl had forgotten the whole affair.

Suddenly, in the middle of the shachrit prayers, the door of the Radziner shtiblopened, and the visitor unexpectedly appeared. His fatigued appearance affected everyone. The shleper's feet were covered in rags. His clothing was tattered. Everyone was so dismayed, no words came out of their mouths. It was as if language had been forgotten.

When the whole crowd surrounded the visitor, he related in broken tones how, halfway there he had encountered Eliyahu Hanavi. Eliyahu looked at him with gentle eyes, extended his hand and greeted him. Then he said with anger, " How does a Jew dare to bring salvation before its time? Go, tell Shebreshin that the time has not yet arrived!"

Then the shleper sat down on a pew and covered his face with his hands. People saw how torn his clothes were, his feet covered in mud. In a loud voice he yelled, " Go home, Jews. The ketz[1] has been postponed. We will arrive in Eretz-Israel in our time!"

I heard this story when I was a cheder boy in the shtetl.

Kiryat Yam

————

Translator's Footnote

1. Coming of the Messiah

————

[Page 146]

"Angels Carried him from Shebreshin to Eretz Israel"
by Avraham Stern
Translated by Yocheved Klausner

I think that the author of "Mar'eh Kohen" also wrote the book "Matnot Kehunah" – a commentary of Midrash-Rabbah. In some of the volumes of Seder Hadorot he states that it all happened in 1624.

I asked some of the Torah scholars in Shebreshin (at the time I was living in the house of my father-in-law Hirsch, the ritual slaughterer from 1896 to 1900) about the event and the man: how is it possible that the tombstone of the author, the rabbi of Shebreshin, z"l, is standing in the Shebreshin cemetery, while Rabbi Chida, z"l(R'Chaim Yosef David Azulay) wrote in his book Shem Hagedolim that he saw his tombstone in Eretz Israel? They replied that according to a tradition, passed from person to person for many generations, angels from Heaven removed his body from his grave in Shebreshin and buried it in Eretz Israel.

Yet his grave in Shebreshin was treated with respect and piety, and people visited and prayed there, asking for help and support; they were assured that the prayers would be answered.

I read in the book by the Holy SHELAH, before the chapter called Yesh Nochalin, that several rabbis (Rabbi Yosef ben Matityahu, z"l, Rabbi Shmuel Eidels [the MAHARSHA], z"l, the BACH [author of Bayit Chadash] and others) agreed that it was in 1624.

Let the cynics, who don't believe in miracles by the merit of Tzadikim, not be astonished: how could angels carry him to Eretz Israel? The wise King Solomon has already written: There is nothing new under the sun. And it already happened that the prophet Elijah, z"l – a long time after he rose to Heaven – buried Rabbi Akiva (Tosefta Bava Metzi'a, 114, 2).

Montreal (Canada), 24 Nissan 5714 (1954)

_____

[Page 147]

Folk Tales

by Mendl Messinger
Translated by Moses Milstein

The groom makes seven circuits...

With a great commotion, in wagons drawn by two horses, and accompanied by music the groom would be brought from Frampol, not far from S. According to an old tradition, a groom coming from elsewhere, along with his guests, had to make seven circuits of the courthouse.

In 1912-1913, this tradition was halted because of the hatred of the anti-Semitic peasants who would stand on the stairs of the court house with boycott posters proclaiming "Buy from our people: "Swoj do swego."

The result of this anti-Semitic hatred was that dozens of Jewish families living nearby had to abandon their homes and businesses.

The marriage of two orphans

In the old shul siddur, where the important events of the town were inscribed, the following story is told.

In 1880, the so-called "Black Plague" broke out in S. and the surrounding area. It struck down large numbers of young and old. The elders of the time decided, after long deliberation, to marry two orphans in the cemetery as a remedy to stop the plague.

With great joy and the musical accompaniment of the Blum family, who were specially brought down from Zamosc, the chupah of the two orphans was erected. The town had promised to support them their entire lives. The orphans were Mendl Ketzeleh's and his wife who were given the exclusive right to sew tachrichim.[1]

*

We find this story completed in the following writings of Yankel Lam (Brooklyn, New York).

There were many deaths due to the plague. First the rabbinical court called for a communal fast. Later, when the plague continued, it was decided that they should mount a "black chupah" in the cemetery for a poor young woman and a poor young man of the town.

All the healthy residents took part in the wedding. Then God came to their aid. The plague ended and the sick were healed.

The revolutionaries are honored

The great revolutionary waves, which broke out in in Czarist Russia, also knocked at the gates of our shtetl.

On a foggy autumn day, when even the church steeple could not be seen, some of the young people gathered at the wooden dwelling of Leibish Schneider. Secrets of the struggle between the revolutionaries and the Cossacks were passed from mouth to mouth.

Breathless and inflamed one of the youths arrived and passed on the news, in the name of Simchele Feldsher (Simchele Rophe), that some of the wounded had just been brought to the local hospital and that in the morgue, lay three dead revolutionaries .

The Czarist authorities permitted visits to the dead. The revolutionaries took advantage of this permission, and with hatred and grief, they marched around the dead bodies and gave the last honors to those who gave their lives for a better tomorrow.

The shul is burning!

Before dawn, still dark, the old shames, R' David Hersh, with his great boots, holding a lantern, goes from house to house, knocks on each door with his staff, and in his deep voice shouts, "Wake up for sliches!"[2]

Suddenly, in the still sleeping shtetl, light entered the windows of the houses.

The bells of the churches began to ring without ceasing. The wind gruesomely whistled and scattered the burning sparks from the roof of old shul.

Young and old, Jews and Christians, ran to put out the fire, some, to save their own houses. The word was passed from mouth to mouth that the roof was ignited because, a large ammunition supply of the revolutionaries had been hidden in the attic.

Haifa

Translator's Notes

1. shrouds
2. Slichot, morning prayers

[Page 149]

Legendary Figures

by Yehuda Kelner

Translated by Moses Milstein

From early childhood, I used to listen to the stories told by the old people in the shtetl. I carried them around in my mind for many years, until I wrote them down for this article. The first two stories are from the 19th century.

The remarkable Lamed Vavnik

Shlomo Frank, or as he was called, the Rabbi, R' Shloimele, Mechele Treger's great–uncle, was usually in the country: he dealt in fish, probably also brought calves on his narrow shoulders. He was small, thin, with a little goatee. He used to wear a thick caftan and big boots. He gave the impression of an ignorant youth who could not even daven.

He was never seen in the streets. He took great pains to avoid talking to his neighbors. But if he heard a baby crying in his crib when no one was home, he would steal into the house, sit down by the crib, sing a lullaby, and rock the cradle. When any of the people living in the house would return, he would get up, and without a word, he would leave. He refused to accept any thanks. He said that thanks should be given to God.

A strange person, the people in town said. A person who seeks no pleasure from this world, but only from the world to come. He ate barely enough to sustain his soul. He argued that it was neither nice, nor Jewish, to eat too much, that a Jew should be tall, fat and healthy.

When he brought his fish to town, he sold the biggest ones, and ate the smallest. "With these little fish, there will be a good Oneg Shabbat." Quietly, he made Kiddushand sang zmires.

Friday evening, after eating, he would lie down to sleep without a pillow, on a bench so small he could not extend his legs, so that he could not enjoy his sleep too much.

He would seat himself at a table covered by a cloth of rough peasant cotton. His chale was of black flour, not properly baked, and burnt. He davened in the small shul. His Shabes clothing consisted of a thin caftan, and since it lacked even one button, he would wage war with the wind, and hold it together with his hands.

During the week, he rarely slept. After midnight, he sat on his doorstep and napped. He spent many a night in the cemetery.

The Jews in town wondered: What does this strange person want? Which Chasidic group does he belong to–maybe the Breslaw? Maybe to the Haskala, or even to the Shabtai Zvi? However, the Shabtai Zvi were an immoral sect, because according to widespread rumor, they carried on orgies with naked women, and for such a Jew as he was, it was impossible to imagine.

He was the object of much speculation until his death, where in his room, many books were found. So much speculation began that he was a Lamed Vavnik. And so the women, perhaps our mothers and grandmothers, visited his grave and inserted kvitlach[1] in order to gain favor from his merits.

The heroic warrior

Everyone in the shtetl knew the Shper family, especially Itche Mayer Shper who had the responsibility for the whole cemetery on his head, and maybe even on his long yellow beard. He guarded the cemetery records, and didn't let anyone see them.

His business was a stall where he sold beverages. Saturday, after prayers, I used to go there with friends to get something to drink. He would take a flask out of his back pocket and ask, " Chevreh, the 45, or the 95?" He would not keep a written tally of what someone drank or ate–a cookie or strudel, but always on Sunday, he remembered what everyone owed.

Neither he nor his family knew that in his family there was a great hero who fought for freedom and for Polish independence. There is no written history of the accomplishments of this Shper and the time it occurred, probably in the previous century (1863).

Outside Shebreshin, there was a great battle between the rebels, the revolutionaries, and the soldiers of the Romanov regime. The commander of the revolutionaries was this legendary Shper. Did he wear a beard? I believe so. He won the battle. In honor of his heroism, the revolutionary command named a village after him. The village is called Szperowka. All Shbreshiners know this village.

The rebbetzin and her seven sons

At the entrance to the cemetery, on the right, the first grave is that of a rebbetzin and her seven sons, Kohanim. The writing on the tombstone is illegible having disappeared with age, and washed away by the rains.

It is said that the rebbetzin, and her seven sons inaugurated the cemetery. If so, it is the holiest place in S. It must have happened soon after the founding of S., because there cannot be a Jewish city without a cemetery.

Something must have happened at the time: an evil decree, an antisemitic law, or perhaps a pogrom and the murderers killed the rebbetzin, and her sons, who died for the Holy Name like Chana and her seven sons in the time of Antiochus. Or perhaps it was a plague that killed them? I believe it was more likely to have been a pogrom.

Why did our ancestors not record this? Our Shebreshiner cemetery is rich with undocumented history. Our pain is great that the holy place began with a family grave at the shtetl's founding, and ended with mass graves perpetrated by Hitler's henchmen who made a mountain of dead of our fathers, mothers, brothers and sisters, threw them into mass graves, and destroyed our Jewish shtetl, Shebreshin.

Buenos Aires, December, 1952

Translator's Footnote

1. Hand written notes to God

———

[Page 152]

A Far Echo from King Solomon's Judgment
by Zanvel Aschenberg
Translated by Moses Milstein
Dedicated to my late mother

The small shtetl of Shebreshin, lay constrained between the mountains and the river, so that in order to grow, it would have had to expand into the goyisheneighborhoods, and this was something they didn't want, and we didn't want. The Gorajec mountains stood at the head of the shtetl. They provided us with lime for the cholent ovens, but nothing else. The river at its feet provided us with a little more–the bath which was located hard by the river had enough water for the mikvah, and to pour buckets of water on yourself, as much as the heart desired.

A little beyond the river, a magnificent grassy area spread covered with a mass of poppies and forget–me–nots that rolled like a green ocean wave with the slightest breeze. The picture was completed by fruit orchards that began the summer with red cherries, sour cherries, plums, and ended in autumn with apples that the Jewish sadovniks[1] stored in their cellars for winter when God might send good merchants from the larger cities. After summer, there was a sadness in the shtetl, which was covered in monotonous, and boggy mud.

A little closer to our time, that is when we, the young people, became aware of the outside world, the shtetl began to assume a different appearance. Awakening in 1918 from a long sleep to a new life, it began to move with giant strides, like water bursting through a dam. The first meeting for an eight–hour day took place in the Bet Hamidrash through the Bund. Respectable Jews were shocked by the news, but kept silent.

From there the movement grew until Shebreshin was called, "Shebreshin the Bundist fortress." The Bundists won all the seats on city council except for one seat for the Citizen's Bloc. Under the influence of this movement, there was a school for poor children, a trade union, and the intellectual cream of the young boys and girls. There were also Zionists of all hues, religious Jews more than others, with their schools, Chasidic shtiblach and so on. In a word, a lively, beautiful, social and religious Jewish life.

Overflowing with superstition

I would like to relate an incident that gave me no rest since my mother told me about it.

In my earliest youth I saw "him" and did not stop thinking about him, until after a plea to my mother, I learned something about him. I would be righting a wrong when I clear him of guilt, especially because his mother's actions deserve it.

About a hundred years ago the shtetl was, like many other shtetls, full of piousness and more than that, full of superstition. Belief in demons and miracles were common.

It was believed that the great fire did not swallow more than the shul because armies of doves brought water in their beaks; that in Tsirl the baker's attic dwelt demons that came late at night, mostly in winter, to warm themselves in the bakery. It was even known that they looked German–like. Woe to him that they wished to harm. If someone was late crossing the shul courtyard, it could happen they would be called to the Torah in the middle of the night. That person was not to be envied. At dawn, when the rooster crowed, the shul was empty again and one could go to prayers without fear.

In general, according to the elders who told themselves stories around the stove in the small shul during the winter nights, life went on as normal along the well–worn paths of piety and poverty without excessive worry.

At that time–and here we come to the point–there lived a poor widow and her only son, Yosele. The mother, very pious and very poor, did all that she was able, all manner of work, the hardest it is understood, in order to send Yosele to cheder. She even performed mitzves, within her means, and the most important was the following: Part of her livelihood involved buying milk from the non–Jews, and selling it door to door. Every morning she brought a pitcher of milk, for free, to the rabbi, in order to gain merit for her son's education.

But fate decreed that her son sought out bad friends, and non–Jewish ones at that. There was no father to instill fear, and he went from bad to worse. He skipped cheder, and disappeared for hours, and later, for days. The more she begged that he should return to proper ways, the less it helped. But to forestall tragedy, she kept at it because she knew in her heart that bad things were to come. She ran to the rebbetsin for help and to ask her to tell her husband, the tsaddik, what was happening with her son. He should stop at nothing. She would have gone to the tsaddik, the rabbi, herself, but she didn't have the few pennies to submit a petition...She believed that the rebbetsin understood her difficult situation, her fear at the outcome for her child. She could not sleep at night, her heart was aching.

On a bad course

Unfortunately, her heart did not deceive her. One day, when her child did not return home, she learned that he had gone off to some village with his friends, and her premonitions were frightful. Days went by with no change. She feared the worst. To whom had she not already run with her troubles? The bad news reached the shtetl, and the mother lay sick in her bed. From the faces of those around her, the mother understood that something terrible had happened. She learned that religious goyim, in order to gain credit in the world to come, to bring a soul to the right way, had promised her son anything and everything, until he agreed and allowed himself to be baptized...

With her last strength, she got up from her sick bed, and ran to the holy tsaddik, like a wounded bird, with a heart–rending plea. Her weakened heart could not support this. On giving the rabbi the news, she fainted. The rabbi already knew. He was silent. She threw herself at his feet. "Rabbi, my only child has been taken from me!" The mother demanded help in her dire need.

The holy rabbi was crushed, and from great pity he said to tell her that he would pray for her, that he who lives forever should take pity on her and remove her shame, and the convert's. She did not understand at first what he meant. She asked again what the rabbi said. It was explained to her more clearly, and she began to stammer, "What? My child! No, great tsaddik, not this! I beg you! Anything in the world, but no harm should come to him. Great holy rabbi! There are so many goyim. Let there be one more!"

Strange. The old people relate that no matter how pious people were in those days, no one bore any resentment against the mother.

Reprinted form "Unzer Gedank"

Buenos Aires, No. 42 (52)

Translator's Footnote

1. A Jew who would lease an orchard from a landowner

[Page 155]

In the Cemetery

by Mendl Farber

Translated by Moses Milstein

The first tombstone at the entrance to the cemetery in Shebreshin, sunken into the earth with age, its letters half worn away, and hard to read, stood between two old, broad, oak trees.

One of these old tombstones was the tombstone of rabbi R' Simchele, who died 150 years ago. It was said that, in his will, he promised that if anyone should come to his grave with a request, he would try to see it fulfilled by God. And indeed, when a person, or the community found himself or herself in trouble, they would come to his grave to remind him of his will.

Among the important graves was the grave of the famous rabbi, R' Shlomo, or as he was called, R' Shlomo the Good. He died in 1840. It was said of him that at Yom Kippur, during "Leyl Kol Nidrei", when all the men and women were in shul, R' Shlomo the Good would go around to the Jewish houses and listen to hear if a child was crying. Mothers would leave their babies in the care of older children during Kol Nidrei night. When the baby started to cry, the older child would also cry. R' Shlomo would enter, and with great love, quiet the children.

Among the tombstones there was also one of a mother and her seven children, Kohanim. People believed that they perished at the hands of Chmielnicki.

Kiryat Yam

————

[Page 156]

The Magnificent Road of the Seer of Lublin
by Aviezer Burstein
Translated by Moses Milstein

Chasidic story

A tenant was usually considered an illiterate Jew, who could daven from the siddurand read the Torah portion, and sometimes not even this. A tenant who could learn a piece of the Mishne was rare, and one who could read a page of Gemora did not exist.

Nevertheless, there once was a tenant in Lukow at Tarnograd who knew tractates of Talmud as a Jew knows ashrei. They wanted to make him a rabbi in Amsterdam, but he was not willing. It seems that Providence settled him in a quiet corner of Poland so that from him could arise the great Jewish figure who would later found Chasidism in Greater Poland, and his name is spoken with glory and praise until today.

He himself, the tenant, R' Yakov Kopel, was not a Chasid. But, he told his son Israel he should not say "Vayitzmach purkanei" in kaddish at his death. And once, when the Baal Shem Tov entered his home by the door, he jumped out the window. He regularly invited the poor to his home, a very righteous man, and a God fearing man. He dedicated himself to fulfilling the mitzvoth of the Torah.

And because he was a proper, pious Jew, he fulfilled the "Veshinantam levanecha." He hired the best teachers for his son, Israel, and for his daughter, Shprintzl–Matel, he sought out a son–in–law, a tsatske, of important lineage, the Shebreshiner "ilui",[1] R' Abraham Laizer Horwitz, and promised to support him for five years.

A year after the wedding, R' Yakov Kopel was blessed with a grandchild. Shprintzl–Matel gave birth to a son, Yakov–Itzchak. The grandfather's joy was not to be described. He loved his grandchild like one of his own eyes. He called him Itzikel, and carried him around all day like a Sefer–Torah. His lips whispered a prayer to the Creator that the child, his first grandchild, should grow up to be a God fearing person and a "Gadol b'Israel."

Prodigal talent

It is known that the prayers of an honest person are heard in heaven. Itzikel, early on, began to show prodigal abilities. At three, he could read from the siddur, and at five, he could read a portion of the Torah with Rashi.

When the son–in–law, R' Abraham Laizer, became rabbi in Josefow, the grandfather kept the grandchild with him. He taught him Torah until his Bar Mitzvah. Afterwards, he sent him to study with the gaon, R' Hirsh Meizlish, in Zolkiew.

In those days, there was a famous yeshiva in Poland run by the Shiniver Rav, R' Shmelke. Itzikle was already a renowned scholar, so his grandfatrher sent him there to study. The rabbi, R' Shmelke had become a follower of Chasidut. He saw immediately that his student, Itzikel, was destined for higher things. So he took him under his wing more than the other students.

Even though Itzikel concealed his erudition, R' Shmelke honored him by having him say the morning prayers for him. Important students, older and well known, were envious of him. R' Shmelke told them, "When Itzikel says the prayers, God and his ministering angels answer, 'Amen'"

Itzikel grew up to be a handsome young man, straight as an etrog. He had large velvet eyes, like cherries, a long, pale face with red freckles, and grew tall as a palm tree in an oasis.

A Bride, a beauty

It was time to talk about a match. A matchmaker from Krasnobrod arrived and suggested a match with an attractive daughter of a rich landowner. The bride herself carried on business, was on speaking terms with the nobility, and was a beauty. The landowner promised a rich dowry, and agreed to pass on all his holdings to his son–in–law after 120 years.

The match was welcomed by the grandfather, and the father. They broke a dish to seal the agreement and decided on a wedding date.

The wedding took place on a winter's night in Krasnobrod. A large crowd attended–relatives and rabbis and a couple of hundred guests. At the groom's meal, before the wedding, there were a couple of hundred guests, and rabbis. The groom turned to his grandfather and said, "I want to see the bride before the wedding!" The grandfather and the father were stunned. How can it be that the young man speaks such nonsense. Itzikel reminded them of what is written in the Gemora. "Asur leadam lekadesh ishah ad sheyerinah[2]" Nu, if the Gemora says so, it must be so.

So they brought the bride in. Itzikel gave her a sidelong glance, and suddenly went pale as chalk. Quietly he whispered in his grandfather's ear that he did not want the bride, because he did not see in her "Tselem elokim."[3]

Escaped from the wedding

The grandfather was shaken and the father almost fainted. They argued with him that you could not shame a Jewish daughter. He should marry her, and later, they would see. They thought he was speaking childish nonsense. He would get married, and then he would see that it was good.

But it did not happen that way. Soon after the Sheva Birchot, while the crowd was dancing the mitzvah dance, he slipped away without anyone noticing, and in his thin silk caftan, he ran away. There was a full moon. The air was gripped with cold. It was hard to catch one's breath. The dazzling white snow squeaked under his feet like broken glass. The cold and silent forest was covered in fearful darkness.

Itzikel remembered that he had not read Kriyat Shema. With numb lips, he mumbled a few holy words. His thin caftan stiffened with the wind, and the cold entered his bones. He had probably been walking for hours, because the eastern sky was getting lighter. It was dawn.

He could see a village in the distance. He came on a Jewish home with a mezuzah on the door. He knocked on the door because he was exhausted. A middle-aged woman opened the door, her face rigid and astonished. She indicated a sofa for him to sit on, and went to light the samovar, to make something warm for her frozen guest. Before the tea was ready, Itzikel's eyes closed and he fell asleep.

Resisting temptation

He awoke when he felt the hot penetrating look of curiosity and desire on him. The woman, who said she was a widow, openly, and without shame proposed to him a sinful act. Itzikel trembled. He wanted to flee the house. So the woman, a sly person, argued with him. Itzikel began to shout–the woman, also. Soon, the neighbors appeared. As Potfier's wife did with Jacob, so did the widow repeat the old libel, and accused Itzikel, whom she had allowed to enter out of pity, of attacking her, and attempting to rape her.

The neighbors, stout Jewish farmers, began to assault Itzikel, and he barely managed to escape from the house. They followed into the street. It was a miracle that a Jewish carriage driver passed by and let him get into the wagon, and berated the farmers, "Even if he was guilty of all the sins, he does not deserve such murderous blows."

At first the driver mocked him. He was certain that he was guilty. But afterwards, when they stopped and he saw how Itzikel davened, he understood that Itzikel was a scholar. He asked him where he wanted to go, and promised him he would take him to Rovno, to the Mezritcher magid[4]. He stayed with the driver for several days in Hrubieszow, and then he brought him to Rovno, to the magid.

When the driver brought him to the house, the magid, R' Ber, embraced him with great affection and said, "Don't worry, Itzikel! Satan has lost the game."

A rare soul

From Rovno, Itzikel sent a divorce notice to his Krasnobrod wife, and then immersed himself, like a fish, in the sea of Torah and Chasidut. He became friends with R' Zishe Anipoler, and R' Zalman Lozhner. The magid also loved him, and said that a soul like his has not been seen since the time of the prophets.

R' Zalman thought the world of him because of something he had seen. Once, Erev Shabes, he saw Itzikel go into the kitchen and prepare a fish for Shabes. R' ZAalman wondered how he knew that that piece of fish would come to him? So R' Zalman tied a thin thread around the fish as a marker. Saturday night at table, the piece of fish was given to Itzikel's neighbor. Suddenly the neighbor was seized with a stomachache, and the shames passed the fish back to Itzikel.

Once a Chasid came to the magid with a request. The magid asked Itzikel to read the request and to make a prayer. That was a sign that he was ready to lead a group of Chasidim. But R'Itzikel was not yet agreed.

R' Itzikel married his second wife, and settled in the shtetl, Lancut. He began to travel to R' Elimelech in Lizensk. It did not take long, and he became the right hand of the rabbi. R' Elimelech began to send young students to Lancut for R' Itzikel to teach them, and to show them the way of Chasidut.

Soon Satan made his way in. People began to gossip that R' Itzikel behaved as if he were a big rabbi. Quarrels began. So R' Itzikel moved to Rozwadow. But the Lizensk Chasidim pestered him there, so he moved back to Lancut where a big quarrel flared up. One day a Chasid appeared and told R' Itzikel a dream he had that R' Itzekel was wanted by heaven to move to Winawow. Where was Winawow? No one knew. That same day, a question about a divorce came to Lancut. It came from Czechow near Lublin, and it is mentioned in the divorce that Czechow is also called Winawow. So R' Itzikel did not waste any time and moved to Czechow. There the Chasidin from Lizensk had no influence.

Honor and glory in Lublin

In a short time, R' Itzikel's name was spread far and wide. Hundreds of Chasidim came to his door. His quarters in Czechow became too small. The wealthy Ephraim Zalman Margolis, the in–law of Ber and Tamarl Bergson of Prage near Warsaw, bought a place for him on Zseroka Street, in the heart of Lublin, and began to build a Bet Hamidrash and a house for him. Why did the rich man do this? Because during the revolution in Warsaw, his daughter was in Prage at his in–laws, and R' Zalman was very worried. So he went to the rabbi for advice. The rabbi calmed him down and said, "Your daughter is kneading noodles and rocking the cradle of a baby with her foot." R' Zalman later found out it was true, "to a hair." So he vowed to build a Bet Hamidrash, and a house in the middle of Lublin.

On the day of the dedication of the building there was celebration in the city of Lublin. The streets were full of people. Thousands of people watched from balconies and windows as a great crowd of Chasidim sang, and carried the rabbi, and the Sefer–Torahs to his new dwelling.

*

When the retinue passed an elegant non–Jewish street, a terrible thing happened. A noblewoman jumped from a balcony, and died on the spot.

Who was she? She was a convert, the wife of a nobleman, the Jewish daughter of a landowner from Krasnobrod, the first wife of rabbi R' Itzikel.

*

R' Itzikel had the honor of laying the foundation of Chasidut in Poland. He raised a generation of tzadikim and Chasidim that stretches to today, and his name is hallowed, and praised as the tzadik of a generation–R' Yakov, the Seer of Lublin.

————

Translator's Notes

1. Child prodigy in Talmudic learning
2. "It is forbidden for a man to marry a woman before he sees her"
3. Appearance of a pious Jew
4. Itinerant preacher

[Page 161]

מעריב של חג

יום ה' 3.6.76 — ה' בסיון תשל"ו

הרב מנחם גוטמן

"מן השמים מעכבים"

רבינו הבעש"ט שמע שבעיירה שברשין
במחוז לובלין יש מסגרה עתיקה ששם הגיעו
גולי ספרד למדינת פולין ויסדו בשברשין
הקהילה הראשונה בפולין מתשע קהילות
שיסדו גולי ספרד בשנת רנ"ם. ובתוך היער
שליד שברשין יש חורשה קטנה ושם לא ירד
שלג שום פעם והגויים קוראים לחורשה זו
בית הכנסת היהודי ואגדה עתיקה מספרת
שמצאו על העצים שחרתו מסכת ברכות,
וקבלה בפי גולי ספרד שיכולים להגיע מ־
חורשה זו בקפיצת הדרך לארץ ישראל.
רבינו נסע לשברשין ושאל אם אמת הדבר
שיש כאן דרך לארץ ישראל? ואמרו לו שיש
בדרך גזלן אחד שיש לו כלבים שמשמש אוכלים
אנשים והוא יודע הדרך להגיע לארץ ישראל.
כל היהודים היו מפחדים לילך בדרך ששם
גר הגזלן.

רבינו הבעש"ט שנכספה נפשו לעלות
לארץ ישראל הלך בעצמו יחידי וכאשר הגזלן
ראה אותו שלח כלב גדול לקראתו שיטרוף
אותו, אולם הכלב עמד על שתי רגליו כמי
שמשתחוה לפניו, אז יצא הגזלן וביקש מהילה
מהרב הקדוש, ובידי הגזלן מפירות שנשתבחה
בהן ארץ ישראל.
— איפה לקחת הפירות?
— מעיירה סמוכה.
— תוכל להוליכני לעיירה זו?
— כן, אבל על הדרך פלג מים תלוי גשר
צר של קרש שצריכים לעבור עליו.

הגזלן הלך מקדם ועבר הקרש וכאשר
רצה הבעש"ט לעבור גאו תלג המים עד
שבקשתי נצל הבעש"ט וחזר יחידי לשברשין.
ואז ראה הבעש"ט שמן השמים מעכבים
בעדו לעלות לארץ ישראל.

Prevented by Heaven
Ma'ariv – Holiday Issue
Thursday, 3 June 1976 – 5 Sivan 5736
by Rav Menachem Guttman
Translated by Yocheved Klausner

Our rabbi the BESHT [Ba'al Shem Tov] once heard that in the shtetl Shebreshin, in the Lublin District, an old tradition prevails: Shebreshin was the place where the exiles from Spain first stopped when they arrived in Poland, and there they founded the first Jewish community, of the nine communities that the Spanish exiles founded in Poland in 5290 (1530 CE). Near Shebreshin, there is a small grove where it never snows, and the peasants call it "The Jewish Synagogue." According to an old legend, the Tractate Berachot is engraved on the trees, and a tradition among the Spanish Exiles in Poland says that from that grove one can arrive, with one step, directly in Eretz Israel. Our rabbi went to Shebreshin and asked – "Is there any truth in the story that a short way exists from there to Eretz Israel?" They said that in the neighborhood there is a robber whose dogs really eat people, and he knows the way to Eretz Israel; but the Jews were afraid to go to the places where the robber was living.

Our rabbi the BESHT, who longed to go to Eretz Israel, went, all alone, to look for the robber. When the robber saw him, he sent his big dog to eat him, but the dog stood up on two feet as if bowing before the BESHT. The robber came out and asked forgiveness from the holy rabbi, his hands full of fruits from Eretz Israel.

Where did you take the fruits?

In the next village.

Can you take me to that village?

Yes, but on the way there is a river, and only a narrow bridge made of a slab of wood can take us across.

The robber went in front and passed the bridge, and when the BESHT approached and wanted to cross, the waters of the river rose and the BESHT barely escaped, and he returned alone to Shebreshin.

The BESHT understood then, that it is Heaven that prevents him from going to Eretz Israel.

Nazis are abusing elders in the courtyard in Shebreshin

[Page 167]

Days of Suffering and Destruction

Page 179 - Yiddish] [Page 167 - Hebrew]

Between life and death

by Yitzhak Stemmer

Translated by Moses Milstein

Itze Stemer and his wife Ruchme

When the Nazis marched into S. in 1939, we were outside the city, in the fields.

With me was my wife, Rochama, my daughter, Sheindele, my mother, Mintshe, and my brother-in-law, Rev Dovid Yoseph. We all lived in S in one house. After a few days, we returned to our house.

A few weeks after this, things changed. The Red Army entered S. But not for long. The Nazis returned soon after, and the dark days began. Horrible acts were perpetrated against Jews in the city and surroundings.

Polish hatred and betrayal

With even greater savagery than the Germans, our Polish neighbors began helping them. At least at the beginning, life would have been much easier, if the Poles had not shown as much hatred and betrayal.

Come winter, the Germans established street kitchens in the middle of the city, out in the open, and handed out food to the people. When a Jew approached, the Poles pointed him out – "Ein Jude" – to the Germans. The Germans handed food to the Jew, while another man took his photograph.

Life became very hard for Jews, worsening every day. They were dragged away to work, and to places from which there is no return.

A few months after the German occupation, they began to build an air-field near the Klemensow sugar factory, not far from the summer residence of Graf Zamoisky. Many Jews and Christians were employed in the building of the air-field. Conditions were very bad. The food was poor. Only bread, and a little warm water they called, "soup".

Life got worse, because aside from the demonic behavior of the German murderers, the Poles, with great enthusiasm, did even more than was required of them. The shtetl found itself in perpetual, chaotic fear.

The Judenrat

The Germans organized a Judenrat of people who occupied social positions. But these honest people soon fled, unwilling to be accomplices to the dirty work.

So the authorities established a new Judenrat of six, who displayed a disgraceful dedication (out of respect for their relatives, we will not mention their names). We had never imagined that such types existed among us.

The new Judenrat proved to be very zealous, and provided more people for the German authorities than was asked for. They sent the poor to work, leaving them no means of support. From the rich they extorted oiskoif gelt. They stuffed themselves with food and drink, while others died of hunger. One of them became a "Kommandant".

Particularly on shabbos, these benighted people took to celebrating and making a "kiddush" in Shieh Pivniak's shenk. [tavern] They cooked the best foods, and invited the German murderers to join their carousing.

Only one of the new Judenrat, Hersh Getsel Hochboim, displayed {virde??}, greatness and courage.

As long as the Germans demanded Jewish money and possessions, he went reluctantly along, and kept silent. But then they began demanding people for "transports", at a time when it was clear that they were being sent to an extermination camp.

Hersh Getsel Hochboim opposed this, and refused to be an accomplice to these shameful acts. He tried to get away and hide. But when they forced him to carry out the German commands, and turn his Jewish brothers over to the murderers' hands, he saw no way out. One evening, he locked himself in his house, and hung himself, ending his own life.

He came from a noble, wealthy family (a nephew of Baruch Hersh Eisen). He was a leather merchant, a partner of Chaim Maimon. He was a modest and learned man. From a young age, he devoted himself to social causes. He was a public delegate {sheliach tsibur} in the Volksbank elections, and in city hall. Politically, he was a General Zionist.

Honor to his memory!

———

The Aktions

Our whole family was hidden in bunkers, pressed together in narrow confinement. Because of informers, we frequently had to change our hiding places. More than once, bullets flew over our heads, and we burrowed deeper into the earth.

German raids, helped by the Polish population, have begun. Jewish martyrs fall daily, in the city, in the middle of the street, outside the city. With every step, you fall on a Jewish victim. If anyone ventured out of the city to find food, he was met with bullets.

The first sacrifice was Yosef Baicher. Later, both Remer sisters (Leibish Shmelia's daughters). They met with death on the Rozlop [Rozlopy] road, when they went to look for a few potatoes to keep body and soul together. Also murdered, were Ben Zion Beker's family. Ben Zion himself was blinded. His oldest daughter, Aidel, and her child were dragged out of a hiding place. Poles betrayed them and the Germans shot them. The Poles threw the child in a {ubikatsieh}...These were not isolated incidents.

Later, the Aktions took on a more organized form. Three Aktions took place in the city. Following the first and second Aktions, the Judenrat, with the help of the Poles, gathered up the victims, mostly old people.

Our house was also home to Avram Hersh Koil's family – Berl Koil's parents. They were no longer alive, and their only daughter, Gitl, was left alone, poor and sick, without help. During the first Aktion, four Judenrat came to see her. She was caring for someone else's child. They tried her to get her to go with them, but she refused to leave the child alone. So they told her to take the child. But she refused this too. They tore the child from her arms. Leaving the child behind, they arrested her, and sent her to where no one returns.

The following happened during the second Aktion. Zeleg Gernshtein was at work at the air-field. His wife and two children who were in hiding were betrayed. They were dragged out, and sent to their doom. When he returned from work, and discovered the tragedy, he ran to the Judenrat, beat everyone there, and went mad. He and the Judenrat were killed in the last Aktion.

There were many such occurrences.

Then came a barbaric act that we have called "Bloody Friday".

One day, a certain number of people had to be supplied for work in Kelikow. Leibl Raz was chosen to go, but he protested. So instead they called for Berl Mochrovski. Then the haggling began. Others said, if they won't go, then we won't go either. Only three or four men were lacking to make up the work party. But the "Kommandant" of the Judenrat could not abide being contradicted. He phoned the head Kommando in Bilgoraj, and reported that he was not being obeyed. Two hours later, several heads of the labor authority accompanied by SS arrived. With the help of the Sonderdienst, they began shooting at the houses. Forty five people fell that day, among them Jews from elsewhere who had come to S. \

It was a tragic scene when they gathered up the bodies, made more tragic by the knowledge that Jews had had a hand in it.

The Judenrein Aktions

The so-called Judenrein Aktion was to have been carried out on a certain date, but it was postponed for two weeks.

One evening someone from the Zaviadow station brought news that six wagon cars had been prepared to transfer S Jews. One can't begin to imagine what then happened in the half-ruined shtetl.

People began to fast, to pray, to visit the gravestones...The wailing and the fear were unbearable. People went mad. They were aware of the results of the first two Aktions.

Suddenly, a miracle happened. That same man from Zaviadow told us that the wagons had been requisitioned for war needs, but not for long...The horrific acts of murder were postponed for two weeks. And then – Woe to our unlucky souls!

Underground, in our bunkers, we heard the hysterical cries of the panic-stricken. In our holes, we felt no more fortunate than our brethren whose suffering had ended. Every day you waited in fear that, any minute, they will come and drag you out.

The first day, they herded together about 2000 people, and sent them to Belzec, to the crematoria on which was written "Wash rooms." ...The other day, the murderers ran around like poisoned mice and searched for hidden Jews with the help of the Poles. They were transported to the cemetery, murdered, and buried in one large communal grave...Until the city was Judenrein.

The first day, Wednesday, Ukrainain murderers worked alongside, dressed in German uniforms.

Before the liquidation, the Judenrat "Kommandant" from Bilgoraj arrived, and announced that they are going to turn S into a "Juden Staat". But this would cost a lot of money...The remaining Jewish people brought their last groschen. Where the money went, I don't know, because the first to be arrested were the Judenrat and the Jewish Militia. They and the rest – innocent, pure, cherished, Jewish souls, were sent away, and perished.

In the evening, they were all taken to the train station. At night, they were held in the ammunition factory which used to be a chemical factory. The place was fenced in and guarded by many armed men, among them, a number of Poles and Ukrainians.

Many children escaped through the windows in the night, and ran for the fields and forests. To this great tragedy, I must add what the children told me later when we met. While imprisoned in the factory with the others, the Judenrat poured salt on their wounds, consoling themselves that this was not meant for them, and that they, the Judenrat, would soon be freed – The children later all perished because of the Poles.

These events we transcribed while in the bunkers, in town, and in the moments when we left the bunkers for some air, or to search for food.

Leaving the bunker

Our family life was, understandably, filled with sorrow. We repeatedly regretted not having perished with everyone. Why did we have to survive and undergo so much agony?

I lay in a hole with my brother-in-law, Yankel Morgenshtern (today in Israel), and my three cousins, the Goldberg girls (yechezkel Yoinale's grandchildren). Thursday morning, some Polish children found our bunker, and began to destroy the entrance. I succeeded in breaking through the other side. I don't know with what superhuman strength I managed to do this, not having eaten or slept in three days. All five of us managed to save ourselves, but everything we had, we left in that hole.

After we crawled out of our hiding place, we ran through the orchards toward the Gorajec hills. Quickly, the Poles informed the Germans, and seeing that we were only 50 meters away, they began to shoot at us. As a result, we lost one cousin, the rest of us scattering away in all directions, until we lost sight of each other. After a kilometer of running, they were still shooting at me.

I fell into water and lay there for two hours until dark. Then I made for a village called Roslop. I walked in my wet clothes for two kilometers. I steeled myself, and sought out a goy I knew. They did not let me in for fear of the Germans. But I pleaded with the farmer, and since it was a very dark night, he covered the windows and allowed me to spend the night. In the morning, he hid me in a stodole.

I knew nothing of the others. A few hours later, my two cousins arrived and snuck into the stodole without the farmer's knowledge. My brother-in-law, Yankel, fifteen years old at the time, not knowing what to do, went back to his parents in town, intending to perish with them. In the cellar where he hid, he found my wife and child. My sister-in-law, Miriam, (Moishe Zilberlicht's daughter) lay nearby in another bunker. Her parents were hiding in yet another place.

At about 2:00 A.M., my wife came to my bunker and called for me. The town was quiet, Judenrein. Not getting a response, and growing more afraid, she called louder, "Itche, Itche!", until three small shkootsim came running. They grabbed her, and pulled at her demanding money. She led them into the house, and with great difficulty escaped from them leaving behind a handful of hair. She jumped out of a window and straight into the bunker. The shkootsim chased her, but couldn't find her.

She had decided to take the child and find me. Peering into the darkness she saw that someone was coming and heading straight for the bunker. At first she was scared, but then she realized that this person knew where the bunker was, and had to be one of ours. It was her brother, Yankel. He told her that everyone was lost, and that he didn't want to go on. He wanted to die together with his parents. They went into the bunker to figure out what to do. Earlier, my wife and I had agreed that if we ran and lost one another, we should have a rendezvous planned. We left signs in three villages. My wife persuaded her brother to come with her. She put the child on her shoulders, and with her brother, barefoot because his wooden shoes were wet and broken, took to the road. Soon, the dark night filled with thunder, lightening and rain. Soaked, they traveled the same road as I was on. It appears the same instinct guided us.

The scattered reunite

After about 100 metres, jumping over bodies in the dark, the night was suddenly lit by a blast of lightning. They came on the body of my cousin Serl Goldgruber, her clothes torn apart. It seems she had been well searched. ... My wife took off her apron and, in tears, covered the innocent victim. She took the soaked baby from Yankel, and set off again in the dark. –Only sky and earth and rain. Instinctively, she headed for Roslop, to the farmer, as we had agreed. Hours passed. Morning was appearing on the horizon.

They approached the house. All was quiet except for the barking of dogs. Afraid of being seen, they stole into a barn, crept up to the hay-filled loft and lay down and slept – wet , tired, and hungry.

They awoke around eleven. The child, then four years old, began to beg for food. It was the fourth day without any food passing her lips. "Mameh, a piece of bread!" she pleaded. Before my wife could cover Shaindel's mouth, the farmer, below in the yard, heard the voices and rushed up in fear. "Who's there?" – Ola boga, tileh zhiduv p186. he called. My wife begged him for a piece of bread for the child. He left the loft, and came back with a piece of bread and some rice and milk. The child revived somewhat.

Then, the farmer told her that my two cousins and I were also here. She begged him to take the child to me, and she and Yankel would come later that night. The farmer agreed.

In the village, out of the village

We could not show ourselves by day, because the farmer and his family could also pay with their lives. In the dark autumn night we came together with feelings of pain, sorrow, terror and joy, more suffering than joy because, at this moment we live, but later...?

After a short time, the farmer's wife appeared. She begged us to have pity on them and leave because, aside from them, the other six neighbors on both sides of the house could also be shot. We had no choice. We begged for a piece of bread for the child, and an old rag to cover her with. For this, we gave her our last gold watch. All five of us, barefoot and in rags because we could not take a thing from home, left for the village, Zrebiec.

We covered the five kilometers in several hours, forced to travel by back roads in order not to be seen. I saw a light in the distance. When we got there, we discovered a house that belonged to a goy we knew. Without asking permission, we climbed into a loft above a horse stall where we spent the night. The farmer discovered us when he came to get hay for his horse. Frightened, he pleaded with us to leave and promised to feed us all. We assured him we would leave that night, but we stayed until the second night with him watching us the whole time. We stole into another loft, and were discovered in the morning. The farmer began to weep at our fate, seeing our appearance, and begging us not to bring misfortune on his family. It has come to such a pass that a goy should cross himself with fear on seeing a Jew.

We decided to separate. The two cousins left for another goy and we stayed with this one.

A tragedy occurred tonight. A Jewish family from S, Simche Limberg and four people, were also hiding in the village. They were betrayed, and they were taken to Silochai and there they were shot. The scene in getting them out of the house was frightful. We almost went mad from fear. The Limberg family pleaded and cried so that the whole village assembled. Many of the goyim were trembling.

After it had quieted down, the goy no longer wanted to hide us. Before morning, we left for the woods, me, and my wife, and child, and Yankel. The Goldgruber cousins, at the terrible moment when the Limburgs were taken, ran away to another village. They were killed by the Germans on the road. Their final resting place is in Teplice village.

In the forest, we came on the children who had escaped from the ammunition factory the night of the last Aktion. They tried to get food from the Rozlop farmers, but were refused. So they stole food from the chickens. There were about 40 children, boys and girls. I heard from the goyim, that about 40 Jews were captured in the forest, probably with the children, and killed.

Help from good-hearted farmers

While we were in the forest, our goy dug a bunker in a field, about one meter wide, and brought us there at around midnight. It was about two km from the village, in the middle of the field. He walked far ahead of us so as not to be caught escorting Jews. The hole was wet and very small. But he had brought a shovel, a bucket for water, a hoe, and a bundle of straw. We carried the tools. He also brought a piece of bread, a pot of unpeeled potatoes, a bit of salt, a knife, and some kindling. We buried ourselves and these goods in the bunker. The tools allowed us to enlarge the pit, and we lay there all winter until Pesach.

When snow fell, no one was to be seen in the field. We often snuck out at night, and searched for stashes of beets and turnips the farmers would store in the fields in winter. We also used to clean the bunker at night and get some air in the frigid winter of 1943. And so we sat with our child in our dark bunker covered with snow. Snow and water entered the hole. Other Jewish families were hidden by farmers in Zrebiec.

Every few weeks, our farmer would sneak up to our bunker and throw in a roasted beet for the child, sometimes a pot of potatoes, some cooked millet, etc. He invariably wept aloud at our fate. He said that our suffering is on his conscience. Had he known the war would last so long, he would not have hidden us. He can't stand seeing people buried alive, the worms eating us alive because we can't change our clothes. Talking done, weeping done, he would disappear for another couple of weeks.

Once, another goy from Rozlop appeared and noticed our bunker. We could see him from within. He caught my eyes peering at him through a crack, and ran away in fright. I recognized the face, so I got out and caught up to him. I wept and pleaded with him not to give us away. He swore he intended no harm. If he had known we were there, he would not have come near. He calmed us down, and told us that on a dark night, we could come to him. He lived isolated in the village, and he told us he would alert us when the time came.

And that is actually how it turned out. On a certain night, he came and took us to his house. He asked me, since I was a tailor, to make him a pair of pants. I could have stayed there a longer time, but the second night the house was attacked by bandits. All the men were taken out of the house, and made to lie on the ground without moving. Three masked bandits stole all the food and clothes from the farmer, had the horses harnessed, and led everything away to the forest. The men were ordered to enter the house, but a revolver was pressed to my head and they yelled, "Jude, you must be killed." I was facing death. Luckily, one of the bandits called out, "Leave him alone. Let him fall into other hands."

Behavior of a good soul

From there, we returned to the bunker. It was full of water, but we had to go in. The earth caved in, and we were forced to dig another bunker in a different place, without the farmer's knowledge. We carried the earth to a spot further away, so that we would not be discovered. After a few nights, the bunker was ready.

As mentioned above, we stayed in the bunkers until Pesach. After that, the owners began to cultivate the ground, and they would not allow us to be there. They were responsible for their land. In the span of nine months, we dug five bunkers. Every time it was discovered, we had to move.

In February, 1943, not expecting to be able to withstand the cold, my wife risked leaving with our half-dead child to go to the village and seek out a farmer called Bartnik. She entered the house and was greeted with fear and shock when they saw her condition.

The farmer's wife, a very good soul, cried and trembled with fear and compassion. My wife told them, "I do not wish you any harm, but I beg you to save my child. I will return to the bunker."

But the woman would not hear of separating a mother and child. She quickly prepared a corner of the house, hiding it with a cupboard so the neighbors would not see it. There, she prepared a bed. She gave the child some warm milk. She bathed my wife and child in a large tub with warm water and soap, and gave them warm clothing. My wife stayed with Bartnik for six weeks. The child got better and stronger. Once, the farmer's wife came and told her that three wagonloads of German gendarmes had arrived in the village. It was said that they were looking for Jews. Someone had said that there were many Jews hiding in the village. There were actually around ten Jews there, among them – Berish Zitron with his wife and two children, who find themselves today on the bloody, soaked with Jewish blood, earth. They too underwent a great deal.

A remedy for the weak

Not wanting to create problems for the good woman, my wife and the child left through back roads to seek out the goy Choropote. But she couldn't stay there, and left in the night for the bunker. We used to go to Choropote for water, quite a distance, but we were afraid to have others see us. As mentioned, we frequently had to change bunkers. Our last bunker was in Bartnik's field with their knowledge. The good hearted woman did all she could for us. But we didn't want to put her in danger. Without their knowledge, we dug another bunker in their field, well supported with wooden boards. We covered it with a deep layer of earth so they could plow, seed and plant potatoes on it. We made a sign, a small opening 50 cm long and 30 cm wide so that we could recognize the spot.

We wandered around in different places for six weeks until the potato plants were tall. Then we searched for the spot and entered our new bunker. It was a dark hole, without air or light. The whole family fell ill from the lack of air. We couldn't breathe.

Whenever someone went out to look for food, we never knew if he would return alive. Every time someone left for fresh air, the child would cry wanting to go with. We had to cover her mouth with our hands. After many scares, she learned that she shouldn't cry, and must remain still and quiet.

We all became weak, and lost all ability to live and heal. We were all sick. In the middle of the winter, during the severe frosts, we were counseled by a farmer to burrow into a pile of horse manure. He led us into a stall one night and left us there. We cleared a space, and me and my brother-in-law, Yankel Morgenshtern (today in Israel), lay down naked in the manure. We were warmed through and through, and sweated, and slowly revived.

Yankel survived great hardship. One cold night in 1943, he crept out to look for food. He was spotted by a bandit and shot at, Yankel fled, and hid in the forest. He was barefoot, his feet swollen and lacerated. He hid all day, and at night came to Bartnik's. Mrs. Bartnik wept at the sight. She warmed his frozen hands and feet with snow, bandaged them and fed him. The next morning he returned to the bunker. That same night, I had searched the snow with a stick for his dead body, thinking he had perished.

Thus, we survived 25 months in the bunkers, nine of them in Zrebiec, until we were expelled with all the other inhabitants to make room for the Volksdeutsche. The exiled were resettled in the Gmina Radecznica. Sitting in our bunkers, we knew nothing of this.

One Friday evening, I went out to look for food at Bartnik's farm. Two strange men jumped out at me from behind a house. I was very frightened and ran back to the bunker. Later, I climber out again and asked a farmer what had happened. He explained it to me. I was able to get some bread from him for my child. He also lent me a razor and shaving brush, because I had not shaved in months. Returning it, was not possible. The farmer was also taken away.

What will be, will be

We stayed another two days in that bunker. We prayed for death. Our fear was great. We could hear the shooting, and the frequent footsteps over our bunker. We expected to be captured at any moment.

Unable to withstand any more, one night, we gathered together our tools, shovels, pots, and set out into the unknown. We headed to Czarnystok through various back roads, carrying the child on our shoulders, and half a loaf of bread on which four people had been subsisting for almost two weeks. We wandered around lost all night. Near dawn, we heard a farmer driving by. He stopped a little way further along, but could not see us because of the darkness. My wife and I decided to approach him. We could see that these were not bandits, or military people because there was a cow tied to the carriage. And it turned out that he was a familiar farmer from Roslop. He was transferring his worldly goods to where he was being resettled.

We could not continue any further, because the man, Gedzusz, told us that a commando headquarters responsible for sending Poles to their new homes, had been set up in Gorajec. We immediately set to digging a new bunker in the forest. It was not far from Szperowka. We hid there an entire day. We had become indifferent to everything. We were tired of living. We were desperately hungry, so I lit a fire in the forest without fear, not caring about the outcome. I cooked some potatoes for us.

The fire attracted some frightened goyim. They told us that they were being hunted too, and they were also running to hide. We were not to be afraid of them but only of the Germans. They could come at any moment. We got through that day. At night, our acquaintance, Gedzusz, rode back and told me that the Germans had left Gorajec. He advised us to wait until later, and he would return for us, and take us to Gorajec.

And that's what actually happened: the Poles had begun to taste our misery…That is why it was now possible to get help from them. So Gedzusz returned. Yankele and my child stayed behind in the bunker. My wife and I disguised ourselves, and walked behind the carriage. He took us out of the forest, and through various routes, to the village of Czarnystok where we met a familiar farmer, Woytowicz. But he would not let us enter his house, because he had been informed that we were long since dead. Through all our weeping and pleading, he refused to believe we were who we said we were. I gave him the names of all of his own family, and the name of the man who slept in the horse barn. We called for him, and he came out of the horse stall and identified us.

Then they let us into the house, and fed us. But they would not let us spend the night. They were too afraid, and I could understood this. They stuck us out in the fields, and there, my wife and I stayed the whole day.

The joy of a reunion

The goy told me that there was another Jew in Czarnistok, Shloime Czarnistokek (Kapenboim). Our joy at hearing the news was indescribable. We had to wait until night before meeting in the forest. For various reasons, the anticipated meeting did not happen until the third night. We had arranged to meet at a certain place, but to our disappointment he was not there. It turned out that he had been there, and waited until dawn, and then he became frightened, and returned to the bunker where he shared with his wife.

When morning came, we hid under kustes. There we were spotted, and the German police was informed that there were "bandits hiding". Luckily, I had left to ask Woytowicz where Shloime's bunker was located. There we learned that the police were coming for us. Woytowicz's son immediately took us to another hiding place in the forest where we stayed until nightfall.

No pen can describe the moment when two Jews – almost the last of an entire community – meet, alone, destitute, homeless and oppressed by everyone in the world. We wept over the fate of our near and dear ones, and over what happened to the large Jewish kibbutz in Poland.

Shloimes's bunker was quite well set up: large, with a stove and a lantern. But air was lacking. We could not live together, because, in such times, we were afraid of too many people being together in one place. Therefore, we dug a separate bunker for us in another location, at a distance from Shloime, and well camouflaged.

That same night, my wife and I returned to my brother-in-law, and my child, enduring a very hard journey filled with fear. There, we had to wait out the day. At night, we took all our belongings, and some potatoes, and returned to Czarnistok.

There was a teacher, Bahan, in Czarnistok, who had worked in S. He was the commander of the A.K. (Armia Krajova – Polish partisans, antisemites). He fought the Germans and shot some of them, but later he was shot. This Bahan discovered that we were Jews, and he wanted to destroy us. My Christian acquaintances in town dissuaded him by telling him I was a tailor and could be useful.

I worked hard for them without money, just for food. Bahan helped us later as well, and I sewed some clothes for him too.

There were heavy snowfalls in the winter of 1943-1944. Everything was waterlogged, and our bunker collapsed. I could not repair it myself . It was the Christian holiday "Trzech Kroli". I ran to the village to beg for help from Woytowicz's son. He came with a horse and wagon and helped me repair the bunker. Naturally, I rewarded him well, and made him a good suit.

Last convulsions

We could no longer stay in our bunker. We were being noticed too often. They even wanted to kill Shloime and his wife because he had a lot of money. The shkootsim wanted him to give it to them. But I stood up for him and pleaded with them. With God's help, I was successful, and they let him live.

It also happened that a Christian had wanted to throw a grenade in my bunker, but he himself was killed when the grenade exploded. My Christian acquaintances said that God had punished him for his ill-will.

When we first entered the bunkers, we were separated from my father-in-law and mother-in-law, and also Miriam Zilberlicht and her children. They had not wanted to leave S after the last Aktion. Later, they perished in the bunkers.

We hid in Czarnistok until the Liberation, in August 1944. We went through many ordeals. Our lives were in constant danger. The area was full of A.K. people, and there were many raids and attacks. We endured horrible days, suffering physically and emotionally. Every day another trial, every day more terrible than the last. Today we had to hide from the German police, the next day from the Polish police, and the following day – from our own...

Our redemption finally came, though we stayed two more days in the bunkers before we heard the news.

The goyim, who had helped us before, were now afraid we would inform on them.

Luck began to shine on us. We left for Zamosc. We stayed there for several months, and then wandered out of Poland, the land cursed by God.

Let the world know what was done to us, the world that had stayed aloof and silent. May the world remember the words of our sages: "And at the end, those who drowned thee shall themselves be drowned..."

May the hands of those who assisted in the destruction of our holy souls be severed –';brothers and sisters, fathers and mothers! God of Hosts, pour out Thy wrath upon the nations and avenge our spilled blood!

Written with Moishe Messinger

[Page 195]

Echad B'Yameinu[1] - Hersh Getzl Hochbaum

by Emanuel Chmielash

Translated by Moses Milstein

Hersh Getzl was "echad b'yameinu." During the time of morality's fall, a Jewish giant, a moral hero, was found, who at the demand of the German murderers to provide 500 Jews, stood in opposition against them. He refused to give up any Jews, and became a martyr by hanging himself.

I am not worthy of writing about him. I would have to purify myself in the mikve hover and over before even beginning.

When the Germans occupied Poland, they also occupied S. They immediately registered all Jewish men between the ages of sixteen and sixty. The day after the registration, they ordered all the men to assemble at the magistrat.[2] If one of the registered failed to appear, they hunted him down, and brought him to the assembly place from which they took all the assembled Jews and transported them under military guard to various work sites.

There were some Jews who did not register themselves and avoided cooperating with the Germans. They were therefore unable to show themselves in the street.

The Jews who were the representatives on the community were responsible for providing the Germans with whatever they needed.

Forced labor

Every day, my father, z"l, my brother, Elkana, z"l, and my younger brother, Noah, were forced to go to work. Every group of workers was guarded by two German soldiers.

One day, the group I was in was working in the outskirts of town cleaning the streets. The two German soldiers were standing by, and beside them, two Polish ruffians, known as the worst in town. One of the Germans came over to us, and silently looked at each of us in turn until he came to Yudl Zuntog, who dealt in boots. The two Poles gave a sign to the soldier by nodding their heads, and the soldier slapped Yudel in the face. Out of fear we kept our heads down until the soldier moved away.

Around the same time, they invaded the Jewish homes and confiscated various things. The mothers left at home in the houses were filled with fear.

Every day more young people disappeared from town. The Germans lacked men to fulfill their quota, so they ordered the remaining representatives of the community to establish a committee whose role was to provide people for labor every day. The unregistered, cut off from communication, were without means to make a living.

In our courtyard lived a young man, Eliah, who drove Pinchas Zelig's wagon. He had a wife and young children. Although he appeared every day for forced labor, he could not feed his family. One day, we discussed the situation , and in the morning, before work began, he and I, and several other friends went to the see the committee representatives on the "pocheneh"[3], and asked, Who will provide food for the children whose fathers work for themselves, and those who are not taken for labor?

It was decided that those who did not register themselves should pay for the days when they would have been required to work. In that way, everyone worked every second day. In our family, I worked one day, and my brother, Noah, worked the second day. Whoever wanted to miss a day had to pay another to work for him. This was what the committee, and the Jews of the city, decided.

With each passing day, the conditions for Jews got worse and more Jews ran away: either disappearing into hiding places, or stealing over the border.

Establishing a judenrat

Then the Germans imposed-as in all cities and shtetls-the judenrat. The Germans used the help of Poles to pick the members.

I know the names of some of those chosen, among them, Hersh Getzl Hochbaum.

I was not raised to judge and criticize others, even the representatives who had done evil. I can only rely on things I have read in other Yizkor books and newspaper articles that helped to establish certain facts.

Up until they began mass liquidations of Jews, the Germans demanded money, goods and slave-labor. At first they shot individual Jews and beat up certain judenratlers. They exploited the egoism of certain individuals, flattered them, got on with them relatively well, and maybe even gave them money taken from the other Jews. In this way they sowed enmity between the judenratlers who hoped for a smile from the Germans.

When the Germans began the mass aktions, transporting Jews, or shooting them on the spot, some of the judenratlers believed that they would avoid death. They even began to fulfill the commands of the Germans with greater zeal. They simply lost their humanity. They only followed their animal instinct-to stay alive.

Before the war, they were decent people, honest, Chasidim, balei tfilis[4], and now-accomplices of the Germans in the destruction of Jews-their neighbors, friends and even members of their own family.

Could we, the survivors, ever have imagined such a thing? Is it to be believed? Unfortunately, that is what happened.

It is said that there are all kinds of people-those with weak characters and those with strong characters. The weaker ones quickly broke, the stronger ones took longer before they too broke.

I am certainly not one to judge. I see before me the words of our sages, "Do not judge your friend until you have stood in his place." The generation of survivors can not objectively judge this sad chapter of the judenrat. Perhaps coming generations can more objectively evaluate their immoral behavior and judge them, or leave it to heavenly judgment.

*

In such immoral times, a light arose, which shines for future generations. His name is Hersh Getzl Hochbaum. I can only add-zichrono l'vracha.[5]

———

Translator's Notes

1. One in a generation
2. City hall
3. a section of the street near the market
4. Leaders of prayers
5. May his memory be a blessing

———

[Page 198]

From the Bunkers to the Partisans
by Yakov Morgenstern
Translated by Moses Milstein

The Germans began identifying Jews from the age of eleven with patches, and yellow Stars of David. Jews had to salute every German soldier. If a Jew did not notice the soldier from a distance, the soldier had the right to beat him to death.

The shul caught on fire when the German poured benzene into it, and set it on fire.

The Germans chased all the Jews together, and assembled them near the courthouse and then to the halle.[1] My parents and I were in the halle.

The fire in the shul grew larger. The halle was shut, and the fear spread that they would set the halle on fire. They tore open the doors, but anyone who tried to escape was shot. Many victims fell as a result. They re–shut the doors and kept us there for two days without food or water.

On the third day they allowed only women and children to leave. The men were kept in the halle, and some were led away under arrest. The Rev was also there. It was said that the Jews were to be killed little by little. So they went to see the Kommandant. He demanded, "Why did the Jews set the shul on fire? For that reason all the men will be shot."

Then a Judenrat was picked. But the chosen ones quickly abandoned their posts. Most of them escaped to the Russian side. Therefore, a second Judenrat was selected.

The Aktions began. The German police, and the Jewish police, with the help of the Judenrat, ran around taking people from their hiding places to be sent to Belzec. Local Poles took part in the Aktions. The janitors of city hall ran around with axes, and when they found a Jew, they murdered him.

At night, I escaped to the bunker where my parents were hiding. It was well camouflaged by potatoes. I was sent out late at night to observe the situation. I saw nothing but piles of dead bodies. The Germans shot continuously at anyone still alive. The goyim carried the dead to the cemetery in tall horse–drawn wagons. The hair on my head stood on end. I saw only dead bodies.

That night I left the bunker with my brother–in–law, and my sister, and my female cousin. Along the way, we were shot at and my cousin was killed. Arriving in the forest, I was alone. In the morning, I joined the partisans.

Hadera

The ribbons with the yellow stars of david

Translator's Footnote

1. Covered market building

2.

[Page 200]

Imprisoned by the Germans

by Ephraim Farber

Translated by Moses Milstein

As soon as Hitler took Sudetenland, we knew war was coming to Poland. Hitler demanded a "Polish corridor." Tensions increased daily. We knew that war with Hitler's Germany was inevitable. Poland responded in August 1939 with a partial mobilization.

In these turbulent times, I was doing my military service in the 27th artillery regiment stationed in Ludmir (Wlodzimierz). Every morning we would stroll out of our barracks to the large exercise ground, lustily singing:

Maruska, moja Maruska
Pojdziesz ze mna spac do lozka.

Or other songs in the same genre. These songs were supposed to strengthen the morale and fighting spirit of the Polish soldier.

Officers with braided mustaches curled upward, boots polished to a high sheen, spurs jingling, the vain "Honor"-these are true pictures of the Polish officer. By contrast, the soldiers were a grey mass, humbled and humiliated. The aim of the mocking words of the officers was to remove the human being from the solder and turn him into a robot blindly carrying out orders.

We were poorly equipped with ancient cannons from the Tsar's era, with artillery drawn by horses, certainly a left over from the Austro-Hungarian empire, and probably used against Napoleon. Horses were groomed three times a day, and cared for like precious jewels. On more than one occasion, an officer could be heard claiming that a horse has greater value than a soldier. We often saw the officers bringing lively girls to entertain at their canteen. The arrogance, the wantonness of the officers made a negative impression on the soldiers.

Anti-Semitic conduct toward Jewish soldiers, from the low to the high ranks, was reflected in the feelings of the Jewish soldier to the military. On maneuvers, Jewish soldiers were yelled at by the NCOs, " Moishe Carabine, Vie azoi gehst du, vie azoi shtehst du?" They cursed at every opportunity. Jews were the butt of the military lexicon. It was a language of vulgar expressions, especially conceived to break the soldier's spirit. Apart from that, we had to worry about the news coming out of Hitler's Germany.

Mobilized in Poland

At the beginning of August 1939, I was on night watch, when I suddenly noticed a commotion. A pre-mobilization was beginning. The mobilization stores for the reserves who had arrived at night were opened. All the windows in the headquarters building were lit up. When dawn approached and my shift ended, and no one came to bring me food, I left my post.

When I returned to my quarters, I couldn't recognize the place. Piles of straw stacked here and there with reservists sleeping on them. I was astonished: straw scattered everywhere? If, God forbid, an NCO found a smidgen of straw in the barracks, he would wake up the whole battery and parade us to a burying-of-the-straw ceremony singing like lehavdil at a funeral. And now, such a mess.

The regiment left for the train station. Artillery was dragged along with ropes on the platform surface. A large part of the population-Jews and Christians-came out to say good bye to the departing soldiers. Many representatives from welfare organizations came bedecking the soldiers with flowers, handing out cigarettes, chocolate and other sweets, in order to sweeten a bitter fate.

Patriotic speeches were made, accompanied by outbursts of "Hit the Schwab!" The orchestra played stirring marches. Slogans were painted on the sides of the cars, "Wlodzimierz-Berlin", "We will repeat Grunwald!" The whistle blew, the hymn, Jeszke Polska" and "The Company" were sung. Tears appeared in the eyes of the onlookers-mothers, sisters, brothers. They looked on mutely, maybe seeing their loved ones for the last time. The train slowly pulled away, and along the route, in the little train stations, masses of people gathered carrying slogans like "Kill the Schwab." The fervor was boundless.

It began to rain that night, which cooled the ardor of some of the excited followers, and they went home to warm beds. We sat in open platforms. The cold and the wet dug into our bones. It didn't help to cover yourself with your greatcoat.

At first, the sky lightened a little and the clouds blew away. We were approaching Warsaw. At the Danzig train station-again flowers, and passionate shouts from the onlookers. They distributed coffee with Saccharin and we warmed ourselves a little after a night under wet blankets. Then the echelon moved on again going towards Pomerania. We debarked at a small train station past Torun.

We were driven to a forest. We put up tents, and arrayed the canons-Howitzers with wooden wheels, no doubt from Napoleon's time. Then the monotonous life of soldiering in the field began. Everyone was wondering what the morning would bring, thinking about home and friends.

The enemy is not far

The political situation got worse from day to day. In the villages where mostly Volksdeutsche lived, we could feel the hatred towards us. Their small acts of sabotage were carried out with the help of German agents swarming throughout Pomerania.

On a Thursday at the end of August, a mounted messenger arrived from division headquarters ordering us to immediately get ready to leave. Amidst the commotion, we quickly harnessed the horses and the battery moved out.

The road went through forest. The foot soldiers walked along the edges, like a flock of geese, wobbling under their heavy load. Rivers of sweat ran from their faces. Their back packs contained extra shoes, clothing, boot polish kits, and on top, a rolled up blanket, a small spade for trench digging, and a bowl. On their shoulders, a rifle and cartridge belt, a gas mask, and a tin cup. By contrast, all the German infantry's equipment was transported by truck.

We artillery soldiers also had to walk, because our horses sweated with exertion, like people, and had to stop to rest. Our advance continued without a halt, but we failed to appreciate the seriousness of our situation. In the middle of the night, the division commander rode up, and told us the enemy was near, and we should load our rifles. A coldness crept through me.

The people-in a state of panic.

We took our battle positions in an open space near the edge of the woods. It was one of those golden Polish autumn days. A road ran by near our position, and we could hear the cries of children. They were coming from the panicked population, fleeing from shtetlach and villages as the Germans approached. Wagons were full of all their worldly goods: old clocks, buckets, sooty pots, cupboards, chairs. Cows and dogs were tied to the wagons. There were flocks of fowl, herds of pigs. Theses were the first pictures of war we saw.

The bleating of animals, the barking, the lamentations from the women and the cries of the children all mixed together in one heart rending cry for the fate brought on by war. The refugees reported that the Germans were burning villages and murdering people. It was pitiful to look at the children wrapped in all manner of rags, only their red frozen noses sticking out.

I asked myself what the fate of the Jews will be, if this is what is happening to the Polish people.

One morning, when the sun appeared just over the tree tops, and the red reflections dispersed on the horizon, we saw a squadron of Messerschmitts. Loaded with bombs, they were an early morning "present" for the peaceful, sleepy population. In the distance, flew some other solitary airplanes we could not identify. We began to fire our machine guns and succeeded in downing one airplane. It turned out to be one of ours. On September 1st, at the beginning of the war, they were the only Polish airplanes, and were supposed to protect us from the skies. The Luftwaffe ruled the skies from the early morning on.

The slogans of our rulers turned out to be meaningless and empty. "Nie damy ani jednego guzika" (We will not surrender even a button) . The polish army was not capable of effectively resisting the German army. We kept on changing our positions. Fear of the unknown crept into our bones-what will our fate be in the coming hours?

However, we did not have to wait long. We saw the first wounded brought in on horse drawn wagons. In the distance, smoke rose from the villages. Flames leapt up to the sky. A little while later, we saw our infantry retreating in disorder, running desperately, leaving their equipment behind.

Retreat

Our division commander fell. Since there was no one nominated to take his place, we soldiers took the initiative and decided to retreat, because the Germans could capture us at any moment. Panic increased as we came under more fire. I ran without concern for what was happening to our battery. My only salvation was to run, even without knowing where to run to. Villages were burning in the entire region. Dense smoke rose to the sky. Cows and horses ran wild. Bleating and barking intermixed with the bomb blasts carrying death and destruction.

Observer planes followed the bombers and strafed us with machine guns. With my friend Berl Babat, I hid under an old dike. Bullets cut the leaves off the branches. The machine guns of our battery opened fire, with little result. We circled our little tree like frightened rabbits. The Germans were literally flying over our heads, so near we could see them making mocking hand gestures at our helplessness.

In a little while, the infantry retreated in panic. Wagons ran into each other. Everyone's eyes reflected fear, and they ran like poisoned rats. Some of the retreating soldiers told us that they had scouted a small village and had not seen any sign of Germans. They were followed into the village by the 23rd regiment. No sooner had they entered than German tanks, that had been well camouflaged in barns, attacked. It was impossible to mount the slightest resistance. The tanks attacked with massive fire power. Many soldiers fell and many were wounded. The survivors fled in panic.

Alongside the infantry, galloped the cavalry, covered in dust and dirt, equipped only with swords. The horses were soaked with sweat, their muzzles lathered with foam. It was a field of shining lances with colorful pennants affixed. A rabble of people, horses, wagons, field kitchens with unused provisions, all running in confusion.

The fire increased. Shrapnel flew. Our battery was firing at 2 km without cover from the infantry. We ended up being the front line on the field of slaughter. Bullets flew over our heads. Communication with the observation post was lost. Later, we learned the commanders fell at their positions.

We quickly dug fox-holes as defense against the whistling bullets. Not receiving any orders, we decided to retreat. The retreat began in great panic. Firing intensified. The bridges which were intact in the morning were now damaged by German saboteurs who worked throughout Pomerania.

I ran. After a few kms, the road entered a forest, and after running some more, I came out into an open field where there were many officers of different ranks standing about, and near them, soldiers with artillery. They stopped me, because they could tell by my boots I was from the artillery. They gathered together other artillery soldiers and pieces thinking that with this they could stop the German advance. When the firing intensified, these latest saviors gave up their plans.

We started running again. Wandering around in the night, I, by chance, came on some war friends. Especially happy at the meeting were two Jewish soldiers, Berl Babat, from Zamosc, and Berl Blum, from Tomasew-Lubelski. A third was Shmuel Beker, from Hrubieszow. We went over the events of the day, and discussed what we should do further.

We continued with the retreat. The main roads were filled with hopeless, beaten up parts of various formations. Soldiers, horses, and cannons were mixed up. The wounded, who had not received any medical care, groaned with pain. Dead bodies lay by the road, horses with bloated bellies, their legs stretched out to heaven like four "shtangen".[1] Masses of flies buzzed around the faces of the dead, and crows picked at the flesh with their black beaks, and cawed with pleasure.

A shudder of apprehension came to all who saw this picture, thinking of their own fate.

My friend, Babat, and I found a hiding place in an abandoned pharmacy near the road. Flashes of fire and bomb blasts carried in from outside. ---Leaving the pharmacy we saw scenes of devastation along the way. ---Terrified and starved we lay on the wet earth.

Small German detachments had been left behind to kill the retreating.

Everyone for himself

In order to free ourselves from this vice, the remainder of our battery decided to send out a scouting party of four riders. I had the fate of being one of them. We rode through a small wood and came out on a paved road. As we approached what must have been a strategic point, a railroad under which a tunnel ran, we came under heavy machine gun fire. We turned around and galloped back. One of us was shot in the hand, and a horse was wounded. Riding back through the fields we were shot at by civilian Germans.

We came back and reported the situation. The officers decided to ditch the cannons in a nearby river so they would not fall into German hands. After doing so, the Christian soldiers removed their hats and crossed themselves as if at a burial. The officers described the hopeless situation to us, and advised everyone to save himself as best he could.

I had inherited a horse from a fallen under-officer, and I decided to ride away to the dense Tuchola forest. When I said good-bye to the battery, I saw tears in my friend, Berl Babat's eyes. Unfortunately, he could not ride a horse, and I had to leave him.

I rode alone on unfamiliar roads. I passed regiment after regiment of hopeless and apathetic soldiers. I came across large quantities of provisions which the military had abandoned: Boxes full of candies, sacks of sugar, coffee, and cigarettes. Tying my horse to a tree, I approached the feast.

At night, I found a suitable place, gathered some branches, and lay down beneath them. My horse began whinnying and I moved further away. Soon after, I heard the calls of a German patrol. They must have heard my horse's whinnies. I wrapped myself deeper in my coat and held my breath.

Deep rooted anti-Semitism.

In the morning, I moved on. I was not used to a saddle and the long riding had rubbed my skin raw, and the wounds bled. When I got to a river, I cleaned the congealed blood and bandaged the wounds. I found some moldy candies on the road, and I cleaned them and shared them with the horse.

I came on a couple of soldiers and chatted with them. They told me that there were large groups of Polish soldiers hiding in the woods. When they found out I was Jewish, they told me that it would go very bad for me if I were to fall into German hands. Nobody likes the Jews, they taunted me. The anti-Semitic hatred of generations was evident in their words. I told them they should worry about themselves-and quickly rode off.

I thought about the hate that surrounds Jews on all sides. If I am so treated by my war comrades, how will the Germans treat me where Jew-hatred is their highest ideal? Dark thoughts worried my mind. How will I be treated by the Germans if, God Forbid, I fall into their hands?

Result of forest living.

Again-spending the night in a new location. Rain fell without end, and I was sopping wet. In the morning the clouds disappeared and the rain stopped. In a moment of hope, I removed my greatcoat and spread it out to dry. I ran back and forth to keep warm. I heard a dog bark, and I quickly remounted my horse and rode off in the opposite direction.

I found an orchard with ripe plums. Some of the trees were torn out of the earth by shrapnel, an indication of the recent battle. I let the horse wander and eat the fallen apples which lay strewn about the orchard. I filled the pouch of the gas mask with plums and ate my fill. Not far away, two dead soldiers lay in a fox hole, and further, a shot-up field kitchen and spilled rotten food. And more horses with swollen bellies picked at by birds of prey and mice. The smell permeated everywhere.

There were potatoes in the field left by the owners who had run out of time to harvest them. I collected a little pile of potatoes and some wood, made a small fire, and roasted them. The horse got a raw potato which he enjoyed very much.

In one of the many nights, I found a half-ruined hut, probably a forest warden's. I decided to spend the night under a roof even though it exposed me to danger.

From day to day, I began to suffer the consequences of forest living. My hair was growing wild. I washed my face with rain water or morning dew. Lice, another war enemy, an unavoidable part of war and forest living, found me.

I resolved to bathe in the river and change my clothes to rid myself of the blood-suckers. I got undressed on a shallow bank, under a bush, and went into the water. It was ice cold and my teeth were chattering and I was seized by shivering when I got out. The lice-filled shirt and underwear, I threw into the river.

A farmer's "guest"

I was looking for a place where I could be sure of food for myself and my four-legged friend. I rode until the forest ended and I saw smoke snaking to the sky. After riding a few kms, I saw small village houses. White flags were fluttering from the roofs of the Polish houses. German flags were flying from others-the Volksdeutsche.

I came to a house with a white flag, and was greeted by an old farmer who invited me into his house. He shaved my beard which had already grown much. He invited me to dine on a "kapusniak" with potatoes, and a red borscht to drink. It had been weeks since I had tasted any cooked food.

According to the farmer, I was near Chelmno which is on the Vistula. The whole area was occupied by Germans. Guests such as I show up every day, but the danger is great. The Germans openly stated that they would shoot anyone who hides a Polish soldier. When the farmer's wife saw me she screamed, "Ole Boga" and crossed herself. Fear shone in her eyes.

The farmer proposed that I spend the night in his barn. I happily accepted. At night, he invited me to dinner and asked that I leave as soon as there was light in the sky. In the morning, he invited me in again for breakfast. He told me that the German army is at the gates of Warsaw. A bitter battle was being waged at Modlin, where the defenders of the fortress displayed true heroism. A small group of Polish soldiers in Westerplatte, on the Baltic Sea, mounted a heroic defense in spite of the shelling from the navy and bombing from the air. The occupied areas are settled by Germans brutally hostile to the population, especially to Jews. New evil decrees issue daily from the Nazis.

I thanked the farmer. He showed me the way to the Vistula, and I took to the road equipped with a food package.

With a friend-in-suffering

I had more forest living to look forward to. I came upon a lost Polish soldier, and we were happy to meet. I shared the bread I got from the farmer. We shared the stories of our adventures, and decided to continue as partners hoping it would help our circumstances.

We gave up on the plan to get to other side of the Vistula. My new friend, Janek, had already unsuccessfully tried several times. We found an abandoned house and agreed to spend the night there. Chickens were wandering around outside and my friend promised me a dinner fit for a king. He found some eggs. There were potatoes in the garden. Janek made a fire and showed his skills in cooking. The roast was delicious. We found a jug of apple juice in the cellar and finished the feast with it.

We decided to spend a few days here to gain some strength for the hard days ahead. Fear of the Germans kept me from sleeping and I envied my friend for his ability to sleep so soundly. Walking around the area in order to learn more about it, we came on a dead soldier, horse carcasses, and destroyed military wagons. We also found some moldy provisions. We sorted through the treasure and took some with us.

Early morning, I was awakened by the sound of shooting that was growing louder by the minute. We quickly saddled the horses and left the house which had served us so well. Returning to it was not an option, as the Germans patrolled the abandoned houses.

To suffer inhumanly would be our fate in the forest, in bad weather, rain and storms. Our skin burned from dirt and dampness.

Riding further, we suddenly heard shooting from a German patrol. We quickly turned and galloped off in the opposite direction. When I looked around, I was, hungry and thirsty, and alone.

With a group of Polish soldiers.

I came to a small house, the dwelling of an old forest warden. He received me courteously and invited me to eat. I washed and shaved. Because of my wounds, I was unable to ride, and I gave the horse to the warden as a gift. After staying with him a few days, I had to leave because of the frequent German patrols in the area.

My goal was to find a place with Jews. As I walked, I came across a larger group of Polish soldiers going in my direction, and carrying a white flag at the front. The group consisted of seventeen soldiers, with one Jew. Because of the Jew, I attached myself to this group. It turned out that the flag carrier was the Jew, Kobziansky. He hailed from Przemyslany, in Podolia, married and the father of two children.

I tried to convince him that we two should detach ourselves from the group because our situation as Jews was more dangerous. But my words did not persuade him. He maintained that being in a larger group was less dangerous. Not having much enthusiasm for traveling alone, I stayed with the group and blindly awaited my fate.

In the meantime it got dark, and we decided to spend the night on the edge of the road under some dense trees. They began to tell jokes about Jews. I thought to myself, they're in deep trouble and they're still swaggering. The tradition of Jew hatred lies deeply imbedded in their bones. Regarding we two Jews, they allowed that we were good Jews. Their problems seem to have been resolved and they were ostensibly very worried about what would happen to us "Zhidkes" in German captivity. Their hatred was not forgotten even in the impossible situation they were in.

Days went by, gloomy and rainy. When the rain stopped, we prepared for our march. In the front, a louse-filled shirt hung on a stick, served as flag. One day, the sergeants decided to change the flag carrier from Jewish to Christian. The great "honor" of carrying a lousy shirt as symbol of capitulation to the Germans was due only to a pure Pole and not a Jew, who, in addition had the look of a Communist about him.

With such "friends", I wandered around day and night, looking for ways to stay out of German hands. My friend, Kobziansky, held to his position that it was better to stay with the group.

On a sunny day, when the sun was shining, we set off to the unknown. Not far away there was a paved road hidden from us by the trees. Columns of Panzers drove along the road. When it quieted down, we continued our march.

Captured

We hid in a small wood and heard the German shout, "Halt!" The Germans were shouting at entire columns of Polish soldiers carrying white flags, their weapons thrown away, their faces downcast, a sign of surrender. The commanders of the "glorious" Polish army, whose only concern was that their boots and spurs shone like mirrors, those who hurled the slogan, "We will not surrender a button", they along with the Commander-in-Chief, Smigly-Rydz at their head, were long gone beyond Poland's borders.

It was a sad picture-thousands of young Polish soldiers with white flags, surrendering to the hated enemy. After spending the night in a small forest, we set off again at noon. We came out on a broad road and straight into the hands of the Germans. Everyone raised their hands. That which I feared most had happened. I was a captive of the Germans.

Two German soldiers with restraint equipment ordered us, a group of seventeen soldiers to sit down on the ground, and throw away our weapons. From a distance came columns of hundreds of soldiers going to their captivity. The white flags, made from torn sheets, from lousy sweat soaked shirts, fixed to the tips of rifles, fluttered in the autumn wind. This large contingent of Polish soldiers surrendered to two Nazi soldiers whose fear showed in their over-fed fat faces.

The Germans kept 30 meters away from the prisoners, and ordered them to lay their weapons in a pile. Hundreds of rifles, bayonets and hand-grenades created a small mountain of weapons. The prisoners sat on the ground, apathetic, grizzled, dirty.

Fearful in such a large crowd of prisoners, they used soft words with us, handed out cigarettes. Using their field telephones, they called in the field gendarmerie who came in large trucks. They carried out an extensive search. Anything of metal, pocket-knives, spoons, forks, was confiscated so they could not be used as weapons.

They loaded us into the trucks with mad shouts, "Los, schneller, Ihre scheiss-bande!" Curses and oaths poured from their mouths. After a short time, we came to the market place of a small shetl which was overflowing with trophies from the defeated Polish population. Thousands of cavalry saddles, thousands of boots, crates of coffee, cigarettes, butter, sweets. The city had become a concentration point for plunder taken from the surrounding area.

They put some of us in the second floor of a theater and stuffed others into a church. The whole town was decorated with white flags on the Polish houses. The Nazi flags with the swastika flying on the houses of the Volksdeutsche put fear into everyone.

Humiliated and tortured

A great number of Jews from every corner of Poland were among the prisoners. As a result of the war, many criminals escaped from the bombed-out jails and were captured by the Germans and treated as prisoners-of-war. One of these criminals, who had been sentenced to life-imprisonment for murder, was my bunk mate in the theatre hall where we were quartered.

The Germans, all with faces like fattened pigs, walked around arrogantly, feeling like super men, preparing to take over the world.

One night we were awakened by wild cries. They ordered us to remain lying on the floor and shone flashlights on us. "You will all be shot, you damned Polacks!" the Germans shouted. It seemed that the prisoners held in the church had disarmed the guards and fled. The Germans fired chaotically into the night. A lot of Poles were killed in their flight. The Germans were afraid that we would also try to run away.

Days went by. Later, the Germans brought a large number of Polish prisoners and concentrated them in the market, under the open sky. They were a pitiful sight-dirty, in tattered uniforms, faces sunken from poor nutrition, bearded after weeks of not shaving. Among them there were many Jews who suffered both from their war comrades and from the Germans. Most of the Poles could not speak German and they were unable to communicate with the Germans. But the word, "Jude," they were quick to learn, and they began to identify the Jews. They competed to show their hatred for Jews before the conquerors.

On a rainy day, an agonizing march was begun. They drove us with wild cries, and shot whoever lagged. We suffered humiliation and derision. In the evening, we halted in a desolate forest. Fatigued, we lay down to sleep in the cold and wet.

Eventually, we were brought to a place surrounded by barbed wire, and fenced in under the open sky. We were not the first to be here. The camp was already occupied by thousands of prisoners. A group of four of us Jews got together, among them my friend Berl Babat, and agreed to keep together, and help each other out to the best of our abilities.

Hunger

One loaf of bread to last for three days was given for four people. Water was more difficult. We were taken to a small river every third day. Thus, the Germans amused themselves with us. It rained for days and nights, and cold winds blew around the sandy hill of our camp. Constant hunger caused fights among the prisoners. People went around with nerves on edge. Hunger led to apathy and madness. Our clothes hung on us like scarecrows from weeks of starvation. Eyes were red from lack of sleep. Can anyone sleep standing up?

At times, the Germans took prisoners for labor. I chose a place near the door where the Germans entered. After many days of watching the door, two armed soldiers and an officer came to select six men for work. The whole camp, thousands of men, flooded the area near the door, like a stormy sea, in order to be one of the lucky ones. The Germans angrily pushed back against the mass of men. I was one of the six, and thousands of eyes glared at us with envy.

They took us to the train station to clean field kitchens which were part of the plunder. When we opened the first oven door, we were assaulted by the stench from the "pentsak[2]" which had been cooked in the first days of September. We fell on the pentsak like starving jackals. When the officer saw this, he drove us away. He led us to the station platform. Luck was with us. German soldiers had just finished eating, and they gave us the remains from their kits. We ate and ate. We ate for the days we had starved, and for the coming days.

The Germans made a "spectacle" out of our hungry condition. They kept on bringing us their remains, and shaking with laughter, they said, " Look at how the Polish pigs eat like horses!" They brought out their cameras. They photographed us from all sides and in all kinds of comical positions.

The officer gave us each two loaves of bread, a coat and a military blanket. Sometimes this happens with Germans. We brought back a little container of soup to camp. We hid the bread and soup under our clothes. We gave the soup to our friends to their great joy. We four kept together, like a small "commune." On rainy days, we slept standing up, leaning against each other, our heads covered with greatcoats. I hid the bread for the next day, but very early on it transpired that the bread disappeared.

Good treatment

One day we were led out of the camp. They took us to the train station and stuffed as many as they could into the wagons. They gave us Polish newspapers which contained German propaganda-a picture of Polish prisoners of war standing in front of the open doors of the wagons with smiling faces and a cigar in their mouths, burned down houses in Warsaw, dead Polish soldiers lying on the ground, dead horses, pictures of President Moscicki , Foreign minister Bek, and Marshall Smygli-Ridz, who were accused of daring to resist the unconquerable German army. The logic of a wolf.

The newspaper wrote about the "treatment" of the prisoners-"they lack for nothing"-and similar lies.

When the train stopped, we found ourselves on cursed German soil. I felt weak as we walked. I probably had a high fever. I felt drunk and out of touch with reality. My true friends came to my aid, supporting me under the arms. If not for them, I would have suffered the fate of others who failed to keep up and would have been left to die on the road, shot by the Germans.

They led us into half-empty military barracks. I began to feel a little better. I did a stupid thing and came out as a Jew. There were about seventy Jews there. In reality, there should have been ten times as many. Jews made up ten percent of the Polish army. The overall number of Jewish prisoners was 10,000.

Germans, Volksdeutsche, and Poles took part in removing our clothing. The Germans gave the commands, the Volksdeutsche carried them out, but the greatest zeal was shown by our "comrades-in-arms", the Poles. We were left with just a shirt and pants and were mocked thereby.

An under-officer, a Volksdeutsche, took charge of us. His first command, to clean out the stable with our bare hands, was accompanied by kicks from his heavy boots and curses and insults from his anti-Semitic vocabulary. An older German from the reserves, amused himself with us and berated us. "You Jews wanted this war, therefore you must suffer. You are all going to be shot." But he quickly caught himself and took it back saying, "Shooting is too much of a luxury for you. You will be hung."

Jews-Isolated

They crowned us with the title, "Jew Company," and made us take our place last in the food line, after thousands of soldiers had received their portions. They separated us form the [Christian] Poles, and housed us in a small barrack. The seventy of us had barely enough room to sit on the floor.

The German soldier chosen to be in charge of us, thought up ways to frighten and mock us. He led us out of the barrack every half hour to muster. We were made to stand in only our shirts in the cold rain and wind. Our suffering gave the sadist much satisfaction. He ordered us to stand on our heads and to laugh. Very few were able to do this. So he ordered us to help the others by holding onto their feet.

He explained to the cook that Jewish beliefs do not permit them to eat pork. So he insisted that a hunk of pork should be placed on everyone's plate. There were frumeboys among us, and they declared that eating pork was permissible under these circumstances because it was pikuach nefesh.

Prisoner-of-war 11022

We were finally rid of the tormented camp and were transferred-under inhuman conditions-to another camp in Hammerstein. A shudder passes through me today when I think of the waiting, half naked in the cold, at the gate of the camp while the guards concluded their formalities.

In Hammerstein, we were quartered in tents. The straw ceiling protected us from the wind. We felt like we were in the Garden of Eden. When the camp commandant saw how poorly clothed we were, he ordered a distribution of military clothing from their Czech plunder. We were registered, and I received the number 11022. From that moment on, I was "Prisoner-of-war 11022."

In spite of the new conditions, we froze. We lay with our military coats over our heads. We warmed ourselves with our own breath captured beneath our coats.

Hungry men are easily provoked, and every night there were fights about suspected thefts. Hunger made us look at everything that could possibly be eaten as food, such as the stinking horse bones that we stole from a vat of liquid where the bones were thrown after the meat had been removed. We would gnaw at the bones to get any remaining bits of meat.

We were led out to work every day. We built barracks for ourselves and for future prisoners that were to come from all the rest of Europe Hitler was planning to conquer. The supervisors were older Germans who had not been mobilized into the Wehrmacht but into labor units. Their behavior to us was correct. There were anti-Hitlerites among them who hated the war and looked on us as its victims. They helped us more than once in spite of the Hitler bible which permitted no humanity especially with respect to Jewish prisoners, who "wanted to destroy the Third Reich, and brought on this war with the help of American Jewry."

This was in distinction with the sadists found here who tormented us.

Some of the Polish prisoners were moved to the new barracks. "Jew Company" were kept in their tents until the end. It wasn't until February that we were moved to a barrack.

Roll call in the night

One frozen night, when all the prisoners in our barracks were sleeping, wild screaming was heard echoing through the cold air. "Alles, schnell raus, ihr scheiss-bande!" We grabbed coats over our heads and quickly ran out of our tents.

Outside in the snow, we saw German soldiers standing with fixed bayonets. A cold winter moon was reflected in the sharp edges of the bayonets. The officers, flashlights in hand, yelled at us to quickly form columns of four, and began the count.

We trembled with fear and cold. What could this mean? Half the night passed in crackling frost, the Jew Company mustered while the Polish soldiers slept peacefully in barracks. What was this devilish scheme? Various thoughts arose. We knew that Germans were capable of anything. The secret was revealed to us when they ordered us to return to our barracks. We overheard the officers saying, "Yes, the prisoner is in the Jewish company, the dog who stole the potatoes."

After ten days, the "potato thief" was returned to us. He told us that one night, unable to sleep from hunger, he crept out to "organize" a few potatoes. (What the Germans call "theft", is "organizing" in prisoner argot). Unfortunately, he was captured by a patrol and placed under military arrest in the barracks. German soldiers arrested for minor offences were his cell mates. He received the same punishment as the Germans even though their offence was four times greater. He was given ample food, good meaty soups, cigarettes. He didn't have to get up and go to work every morning. Truly, a paradise. He was ready to stay under arrest until liberation. Instead of a penalty, it was a vacation.

We "organize" wood for heating

The cold got worse in the evenings. The single iron stove in our barrack could not heat the entire length. The main duty of the guard who walked around our barrack was to guard the wood which was dedicated to building materials. On changing of the guard, the replaced guard would call in a loud voice, "Don't let the prisoners steal the building lumber." We, on the other hand, had the opposite task, to "organize" the wood, because the cold was unendurable. Because of poor nutrition, we felt the cold doubly.

The lumber was located not far from our barrack. The organizing was carried out with several variations. When the guard's back was turned, we quickly grabbed a plank and disappeared into the barrack. Another method was the following: Two prisoners would engage the guard in conversation about the weather, about the war. One remained with the guard ensnaring him in conversation while the other crept away and, on a signal from his friend, grabbed the wood and disappeared.

We haul potatoes

The news that three large trucks filled with potatoes had arrived and men were needed to unload them, spread like lightning through the barracks. Outside, the camp was buzzing like a disturbed beehive. A mass of prisoners fought to unload the potatoes. The Germans understood the intentions of so many "volunteers", but it was difficult for them to disperse them. They threw themselves on the trucks like a pack of wolves.

The officers screamed at the soldiers to drive away the "Scheiss-gezindl", or the trucks would be removed. They beat at us with their rifle butts and yelled at us until they were hoarse, "Get back, Scheiss-bande." My barrack commander, a tall, brown-faced man, recognized me. He yelled at me loudly so the officer would hear, "Los wek!", while winking at me to go and get myself some potatoes.

Every month we received 24 Marks in ration cards, which were valid only in camp. This was paid by the building company. We could use them to buy things in the small canteen-shoe laces, polish, shaving things, cigarettes, but no edible products.

I sold the cigarettes I received to our guard for real money. Many others exchanged their rations in similar fashion.

Part of the ration money had to be paid back to the commander as a bribe. Every Sunday he came for his cut in schnapps from our Jewish commandant, Jagoda. In return, we received certain privileges.

He would give us a day's notice before inspections so that we could ready ourselves. We hid the "organized" potatoes. The clothing we all had, we hid under the bed. As a result, the Jewish company had a good name in the camp administration for not stealing potatoes, or clothing, or wood, and other things.

Slipped on the ice

The cold worsened. Cold, icy winds blew which we felt most on the way to work. Cold and hunger followed us day and night. We thought less about our future than about receiving a bowl of soup from the kitchen. Getting a bowl of warm water that the Germans called soup, awakened my hunger. It wanted more, and was angered when it was denied.

I got an inspiration and broke my plate. I went to the kitchen officer with the shards in my hands, and told him that I slipped on the snow and spilled the soup. He believe me and told the cook, "Give this dog another bowl of soup." To me, he said, "The plate is the property of the Reich. If you do it again, Schwein, you'll get it up the ass."

I gave up the slipping gambit and thought up another one.

A portion of soup under a cape

I wore a Czech cape tied at the throat with a string. I attached a wire to the inside bent into a hook and hung a mess kit from it so that nothing was visible from the outside. The pots in the kitchen barrack were arranged in a long row and the steam from the pots enveloped half the kitchen due to the cold.

Coming into the kitchen, I went to the first pot and put a portion into my mess kit and quickly hung it on the hook under the cape. Then, I put another portion on my plate.

The ruse worked for me for a long time until the weather changed and the pots weren't as steamy. I used it until a German officer spotted steam coming out of my cape around the collar. He yelled at me, "Halt, halt!" and a soldier blocked my way. He opened my cape and saw the kit with the soup, and he hit me on the head with the wooden spoon used to stir the pots, and I fell to the ground.

I still remember today how a thousand stars swam before my eyes. How long I lay on the ground, I don't know. A stream of cold water got me back on my feet. The head wounds healed in a few days, but the headaches lasted a long time.

I lost a "gravy pit" and I began to think of another scheme to still my hungry stomach.

Oats in the pants

One frosty morning, they took us to work in a large grain elevator of oats in Hammerstein. It was a hard journey, the frozen snow breaking like glass under our feet. The snow sparkled like many-colored gems that dazzled our eyes.

The work consisted of shoveling the oats from one pile to another with big wooden spades in order to prevent them from getting moldy. The elevator doors were wide open and the freezing wind came in. We worked fast in order to keep warm. The dust floating in the air penetrated our mouths, ears, and made it hard to breathe. A ration of dust instead of food. The guard ran around knocking one boot against the other to keep warm.

Shoveling the oats was hard work for starving men. The cold and the dust made our eyes burn. And the hours dragged by so slowly-"a sho a yohr"[3]-as we used to say in our shtetl. So many hours to go until the day ends.

After the guard finished his coffee and lit a cigar, he felt it was time to begin to hurry us.

My best friend Berl Babat (a Zamosc boy) worked with me. He began to describe all the dishes that can be made from oats. We were faced with a problem: How to get the oats to camp. It was impossible to put them into our satchels because we were being constantly watched.

We worked out the following scheme: I unbuttoned my pants and turned my back to the guard. My friend shoveled oats into my pants which I had previously tied around my ankles. Then I did the same to him.

Throughout the course of the work, we slowly filled our bags with oats. We even tried to eat them raw, but they were too spiky and the guard saw this and yelled, "Stop this Schweinerei immediately. What are you, horses?"

Back at the camp, we busied ourselves with the oats. We heated an old piece of tin and dried the oats on it. Then we ground them with two bricks making a kind of oat kasheh. We boiled them in an old marmalade can. We added some potatoes and it was very tasty. Then we understood why horses like oats so much. Evidently a starving man would like it too, since we also ate moldy bread plucked from the garbage cans.

Unloading coal ore

One morning, the guard came to take us to work. He asked, with a sly smile, for volunteers to unload coal ore at the train station. I was suspicious of his asking for volunteers, and his mysterious smile. I and five others stepped up to volunteer. The guard then said to the others, "So you did not want to unload coal. These people, who freely volunteered, will be unloading bread."

We dared not believe his words. We knew that the Germans liked to amuse themselves at our expense. As we approached the station, we saw a freight train sitting on a side-track.

Our curiosity increased with each step. What awaits us in the locked cars-bread or coal?

To our amazement, when the doors were opened, we saw bread. Bread! Cars full of bread. Each one of us was feverishly engaged in figuring out how to organize a few loaves for himself. Before work started, our guard distributed one loaf to each of us, and promised another at the end of the job.

We arranged ourselves in a row: three in the freight car, three on the ramp, and two soldiers in the automobile. We passed the bread from hand to hand. The one who was furthest into the car, took a bite out of each loaf. When the Germans inspected the bread, they thought it was done by mice. Standing near the two soldiers I could hear them talking about it. One held that they were signs of mice teeth, and the other that it was human teeth.

They ordered us to stop unloading and called over an officer to settle the dispute. After long study of the bread, the officer declared that these were not only human teeth marks, but fresh ones as well. He became angry and started to berate us. He ordered us to "fall in" and gave us a lecture. "Why are you sabotaging? This bread is meant for the victorious German soldiers." He sternly warned us that this must not happen again. Nevertheless, he ordered that we be given another loaf each.

No more loaves were bitten into after the strict lecture. After the unloading was complete, he tallied the numbers and said that there were six loaves missing. He addressed the soldiers, "The count is exact. The missing bread was obviously stolen by the prisoners." They ordered us to get on a truck open to the elements, and we froze on the way back.

We got to the Hammerstein barracks and unloaded the bread in the stores. German soldiers in the magazine arranged the loaves in rows and counted them. I and a friend decided to "organize" two more loaves and hide them in the snow. An opportunity like this to acquire bread-the dream of thousands of prisoners-must not be wasted. We buried two loaves in the snow so we could get them at the first opportunity.

The Germans could not believe that there were now two more loaves missing. They recounted and asked us again if we had not stolen them. Understandably, we denied it. They yelled loudly at us. We tried to show them that there was an error made at the station. This enraged them more. They yelled, "Silence, you gang of Jews."

My friend and I planned how to get the two loaves. The idea was simple. Every afternoon, two prisoners were taken out under guard to chop wood near the magazines where we had stashed the bread. We told the two about the bread. They told the guard they weren't feeling well and pointed to us as their replacements. The guards agreed.

At the spot, I hid one glove in my bag and claimed that I had lost it. I searched the snow thoroughly "in order to find the glove" but I did not find the bread.

Kiryat Yam

Translator's Notes

1. Four "shtangen" could be an allusion to the four pillars of the Chupa canopy, as in "Unter die fier shtangen."

2. Gruel

3. An hour like a year

[Page 223]

With the partisans in the forest

by A. H.

Translated by Moses Milstein

When the Germans arrested the Judenrat leaders, it became clear to everyone in town that no one would be able to save themselves. Like many others, we prepared a hiding place in a cellar. It could hold twelve people, but there were forty of us.

The Gestapo, with the help of local Poles, were busy dragging new victims out of the hiding places. The streets were overflowing with dead bodies. Other Jewish citizens were taken to the jail, then taken to the cemetery at night, and buried alive.

My father brought us these reports when he stole out one night to get some water some five days after we first holed up here. The reports showed our situation was hopeless.

After the fifth day, around three o'clock, we suddenly heard a commotion. Every one held his breath; mothers covered their little children's mouths so they could not cry. We were certain this was the end. From above, we heard horrible laughter. Then a light shone on us through the cracks in the floor, illuminating everyone. Everyone saw the Angel of Death before him. I will never in my life forget the moment when my father, sitting next to me, clasped me unusually tightly to his breast, and said in the silence: "My child, don't scream. " At the same moment, we heard the bandits talking, and deciding that there was nobody down below.

For several minutes, we dared not admit to ourselves that we had experienced a miracle. From certain death back to life. But what do we do now? That evening my father said, "Enough waiting for death. Now we will try to resist, and maybe we will be lucky, and escape from the bandits' hands, and escape to the forest."

Escape to the forest

Back in quieter times, we had made an agreement with a forest watchman that, at the critical moment, we would try to hide out in the forest. Time was short: we had to decide and go. My mother's opinion was that, "Where God leads, we will go." But my father was a very forceful man, and he persuaded us that there was no other option.

We quickly got ready for the road. Packs in hand, and out of the house. The night was as bright as day. We could hear the wild shouts of the SS coming from the shops and restaurants. The streets were smeared with blood and full of dead bodies. My father led and we followed behind. The worst part was passing by the cemetery where the murderers were finishing off their long day's work.

After we had gone a good distance, we suddenly heard the barking of dogs. This made the situation dangerous for us, because the murderers heard, and began shooting with automatic weapons, and shouting, "Hent Hauch, Stehen bleiben!" It's a miracle we were already so far away from them. Because of the danger, we mustered our strength, and we ran without stopping. We covered two kilometers this way, until we were no longer in danger, and we rested.

We continued a little more calmly to the Kovenczniker (p224??) forest. There the watchman helped us to find a good spot. We were lucky to have escaped from that hell.

The days passed slowly and sadly. For food, we had to get by with what our good clothes could sell for in the village.

Killing Germans, blowing up train tracks

One morning, our hiding place was assaulted by partisans of the AK. They forced everyone out, took them to the valley, and shot them. By chance, I was not there. The evening before, I had gone to the village for provisions. When I got back, I saw the great calamity that had occurred. My first thought was to take my own life. But the only way to do that was to starve to death, and death from hunger comes too slowly.

After a day of terrible experiences, left all alone, I came to the decision that I must continue to live. I went to the village, and with the help of a farmer I knew, I buried the whole family in one grave.

I had often met partisans when I went to the village, so I decided to join them.

At first I found it very difficult, but in time I learned to live with these strangers who became my saviors. The group was small from the beginning: some 40 Russians, and a very small number of Poles and Jews. With great joy, one day, I unexpectedly came across Raizel Berger in the group. We treated each other as sisters, because we had no other family. We supported each other whenever we got together.

Unfortunately, it did not last long. I got an order to cross the river Bug with a group of about 30 partisans. We had to fight our way to the larger Russian division in Pinsk. The conditions were very dangerous, as the farmers used to betray us.

The road was hard. No sooner did we get over the river onto land than we were attacked by Ukrainian nationalists. We lost two partisans. When we got to our destination we were hailed as heroes for making it through.

The partisans in White Russia were well organized. Our task was to ambush and kill Germans, demolish bridges, and train tracks, blow up military trains, and so on.

This lasted until 1944. When the Russian army arrived, we joined them, and together, we retook Pinsk. Later on, the partisans were disbanded. Many men joined the army. Others were given good civilian postings.

Among the scattered ruins

My job was, however, not over. I received an order to transport sick soldiers to the Russian interior. I got everything organized and completed my task, but I fell very sick myself. I spent three months in hospital. When I left, I found myself in a strange city, knowing no one, in broken health. But, after a short time, I got myself organized, and found work, and stayed in Russia for a whole year.

During that time, the Lublin region was liberated, and I decided to go home.

How sad was the day I got home. No sign of living family, not a drop of hope that anyone had survived. Even my brother who I had always [gericht p226??] showed no sign of being alive. The whole shtetl was dead, only the scattered ruins accompanied my tears.

The Poles, who with their own hands added to the fire, tried to console me. But I fled from them, the earth burning beneath my feet.

I came to Lublin, and, finally, met various people from Szczebreszyn: Dora Fleisher, Yehuda Weinstock and my friend Raizel Berger with whom I spent over a year in Lublin.

Still today, my greatest pleasure is to get together with people from my shtetl, Szczebreszyn.

———

[Page 229 - Yiddish] [Page 227 - Hebrew]

Taking Part in the Battle

by Zvi Treger (Tal)

Translated by Moses Milstein

When the Russians retreated from our region, many Jews left for the area around the river Bug in order not to fall into the hands of the Nazis. Our whole family left with them. The Red Army retreated beyond the river Bug which had become the new border between the Soviet Union and Germany after the Ribbentrop-Molotov Pact of August, 1939.

We went to Wolyn, and after a short time, we were sent to the Ivanov-Vosnesensk area, to a small town, Privolsk, along with the Farber and Greber families. We worked in the textile factories, and our standard of living was typical of the area. No one was dying of hunger.

At first, I and my brothers, Shimon and Yerachmiel, were there alone. Our parents and other family members were in the Veligotsiker forests. With great difficulty we managed to bring them over to us. This was in 1941, when the Germans had attacked the Soviet Union.

Hunger in Uzbekistan

We were all sent to a kolkhoz in Uzbekistan. There, we suffered from hunger. The Uzbeks did as well. We were mobilized into a "Torud army", in the Ural mountains, where the conditions were abominable. We worked from dark to dark. Whoever could, ran away.

Many of the conscripted died. My brother, Yerachmiel, z"l, died of malaria. The doctors paid no attention to him because he did not display any fever. Whoever was in Russia in those days knows full well that the sick received no help. He had to work like all the others.

Not long after, I received news that my family in Uzbekistan had died of hunger. My mind became so disordered, that I did not react to people around me. The terrible news, the hunger, and the cold led me to expect death myself.

Revenge against the Germans

I managed to regain a little of my strength, and when I returned from the Leningrad area, I decided to enlist in the Red Army. We had heard about the barbaric actions of the Germans toward our Jewish brethren in Poland. I wanted to seek revenge against the murderers. I fought against the Germans as part of the Polish-Soviet army. I took part in the battles around the suburbs of Kolberg, the crossing of the Oder river, and the taking of Berlin. I did not display any particular heroism, but I took revenge wherever I could. I saw it as my holy duty for those murdered, and for the Jewish people.

Back in Poland

After the German surrender we were sent to Chelm to fight against the Polish reactionary groups. Day in and day out, we "sanitized" the Zamosc and Tomaszew-Lubelski area. We fought major battles against the Ukrainians in Jaroslawiec, Rzeszow. Many Jewish boys fell in battle against the Ukrainians and the Polish AK bandits.

I remember Chelm well, because many Jews from the Soviet side gathered there. They were those who had been hiding in bunkers and in the forests. We Jewish soldiers, even though we were few in number, did everything in our power to protect them from the Polish hooligans. In spite of our efforts, they managed to kill several Jewish families, among them a doctor and his wife.

I met my wife Sima in Chelm and we got married there. She comes from the shtetel, Manevitch, near Kovel. She lived through the war with Jewish partisans bands in the forests.

I met Shebreshiner people for the first time in the war, when I was sent on a mission from Chelm to Lublin. The first ones I met were Yehuda Weinstock and Raizel Berger. From them I learned that Ephraim Farber and Hersh and Leibl Shtil were in Lublin. In the evening, we got together at Yehuda's house and we drank a heartfelt l'chaim both for our survival and for having avenged the murders of our people.

We came to Israel via Italy, where one of our three sons was born. Today, they have all had children of their own. They followed in their father's footsteps and volunteered for the paratroopers. Two of them took part in the Six Day War and the Yom Kippur War.

Tel-Chanan

[Page 232]

In the Hell of Belzec

by Ephraim Farber

Translated by Moses Milstein

From the beginning of the Nazi occupation until 1941, Belzec (Tomaszew Lubleski area) was a forced labor camp. From 1942-1943, it was an extermination camp. About 800,000 prisoners from Poland and other places, mostly Jews, were killed here. The majority of Shebreshin's Jews perished in Belzec.

The following account is from the time Belzec was a forced labor camp.

In late summer, 1942, when I returned from German detention, the shtetl of Shebreshin was unrecognizable. Germans from all sorts of units were seen in the streets. The gendarmes had occupied the Rathaus building. The Jews who had not left town with the returning Russians were left dependant on the kindness of fate or the Germans.

Older Jews comforted themselves with the belief that the Germans were a cultured people. Some remembered the Germans from the First World War as fine people. In order to console themselves, they forgot that, in the intervening years, drastic changes had occurred in the political arena. In Germany, Hitlerism came to power, and among its political slogans was war against the Jewish people.

Right from the start, various decrees were promulgated, such as capturing people for work, and levying large sums of money from the judenrat. Poverty reigned among Jewish families. Many families were separated. A large number of men had fled to the Russian side. Women and small children had to worry about sustaining themselves. Anti-Jewish laws were carried out with typical German precision. Bearded Jews left in the shtetl wrapped their beards in rags to pretend that they had a toothache in order to protect themselves from the German beasts.

The dedication of the Judenrat

In the short time after my arrival in S., events evolved quickly. Not one day passed without an edict against the Jewish population. The judenrat, willingly or unwillingly, helped the Germans carry out the sentences. Life as a judenrat member was not easy for those who had compassion for their suffering brothers.

Among the judenrat, there were those who were willing to sacrifice themselves for their brethren. But there were also others who believed that they would save themselves and their families by carrying out everything the German murderers ordered. Some members carried out the inhuman orders against their suffering brethren with great zealousness and initiative.

I remember the time when the judenrat, on the orders of the Germans, had to supply 300 young men to be sent to Belzec. The chairman of the judenrat, an honorable Jew, a shomer mitzvoth, met me in the street and asked me to register myself. I told him, "I do not obey German orders!" He said scornfully, "Don't be a choochim. I'll send the Gestapo after you!" (I do not want to mention his name, because his relatives live in Israel.)

I was stunned, and couldn't believe what my ears had heard. I thought this was a bad dream. Unfortunately, it was real. Reeling from the shock, I told him, "Woe is to you if the Gestapo turns its attention to you. I know, from long experience, what the Gestapo can do!"

The first edicts

This was shortly after my return from captivity. The burned shul stood, walls blackened with soot. The old walls, that had absorbed Jewish prayers for hundreds of years stretched to the heavens, the wind blowing through its empty windows. But the heavens were closed to Jewish prayers. The tears of Jewish mothers, whose only sons were taken away to the camps, had no effect. On the contrary, the murderers looked on mockingly. On their belts was engraved in large letters, "God is with us".

The shtetl Rav went around with his beard wrapped "in order not to antagonize" the Germans. On Shabes, Jews gathered in small minions, stealthily, to pray in private houses like their brothers in the time of Torquemada's Inquisition in Spain. The Jewish population was forbidden to leave their houses between 6:00 pm and 7:00 am. Stores were half-open—one door was closed, the other partly open. The Gestapo constantly levied more sums on the judenrat, either in cash or in goods. Jewish residents had to present themselves for all kinds of work without payment.

I remember the Germans found an old Polish flag in Groisse Shloime's budke, the kind that used to be displayed during Polish national holidays. The owners had forgotten to hide it. This gave the Germans a pretext to arrest those found in Groise Shloime's budke, along with its owners. After much negotiation on the part of the judenrat, and payment of a large sum of money, the arrested were beaten, then freed.

The Gestapo arrived from Zamosc with Jewish helpers who led them to the homes of wealthy Jews, and demanded their money. The shtetl panicked. Germans captured any Jews who fell into their hands.

I, and other young people, fled and hid in the peat meadows where the Germans could not get us. I knew the swampy meadows from my earliest childhood. We hid under low bushes between the villages of Blonia and Little Broid. After noon, when hunger began to gnaw at us, I and a friend, headed in the direction of the village, Bloina. Arriving there, the farmers ordered us to leave immediately. They had received a warning from the Germans not to hide any Jews, and they themselves were no friends of the Jews either.

We left for the Gorajec hills and hid in a cave. Many Jews were hiding in the caves and hollows. Towards evening, we headed back to town, because after the curfew we could not be seen outdoors. Most of the Poles collaborated with the Germans in persecuting Jews. They quickly learned the word "Jude". People were grabbed for work, whether the work was needed or not, in order not to allow them one moment of freedom in their sorrowful lives.

The Germans heaped prohibitions on the Jews in order to break their will and make them passive, a state which takes away the will to rebel. Orders were posted in town for all the inhabitants: Tomorrow, from early morning to night, it is strictly forbidden for anyone to show themselves outside. The reason: The governor-general, Hans Frank, will be passing through our shtetl.

One becomes accustomed

A multitude of homeless Jews, expelled from Pomerania and from fire-ravaged Bilgoraj, became the responsibility of the S. Jews. Yesterday, they were self-sufficient people, and today they wander around among strangers, homeless, no roof over their heads, humiliated. Everything possible is done for them. They are divided among the homes, food is provided for the needy. Some of the expelled families are made up of women and children, the men having been taken away to camps.

Slowly, you become used to the problems. The Nuremberg laws are brought in slowly, but covertly. All the orders against Jews are passed from one Jew to another: Jews cannot engage in trade, can't buy, can't sell, can't apply for open positions, can't leave town. They must wear the yellow star. Even this, we slowly got used to. But we felt that this is not the worst yet. Worse could still befall us, and we were afraid.

The Germans identified Jews not by their passes or documents but simply as, "Jude." "You are a Jew." This underscored for them that they are free to do what they wish. The Germans amused themselves: they caught a Jew with a beard on shabes, and shouted, "Cap off!" forcing him to kneel. A soldier went by carrying a box of Kielbasa, and forced him to eat the treif sausage. Officers with cameras stood around and took photographs. They ordered the Jew to carry the box to the market where they have their canteen. The soldier led the way, smiling. Every few steps, he made the Jew put down the box and kneel, and with uncovered head, to pray to the Jewish god.

But this "humor" was child's play compared to future criminal activities directed against Jews.

"Good Jews", we learn how to behave to the Germans. My father's uncle, Zalman Kliski, with whom I was raised for a time, begged me to put on the yellow patch of shame and not be an exception. While in S., I kept it in my bag. I was sickened and humiliated to have to wear the mark of shame. I only put it on in exceptional circumstances.

Another one, who was concerned that I should be "in order" and register myself at the magistrat, , because it was demanded by the Germans, was a member of the judenrat. This provided them the exact number of the Jewish population—how many were at their disposal—all with German meticulousness. At the end, I decided I could not be an exception and registered myself.

One Saturday morning, I went to the city clerk, Leszczinski, to register. Upon hearing that I had been a Polish soldier, he exhorted me not to register. He praised my father for not having taken part like other "zhidkes" with the Bolsheviks when they had been in our shtetl for a short time. He said to me, "The Germans don't have enough to persecute, they need you?" I thanked him for the good suggestions. Going down the stairs, I encountered the member of the judenrat. He asked me if I had registered. When I answered, yes, with a smile, he understood that I had not. Then Leszczinski called me back and said that I had to register because the judenrat forced his hand. The Germans found loyal servants in the judenrat.

Forced out of home

You never knew what could occur to a crazy kommandant or any crazy German. The judenrat received an order to provide 300 young people for transport to Belzec, and they swiftly undertook to carry it out. They were not successful, because most did not want to go, knowing what awaited them.

The assembly point was in front of the rathaus. Early in the morning, I watched the assembly point from the house of my uncle, Moishe Ledereich (Turbiner). The streets were empty. Only the judenrat, the SS, and the assembled Jews sitting on their bags, were seen. The SS counted the assembled Jews. Half of the required number were missing. So they began to beat the judenrat, forcing them to kneel. The curses of the SS echoed through the empty streets.

The SS, led by the judenrat, began to search the houses for the missing Jews. The scene in front of the rathouse was horrible. Jewish mothers wept as the Germans prevented them from approaching their loved ones. The Poles were happy that the "zhidkes" were abused. The pious ones said, "This is punishment for the torments of our beloved Jesus Christ."

I could not stand to see anymore, and I stole out of town. I hid in the swampy meadows where the Germans could not get to me. As I lay hidden, I saw a black mass heading to the train station—our loved ones being led by the Germans to the train station on the way to Belzec.

Hitting the road

It made no sense to stay in town any longer. The situation was deteriorating daily. I decided to hit the road. My goal was Tarnograd. Not far from there was the new border between the Germans and the Soviets. My route was through the back roads; the main roads were full of Germans. I spent the night with a Jewish family in Bilgoraj. There were few Jews left there. Most of the town had been burned down.

After traveling all day on foot, I came to Tarnograd in the evening. It gave the impression of being a quiet shtetl. I met a few Shebreshiner there, like Tslal from the butchers. Towards evening, I noticed a large movement of Germans arriving by truck. That got me thinking that they were preparing an aktion.

My premonition was correct. In the middle of the night I was awakened by the sounds of rifle butts beating on the doors, mixed in with wild shouts—"Auf!". The old Jew I was spending the night with jumped out of bed and opened the door. SS burst in with shouts and curses. They beat him brutally and led him outside.

I was sleeping on the floor. The SS shone flashlights in my eyes. They asked me how old I was. Thinking quickly, I answered, "14 years." One of the SS said, "The schwein is too young." The same thing happened with the son of the house owner. He was really only 13 years old. The SS left the house. I thought I had succeeded in escaping their clutches.

Captured

However, I was wrong. Half an hour later, I heard the Germans shouting again. The home owner had told them, in his Tarnograd Yiddish that they could barely understand, about a document he had left at home. The SS, different ones this time, asked me again how old I was. When I told them—15 years—they unleashed a torrent of blows on me. I heard them screeching, "Get dressed immediately—Verfluchter Jude!" In order to avoid more blows, I grabbed my clothes, and left the house as quickly as possible. It was dark outside. On the other side of the door, an SS man hit me in the teeth with the butt of his automatic weapon. Blood poured out of my mouth.

I was placed with a group of other Jews taken from their homes. In the darkness, we could hear the screaming of the Germans and the barking of dogs. From time to time, shots cut through the air.

The Germans concentrated all those captured during the night in a lerer mill outside of town. The mill was encircled by gendarmes and Ukrainian police. It was not possible to escape. Women and children were standing at a distance with bundles of food for their loved ones. They were beaten mercilessly by the Ukrainian guards who kept them from getting near the prisoners. They kept bringing more Jews who had failed to escape. The shtetl was hermetically sealed by the Wehrmacht and the SS.

After the captures had ended, a Gestapo officer appeared. He stood on a slight rise in the courtyard and delivered a harangue in the Nazi style. "You Jews have never worked, you just engage in criminal activity. You are going to Belzec to work. You will be well-paid and well fed." Many of the captured Jews cried out ecstatically, "Long live the Herr kommandant." It is sad that a large part of our people so wanted to believe the German lies.

After the lecture, a German commission and the head countyman [kreizman] from Bilgoraj, seated themselves around a table. Everyone had to pass through the so-called commission. They asked our ages. There was no medical exam and no one was let off. The sickest ones, who suffered from all kinds of ailments, were yelled at and told to "halten die schnutze".

To an uncertain fate

The Jewish prisoners of Tarnograd were lined up in rows of six, young and old together. The columns marched through town to an unknown fate. Jews who had lived in this small shtetl for generations were leaving without knowing if they would ever return. I marched along with them. The Germans kept shooting into the air—out of fear and to bolster their courage. On both sides of the road, stood Poles who greeted their co-citizens—some with curses, others with regret. With tears in their eyes, the relatives—mothers, sisters, children, saw their loved ones off on an uncertain journey.

Outside town, Poles from the surrounding villages waited with wagons to take the Jews away to Bilgoraj. The guards split up: For every three wagonloads of prisoners there was one wagon carrying two gendarmes armed with automatic weapons. When the distance from the rear gendarmes increased momentarily, some of the younger people tried to run away. I was seated in a wagon next to the gendarmes, and escape would have met a predictable end.

At the small railway station, Ropi, they loaded us into freight-cars—as many as could be stuffed in. We were tightly packed, standing on each others feet. The cars were hermetically sealed. Older people fainted from lack of air. After being unloaded in Zwierzyniec, the Germans ordered us to crawl on all fours. This is how they sated their sadistic hearts with the suffering of others. Debased and broken, we had to sing and dance for the amusement of our guards.

Evening slowly descended on God's world. We were sitting on the ground near the train tracks. The Polish train workers started to make fun of the "Zhidkes". This annoyed the Germans and they asked us, "Why are the verfluchte Poles so happy? Did they win the war?" The Germans believed only they had the right to be happy. Then the Germans ordered us to sing "Yesh polska nie zginenla". We sang it paraphrasing. "Alia zginontch mushi". Then, the Polish workers drew back ashamed.

A piercing whistle cut through the night—a signal we were about to leave. Woeful moans issued from everyone's heart. Now everyone felt the horrible pain of being torn from home. Pious Jews recited the tefilot haderech and some psalms. The others listened reverently. We asked "Him, whose name we are not worthy to mention", to help us. Young Christians stood along the route. They looked at the train windows and passed their hands along their throats. Fear gripped all those who saw.

The train stopped. We all held our breath. Teeth chattered from fear like with the ague [kadoches], and hearts beat faster. The mass of people in the car waited with deadly anxiety for what lay ahead. Shocked and panicked Jews, a doomed people, peered out of the windows, searching for a ray of light in the darkness. Their search and hope was futile. From time to time, the wagons were lit by the lights of the German bandits. It was the middle of the night. The whistles of the departing trains could be heard.

Anti-Panzer ditches

We arrived at Belzec. The wagons were unbolted and we were unloaded with blows. I got ready and jumped out of the car. Thus, I was able to avoid a couple of cracks on the head. This was the welcome the SS provided for the prisoners.

Day is ending. Barbed wire stretches around the camp. Tea is being served in the middle of the yard near the kitchen. Masses of people stand in rows. A deathly silence reigns. Suddenly, a commotion occurs. "Stilstand! Caps off!". After a while, comes the command, "Caps on! The roll call is over."

Belzec lies on the way to Tomaszew-Lubelski—Lubycza-Krolewska, on the Warsaw-Lemberg line. Before the First World War, the border between the two great empires of Russia and the Austro-Hungarian monarchy ran through here. The small train station, isolated from any larger centers, slept dreamily amidst pine forests, surrounded by many villages. In 1940, the German Russian border lay about 600 meters from the Belzec train station.

When I arrived, Belzec was a forced labor camp. The work consisted of digging three- meter-deep "anti-Panzer ditches" the length of the Belzec sector. On the German side, there was a moderately sloped earthen rampart. On the Russian side, a steep wall. To carry out this goal, the Germans brought tens of thousands of Jews from the whole "General Government" to Belzec. In summer of 1940, this included about 300 Jews from S.

What were the ditches for? Were the murderers preparing to defend themselves? They spread the news that they were reinforcing themselves against the Russians. At this moment, plans for Operation Barbarossa—the invasion of Russia—lay in Hitler's Reichs chancellery. Were the Germans already preparing mass graves for their victims? Later, the purpose of the ditches was revealed. The "anti-Panzer ditches" served as mass graves for Jews, among them, the Jews of S.

German methods of "productivity"

The depot where I was stationed was once an old building now converted into a camp. Tracks went through the middle of the hall. We called the building, "Parovozovnie". Three- storied bunks filled the hall. The yard was encircled with barbed wire. There was a large trough of water in the yard. The other half of the camp was on the other side of the road—the mill. The highway, which ran from Tomaszew-Lubelski to Rava Ruska, cut the camp in two. Most of the Shebreshiner were housed in the mill. In the Parovozovnie, were Shenbreshiner—Motele Shochet, David "Leb", Baruch Fink "the menaker", Tsaler Beitcher, "Der Groiser Tsaler", Ephraim "Bazhak", and I.

The same day I arrived in Belzec, the sadist and murderer of Lipowa 7 in Lublin, SS Obersturmbannfuhrer Dolp, came riding in on a white horse. The white horse was a gift from the Lublin judenrat. His face was frozen, his gaze fixed—like a statue, immobile. He examined the victims, and pondered how to afflict the unfortunate.

The Jewish community in Lublin had earlier had the misfortune of knowing this beast in human form for his actions in Lipowa 7. Among his "good deeds" was the shooting of the "liberated" prisoners of war who, at his command, in the winter of 1940, were driven out of Lublin to Biala Podlaska, their blood marking the route. The majority of the Jewish prisoners were shot at his command.

Under the command of this subhuman beast, the Shebreshiner Jews had to "produce", the German word for persecuting the Jews in the camps. His assistants were: Barteczko, SS units, and Volksdeutsche. We called Barteczko, "the boxer"—built like a Colossus, with a big head and a broad face. His two fists were always at the ready to break your teeth. He did not know how to speak—his fists did the talking.

The Volksdeutsche, the sonderdienst, we called the "Blacks", because of their black uniforms. They were a mixture of Slavic bandit and German barbarian, and afflicted us sorely. Every piece of Belzec was soaked with the tears and blood of the Jewish prisoners from all over Poland.

Shebreshiner Jews, all the time they were in the camp, kept warm, friendly relations with everyone. We shared our last piece of bread with the hungry.

The Dance of Death

We would go to work at moon rise, accompanied by blows and curses. We suffered from illness, hunger and lice. At night we slept on hard wooden boards, amid stench and filth, unable to find rest for our work-battered bones. Executions took place in the middle of the night.

There were also 300 Gypsies and their families, during my time in Belzec. The SS would lead the young Gypsies out in the evening, force them to strip naked, and bathe in the trough. Drunken SS carried out an orgiastic spectacle with them by the light of the moon. Wild screams cut through the stillness of the night. Dead tired, shaken by the work day, we could not sleep because of the savage orgies.

A Lubliner Jew went mad from the horrific deeds. The barbed wire, the SS, the whole camp disappeared from his insupportable reality. In his mind, all danger was gone. One day, he headed towards the barbed wire, and was stopped by a bullet.

His dead body was placed in the yard, near the trough, as a warning for would-be escapers. One night, the guard at the entrance brought Hersh Steinberg (Retech), and another youth, to the dead body, ordered them to pick him up by the hands, and dance with him.

"When will we be rid of you?"

It is autumn. We, the slaves, accompanied by shouts and curses, and shots in the air, walk in the rain, our feet sinking into the limestone mud. If anyone stops, he is shot by the SS. On such a rainy day, I was walking in the same row as "menaker" and Motele Shochet. Obersturmbannfuhrer Dolp rode up on his horse and stopped next to us. He ordered my two friends to step out of the row. "Jews must be happy!" he said, and ordered them to sing.

They sang a song with a "chazunish nign" for the murderer. "Oy, oy, enemy of Israel, when will we be rid of you." The song echoed through the wet forest. They sang with heart and soul. Their eyes were shut, distancing themselves from the evil which surrounded them.

To everyone's astonishment, the murderer, Dolp, shouted, "Jews, well sung!" Then he ordered Motele Shochet to sing something by himself. Frightened, Motele was unable to produce a sound. Dolp's eyes reddened. He jerked his horse toward Motele, wanting to crush him under the horse's hooves. He lashed him bloody with the whip, cursed him with "zaftige" curses, wheeled his horse around, and disappeared.

Gripped by rage, Dolp would take out his whip and beat his own dog. If that failed to quell his rampaging blood, he would go into the forest and beat a tree until he collapsed. He would also quiet his sadistic urges with the following game: He would place bottles of water on a Jewish head and aim his pistol from a distance. What deathly fear the suffering victims endured. More than once, a head was smashed instead of a bottle.

His sadistic pleasures also entailed locking Jews in his cellar and denying them food. Only thanks to his wife, who was sometimes able to smuggle some bread or water to the prisoner, were some able to survive.

A way to meet

I was able, occasionally, to meet Shebrishner imprisoned in the mill. One evening, I helped carry the field kitchen in the "porovozavnie" to the mill. It was the only way available for us to meet. In the mill, I was able to talk with my townspeople—and there was plenty to talk about. I decided to spend the night with them. When those I came with were getting ready to leave, they noticed they were one man short. The eldest of the group notified the SS immediately. He didn't have to do it, since no one kept a count.

Even if I wanted to, I could not go back. Now a game of life and death ensued. The SS immediately ordered a roll-call. Reflectors lit up the place, and we were ordered to line up by city and shtetl, every group separately. The SS announced through loudspeakers, that if the missing person was not surrendered, ten men of his group would be shot.

I placed myself in the Shebreshiner group: not one person objected. When the SS asked if all was in order, they answered, "yes." Our group stood trembling, our nerves on edge. The SS searched and failed to find the "culprit". They decreed that everyone must go before the blood-thirsty Obersturmbannfuhrer Dolp.

When it was the turn of our row, lights blinding us, I passed before the commission with forced boldness, my fate hanging on the answer to, "Is this the dog?" "Not him," was the reply. I felt my life was granted to me.

The remnants of Wroclaw after the war

Indescribable horror stories

Our camp in Belzec was part of a collection of camps stretching over a huge area. The forest work camps were closed off, encircled by barbed wire and guarded by armed SS. Anyone trying to escape was shot on the spot. In every sector of the camps young Jews worked —barely clothed, barefoot, starving, emaciated skeletons.

The horrible events surpassed Auschwitz. On a daily basis, Jews were forced to dig deep, narrow holes and stuff someone in. They forced every prisoner to defecate on the prisoner's head. Whoever refused to participate received 30 lashes with a wooden stick. This went on all day until the prisoner was suffocated in feces, and died.

It is hard to believe the German's sadism. Every Sunday, the SS brought baskets of rotten tomatoes and carrots. Then, one by one, they were brought to the place where the Gypsies were concentrated. One tomato was fought over by hundreds of Gypsy men and women. Fights broke out. The Gypsy women tore at each others hair, the men fought with their fists, the children bit. The screams reached to the heavens. This gave the Germans great satisfaction.

Because of poor nutrition, the majority of the Shebreshiner youth suffered from dysentery. The filthy conditions led to skin infections.

Across the Russian border

It is autumn. The rain doesn't stop. The forest we pass is covered in fog. Visibility is reduced to short distances. The Soviets are on the other side of the barbed wire. We look at the Russian side as in a dream: there, Jews aren't persecuted. From time to time we hear a shot and a cry, "Stoi!" Every time I pass near the border, the other side appears to me like a ray of light in the darkness. I waited impatiently for the day when Shebreshiner would be released from the camp. The judenrat had been negotiating with the SS for a while, trying to ransom us.

My plan was to escape over the border when the Shebreshiner were released. The day of realizing my plan arrived. The push came when an SS man overheard me talking to a group of Jews I was working with. He pointed his gun at me, and I thought I was done for. He said to me, "Shut up, you pig. If it happens again, I will kill you." I told him, it wouldn't happen again.

I decided to escape. That evening, I got together some bread, sugar, and cigarettes for the journey into foreign territory. I didn't sleep that night. I discussed my latest plans with my brother in sorrow, Berl Singer from Piotrkow Trybunalski.

In the morning, we went to work, waiting for an opportune moment when the SS were looking in another direction. The moment came, and we threw away our spades and began to run. By the time the SS noticed, we were between the dense barbed wire. Injured, our clothes torn, we escaped from Belzec. We fled to the unknown, to the East.

*

After years of ruin and devastation, Belzec is still again. Occasionally a farmer's plow catches on a shard of our loved ones who perished in the hell of Belzec.

To this day, my blood boils when I hear the name, Belzec. The earth of Belzec has forever swallowed the holy souls of our unforgettable shtetl, along with those of many other cities and shtetlach of our Polish diaspora.

Kiryat Yam

———

[Page 246]

Quietly Weeping

by Shalom Stern

Translated by Moses Milstein and Yocheved Klausner

Elul, sad and beloved!
My dusty footsteps
pass through empty houses
with shattered windows.
Elul, haunting and beloved,
to your skies tinged
by the dust of ash–pits,
hungry crows flock.
Elul, sad and sweet
strides feverishly
through the dessert–like land.
And in the shtetl, desolate and empty,
the soil turns to sand
and, in my eye, no one can see anymore
the swimming tear.
Elul, the sky still, thoughtful,
swims over the land pierced with thorns.
And in the gloom of dawn
no one hurries to slichot
no store–keepers, no tradesman.
Only a peasant woman carries
a bucket full of clear water
from the sobbing brook.
Elul, haunting and dear,
around the stream that gleams
with sun–gold flecks

peasant houses, village fields,
and sweet smelling hay.
But the town's desolation, spread afar,
ignites the sorrow in my eyes.
On sill and wall
wild grass spreads.
And my shadow shrouded in fog
trembles in the darkness
of the Bet Hamidrash.
Elul, sad and dear,
in the sundered graves
of the plundered cemetery garden
cracked vessels lie about
and from beneath sand and wire
hollowed–out skulls protrude.
Desolation and silence
everywhere around.
There is nowhere to hurry.
The shul with its white halls
and painted walls
is burned to the ground
Desolation and silence
everywhere abound.
Rotted shawls,
bloodied kerchiefs.
In the emptiness, the wind blows away
the old pages of siddursand books.
Gone is the joy
of children's play.
Parchments of sefer–Torahs,
copper branches of menorahs
yellow and rust
under the still, autumn sky.
Elul, sad and beloved,
the shtetl of empty houses
guards the deep, thorn–covered graves.
Desolate and empty.

No one sees in my eye
the swimming tear.
Ruined threshold
wall destroyed.
Under my tread
The soil turns to sand
in the dessert–like land.

Autumn

The windows are
shrouded in pall.
A hard autumn rain
falls.
Familiar faces
silhouetted on the walls.
Sorrowful,
pleading Gemaramelodies
tremble through the
cracks in the synagogue's
halls.
What is so surprising!
Jewish faith is buried in
the holy books.

From the poor trade
unions
the battle songs sing
of our heroic comrade
workers.
Why the wonder?
Songs of freedom ignited
in the simple hearts of
the people's children.

The shadows paint

horror pictures.
How can a human hand
from such great terror–
become a creator?
In the sad cold, autumn
they are driven to the Bet
Hamidrash, the old one.
Hands are broken, heads
split open.
Warm blood drips.
The Nazi killer pierces
the heart.

The boys and girls
from libraries and trade–
unions,
always the first to go
forth in battle.
Their honest faces,
magical, with Jewish
charm,
illuminate
the poor, gloomy, shtetl.
Now they go bloodied
to the killing field.
They go, and they weep–

Autumn, windows
shrouded in pall.
Wailing, hard rains fall.

Alef–Bet

The shul yard has
burned,
and the field and the
grass.
The time for
midnight prayers
has come to pass.
Listen well, repeat

every letter after me
until the break of
dawn.

My sole survivor, my
boy,
you are not the last
of your generation.
Recite with faith, the
melody ringing
loud:
Our blood will not be
silenced.
God is with us; our
enemies will fall like
flies.
Together we arose,
together we will
triumph.

Listen well and
learn
the pure melody
of the beautiful alef–
bet.
See, how the letters
shine.
They burn with our
blood and pain.

Repeat after
me, alef–bet.
Every letter clear
and white
Every dot a symbol–
a comforting sign.
You are still young
and small.
Prepare yourself to
be a Jew.
Our Torah stands
complete and clear.

Stand before death
without any fear.
Repeat, sing the
melody again:
Alef
God's word–a
lightning sword.
Cholem bet–B, after
an alef,
makes boh [1].
That is God's will.
Kometz yod–Ya,
cholem bet–Boh,
after which an alef,
makes yavoh [2]

Through your mouth
my child, God's word
falls like dripping
dew.
Cholem yod–Yoh,
after that, a mem,
makes yom. [3]
Be mekadesh
hashem b'chol yom
vayom. [4]
Now repeat
together:
Israel is a strong
tree
Boh yavoh yom, [5]
Rome will be
ruined.
God will erase Berlin
like Sodom.
God's punishment is
already inscribed,
written on the black
edges of the sky.

Pitch–black night.
God watches over
Jacob's tent
God's wrath has
overflowed,
He went out against
our enemies in
battle.
Have faith, you will
grow.
No one can destroy
Israel's home.
See,
the chalutz [6]with
his blue–white flag.
You shall, like him,
the killers attack.

You must arise
little boy
with vengeance full
repay the killers:
Tooth for a tooth,
eye for an eye,
hand for a hand,
for the murdered
Jews
behind the ghetto
wall.
Come closer
pull yourself in
snuggle in
little man.
You are no longer
alone.

You have memorized
the whole alef–bet.
Now you are a Jew,
know it, know.

Praised be the

creator,
I have lived to study
Torah with you.
Wash your little
hands, like for se'u
yedeichem[7]
With a pure face,
say to the surviving
Jews, shalom
aleichem.

Dawn has broken.
The first shot has
thundered.
The first bloodied
letter has sung:
Alef–bet–no harm
will come to the
Jews.
Alef–God's word, a
lightning sword over
our foes.

Eliyeh Maier

A.

Hands folded behind
him,
bent to the ground,
Eliyeh, the village–
traveller
sobs softly in the
little house of
prayer:
God, your people are
a frightened
congregation.
Mother and child–
both shot in one
day.

Always ready to flee
to be afflicted among
strangers.
Ashes and
sackcloth.
forever on their
heads.
Fear and sorrow in
our lands.
Where are you
chasing us, to what
end?–

Blind Pinchas lies
on the long table, as
on a sacrificial altar,
and groans a prayer.
His hunger smells
the scent of bread
His face pale and
calm, soft.
The river runs clear
in the gardens.

B.

Horse and wagon in
the smoky dust.
Cries of despair from
the ruins.
In the cemetery,
with bedding, sefer–
Torahs and Gemaras.
half a shtetl lies
hidden.
The day drags darkly
through the trees.
Behind the tomb
stones–
Fear in every sinew.

The tall grass

by Meshiach's grave
does not hide the
living, pleading,
bundles of bones.
Nazis drive, harass,
shoot.
Jewish blood flows in
the streets–
Hands held behind
him,
Bent to the ground,
Eliyeh Maier, the
village–traveller
sobs softly in the
little house of
prayer:
I am ready for death.
Let the wicked, as
with R' Akiva,
tear my flesh, my
skin
with iron combs.

At the wall, hard
battle,
sharp clang of
knives.
A crash at the door.
Eliyeh Maier stares
at the rifle, at the
bloody bayonet:
The muddy valley is
full of Jewish blood.
God, shafuch
hamutach al
harotzchim, [8]
Take revenge on the
beasts,
for all the Jews, and
for my brother,

Ephraim.

The bayonet buries
itself in him.
Imprisoned in pain,
the world stands
still...
Blood drips from his
bones.
Eliyeh Maier, a
martyr–whole and
pure.
Among the ruins,
God's presence
weeps silently.

Montreal, Canada

Translator's Notes

1. Come

2. Shall come

3. Day

4. Every day you shall sanctify God's name

5. The day shall come

6. Pioneer

7. The blessing of the Kohanim

8. Pour out your wrath on the murderers

[Page 253]

Uprooting the Szczebrzeszyn Jews

Excerpts from the diary of Dr. Zigmunt Klukowski

Translated from Polish to Yiddish by M. Melman

English translation of the Yiddish version by Moses Milstein

From the editors:

The excerpts of a diary, which we present here, were written between October 13, 1939, and March 22, 1943 during the Nazi occupation, by a Polish doctor in the town of Shebreshin, Province of Lublin, Zygmunt Klukowski.

Because it was written during the German fascist occupation, the diary, which gives a picture of the annihilation of the Shebreshiner Jews, stands as a significant source of information for future studies of the destruction of a Jewish-Polish shtetl.

It is an objective work. The author does not conceal the facts of betrayal and collaboration of the fascist-hooligan part of the Polish population. He also reveals facts about the life-saving aid given by Polish farmers to the stricken Jews. He gives an accurate description of the process leading to the Jewish holocaust. And he also presents facts about Jewish participation in the partisan movement, from sabotage of German assets to passive resistance, and so on.

Oct.13 1939

...New decrees were issued. I will set out several of the more important:

"All Jewish men, from 15 to 60 years, of age must present themselves at city hall on X –14, at 8:00 in the morning, for compulsory work. They must bring brooms to sweep the streets, hammers and shovels. As of this day, Jewish residents are permitted in the streets only between 600 hours and 1800 hours. Their homes must always be accessible to the security forces. (Gendarmerie and local groups)." The Jews have hidden themselves behind tightly closed doors -- hardly any are to be seen in the street.

Oct 14, 1939

... In spite of the fact it was the Sabbath, the Germans ordered the Jews to clean the streets for the entire day. They treat them brutally; cut off, or even tear out their beards, curse them, beat them, etc.

Oct 15, 1939

... A militia[1] has been formed in S. composed of 60 men, appointed by the Platzkommando with the agreement of city hall. During the training sessions, the German Platzkommando, Meyer, instructed them that they should look the other way at any wrongs or acts of brutality against the Jews, that persecuting Jews is not merely tolerated but encouraged from "higher up". The Germans themselves create unheard of woes for the Jews—they beat, kick, prod them, and choose the filthiest work to allocate to the better dressed. Before work begins, they order everyone to perform calisthenics, which for the oldest Jews is truly painful, and only then are they driven to work singing "Hay Shcheltsi vraz" or similar songs.

Oct. 16 1939

... Brutalisation of the Jews is becoming more frequent. They are beaten mercilessly. Today, two devastatingly beaten Jews were brought to me -- their buttocks as purple as plums. They begged me to issue them certificates. However, I had to refuse, because that could lead to worse consequences. I advised them to see the German army doctors in town who would often also see civilian patients.

Oct 17, 1939

... More and more Jews come requesting certificates. Mostly, we refuse them. My colleague, Spoz, and I, issue them only in cases of true suffering. Today, I visited an ailing Jew in town who was terribly beaten by the Germans yesterday at work. But in such cases, other than writing a prescription, we can be of no help.

Oct 18, 1939

...This morning, a truckload of Jews was driven beyond the city limits to work. Up to now, some of the richer ones have managed to get out of this kind of work, or from the forced exercises, etc. But the Jewish women—the wives and mothers of those taken away—assembled in front of the houses of the privileged Jews, and made such a commotion that the Germans detained these Jews and took them away under arrest.

Oct 19, 1939

...This afternoon, a German doctor brought about 20 Jews, bakers and butchers (only five were Poles), to examine their health status. The examination was terminated with a long lecture in German, afterwards translated into Polish, about the necessity to maintain hygienic personal and workplace conditions.

Oct. 20, 1939

...Today, they brought me a poster from city hall listing new orders from the German Platzkommando.

Several items are so characteristic and interesting that I will transcribe them literally:

...“Jewish residents will be tolerated and will benefit from the protection of the army contingent on their behavior.”

...”Jewish tax-payers belonging to the S. municipality are obligated, before the 25th of October, to declare their entire estates...all manner of assets must be declared (cash, real estate, immoveable goods, mortgages, debts, merchandise, etc.) Failure to follow this order, giving false or inaccurate declarations, will result in confiscation of the entire estate with no appeal.”

Oct 22, 1939

...The day was full of fear and unrest. Around 10:00 am, the Germans declared a state of emergency. They began dragging the Jewish men from their homes and to herd them to the city hall building at the market. The Jewish women were forbidden to step outside their houses. No one was allowed to approach the market at all, except for the militia. Everyone who had come in on foot, or had ridden into town from the countryside, was forced to return.

Around noon, the Jews were marched from behind city hall in rows of four to the magistrat, and made to stand in the yard. In the meantime, we had no idea of what was happening, or what was to follow, until a well informed militiaman came to us, the mayor's son, a student from the Lvov Polytechnic, Franchak, and told us the whole story.

Earlier this morning, the Germans had gone around to the Jewish houses dragging men out for work details. At one place, a Jew tried to hide by clambering up to an attic. The Germans pursued him, the ladder overturned, and in falling, lightly grazed one of the Germans who then ran to complain to the Platzkommando. Eleven Jews were arrested. They were arraigned, and the state of emergency was declared. The Jews went to Tczeszlewski, the priest, to beg him to intervene with the Germans. A delegation made up of several Poles immediately went to see the German authorities.

When all the Jewish men were assembled in the city hall courtyard, the real looting began. Jewish stores were thoroughly emptied out, merchandise taken out onto the street. Later, they were collected and laid out at the courthouse and city hall and then transported away in trucks. In the evening, the trial of the arrested Jews was held. All were released, including those held in city hall. The general opinion is that the whole affair was fabricated in order to provide an excuse to issue still harsher ordinances which would, in turn, allow the thefts to proceed quietly and smoothly.

Oct 23, 1939

...The city is unnaturally quiet, but the Jews live in constant fear. I was told today that yesterday everyone in the courtyard at city hall was beaten, without exception. Even the Rav was not spared. Today, the rebbetzin came to me in tears, asking if it was true that all the Jews were to be slaughtered tonight, and begging to be saved.

Oct 30, 1939

...Even the German officers today were going through the houses of the richer Jews, and confiscating money, jewelry, and clothing.

Nov 1, 1939

...Every day now, many Jews pass through S—on foot, in wagons, men, women, children—carrying sacs, packs, bedding, chased out by the Germans from the western parts of Poland and heading somewhere East.

It is not known, however, if they are heading for the other side of the river Bug to the Soviet Union, or whether they will remain in the Lublin region.

Nov. 7, 1939

...Tonight, two Jewish women from the countryside who were wounded by bandits were brought to me. Such attacks are occurring more frequently in the region.

Nov 14, 1939

...The Jews have been left in peace finally. Now they are after the Christians...

Nov 15 1939

...Last night at ten o'clock, having just fallen asleep, I was awakened by a commotion in the street. I jumped out of bed and, through the window, I saw that the area across the street from the hospital was on fire.

In an instant, I alerted the staff and ran out into the street. Jewish houses near the shul were in flames. I was struck by the fact that one didn't hear the wailing and crying common to such circumstances from the Jewish women. The Germans were engaged in energetically fighting the fire, obviously in order to insure that the fire should not spread to the adjoining non-Jewish houses. The civilian population was kept away. There was none of the usual mob as is always the case at a fire. No one was allowed to leave his house with the exception of those whose homes were engulfed in flames. Rifle and revolver shots were heard incessantly. The Jews were not allowed to save their belongings, or, at best were not helped in that endeavor. The Platzkommando and his deputy were at the fire the whole time, and endlessly repeated that the Jews were responsible for setting fires at four places in town simultaneously. In three places, they succeeded in extinguishing the fire, but opposite the hospital, the fire spread with dangerous speed... the Germans assured me that they would not allow the fire to spread to the hospital. German guards were posted at the entrance doors. The Jews were treated in a frightful manner -- they were yelled at, pushed around, beaten, and I was forbidden to admit any to the hospital. They brought me a Jew who was shot through the hand, and they watched to make sure that he left the hospital as soon as his hand was bandaged.

After about three hours, the fire began to die down. Then an order was given that all the Christians should be in their houses by two o'clock, and that the Jews were to go to the targhalle at the market. They then began to drag the Jews out of their homes and to drive them to the market. Every so often shots were heard. Wailing and crying began among the Jews. I saw old Jews being driven at bayonet point by the Germans. I saw a very old man barely able to stand being supported by two Jewish women, quietly, without a word, only the curses and oaths of the German soldiers could be heard...

In the morning, several Jews were held as hostages and led away under arrest. All the others were released. A contribution of 10,000 ZL was levied on the Jewish population.

The whole story of the simultaneous firing of four locations, the burning of the shuland about ten houses, including the house of the Rav, and the bet hamidrash, appears to be very suspicious. What reason could the Jews have to burn their own nest?!

I accepted a Jew who had been shot in the face, to the hospital. In ordinary circumstances, there would have been an unbelievable commotion to do with the shooting, half the city would have assembled at the hospital. But, instead, today, the hysterical, half-crazed wife of the wounded man came to me and asked me, quietly, if I would admit him to the hospital. She was afraid, that in today's conditions, I could refuse to accept the patient because of his Jewish origin! -- I also saw a Jewish woman with a bayonet wound in her buttocks.

I went to look at the scene of the fire. Everything is still smoldering. The city is oppressively silent. Everyone is convinced that this is just the beginning.

Nov 18, 1939

...We constantly hear about new house searches and arrests; we live in continuous tension and expect the same will happen to us. The Jews tell me that, among them, no one gets undressed at nigh. Even the children sleep in their clothes, so frightened is everyone since the fire, the looting, the house invasions, etc.

Dec 11, 1939

...The last days reveal a certain aggravation of the course of events concerning Jews. Fifty of them a day are required to report for work. For a while, they were permitted to provide substitutes, but now they must personally show up. Yesterday and today, they were led through the streets to work with bare heads, forbidden to wear caps or hats.

Dec. 19, 1939

...180 Jews arrived last night in S.. They were driven from Wloclawek. Mostly women and children, men very few and these elderly, because the younger ones have been detained in Zamosc. The local Jews immediately occupied themselves with them, and distributed them among themselves. Rumor has it that several hundred more are expected.

Dec 20, 1939

...In the afternoon the town crier went around banging his drum, and new orders were read namely:

As of Friday, the 22 of Dec., all Jews from 10 years of age upward must wear white armbands, bearing a six pointed star, on their right arms. A sign must be visible in front of every store indicating whether the store is an Aryan or a Jewish one. The armbands will be sold at city hall for 1 Zl. each.

Dec 22, 1939

...In spite of the clear order that Jews are, from this day on, to wear the special armbands on a "conspicuous spot", I did not meet one Jew in town with such an armband.

Dec. 25, 1939

...Order number 8 from the commander in S. of dec. 9: &&$137;In order to differentiate the Polish from the Jewish population in the S. county, I have determined that:

All merchants must get signs available from the commandant stating, "Aryan shop", or "Jewish shop", and display them in their stores in a conspicuous spot.

All Jews, whether women, or men 10 years of age or older, must immediately obtain from the commandant a white armband with Star of David, and wear it in a highly visible spot.

This order enters into force on the 22nd of Dec., 1939.

Not complying with the aforesaid orders will be punishable with a fine or arrest.

Jan 4, 1940

...The Jews began to wear the armbands just yesterday. Some wear them on the right, some on the left.

Jan 11, 1940 ...I was called today to attend an old Jew suffering from frozen feet. He was traveling on the train from Warsaw with merchandise he had purchased. He tearfully related to me how, while still at the station in Warsaw, he was thrown off the train by the Polish passengers who also stole some of his goods. The conductor put him in the baggage car where he traveled for 12 hours until Rajowiec, then another 12 hours in a passenger car, but also unheated. German methods are finding fertile ground among certain segments of the population.

Jan 26, 1940 ...I admitted to hospital a Jewish couple driven from Lodz. They are suffering from Typhus. I reported this to the Platzkommando. Strict security measures were undertaken. A militia guard was posted at the house where the sick were staying, and all the residents, 53 of them, must undergo a 14 day quarantine.

Jan 30, 1940

The most important events of the last few days are the first few cases of Typhus among the Jews on the Zamosc street where there are also German barracks. The German authorities issued strict orders. Absolutely no one is permitted to enter the barracks. They no longer employ Jews there or the city's unemployed—they do everything by themselves. The soldiers are not allowed to leave the barracks to go into the streets. Even walking on the sidewalks near the barracks is forbidden...I am obliged to inform the Platzkommando immediately about every new case of Typhus. Today, I informed the commandant about the first Typhus patients among the Krasnobrod Jews. The lice infestations of these Jews is shocking.

Feb 5, 1940

...Today the gendarmerie raided Jewish houses, and confiscated textiles, soap, food, etc.

Feb 7, 1940

...This morning, I watched the lineups in front of the bakery opposite the hospital. The bread was sold to Poles until 8:00 o'clock, and only afterward, to the Jews, although there was no bread left. Went to City Hall. I was informed that currently S. has eight bakeries: three Polish ones and five Jewish. Jews were told that they could buy bread only in Jewish bakeries. They do not obey these orders, and push themselves in great numbers into the Polish bakeries in which they seldom used to buy baked goods. Because of that, the Polish bakers and militia received an order not to sell to the Jews.

Feb. 9, 1940

...They've changed the orders again about providing the Jewish population with bread. The Polish bakeries are allowed to sell baked goods to Jews, but only that which is left after all the Christians have done.

Feb. 10, 1940

...The cold is unrelenting. Very few people out on the street. The stores are closed, only here and there can one see a larger group of people in front of a house, mostly Jews: in these houses the Germans, gendarmes and militia are carrying out searches. They look for hidden goods and confiscate them. This has been going on for several days. They do not yet enter Polish stores and homes.

Feb. 26, 1940

...German police, speaking Polish quite well, constantly go through Jewish stores and homes to look for hidden goods, levy fines, and mercilessly beat the Jews.

Mar. 5, 1940

...Deadly weather. Snow is falling in giant flakes, and the blizzard blows and covers all the roads. The snowfall has stopped all auto traffic. The Germans send Jews to clean the streets. In Zamosc they force them to sing: &$147;Rydz has taught us nothing, our golden Hitler is teaching us to work" -- They brought me several Typhus cases from Zamosc. All were Jewish, driven out of Kalisz.

Mar 6, 1940

...An announcement in town: all Jews from 12 to 60 must be accurately registered. Understandably, considerable unrest reigns among the Jews because this is certainly to do with rumored, so-called, work camps.

Mar 16, 1940

The days are warmer, the snow is beginning to melt, the roads are impassable. The Germans have mobilized the Jews who zealously clean the streets... New orders were passed out forbidding the Jews from promenading on the main street on the Sabbath.

Mar 20, 1940

...We have received a new circular from the Health department in Lublin. This circular states that Jews can only be treated by Jewish doctors. This order is obligatory for all doctors, dentists, lay doctors, and midwives.—the following justification was issued: whereas Typhus and other contagious diseases are mostly found among the Jews, other doctors and personnel who find themselves in close contact with sick Jews could transfer the disease to the Aryan population. –We don't know how this will work in S. where there is not one Jewish doctor.

Mar 27, 1940

...A constant stream of Typhus cases comes from Zamosc—All Jews, driven from Lodz and Wloclawek.

Mar 29, 1940

...Dr. Spoz traveled to Zamosc yesterday to clear up the question of our treating Jews. He discussed this with the director of the health branch of the starostve. This individual categorically declared that we are forbidden to offer any kind of medical help to the Jews, nor even to allow them into the clinics or hospitals. It is, however, difficult to comply with these orders as there is not one Jewish doctor in S.

I had a strange experience today. I was called to see a sick Jew. I went, looking about in all directions, to see if anyone one was spying on me, because you can expect anything from the Germans. I did not write the name of the patient on the prescription. We have reached the stage where the fundamental basis for being a doctor—helping the sick—has become an illegal activity, meriting punishment.

April 1, 1940

...Along with Dr. Tyszkowski and Dr. Bonicki, I went to the standartarzt in Zamosc. Again we raised the question of admitting Jews to hospital. The Germans are unwavering on the point that it is simply a necessity to separate the Jews from the rest of the population. Moreover, a sort of "Jewish laza-et" is supposed to be established where Jews from Zamosc and surrounding areas are to be admitted. Until then, we can continue to admit Jews to hospitals, as now.

June 10, 1940

...A new order has been announced concerning the curfews: Aryan men can be out until 10:00 pm. Jews, still, only until 7:00 pm.

June 11, 1940

...A truckload of Germans arrived from Zamosc, and a real police-raid on the Jews took place. They organized a hunt, like dogcatchers after dogs. Afterwards, they drove them away to Zamosc for a work detail and brought them back in the evening.

July 17, 1940

...This day was a very hard one for the Jews. For the last few months they have been relatively unmolested. They just had to provide several dozen men for work in Zamosc every day, for the farms in Badaszow, and for the local barracks. Aside from that, they were left alone. That from time to time, a Jew received a beating from a gendarme, or the police, is not counted. They have already regained a certain self-confidence. But suddenly, in the last few days, an announcement arrived that 500 Jews from S. will be taken to work camps. Terrible consternation and turmoil runs through them. The Jews have thrown themselves on the doctors for certificates, begun to claim admission to hospital for the slightest ailments, sent delegations to the starostes in Bilgoraj and Zamosc, to the labor department, etc. Finally, after such strenuous efforts, they succeeded in reducing the number to 130. This transport of Jews was to take place this very day. The Judenrat decided on 130 young boys, and gave everyone a mobilisation certificate. Only 98 showed up. The rest ran away or hid. The Gestapo arrived from Zamosc. Twenty soldiers mounted on horses were attached to them. The hunt for Jews began. The mothers, sisters, and fathers of those boys lined up at the market tried to get as close as possible to them in order to give them something, to talk to them, to say goodbye, but were driven away. More than one got a stick across the back. The soldiers were dispatched in all directions to search for the escaped boys. They rode over the sidewalks on beautiful, obviously Polish, horses. Some of the escaped boys were found, and instead of them, their parents were taken. The members of the Judenrat were also beaten. The Germans beat the vice-president with clubs, and then forced him to lie face down in the market for an hour. Finally, the market and the neighboring streets were cleared of most of the Jews and the arrested were taken away in columns of three in the direction of the train station. They were surrounded by the mounted soldiers. The train was greeted with wailing and cries from the Jewish women who were hiding in the doorways and in the nearby streets. The whole police-action was watched by a large part of the Polish population. Some of the onlookers showed no sympathy and even joked throughout.

After the first group left, various repressive measures were instituted because of the failure to deliver all the workers. Jewish stores were closed all day, very few Jews were out in the street.

July 18, 1940

...There is tremendous unrest among the Jews. They fear that many more of them will be taken to the work camps. Through the old fashioned town crier, and by postings on the walls, an order from the mayor was posted that all Jews between 16 and 50 must present themselves daily to the Judenrat. No Jew is permitted to leave the city limits without special permission from the Judenrat. Any Jews found outside the city without permission will be severely punished and sent to the work camps.

July 23, 1940

...Dr. Snotski, the powiat doctor from Bilgoraj, during his inspection visit in S. today, called all the doctors together to relay certain orders from the German authorities regarding the Jews. Not only are we not allowed to furnish certificates for Jews, we are not allowed, above all, to treat them. But since there are no Jewish doctors in S., they agreed that we can see Jewish patients, for one hour set aside only for them, so that they will not meet any Aryan patients in our waiting rooms. Later, they forbade us to admit them into the hospital with the exception of contagious diseases.

The conditions in the work camps are terribly difficult. There are such camps for Jews in Kartoticz and in Bialobrzeg outside Zamosc. The work consists of digging ditches in order to drain the swamps there. They must work standing in the water, they are fed very poorly because their families are rarely successful in getting food to them, they sleep in barracks which are incredibly dirty, and crowded, and several kilometers away from the work. They must make this trip every day, and for the slightest mistake, they are beaten with clubs. They are covered with lice. The clothing of some of them looks as if covered with poppy seeds. I had the opportunity to see this for myself, because in the Bialobrzeg camp a Typhus epidemic broke out, and all the sick are sent to me until the contagious diseases pavilion in Zamosc is finished. They are mostly boys, 17-20 years old, rarely do we find an older Jew.

August 5 1940

... Borotski the mayor has decided to convert the fire damaged shul to a movie theatre. He brought the engineer Klimak from Zamosc who, in two days, measured and produced pretty drawings. Learning of this, the frightened Jews sent a delegation of the three most prominent community members to see me, begging my advice as to what to do to prevent this.

Today, from early morning, turmoil reigns again among the Jews, but for another reason. Unexpectedly, a large number of gendarmes together with the local police, blockaded the Jewish stores, and began to confiscate goods.

Aug 8 1940

...More crying and wailing among the Jews. 300 men must go to the work camps. They must all present themselves on Monday the 12th of August.—The second reason for the unrest is that the Germans intend to expel all Jews from Zamosc Street and the market. Where they are to move to and where they will live—this no longer interests anyone anymore.

Aug 11 1940

...there is anguish and unrest among the Jews on the eve of the work camp conscription. The Jews themselves told me tearfully that many of those that have received summonses to present themselves have run away, consequently others are afraid that anyone who falls into German hands will be taken. It seems to me that they are afraid of excesses not only from the Germans, but because of other cases that have already occurred. Last night, 12 year old Israel Groisser was hit in the head with a rock and was killed. This evening, a Jewish woman was brought to hospital with her head split open.—Many Jews come to the hospital begging to be admitted, or at least to be hidden for just the night.

Today I traveled to Zwierzyniec with my wife. On the road we saw many Jews escaping from town. Their fear was greater than I have ever seen it.

Aug 12 1940

...All night the Jews quietly snuck out of town. For several hours tonight, and at dawn, I stood at my window, and through a lorgnette, observed everything going on. Almost all the Jewish men, not only those who had received notices, were running away! As a result, instead of 300, they barely got together 50 Jews. Police searches began in town and in nearby villages. Aside from the police and two militia, many citizens of S. joined in of their own free will with Borotski at their head. The searches produced little, as they only caught about ten Jews. The old ones were held under arrest, and the rest taken to the train station. Only Jewish women and children are to be seen in the streets. Their mood is desperate. They are overcome with despair and hopelessness.

At noon, the Germans announced that every Jew who is issued a work summons, and does not show up, would be immediately shot on sight. No one knows what will happen next. One thing is certain. The Germans would not make idle threats.

Aug 13 1940

...A strange market day today. A large crowd, yet not one Jew is to be seen. Only a few Jewish women.

At night , there was a bit of a search for Jews, but with little success. Everyone is in suspense waiting to see what will happen further to the Jews.

Aug 14 1940

...Halfway through the night, the hunt and capture of Jews began. We were awakened by the sound of break-ins into the Jewish houses opposite. On our street, the janitor of city hall, and two young civilians, took part freely in this "work". The magistrat declared a bounty of 5 ZL which had to be paid by the captured Jew.— The searches carried on all night until 5:00 am. We heard constant shouting and banging on windows and doors. The screams and the racket intensified after two o'clock. I stood by the window almost the whole time and watched the goings on. Then soldiers arrived from Zamosc, and things really got going. They went around searching the houses where searches had already been conducted by the civil forces.... The result of the night's raid was two truckloads of Jews taken to Zamosc. The captured were, of course, beaten mercilessly.

—All the Jewish homes are filled with a painful silence, and in some, desperation. The conditions are aggravated by the fact that many Jewish women are penniless, and the Christian merchants will not sell them anything anyway. Furthermore, the wives of the S. Polacken drive the Jewish women away from the farmers who try to sell them food at the market.

I am well informed on this mostly through the family of the hospital butcher Laizer Zero. He ran away alone to the country, and left behind his wife, and mother, and four small children. We have to help them not only with money, but by buying bread, potatoes, etc. for them. How curiously the roles are reversed?

Aug 16 1940

...We have learned that the Germans are capturing more and more Jews from our area. The same is happening in all the shtetlach in our and in neighbouring counties. Trainloads full are being shipped to Belzec.

Aug 21 1940

...Over the last few days, no Jews have been captured. They have begun slowly to creep back to town, and we see more and more of them in the streets. Suddenly, today, a contingent of gendarmes and soldiers appeared, and the raids on Jewish homes began again in the hunt for Jews. A fair number were detained, but around three o'clock, they were all released with the injunction that all the men must present themselves to the work authorities in Zamosc where their precise selection will occur. The old, the sick, and those of certain trades (e.g., shtepper) who cannot yet be replaced by Christians, will be freed from work in the camps, and will receive special cards which will exempt them from future detainment.

Aug 22 1940

...This morning all the Jews living in residences fronting Zamosc Street must vacate. An exception was made for the dentist Bronstein.

Aug 26 1940 ...A new announcement appeared today, and was quickly disseminated in order to increase attention to it. I cite it in its entirety as an example of the times, and of the nature of the ruling regime:

August 24, 1940. The city administration declares that it is forbidden for the Jewish population to walk on Zamosc Street.

Jews are also forbidden to enter city hall.

Failure to obey this order will be severely punished.

Jewish affairs will be conducted through the mayor at the Judenrat offices.

This order does not apply to the members of the Judenrat, workers on their way to work, and the porters who drive through Zamosc Street with their wares.

Mayor—Borotzki

Aug 29 1940

...All the Jewish stores in town have been closed—the beer stores, cafe and pastry shops, soda water stalls, etc. These and similar businesses were quickly put on auction. They were attended mostly by the newcomers from northwest Poland who are called by everyone here "Poznaniakes". Some local citizens concluded a silent partnership with the Jewish ex-business owners.

The above mentioned edict forbidding Jews from being on the Zamosc Street is generally ignored and they are everywhere still.

Sept 7 1940

...A Jewish doctor, Pomerantz, from Krakow arrived in S. He was ordered by the German authorities, through the Krakow physicians' society, to leave Krakow, where he had practiced as a gynecologist for many years, within 24 hours. He visited me today. He is, understandably, very unhappy to be forced to settle in S. He dreams of returning to Krakow.

Sept 9 1940

...While standing at my window after lunch, I was the unwitting witness to the following events. Across the street from the hospital and towards the market stand several Jewish houses ruined by fire. Near one of these stood an old Jewish man and several Jewish women. At the same time, three German soldiers were passing by. Suddenly, I saw how one of the soldiers grabbed the Jew and shoved him through the ruins of the doorway into the pit where the cellar used to be. There was a great outcry, and, quickly, a large number of Jews came running. The soldiers calmly walked on. No one knew why this had occurred. A few minutes later the bloodied old man was brought to me at the hospital. It appears that the old man, called Briks, had not noticed the approach of the soldiers and had not removed his hat as is required for Jews. And that is why they threw him head over heels into the deep cellar. After I bandaged several wounds on his head, they led him home. –In the last few days, stories of Jews being beaten on the streets are heard again.

Sept 25 1940

...Today, the Gestapo from Zamosc came to the city hall, and demanded that certain Jewish women be brought to them. When they had presented themselves, frightened and trembling, they were officially informed that their husbands, arrested several months ago for something to do with transporting merchandise, had been shot. The Jewish women, in their anguish, began to scream and cry, and the Gestapo looked at them, and laughed.

Sept 27 1940

...Military patrols roam the city in significantly greater numbers than before. At 7:00 o'clock, they patrol the city to make sure that no Jews are about in the streets.

Oct 1 1940

...The Jews had a happy day today. Almost all of those sent to Belzec returned today. For being freed from the camps, the Jews paid 20,000 Zl.

Oct 8 1940

...At today's market, German air force pilots with rifles suddenly appeared and began to grab Jews on the street for work on the air-field near the sugar factory. A stampede began among the Jews, but the Judenrat quickly intervened obligating itself to present the required number of workers. The fear of renewed detention will not now leave the Jews. They had some relative peace for a little while only.

Jan 4 1941

...For several days now, a raging blizzard has covered all the roads and train tracks. Thousands of people are working on the roads and train tracks. The Germans have herded together a multitude of Jews and country peasants.

...Aside from this, there isn't anything worth recounting. Complete stagnation.

Just yesterday, the people had a certain surprise observing the mayor, Boritski, personally beating Jews who were late for work on the roads.

Jan 22 1941

...In Zamosc, The Jewish architect, Braunstein, was arrested. He was charged with sabotage. He was employed at a Gestapo construction site.

Jan 28 1941

...The German administration is readying itself for a spring campaign. Today, yet another registration of all the Jews was carried out—certainly with a view to more labor camps.

Jan 31 1941

...As of yesterday, the duty of Jews to remove their hats to Germans was repealed. We don't know how to explain this. In every instance though, the Jews still doff their hats because when they failed to do so, they were still beaten.

Mar 2 1941

An order appeared in the city signed by the chief of Lublin district. It forbade the Jews from leaving their residences and required them to punctually comply with the curfew under pain of three months imprisonment or a fine of 1,000Zl.

May 6 1941

...There is panic in the city from early morning on. The Germans were grabbing men on the streets and in their houses, Jews and Christians, for work on the air field. It did not pass without beatings. I saw how this happened from my window. With particular relish, they searched for, and herded, the intelligentsia, and the better dressed people.

May 8 1941

In Jozefow, the Jews who had fled from Konin came down with Typhus. They brought me the first group yesterday, nine patients.

Work on the air field is hard especially for those not used to physical labor. I am being sent increasing numbers of people from there for treatment and observation. I have had to set aside one hall especially for Jews.

June 3 1941

...The first day of Shavuot, (June1), the SS carried out a pogrom on the Jews of Rudke and Zwierzyniec. They were beaten and robbed of anything possible. As it happened, some Poles were also beaten. The same happened in Gorajec. Three Jews died there.

July 8 1941

...Last night, in the Jewish quarter, a German pilot shot and killed a young 22 year old Jewish girl on the street. Understandably, the Jewish population is deeply shocked at this new barbaric German action. All the Jewish women in town took part in today's funeral for the murdered woman.

July 11 1941

...More Jewish Typhus cases from Jozefow. One of them is called Wolf Bondzow.

Oct 16 1941 ...A delegation from the Judenrat came to see me today about something very odd. They begged me to intervene with the authorities in Bilgoraj to prevent any Jewish doctor from being assigned to S. because the Jews absolutely do not want one.

(Dr. Pomerantz, who was sent here from Krakow, left one day for parts unknown).

The idea is that if there is in S a Jewish doctor, then no Aryan doctor can give medical aid to sick Jews.

Oct 23, 1941

...Typhus is spreading through the district at an alarming rate, especially among Jews. More and more are coming to the hospital. The German authorities decided to hold a conference at my hospital with the participation of the doctors, mayor, police commandant, and the Judenrat under the chairmanship of the district doctor Snotski, in order to study preventive measures. The new Jewish doctor who had been sent here, Dr. Bolotni, also attended. According to the order of the staroste, the Judenrat must immediately see that baths should be taken daily. All Jews must shave their heads and their beards, as occurred in Bilgoraj. Those not obeying will be severely punished. There must be some control over bathing, disinfection, etc.

Nov 2 1941

...Several doctors have contracted Typhus in the region: in Zamosc. Dr. Rosenbush, Dr. Spiegelglass, in Tyszowce, Dr. Atlas, and another Jewish doctor in Nori.

Dec 21 1941

... I went to Zamosc a few days ago. The Zamosc hospital is full of the sick, many with Typhus. No Jews are admitted, however, to the infectious diseases department. They are taken to special barracks in the Jewish quarter.

Dec 31 1941

...The German gendarmerie has its hands full confiscating fur items from Jews. On Dec 26th, it was announced that all Jews must immediately, under penalty of death, hand over all fur collars, handkerchiefs, hats and earmuffs. Turmoil ensued. Some tried to hide the furs, others gave away everything they had. So, for example, Dr. Bolotni gave up all the furs belonging to him and his wife to the Judenrat for a sum of 12,00 Zl.—Any day now, we await the same orders for the Aryan community...

In Gorajec, a number of Jews were thrown out of their house to accommodate other exiles.

Jan 14 1942

...Great agitation among the Jews. Two Jews who were found with hidden furs, were arrested and quickly shot. Six Jews were taken as hostages today, because not enough furs were forthcoming. For the same excuse, the whole Judenrat in Bilgoraj and Tarnograd were arrested.

Jan 20 1942

...One can sense a significant aggravation in behavior to Jews. In the last weeks, several Jews were shot for being found outside city limits, for leading a calf, for hiding a fur pelt, for not wearing the arm band, for selling flour. We constantly hear about other executions in neighboring hamlets. Among some, especially the exiles, there is terrible need. Yesterday, I visited the sick Winower, a near relation to the well known literary figure Bruno Winower, who lives in deplorable conditions in a sort of cell, nailed together from boards, on a cot, on which, besides the patient, his wife, and little daughter also sleep. The Judenrat refuses to give them any help at all, because they did not register themselves, and secondly because they are converts whom the Polish community will not recognize.

Jan 21 1942

...We are exhausted with the Typhus. It is spreading violently everywhere, lately especially among the Jews of S. I have not seen such privation before. The Germans issue yet harsher orders. So, for example, the Jews of Gorajec are not permitted to step more than 10 meters from their houses, they are not permitted to use the footpaths, only the roadway.

Feb 18 1942

...Several days ago, the gendarmes detained a 20 year old Jewish girl on the street for not wearing her armband. They led her to the outskirts of the city in the direction of Zwierzyniec, and shot her.

Mar 25 1942

...The situation of the Jews is becoming more acute. News about exiling them to the east comes from various quarters.

To our knowledge, 250 Jews from Bilgoraj were exiled to Tarnograd.

There are more frequent cases of Jews being killed on trains, or for illegally leaving their permanent residence.

Either in packed train cars, or several at a time, civilians, mostly Jews, are taken somewhere, sometimes in one direction sometimes in another. Whereto—no one knows. Rumor has it, to the East, closer to the front, to some sort of work...

Provisioning difficulties become ever greater and more circumscribed...In certain places, e.g. Bilgoraj, Jews are only sold horse meat. And in spite of the proscriptions, the Jews carry on a lively trade. You can get anything from them. Without leaving their places, they have an excellently organized assortment of country produce. At all the small streets leading into town, stand Jews and buy everything that the peasants can carry. From my window, I can see this going on in front of my hospital from before daylight to night.

Mar 26 1942

...The Jews are experiencing tremendous fear and disquiet. News comes in from everywhere about unbelievable atrocities committed against the Jews. Full trainloads of Jews from Czechoslovakia, Germany, and lately even from Belgium, pass through. Here too, the Jews are being driven out of various towns and cities, and taken mostly to Belzec. I heard a story about what they did to the Jews in Lublin. It's hard to believe that it's not true. Today they expelled all the Jews from Izbice and took them also to Belzec, which must be a horrible camp. Very many Jews are dying there, because for the slightest thing they are shot on the spot.

Mar 29 1942

The Jews send out special Aryan emissaries for reconnaissance. From Izbice, certain particulars to the effect that about 2,000 Czech Jews, completely assimilated ones, were brought there, and because it was impossible to house them all, they sent more Izbicer Jews to Belzec. Today, an emissary was sent to Belzec to find out what goes on there. The Jews in town are completely disoriented. They don't know what do; whether to hide or to sit still and wait. They are even afraid to go out, because the Germans will kill any Jew they see on the street, with no qualms.

Apr 8 1942

The Jews are severely depressed. We now know with complete certainty that, every day, one train arrives at Belzec from the Lublin district and another from the Lvov area, with over 20 cars each. Here the Jews are unloaded, they are driven behind a barbed-wire fence, and they are killed with electric current, or gassed, and then their dead bodies are burned. Along the route people, particularly train workers, are witness to terrifying scenes, because the Jews well know where they are going, and why. They are given neither food nor water. At the train station in S., the train workers saw with their own eyes, and heard with their own ears, as a Jew handed over 150 Zl for a kilo of bread, and how a Jewish woman took her gold ring off her finger for a glass of water for her dying child. –Lubliner people told me of unimaginable things being done to Jews there, of children being thrown out of windows, of the sick being shot on the spot, of the healthy shot in the outskirts, of thousands being transported to Belzec, and so on.

Apr 11 1942

...The Jews received news today—and their intelligence is good—that today they transported the Jews of Chelm, and after unloading them at Belzec, the empty train, the so-called Jude-Zug, went off to Zamosc. –Before evening, news spread that Zamosc is already surrounded. Everyone is sure that the capture and transport of the Zamosc

Jews will follow. Here in town, fear is high. Some are completely resigned, others run through the streets looking for safety, because they are all convinced that, any day now, the same will happen in S. A lot of Jews come to me asking me to admit them to the hospital.

Apr 12 1942

...From Zamosc, through various avenues, we receive news that terrible things are going on there.—This was predictable. It is said they rounded up 2,500 Jews. Several hundred were killed on the spot. Certain Jews mounted a revolt. We have no particulars, and in general nothing is known with certainty.—Among our Jews, the mood is completely hysterical. The old Jewish crones spent the night at the cemetery. They want to die here, in their shtetl, among the tombstones of their near ones rather than somewhere like Belzec, after first undergoing torments. Some take a chance and flee to the countryside. Very many hide out locally. Still others send their children with trusted Aryans to Warsaw.

Apr 13 1942

...The night passed quietly, but the panic among the Jews has increased. From early morning, they have been expecting the gendarmes and the Gestapo to appear. A significant number of Jews has disappeared. –They left for the outskirts of town to hide in some unknown place. Others feverishly carried something out, settled their pressing affairs. All manner of hooligans crawled out, spent the whole day waiting for the looting to begin.

The Jews gave over a great quantity of things for hiding to the residents of the city, and to the peasants. All day, people could be seen carrying around baggage, baskets, sewing machines, etc. For hiding young children and older ones for a few days, huge sums of money were paid out. However, the peasants of the nearby villages are afraid, because the penalty for hiding a Jew is death, and informers are everywhere. Children are therefore taken to the villages further away. About this, I'm certain.

In the afternoon, there were hardly any Jews to be seen. This led to a significant decrease in the price of village products, because there were no Jewish buyers. The whole population feels the tremendous strain. A lot of people would like this to finish quickly—one way or the other, because this hysterical condition of the Jews is contagious.

Apr 15 1942

There was not one train to Belzec yesterday, and no bad news arrived from the neighboring towns and cities. Today the same, although the majority are still in hiding, and we see very few Jews on the street. That's why, however, the telephone booth at the post office is besieged. It's difficult to get near it through the mob of Jews who are waiting to be connected to other cities.

Last night, the station reported to the gendarmerie that among the crowd waiting for a train are several Jews. The gendarmes grabbed the first horses they came across—by chance they were from the hospital—and headed straight to the station. They detained eight Jewish men and women who wanted to travel to Zwierzyniec where the executions are actually taking place.

Apr 19 1942

...Several days have passed utterly quietly. There are no trains going to Belzec. The Jews are gaining courage and hoping that maybe the storm has passed. But there is absolutely no certainty. They are trying to understand why the sudden cessation of their mass extinction.

Apr 23 1942

...Since yesterday there is an active Jewish police force. It consists of eight young Jews in hats with blue brims and armed with rubber batons. They even have some kind of rank signified by two or three stars on their hats.

Apr 24 1942

...Masses of Jews have gathered in front of city hall since the morning. A German inspector arrived from the labor authority in Zamosc in order to press gang 350 Jews for the work camp in Kolikow, not far from S., where they are to do some sort of improvement work. They could scarcely muster 63 Jews. Because of the unsatisfactory number, we will now have to await further police actions and other repressive measures. So I was told today by the new mayor who, as a German (actually he is Ukranian), is well informed.

Apr 29 1942

...Yesterday, in Bilgoraj, a decree was issued forbidding the Jews from walking on the main street. This morning they shot four Jews on the street for defying this edict.

The mass deportations to Belzec have stopped. On the other hand, we hear more and more often from all sides about shootings in the street, on the roads, etc.—Several days ago, they shot four members of the Zwierzyniec Judenrat.

May 5 1942

...Several days ago, three Gestapo and their chauffeur arrived in Torobin. They killed 107 Jews, in groups of four. –Now we hear unsubstantiated rumors that two Gestapo were killed in Izbice. Clearly, the Germans have received a scare. The gendarmerie is shut so tight that no one can get in, even in the daytime, without special reasons.

May 7 1942

...This morning the ""blue" police, and the Jewish police, along with several Polish civilians, arrested five Jewish men, and eight Jewish women, among them the dentist

Bronstein, and his 75 year old father. First they were taken to the police station, then they were taken to city hall jail. Nobody knows if they were taken as hostages in place of those they couldn't find, or as communists, or something of the sort. In any case, their fate is uncertain. I telephoned the district doctor, Spasky, to beg him to intervene in favor of the dentist Bronstein who had written a desperate "grips" to me.

May 8 1942

... We endured a terrible day today. I can't quiet my agitation. At 3:30 in the morning, two Jewish women, and five Jewish men, were led away out of the city in the direction of Zwierzyniec: Bronstein, father and son, and the old, rich merchant Bronspiegel, the young and rich merchant, Fersht, and the divorced shoemaker, Sher. Hard by his house, Fersht jumped out of the carriage and ran away. He was, however, killed right there. No one doubts that they were all shot in Zwierzyniec.

Hell broke out in town at around 3:00 in the afternoon. Several armed Gestapo units arrived from Zamosc. First, they demanded that 100 Jews present themselves for work within one hour. Then, with the help of the local militia, they initiated a bloody business with the Jews. One could hear continuous shooting. They were shooting at people like at ducks. They killed people even in their houses—men, women and children. The number of dead and wounded is impossible to know. We can only say with certainty at least one hundred.—When the first casualties occurred, Jews came running to me begging to be saved, for first aid, or admission to hospital, even though the district doctor in Bilgoraj told me in no uncertain terms that we can not admit Jews under any circumstances even those wounded in such a mass aktion.

Around 4:00 o'clock, I was visited by two Gestapo, a local gendarme, and a "blue" policeman, all with rifles, as if their blood was still inflamed, and in a brutal, sharp, way asked me if I hadn't helped wounded Jews, and if I was not hiding any Jews in the hospital. I assured them that I have no one. They threatened me that if they found someone they would take me too. They said the same to my attendant. They left through the main entrance, and in a little while, they returned through an opening in the back fence in the shadow of the hospital. They captured one Jew who was legally working here, and had been sent by the general work authority. They took him to the police station, but soon released him.

Around 5:00 o'clock, the Gestapo, sated with blood, left S. The Jews are sunk in despair. The women tear their hair out and lament, but differently than usual, quietly, with no cries. The men went to the cemetery carrying shovels to dig graves. They began to carry away the dead in horse carts. The Jewish doctor, Bolotny, came running to me for help, because he is completely helpless with the large number of casualties. This shook me up as never before. –I see forever before my eyes the wagons loaded with the bodies of the dead thrown upon each other. A Jewish woman who, with quiet despair, sneaks away with a dead child in her arms; the stretchers in front of the hospital with the bloodied wounded.

May 9 1942

...The only topic of conversation in town now is yesterday's pogrom. Several of the wounded who had been taken to the isolation house for Typhus patients have already died. There was a constant stream of people coming to me and the other doctors, Jews, as well as Dr. Bolotny, begging for help for the wounded. Before daylight, a number of Jews fled town. Others stood along the way to try to stop them so that a greater tragedy should not befall the remainder. Eight o'clock in the morning, 60 Jews presented themselves at city hall, and were taken away to Kolikow to the improvement work.

We all have the impression that this will not be the end yet.

I learned today that for yesterday's Gestapo visit, I have to thank one of the town's big shots who went to the "blue" police, and then to the Gestapo, to say that I am hiding Jews in the hospital. He even gave several names. A lot of hooligans are waiting for the moment when they can begin to loot the abandoned houses in the Jewish neighborhoods.

As an interesting detail, I was told that the Gestapo demanded three kilo of coffee, and 2,000 Zl from the Judenrat for the bullets used!

May 11 1942

...Today, before 6:00 am, they arrested and shot the Jew, Klieger, the owner of a small print shop.

May 13 1942

...Monday the 11th of May in the afternoon, three Gestapo carried out a terrible pogrom in Jozefow ordenatski killing over a hundred people. Even the German, Becker, the treuhendler, at the company Alwa, who happened to be in Jozefow, told me afterward in the office that this was something dreadful, indescribable, an indelible impression, although he was always slandering Jews, and saying that they should all be exterminated.

May 15 1942

Yesterday afternoon, two local gendarmes, and one "blue", drove out to Gorajec to hunt Jews. The special messenger that the Jews sent out, brought the news that 14 Jews were killed.

May16 1942

...Before daylight the gendarmes shot three Jews. They were in the city jail, and when they were led out, they began to run. They would rather die her in their birthplace than be executed in Zwierzyniec. Among the murdered is the wife of Levnik

Berger, a rich metal merchant, who left with the Soviet army for the East. One of them, Dailes, succeeded in running away.

May 18 1942

...The gendarmes shot two Jewish women today on the Rozlop road outside S., daughters of old Malazh Leger.

May19 1942

...This evening, Gelernter, was killed in front of city hall. They were leading him out under arrest in order to execute him at Zwierzyniec. He refused to get on the wagon, better to die right there. The body of the dead man lay in front of city hall until 8:00 in the morning.

May 24 1942

...News has arrived of a new wave of killings—in Krasnobrod, Zamosc and Tomaszew. Fear and unrest again runs through our Jews. It's not much better for us. We are constantly on the alert for arrests.

May 27 1942

...I went to Zamosc today, and spent several hours in the hospital...I really wondered why they have not yet instituted any decrees limiting the admission of Jews to hospital. They are admitted exactly as before in all departments, with the exception of Typhus for which there is a special isolation house. Even the Jews wounded in the last horrible pogrom were admitted with no complaints.

In Zamosc and in various shtetlach, masses of Jews are again being taken, mostly the elderly, over 60, and they are taken to unknown destinations.

May 28 1942

...The Jews of S. are constantly anxious about their fate. Everyone—old, young, man, woman, strive to find some employment locally. They hope it will keep them from being taken away. Many come to the hospital pleading for work. As a result, about 15 Jews now work in the garden. And all think they are really fortunate.

June 17 1942

...In the early morning Gelernter, the brother of the one shot a few weeks ago, was shot.

June 23 1942

...We thought that the calm would persist a little while, as it usually did after mass arrests. Meanwhile, I learned that last night, arrests began among the Poles, as well as a hunt for Jews. They were dragged out of their homes, and later taken to work at the air-field. In the process, two old Jews were killed—the sick Gelernter, the father of the two murdered brothers, and a shoemaker. The arrests, and the Gestapo patrols throughout the city, went on until 6:00 pm. They entered many homes, stores, etc. Later, they transported the arrested in the direction of Bilgoraj. I don't know exactly who yet. –53 Jews were among the arrested.—The mood in town is frightening.

June 23 1942

...In the afternoon, 20 old Jews were taken from jail at city hall to the field at the end of Pamfiger street. Cries, tears, and exceptional turmoil among the Jews: All 20 were shot in the field, the rest were freed.

June 24 1942

...I found out more about the Jews who were killed yesterday. A grave had been dug by some Poles in the field. When the praying old men were brought to the field, several at a time were forced to lie face down in the grave. After they were shot with a machine-gun volley, the next bunch were forced to lie on top of them. And that's how, in three layers, they were all killed.

July 17 1942

...A terrible pogrom carried out by the Germans in Jozefow a few days ago. It is said that 1,500 people were killed there, mostly women and children. The men were taken away.

July 17 1942

...Six Jews were killed here tonight.

Aug 8 1942

...11:00 am. The Jews are extremely tense and depressed. Last evening, they knew that their situation was precarious. Alarming news came from Bilgoraj and Zwierzyniec. From evening on, numerous patrols wandered about town, checking passersby. Around 1:00 am, we were awakened by a commotion opposite the hospital. They were hammering at a Jewish house. We heard, screams, cries, calls in German, Polish and Yiddish. They took so long in the first house that by the time they broke into the second, there was no one there. A Jewish woman and her four children had hidden in the attic, but they did not look there. –

From morning on, there are no Jews to be seen on the street. I went out to see what was going on. All Jews without exception were ordered to show up at 8:00 am in the market by the Judenrat. They were permitted to bring 15 kg of baggage, food for five days and 1,500 Zl. The mayor told me that 2,000 Jews were to be transported to "the Ukraine". The train workers said that a train with 55 wagons was waiting at the station.

None of the Jews volunteered to go. They were grabbed and taken to the market hall. I asked a gendarme from the local station, who spoke Polish exceptionally well, what would happen if the Jews refused to go. He answered curtly," We will shoot them all."

It's almost 7:00 pm. For most of the day, gendarmes, Gestapo, soldiers from the Sonderdienst, "blue" police, city hall workers, members of the Judenrat, and the Jewish police, search the town for Jews, drag them out of various hiding places, and drive them to the market hall. The appearance of the Jews is awful, mostly in torn, old rags, women with small children in hand. It is completely still, no crying or wailing is heard. The Jewish houses are deserted, some wide open. The city hall workers carry out the abandoned and hidden goods. I saw wagons full of packs and bags containing various things. Most of the Jews had hidden, and could not be found. There are hooligans among the Polish population, mostly young boys, who zealously help in the search. –There is great tension in the whole town.

9:00 pm.—Beginning at 8:00 they began to lead the Jews out of the market hall. Some began to flee and a dense, scattered, shooting began. The Poles, who were gathered in numbers on the street, began to stampede, running madly, taking shelter in houses. A little while later, they drove the Jews in the direction of the train station. Some old women and disabled old people were driven to the end of the train by horse wagon. The latecomers were beaten with clubs, whips, etc. I saw everything with my own eyes, because I was standing at the hospital gate by the road. This was so shocking, so terrifyingly inhuman that it is even hard to describe.

From Bilgoraj and surrounding areas they deported about 1,000 Jews. They were driven to the train station at Zwierzyniec. No one believes that they are to be taken to the Ukraine, everyone is sure they will be murdered. After yesterday's nightmarish day, no one can feel easy. We have the impression that we have not yet come to the end.—Today, 13 Jews shot in S.

Aug 10 1942

...No Jews to be seen in town yesterday.

At night, three Jewish women who left their house were shot. Regarding the ones taken away the day before yesterday, we only know that the train went in the direction of Belzec. Everyone is certain that they are no longer alive.

Aug 11 1942

...There is no market today. The villagers are afraid to come to town. It is forbidden to sell anything to Jews. The city hall staff go through the abandoned houses and take out everything, furniture, bedding etc. and collect it in one place. Only the Jews engaged in some trade are allowed to remain in town. The rest will be "relocated", meaning murdered.

A state of emergency has been declared. No special regulations or limits are involved, just the permission to shoot with impunity for the smallest trifle.

Aug 12 1942

...A Jewish woman with a child, as well as a man, were shot in the street this evening.

In the afternoon, the district doctor from Bilgoraj, Dr. Snotski, came with a warrant for requisitions. They sealed the equipment of Streicher and Bronstein's wife's dental cabinets. Part of Steicher's cabinet they took with them. They made an inventory of Dr. Bolotny's medical cabinet and declared that he can not sell anything. He has thus become merely a temporary user of his own assets. The mayor Kraus, and Dr. Snotski, assured me that the Jews will be completely liquidated soon.

Aug 20 1942

...Hardly a day goes by without several Jews being shot. People are so used to it that they don't get upset anymore. Gunshots in the night don't have the same effect on people as before.

Sept 17 1942

...Yesterday a lot of Poles were arrested...Also arrested were the two Streicher brothers, Jews: a dental technician and a barber.

Sept 19 1942

...Yesterday in Bilgoraj, both Streicher brothers were killed.

Sept 30 1942

...All the Jews from the Radecznica Gmina were brought to S. Most from Gorajec and from Radecznica proper, around 400 people, so the mayor informed me.

Oct 15 1942

...We were deeply shocked today by the shooting of Laizer Zero. He was our butcher who provided meat for the hospital for more than a decade, leased our orchard, took care of various legal matters for us, and was thought of as one of us. Lately, he was officially assigned to the hospital by the work authority and was always here, day and night. He was an exceptionally likeable Jew, we were all extremely fond of him. He proved to be very helpful to me in this war. Every day, he brought me the latest radio and local news. This morning, he was quietly standing in the market, and the gendarme, Siriez, requested that he accompany him to the station. Since he was occasionally asked to go there, he went not thinking anything of it. Half an hour later, three gendarmes led him out toward the city hall. There, they brought from jail another Jew arrested a few days ago, the barber Tuchschneider, put them both on a horse drawn wagon, and went towards the sugar-factory. In a few hours, we already knew they had been taken to the outskirts of Michalow, in the so called Remyza woods and shot.—Just last night, we had a long talk with Laizer about the general situation.

He always maintained that "he" [the Germans] had lost the war but worried, "Will we survive?" We truly mourn Laizer.

Oct 18 1942

...As of several days ago, the Jews have been definitively liquidated. There remain just a dozen tradesmen,. The older ones were shot on the spot, those who could walk were taken to Izbice. Tonight the Jews of Turobin were liquidated. We are certain that the S Jews will suffer the same fate.

Oct 19 1942

...Oppressive silence in town. The Jews fear a liquidation. The Poles—arrests.

Oct 21 1942

...I had to go to Zamosc today. I got up early to get ready for the trip. Suddenly, I heard, and saw, through the window unusual movement in the street, in spite of the fact that the streets were empty. It turns out that as of 6:00 am the "relocation" of the S Jews had begun—in point of fact, their liquidation. Throughout the whole day, until evening, the most horrible things transpired. SS and "blue" soldiers ran around town looking for Jews. They were rounded up and driven to the market in front of the court house. They were dragged out of hiding places; gates, doors and shutters were broken in; grenades thrown into cellars. They were beaten, kicked, and in general tortured in inhuman ways. There was fire from revolvers, rifles and machine guns. Around 3:00 in the afternoon, around 900 Jews were led out of town—men, women and children. They were herded with clubs, rifle butts, etc. and shot all along the route. Only the members of the Judenrat, and the Jewish police rode in horse-drawn wagons. The Aktion continued even after they had been led away. They found more hidden Jews. It was announced throughout town that the penalty for hiding Jews, or their goods, was death. Special rewards were promised for disclosing the hiding places. Those Jews now captured were shot without delay. The Polish population was conscripted to bury the Jews. The number of dead is difficult to ascertain. It is said 400 to 500. I will try to verify the exact number at city hall. From the numbers given one can assume that there are still around 2,000 hidden.—The captured were taken to the train station, and from there, I don't know.

It was a dreadful day today. I can not describe all that has happened. It would take a special literary talent to describe the horrible barbarity of the Nazis. No one ever **dreamed that such things were possible.—I am shaken, I can't settle down.**

Oct 22 1942

...The hunt for Jews does not end. The foreign gendarmes and SS left yesterday, and "our" gendarmes, and "blue" police are ordered to kill captured Jews on the spot. They carry out these orders very zealously. From early morning on, they bring the bodies of the murdered Jews in wagons from all sides of the city, and especially from the Jewish so-called "Zatili" quarter. They are buried in mass graves in the Jewish cemetery. Jews were found in various hiding places throughout the day. They were either shot on the spot, or taken to the cemetery and shot there. The group was led by two gendarmes, Pryczing, and Syring, and one "blue" policeman.

Those driven out of town last night were held in the open air at the Alwa factory near the S. station. Around 9:00 pm, the Jews of Zwierzyniec were brought there. Today at noon, they were loaded into the railroad cars. At 4:00 pm, the train was still standing in the station. It's cold out, a fine autumn rain is falling.

The Jewish houses are sealed. Nevertheless, the hooligans break in. A lot of hooligans took part in the hunt and capture of Jews. They pointed out where Jews were hidden, took part in the hunt, even of little children, whom the police killed in front of everyone's eyes.—In general, horrible things took place, nightmarish, to make your hair stand on end. The Jews of S. no longer can be said to exist. Even the indispensable tradesmen are gone, the loss of whom is strongly felt. And in spite of that, there are still large numbers of hidden Jews. All will die when they emerge from their hiding places, where they can't stay forever.

Oct 23 1942

...The Gestapo carried out its deadly work with the help of the local gendarmes, and the "blue" police, and with the active participation of certain inhabitants of the city. The young policeman from Polow, Matysiak, "distinguished" himself. Some local amateurs also zealously helped out hunting, herding Jews to the city hall, beating, kicking, etc. Some conducted the hunts for these unfortunates, others collected bodies and dug graves. Form time to time, shots rang out.

Oct 24 1942

...This is all still going on. The Gestapo from Bilgoraj are still rampaging. With the help of locals, the gendarmes and police still drag out the hidden ones from various holes, shooting them on the spot, or taking them to the Jewish cemetery and killing them there. Some are taken to jail, and then taken in larger groups to the cemetery. I saw them leading one such group. Gendarmes, police, and Polish citizens recruited for "gehilf-wach-dienst", unarmed, in black German uniforms, walked by their side. The rear guard kept beating the Jews with clubs across the backs, on their heads, wherever they could. The captives' appearance was horrible.

At noon, the Gestapo announced that all men over the age of 15 should assemble with shovels at 2:00 pm. Until then, it is forbidden to sell alcohol. To go into restaurants is forbidden anyway.

Jews were brought to the cemetery without let-up. Dead bodies were brought continuously in wagons. All kinds of things were brought to the market hall from Jewish homes.

Today was a nightmare, and this is the fourth in a row. No one will be able to determine how many Jews have been killed. And this is certainly not the end, because tomorrow at 8:00 am., the men must show up again with shovels, and the peasants with horses and wagons.

Oct 26 1942

...Yesterday, Sunday, around 50 bodies of the murdered or those dead from privation were brought in. They brought a group of about 100 men to the cemetery, and in a separate group, women and children. And they are still hunting Jews everywhere.

I saw how, in the nearby buildings belonging to the rope maker Dym family, whom I knew, they led away about 50 Jews. Hooligans were standing by and watching. Some freely participated, breaking down doors and walls, and then beating the Jews with clubs.

One of the most active participants, the city official Kercher, told me that two Jews in the isolation house suffering from Typhus were killed, and buried together with their bedding in a grave four meters deep. He brought me this news in an official capacity so that I could relay it to the district doctor.

The fate of Dr. Bolotny is unknown. The dentist Bronstein, and her two small daughters, were taken to Belzec on the first day. The female dentist, Stricher, was killed near her house. –Scoundrels loot whatever they can from the open Jewish houses, taking, without shame, Jewish household goods, or merchandise from the small stores.

6:00 PM...People from town come and tell us about the latest atrocities committed on the Jews. Our nurse saw with her own eyes how the gendarmes chased down a fleeing young Jewish woman, threw her on the ground, kicked her savagely, and then dragged her through the whole market by her hair to the station. My colleague, Dr. Matewszewski, was witness to the killing of five Jewish women, one after the other, by the Gestapo's Majewski from Bilgoraj. You can see puddles of blood on the sidewalks of S. –At the city jail, you can hear constant crying, moaning, groaning, and cursing. From time to time, in the city hall courtyard, Jews are shot. The clerks at city hall are nervous wrecks, women are crying and no one, of course, does any work. The only ones working are the secretary, Babiasz, who is replacing the sick mayor, and those who have an active role in the Aktions. Some clerks have fled the offices, because their nerves can not take it anymore. Others have become indifferent to everything.

All together, a horrible scene has been created that is difficult to describe. Something this dreadful and nightmarish has not been seen or heard of before. My recollections have a chaotic quality, awkward, because my equilibrium has been destroyed. I am, however, convinced that even such observations will someday be a sort of document of the times we are living through.

Oct 27 1942

...It has still not ended. The extermination of the Jews still continues. We have become so used to seeing dead bodies on the street that people pay relatively little attention to it, passing indifferently by. The dead body of the young boy, who was shot yesterday for robbery, lay on the sidewalk almost a whole day and night before it was taken away.

Oct 28 1942

...Two times I stepped out today, and both times I came across a group of Jews being led to their death. I saw one old lady, who could barely walk, killed with a rifle shot by a Gestapo. He took careful aim, shot once and failed to kill her, shot again, and then continued to drive on the rest of the group.

Oct 29 1942

...With the Jews, always the same. Wagonloads of Jewish goods continue to be unloaded at the market hall. There is no more room within, and beside the hall, a mountain of possessions grows.

Oct 30 1942

...Today too, Jews are being brought to the cemetery. A few Jews that were captured in the villages were brought to S.

Oct 31 1942

...They are still pulling exhausted Jews out of hiding places. Besides the Polish "helpers", three Jewish boys hang about. They know where their Jewish brethren are hiding and are hoping, thereby, to have their lives spared. An empty hope, because in the end they will also be shot.

I heard from a Polish source that about 3,000 Jews have been liquidated. It is believed that about another 1,000 are still in hiding.

Nov 2 1942

...Went to Zwierzyniec yesterday. There the Jews were liquidated exactly as in S. They are still able to drag the odd Jew out in S., but not in the mass numbers they did before. The "helpers" are now combing the woods and catching Jews. They have already brought in a few.

Nov 4 1942

...The occasional Jew from the forests, the villages, or the city, is brought in to the city jail. Mayor Kraus, a well informed person, told me that, in the first Aktion, they rounded up exactly 934 Jews and around 2,300 were shot in their homes, on the street, and in the cemetery. Here, there is no one in a position to give an exact number. There were obviously cases where the peasants killed certain Jews in the countryside, afraid to hide them. This happened in the forest as well. There were also absolutely other cases where peasants hid Jews for many months, or even until the end of the occupation , without regard for the danger to themselves.

Today, a fairly large group of Jews was liquidated by the Gestapo, mostly men.

At the end, the four Jewish boys who had been helping the Germans find hidden Jews were shot.—There are three large, long, graves at the cemetery. The last one is not yet filled in. Uncovered bodies lie in it, awaiting further sacrifices. They were shot mostly having been ordered to lie face down in the graves. Witnesses said that not all the Jews died at once. Some got back up, screaming, begging for mercy, and were covered by the next layer.

It's now the third day of the liquidation in Bilgoraj and Tarnograd. There, the Jews in one house mounted resistance, threw themselves on the Gestapo officer, and beat him up.

The whole route from Bilgoraj to Zwierzyniec where they transported the Jews is littered with corpses.—In the same way, the extermination of the Jews of Jozefow was carried out.

Everywhere, horrible things that are hard to believe took place, and I would not believe it myself had I not seen it all with my own eyes in S.

Nov 10 1942

...From time to time, they still find the odd hidden Jew. In principle, all the Jews in the settlements of the Bilgoraj district, to which S now belongs, have been liquidated. The only ones remaining are those in the forests, valleys etc. They sometimes steal into the city at night looking for food, but the guards on the roads, and the night patrols, catch them.

Nov 14 1942

...The last few days have been quite quiet. Every day, a couple of Jews are found. Certain people thought that the whole attention of the Gestapo and gendarmes was focused on the Jews. Therefore, the surprise was greater when the Gestapo started showing up in Polish houses, and making sudden arrests.

Nov 17 1942

...They are still dragging Jews out from various hiding places. Their appearance is frightening.

For almost two years now, the household of the gendarme station was carried out by a certain Oberweiss, a woman of some thirty years of age, a convert, from a large Jewish family that had converted many years ago, and settled in the village of Gorajec.

She tried to accommodate the gendarmes in any way possible, and they were happy with her, and behaved well toward her. It was thought that she could be completely secure and certain regarding her fate, especially as the biggest wave of the Aktions had already passed. Nevertheless, she was shot yesterday. They sent her into the city for something. A gendarme followed her, and from behind, put a bullet in her head. At least, they spared her the knowledge that she was going to die.

Nov 18 1942

...Again today, they shot captured Jews. They are mostly now found in the forests and villages, haylofts etc. Much less in town. I was told today that two Jewish women with small children gave themselves up at the jail. They could no longer hold out without food, or clothing, which was stolen from them in the forest. The children were barely alive.

Nov 20 1942

...I saw two Jews today being led through the street by local "helpers".

They were emaciated and exhausted. They were walking unsteadily, like drunks and could hardly move. When they had to bring out some Jews from jail who could not make it on their own, the gendarmes stopped a passing wagon, threw the unfortunate victims on it, and took them to the cemetery. –More often now, we see Jews giving themselves up, and begging to be killed.

Nov 26 1942

...Among the "bandits", there are now a lot of Jews.

Jan 5 1943

...A gendarme patient of mine told me that they found two Jews yesterday in some sort of hiding place.

Jan 6 1943

...Tonight, in the outskirts of S, they found five Jews in the loft over the stable at Kologiczik's. He was hiding and feeding them.

Mar 22 1943

...I saw the badly wounded farmer, Solewski, from Gruszka Zaporska. He had been hiding six Jews from Radecznica in his stable. When the police came, he tried to run away and was wounded. He died tonight. The police refused to give his body back to his family, and ordered that he be buried as a bandit. The Jews were shot in Radecznica by Polish police. The gendarmes came back and shot the farmer's wife and two children—a boy of three, and a girl of eight.

Translator's Footnote

1. Police

———

[Page 290]

Observations on the character of Dr. Klukowski

by Devorah Fleisher

Translated by Moses Milstein

In 1942, ten of us, women, worked in the hospital garden under the supervision of Dr. Klukowski, from 6:00 am until 5:00 pm. We were not allowed to buy bread from Christians, and Jews were not allowed to do any baking. We worked without wages, just in order to have a work place, although this did not guarantee that we could not, at any moment, be taken by the Germans.

Dr. Klukowski, the doctor-historian, worked us without supplying any bread, at a time when even the German murderers provided bread and soup for their workers. Dr. Klukowski took advantage of our misfortune and treated us as slaves. When the time finally came when there was some green in the garden, we could only steal a carrot or tomato and quickly eat it, because we were being watched from the hospital windows. Vegetables were plentiful; there were 800 tomato plants.

Do you know what it is to be hungry and not to be able to touch food while you're working with it?

Dr. Klukowski emulated Hitler's methods. Before annihilating them, he humiliated them, and that is worse than death.

We were not allowed to shop at the market. But sometimes, before work, we might catch a Christian woman behind some gate and quickly pay her whatever she asked, and even more quickly, run off. Once, on the way to work, we bought some cucumbers and brought them with us. When we were leaving work, the hospital watchman searched us and found the cucumbers. However, he immediately saw that they were not from the hospital garden. We began to weep, ashamed at what had befallen us,. The guard apologized and cried with us...He pointed to the windows, meaning it comes from the Prince.

Once I came to ask about the status of my husband who was in hospital. Dr. Klukowski threw me out of the hospital corridor.

So basely did he behave.

[Page 291]

Szczebreszyn under Hitler's occupation
by Devorah Fleischer
Translated by Moses Milstein

The whole town of Szczebreszyn was enveloped in horror. Young and old, Jew and Christian, awaited the future with sorrow and despair.

Sept 1 1939

– That cruel date marking the outbreak of the Nazi war. Like everywhere else, the news hit S like lightning.

Nursing classes were offered, for Jewish women as well. We had hardly had time to have a few classes before the German airplanes began flying over our heads. People hid where they could: orchards, gardens, fields, villages.

Sept 8 1939, Shabbes

– A large armada of bombers flew over, and dropped hundreds of bombs on our little shtetl. Instantly, we came face to face with horror. There were many wounded and killed – among them, Yosele Warman and his wife, Shmuel Yankel Grant, and Binyamin Shmacher's daughter.

Sefer torah burned with our own hands

Sept 13 1939, Rosh Hashanna

– The Germans are here. The first thing they did: they took Yechazkel Ehrlich who worked in the soda water factory, and forced him to take the sefer torahs out of the ancient shul, and burn them, with his own hands, on the street.

He told me later, through bloody tears, about his great anguish and feelings of guilt. He has not forgiven himself to this day.

The Germans refrained from other dirty tricks, because the second day of Succoth, the Soviets arrived. We thought our salvation had arrived, and we were saved from humiliation and extermination. However, after a few days we heard news through the radio that the Soviets were withdrawing from our shtetl, and the Nazis were coming back.

That night a large part of the Jewish population fled. – Some left with the Russian military, and some hid outside town.

The next day, the Germans returned, and showed again their bloodthirsty nature. They grabbed people for work, forcing them to clean the streets, the latrines and outhouses with their hands. Every day, tortured screams, every day, human sacrifices. By day, you had to work, at night, you hid where you could.

A story about a ladder

Sept 26 1939

Hiding in an attic, Abraham Reichstein's son-in-law was about to pull up the ladder, but on seeing an SS officer below him he panicked, and dropped the ladder on the German's hand.

After this, an order immediately went out that Jews could not leave their houses. All Jews, men and women alike, were driven from all over the city, like animals, to the Magistrat [city hall] which was heavily guarded on all sides.

When the lawyer, Paprotski, heard about this, he went to the priest, Tczeszlewski, and both went to the mayor, Franchak. All three then went to the German commandant and explained to him that the issue of the ladder was an accident, and assured him it would not happen again. The commandant made a big speech to everyone that if this or a similar incident happened again, every tenth Jew would be shot. Before this was even published, Rev Yichiel Blankman and Shlomo Maimon, and others had already been beaten up.

Oct 30 1939

The city is trembling with the news that Gestapo have been running around with a list of prosperous Jews. They beat them viciously with truncheons. Badly beaten were Baruch Shisl, Abraham Reichstein, and others.

A lot of people fled to the Soviet side last night across the Green border. My husband and son left then too.

In October 1939,[1] the Germans burned the shul.

Refugees arrive

Winter set in. People fled to Zamosc on sleighs. Captured together near the agrar school, which has become a Gestapo post, were Israel Pope, Yosel and Getsl Weinbleit (Zelig Fisherl's son), Moishe Shpool's wife, Moishe Wolf, and Miriam Ziser. Only Isrulke Pope returned, because they took him for a Christian.

In December, on a fiercely cold night, a train arrived full of Jews expelled from other parts of Poland. Their cries rent the night. A lot of them were brought to the beit hamidrash from Rev Mordechai's court. In the morning, whoever had the means, took people into their homes. Later, a kitchen was established for the homeless in the beit hamidrash.

A few quiet months passed. People slowly went back to work. But on the Soviet side, conditions became very bad. People were sleeping in train stations with no means of supporting themselves. People began to return home. Along with many others, my husband returned. My son remained in Bialystok.

Problems from the Judenrat and the Poles

A Judenrat was established. Nobody willingly wanted to become one of them. They were constantly drinking with the Nazis, and betraying the Jews.

The Germans took Jews for street work, and to Belzec to dig canals. In order not to be sent away, every one tried hard to get work at the air-field near the sugar factory. My husband found work there as a foreman of the qualified workers. In order to lighten the lot of the Jews, my husband took on a large number of unqualified people, anyone who approached him. Because of this, he received a lot of trouble from the Judenrat who were trying to make a business out of this by squeezing more money out of the Jews.

There were other reasons they wanted to work at the air-field. They preferred to work under a Jewish overseer, it was near to home, and they received bread, soup, and some vegetables.

The Polish underclass contributed to German chicanery and the downfall of the Jews. They fingered Shimon Goldman, Hillel Eisen, and Leibkele Glaser and his wife as Communists. They were arrested and sent to Zamosc. After 2 months, Shimon Goldman and Hillel Eisen returned. But Leibkele Glaser, and his wife, perished in jail.

Conditions were deteriorating from day to day. Jewish stores and their merchandise have been long since confiscated. Only some merchandise has been secreted with amenable Christians. You had to steal it back little by little in order to try to survive. So time passed until June 22, 1941 when the war with Russia began.

For the last month, we have seen the German military continuously massing during the night. Jews have been increasingly oppressed, forbidden to go to the countryside, or to buy from Christian stores in town. For such a transgression, Itsku Minzberg (my brother-in-law's son) was taken to Lublin to the famous number 7 Lipowa Street to be seen no more.

Evicted from homes

In the winter of 1941, every Jew had to relinquish any furs he might have. For not obeying, the penalty was death. Because of one fur, found hidden between 2 walls, Haim Maimon and Gershon Staatfeld (Shloime Maimon's brother-in-law) were taken out to Zwierzyniec forest and, there, killed.

The Jews were driven out of their houses and concentrated in the back streets. Only on Green street where we lived, in the market near the church, and on the "potchene" were the occasional Jews still living. The confinement, the crowding, and poor clothing brought Typhus.

Many people died then. My husband became infected from the newcomers who used to come to the kitchen to eat. He could not permit himself not to help the unfortunate. After two weeks of illness in hospital, he died on the 8th of January 1942. At the same time Binim Rosenfeld also died.

Two days after this tragedy, I too was taken to hospital. The doctors held out little hope for me. But I survived. I was bed-ridden and sick until Pesach. At that time, baking bread was forbidden, much less matzos. We got a small portion with our ration cards. With great difficulty, we managed to get a couple of kilos of flour from Christian bakers and, at night, with stealth, we baked at home.

Bad news, terrible events

Before Pesach, we heard bad news about Jews being transported out of Lublin and all the little shtetlach. We waited fearfully for the Aktion to happen here.

Rav Yichiel Blankman, at some risk, gathered a minyan and went to the grave of Rev Simchele, and begged for mercy for the Jews of S. Rev Simchele stated in his will that whenever there is danger in the city, he would help, if his grave were visited for the next 10 generations. This is the 9th generation. I don't know if it was a miracle, but the rail cars were already at the station. People wandered around in a daze.

Everyone saw his death before his eyes. And then an announcement: the quota has been filled without S.

Our relief did not last long. Right after Pesach, it was rumored that "there is a list of 70 people." I did not know if that meant women too. But I had a feeling they would not be spared.

One day, 6:00 in the morning, we heard a commotion. Through a window, I noticed that they were leading the Bronsteins, father and son, (the kazioner Rabiner and his son, the dentist).

I realized that their house would not be visited again, so I snuck into Natan Bronstein's house through Jodcikovski's orchard. There, I witnessed the heart breaking distress of both the wives and the children. They told me immediately that I was being sought too.

The murderers took away 13 people: both Bronsteins, Moishele Fersht, Liba Itta Berger, Shloime Dales, and others. Shloime Dales ran away. Liba Itta Berger, Moishe Arieh Gelernter and Moishe Fersht were shot near the Magistrat. All the others were taken to the Zwierzyniec forest and killed.

Also on the list were: Abraham Finkel, Abraham Rothstein's wife, Beile Berger, Esther Mantle, Heshl and Itzhak Haim Eisen, Itsele Fersht, Menachem Neitel, Shimon Rice, David Sapir (my brother-in-law), and Sala Danziger. We all hid away. The Polish police took huge sums of money to keep quiet, but we still had to hide. For four months, I slept in a tiny attic in our wooden house with two other people. Life became a monotonous misery. People went around like lunatics, not knowing what to do with themselves. Everyone was tortured by the thought: I am going to die. We had no peace, day or night.

Now there were shooting sprees on the roads. It was no longer permitted to go to the sugar factory, only to the air-field with proper documents. Everyone had to be find work. The unemployed were sent off. Half of the men and women of S. went to the Krasnobrod forest every day to work.

I and nine other women worked in the garden in the hospital. Among them: Hadass, (Moishe Buk's daughter), Hadass (Leib Doktor's daughter), Tzviah Fersht, and Ruchel Shpool. We hid ourselves: at night in the attic, or in another hiding place, in the daytime in the garden – often without a piece of bread.

The Poles exploited the Jewish labor. We had to work with absolutely no wages. They were, moreover, doing us a favor by employing us. Even Dr. Zigmunt Klukowski, the famous physician-historian, understood that Jews should work without bread. The Poles treated us like slaves. We were powerless, and endured all kinds of sorrows and humiliations.

The aktions

Shavuot, 1942, saw the first Aktion. The Judenrat fulfilled the German orders and rounded up Jews for shipment to Belzec. The work cards did not help. 280 people were shipped out. A lot of people also died in S that day.

Every day we received depressing news brought to us by the train workers: Every day 5-6 sealed cars full of people go through, bound for Belzec. Jews wandered around terrified, weakened, at the end of their strength. Seeing that even work can not save you, they gave up and avoided work.

In June, 1942, more people rounded up. Twenty six men were taken, among them: Hershel Ingber, Mordechai Frank, Baruch Frenkel, Yehoshua Glattman, Nathan Shtibel, Haim Nie. The Germans herded them in broad daylight through the streets to the "vigon", and there killed them.

Right after this, they made sure we understood that Jews were not allowed in the countryside. The assassins in Deszkowice shot Yankel and Etele Bricks, Hadass (Moishe Bik's daughter who had fled there to hide) and her uncle's family. At about the same time, they sent away to Mecholov, Laizer Zera and Leibish Shmayele's son, Yoseph (a barber), and shot them. People were crazed. We had to go to work, and every day, wait for another Aktion.

Hiding in an attic

The news was out that S will become Juden-rein. We saw no escape. What can you do? How do you disappear?

In the still of the night (so that the Polish neighbors would not hear) people dug deep cellars underground, under the latrines, or searched out hiding places in attics, well camouflaged. But all our toil and ingenuity was for naught. We envied the dead. The end arrived for us Jews who were so brutally annihilated by the murderers.

The following happened on October 21 1942: Quite early in the morning, we heard shooting. I barely made it into Isrulke Germanovitch's house. There was nobody left there except for his little 4 year old daughter, Ruchele, who, in the turmoil, was left behind. I took her to me, and calmed her down, and together, quickly, we got into an attic cupboard. There, we found her mother. We could not get to the prepared hiding place at Germanovitch's.

We lay there a whole day in great fear. We heard the houses being demolished. The murderers were running around searching every hole. Sometimes they were in our prison in the attic. Shooting could be heard from all sides mixed with the cries of parents, the wailing of children. You could go mad listening to this.

I don't know what happened to those closest to me in the last moments. Beile Berger, who lived with me, was sick and bedridden. Reizl Berger tore herself free from the murderers' grasp, and escaped to the fields, and later to the forest. Before, she had not wanted to hide with me, thinking there was still time.

At night, I went down to my house. I crawled on all fours so as not to be seen from the street. Everything was demolished, the doors and windows shattered. I took along a little water, and a piece of bread, and went to the second hiding place which was behind a separate wall in Germanovitch's house. There were 14 of us there. We had to crawl up to an attic through an opening in the kitchen which was covered up after. We lay there in fear, the Germans passing by frequently in their searches. It was so comfining, there was no air. The lamp would not burn. At night, we went out to get some air.

A funeral of the living

I realized that I could not stay there. So I went to the previous hiding place in the attic. Hidden in other attics were Zelig Fisher's children, the Ketselech, and the shochet's family. Through the cracks, we saw them lead away Moishe Ketsele to the yard. The Polish policeman, Gall, who collaborated in the Aktion, shot him. This was 23rd October, 1942.

That same day, we saw them lead out the whole courtyard full of people. The heavily armed murderers, aided by guard dogs, led them. Polish children ran after them. I will never forget the horrible picture: a funeral of the living! Exhausted, filthy from hiding, resigned to their fate, they went wretchedly to the slaughter.

Lying in the attic, all manner of thoughts crossed my mind, thoughts of being doomed to die. I saw how people from other hiding places expired from thirst and hunger. I decided to run away to the forest. Also fleeing with me were Itshak Haim Eisen, and Latche Eisen.

Fleeing to the forest

On the 24th of October, early, we escaped through the fields to Klemensov station, and from there, into the forest. We were certain we would not live, but if we were to be killed by a bullet, better to die in freedom.

In the forest, we came across many people. They came here by crossing the river. We reckoned that there were more than 1000 people in the forest. Regrettably, most died at the hands of the Poles.

Among others there were: Motel Blatt, Israel Zirer, Laizer Untzig, Binyamin Shuk, Yankel and Shmuel Miller, Aaron Shea (Grishker's son), Hadass Beitcher (Leib

Doktor's daughter) Feige Reiber, and her family, Zeftl Reiber and her family, Sarah and Breindl Shisl, both Hochgelernter sisters, the Dym family, Pessl Mabeh, Yosef Tuchschneider (Leibish Shmeieleh's grandson) the Eisen brothers and their sister, Hershel Bricks, the Kulpes, the younger daughters of Yankel Lutwack, the Herring family.

Out of all these, survived Itke Herring, Raizel Berger, Zindl Reiber, Itche Shtemer and his family, Gershon, Roizele, Zhiletts, and Yenkele – Manker's boy.

After two days, I left the forest. We did not meet again until after liberation.

I want to add that there were Christians who empathized with the Jews and helped and suffered because of it. One such was the milner Brilowski whose garden bordered the hospital garden. He showed us an escape route in case the Germans came for us. Behind the barn, he cleared away obstacles and made a clear route to the river. I would also like to mention Dr Spaz, the priest Tczeszlewski, the vicar, the organist Stets and his daughter, the pharmacist, who helped Jews. Hidden Jewish things found there caused them much grief.

But people like these were few. Most of the residents declared themselves to be Volks Deutche, and collaborated with the murders and the aktions against the Jews.

Bad Reichenhal, June 15 1947

———

Translator's Footnote

1. Dr. Klukowski puts this at Nov. 15, 1939 (MM)

———

[Page 299]

„טשאָטשאַ מאַרישאַ"

(×) לאָט לאָט חם מתקבצים ובאים
אלינו מעמק הבכא. הלוחמים האמיצים,
המצילים האלמונים. בימים אלה הגיעה
לאָרץ אחת מהם, אשה ששמה נפשה בכ־
פה ועשתה כדלום כדי להוציא נפשני
הכליה והשמד עוד נפש ועוד נפש. היא
עברה את פולין באורך. וברוחב כרוזנת
פולנית. כנוצריה פושטת־יד. כרוכלה.
כגיבנת. כצולעת – וחיפשה ילדים יהו־
דים אבודים ונידחים. במנזרים. בבתי
היראה. בבתי איכרים גישה וחיפשה
והצילתם מיד צכו"ם. שמה של האשה –
דבורה פליישר. בקרב הגוים היתה
ידועה כמריה דובז'ינסקה. המפעל הנגרז
של הצלת ילדי ישראל התנהל בפיקוחו
של חבר קבוץ יגור. לייבעלע גולדברג:
שליח ארץ ישראל אשר הופיע בשם
מוסוה טוארק. במסירות אין־קץ פעלת
„טשאָטשאַ מאַרישאַ". או „פאַני מאַרישאַ"
– היא דבורה פליישר. הודות לידיעתה
שפות הרבה ולהשכלתה הגבוהה היא רו־
כשת אמונם של ראשי המנזרים בסבי־
בות חרוביאשוב. לובלין. צ'אַנסטחוב
ועוד. ילדים ששבחו מכורתם דתם וגזעם
מוחזרים לחיק היהדות ואף הועלו לארץ
ישראל.

עתה הגיעה דבורה פליישר לצרץ.
וראויה היא לברכה כבואה להקיב מחדש
את קנה שבחרס בגולה פולין. א/ג/

Tchotcha Marisha

by Mendel

Translated by Yocheved Klausner

Slowly, one by one, they gather and come to us from the "valley of tears" – the courageous fighters, the anonymous rescuers. Now, one of them has arrived in our country–a woman who risked her life, and did everything she could to save soul after soul from conversion and extinction. She traversed the length and breadth of Poland disguised as a Polish baroness, a Christian beggar, a peddler, a hunchback, or a limping invalid – and looked for lost Jewish children. She searched and combed through churches, convents, monasteries, peasants' houses, and rescued the children from idolatry. The name of the woman – Devora Fleischer. Among the Christians she was known as Maria Dovzhinska. The daring enterprise of saving Jewish children was supervised by a member of Kibbutz Yagur, Leibele Goldberg, an emissary from Eretz Israel, who acted under the assumed name Tuarek. "Tchotcha Marisha" or "Pani Marisha" – a.k.a. Devora Fleischer – acted with endless devotion. Thanks to her command of several languages and her extensive education, she gained the trust of the heads of the convents in the neighborhood of Hrubieszow, Lublin, Czenstochow, [Chestochowa] and others. Children who have forgotten their homeland, religion and race were returned to Judaism, and many of them made Aliya to Eretz Israel.

Devora Fleischer arrived in Israel. She deserves thanks and blessings as she came to reestablish her home, which had been destroyed in the Poland Diaspora.

———

[Page 300]

Twenty-four Children Saved from Christian hands

by Devorah Fleischer

Translated by Moses Milstein

In 1945, after the destruction of Polish Jewry, the few families that survived wandered from city to city looking for a trace of their relatives. I too, as one of the survivors, dragged myself around for long months, on highways and byways, looking, asking, hoping, but without any sign of my only child, or my sisters and brothers.

Bitterly dejected over my fate, and after endless wandering in cities and villages, I settled in Lodz where there was a larger Jewish community. Few there were from Poland, most were returnees from Russia. They were in a terrible depressed state. They had come from the forests, the bunkers, and they were homeless, unable to start their lives, with no one to turn to, and no where to go.

It was then that each person first became aware of the great tragedy that had occurred, and the fact they were now alone. Anyone who came back to his home town, and saw that no trace of Jews remained, when it seemed like only yesterday that the streets were alive with thousands of Jews, was overcome with great melancholy. The towns were dead, like a huge cemetery with no graves.

There were just a few Jews in the larger cities. They lived in fear of the Christians who were still filled with hatred and often fell on the remaining Jews, and shot them for no reason other than that they were Jews. After years of suffering in their hiding places, their lives in constant jeopardy, often going weeks without food or water in the dark holes-now, having gained their freedom, they were killed by a bullet shot by the murderous Poles. Even now, after the liberation, those with a characteristic Jewish appearance were afraid to show themselves in the streets, or to take the trains which were often stopped, the Jews taken out, and shot.

Influenced by an Israeli emissary

In November, 1945, among the emissaries bringing the first greetings from Israel, was Leibele Goldberg (from Yagur), under the alias Turek, who came with the goal of returning Jewish children to the Jewish people.

I first met him in Lodz at the Bregman family. The Bregmans displayed great care for the reclaimed children, keeping them for many weeks like children of their own, sometimes paying out money to ransom them from Polish hands. Leibl was introduced to me by chaver Sheftl, chairman of the Central Historical Commission of Lodz.

Leibl, an intelligent young man, unassuming, energetic, persuasive, fervently explained the goal to me: Finding Jewish children kept by Christians, and rescuing them. Without a thought for how dangerous travel would be, I immediately agreed to help in this important work.

He pointed out the difficulties of the clandestine and illegal undertaking. We had to be ready to pay with our lives since these were turbulent times in the cities and on the trains. He affected me so strongly that nothing was going to hold me back. I thought to myself that with his characteristic Jewish appearance, he was putting his own life in danger. I then dedicated myself to one goal-tearing the Jewish children away from Polish hands at any cost, and with this, stilling my own pain.

I met him on a Friday night, and by Sunday, I was already on the road as a Christian. I went to the Lublin area which was the most familiar to me, but also the most dangerous at the time. It was, after all, the region of Majdanek, Sobibor, Treblinka, and Trawnik in the time of the Germans, and, later, the biggest zone of anti-Jewish terror perpetrated by Ukrainians and Poles. My acquaintances and near ones tried to dissuade me from going. My only remaining father-in-law traveled from Chelm to Lodz (a considerable distance), putting his own life in danger by traveling by train, to plead with me, "Why do you need to do this? You have survived the war and now you are putting your life in danger?" I answered him, "There is nothing to hold me back. I have no one left! It's all the same... earlier, later. And since I have survived, I must accomplish something!"

I was in constant contact with Leibl during the year I was involved in this difficult, stressful work. I often had trouble locating him. He himself usually didn't know where he would be at any given time. He was often nervous when he left, and failed to write or telephone while on the road.

I remember that once, returning from travel, I was told that Leibl had been desperately running around in the Zionist "coordinatsye" looking for me. "Who knows what could have happened to her?" I, in turn, began to look for him. I ran to the organization on Narutowicza Street, to the Historical Commission on Srodmiejska, and to his residence. Finally, resigned to not finding him, I returned to the "coordinatsye" where I found him in a room with the newly founded Aliyat Hanoar[1] teaching Israeli songs. He was active in all domains.

More than once, he put his life in danger traveling by train. Once, on July 1st, 1946, while traveling with the emissary Nathan Blizowski, from Warsaw to Szeczin, the A.K.[2] stopped the train at Malkin and killed three chalutzim from the Bialystok Gordonia[3]. Leibl and Nathan were shattered by this as well as by the news from

Israel that the English military, on June 29th, 1946, had attacked Yagur where they had left their wives and children.

On arriving in Warsaw, they agreed that if one of them should fall, the other would transfer his body to Eretz-Israel.

The well known author, Chaim Grade, was present at this discussion, and it made a very deep impression on him. He asked them to describe the work that had motivated them to leave their families behind in Israel where their lives were in danger from the English, and to come alone to Poland, endangering their own lives. He later visited the orphanage in Lodz (Piotrkowska 88) where he saw the children rescued from Polish hands sleeping innocent and carefree in white beds, clean, well-fed, but lonely orphans. Deeply moved he wrote the poem. "Yosel From Yagur."

There were four such orphanages, founded with great effort and difficulty, but with much love, and staffed by specialized supervisors and educators. Two on Piotrkowska 88, and Narutowicza in Lodz, and two on Pietrolesia and Kamienec in Lower-Silesia closer to the border, from where they were transferred to Germany and, after, to Eretz-Israel.

By various means

During the war, Jewish children came to live with Poles in various ways. The majority were given up to Christians by their parents who knew they were going to their death and still had the opportunity to do so before the aktions which took place in 1942-1943. At the same time, they also gave up all that they possessed. There were also cases where compassionate Christians, finding a child wandering around alone in the forest, or in a village, took them in. But such cases were few, because the farmers often betrayed and gave up the children. A blonde child with blue eyes, who could speak Polish, had a better chance.

Christians who kept Jewish children were mostly of the Polish intelligentsia, good friends of the parents. This was mostly in the larger cities, because in the smaller shtetls it was more difficult. The neighbors lived too closely, and knew each other too well, and often betrayed them, sometimes out of enmity, sometimes out of envy because the child could be exploited, or his fortune stolen.

Many Jewish children-I believe the majority of those alive after the war-were saved with the help of the Catholic clergy who took them into the church notwithstanding that they put their own lives in danger.

The Red Cross also helped. In 1943, when the Warsaw ghetto was burning, the Red Cross drove around in cars on the Polish side, and, quickly, so the Germans would not see, picked up the children who were wandering around, and afterward transferred them to the churches. There, the children found themselves among hundreds of Christian children, and were well protected from the murderous Germans.

Polish clergy does not want to relinquish

It is regrettable that still today there are many Jewish children in these same churches because the clergy converted them, and considered it a great sin to give them back to Jews.

In 1946, R' Herzog visited the Pope in Rome in order to see about reclaiming the children from the churches, but to no avail.

Getting the children back from Christians families was met with great difficulty, because they did not want to give them up. Everyone had their own interests in mind.

Many of them saw them as a source of income. The Jewish committees which were established soon after liberation in the large cities such as Warsaw, Lodz, and Lublin, gave the Christians holding Jewish children large sums of money practically every month, as well as clothing, food etc. Every Christian hoped that a rich uncle from America would materialize and pay him thousands of dollars.

The farmer in the village had, in the ten to twelve year old Jewish boy, a dedicated shepherd, working for free, whereas he had to pay the parents of a Christian boy to look after the cows, or geese, four to five measures of wheat annually, as well as clothing him. The Jewish shepherd, without a guardian, barefoot and poorly clothed, looked after the cows until late autumn, in rainy weather, and also in the frozen days of winter. The child also had to work and do the cooking in the farmer's house. A twelve year old girl told me that she had to cook for the whole family of seven during the harvest.

There were also cases, particularly in the cities, where the Christians became very attached to the child, and loved it as their own. These people did not approach the Jewish Commissions about their Jewish child, because they were afraid to lose it.

The Jewish committee after the war in Poland was pro-Communist and was not interested in reclaiming Jewish children from Christians. And if they were reclaimed, they were content to leave them in Polish orphanages in order to build a Greater Poland. The committee was also absolutely against transferring the children to Eretz-Israel. Furthermore, there was no expectation that the committee would help the Zionist organization in reclaiming Jewish children from Christians. They also did not want to share the lists of Jewish children. But we did find some interested people in the communist committee that did come to our aid, and gave out the lists.

Haifa 14.12.1950

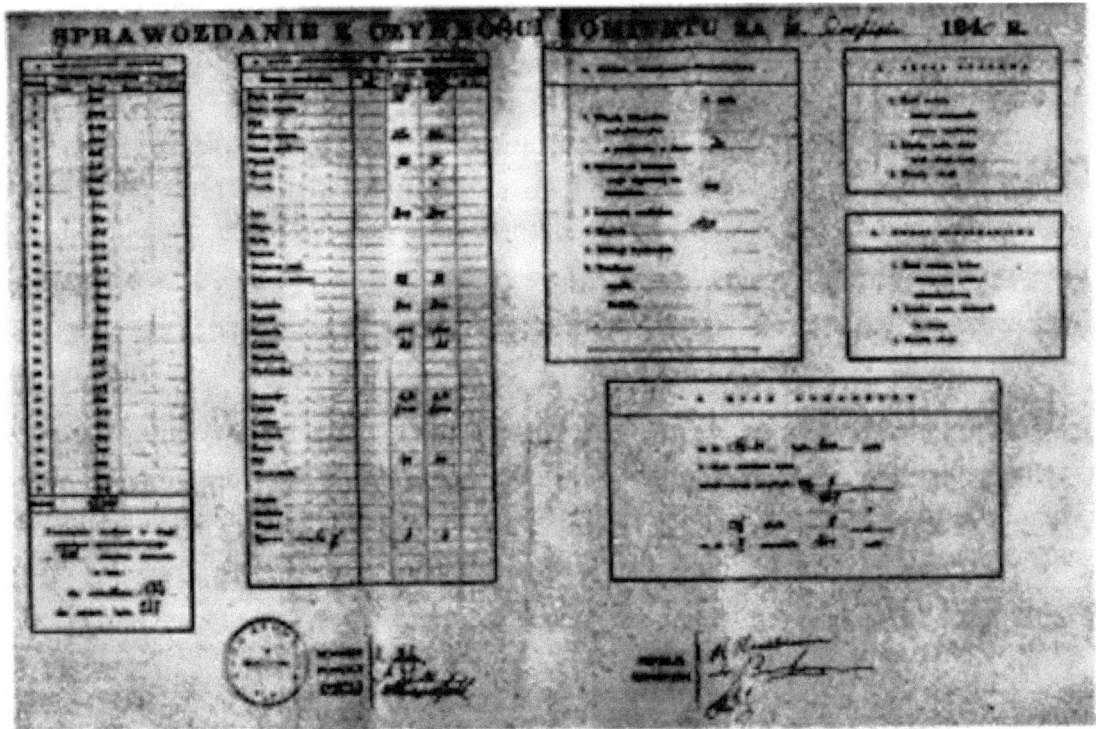

Resolution of the relief committee 1940

———

Translator's Notes

1. Youth Aliyah
2. Polish Home Army
3. A youth movement

———

[Page 305]

The Last Train
by Aaron Shrift
Translated by Moses Milstein

My father worked hard all his life. Hard is an understatement. He would leave the house very early and return late at night. He would come home late in the winter night, broken by hard work, eat his poor meal, and sit down by the warm oven to learn Tanach with us. We children would eagerly swallow his every word.

But not everything proceeds as we would wish. Sometimes my father's hand would swell up from his labors and he would not be able to work. Then, there would be nothing to eat. There were seven of us small children and we had a healthy appetite. We didn't have to be coaxed to eat, we would have eaten stones.

The whole responsibility for making a living lay on my father. My mother was also not in the best of health, but she would do everything in her power so her children would not go hungry. Sometimes times were better, sometimes worse, but more worse than better. I was in Shebreshin until I was 18 years old, and I remember that even in the worst of times, I never saw my father cry.

My mother, however, would, from time to time, have a good cry. It's easier for women. There was no lack of opportunities. For example, Friday evening at candle lighting, erev Yom Kippur, and sometimes, when the soul is burdened, it doesn't hurt to cry a little. But my father was unmoved and he did not cry.

I don't think there was anyone in the shtetl who did not know my father Reuben Shrift (Sapuch), a tall man with a copper, a little grayish already, beard. He was a very intelligent man. He was always ready to give advice to others, but he could not help himself. He also liked to joke around. For this he had his friends-Yosel Kandl, Atchi Shiser, his brother Beirach, and many others. He went through life with a light heart.

So life went on until 1939, when the Second World War broke out. As soon as the Germans entered, the troubles began. First Chaim Laizer Shtreicher was beaten up. The goyim immediately began to steal. When I saw a goy carrying out bolts of cloth from Arish Maimon's store, I grabbed the goods from him and ran to Simchele Roife's house. The Germans saw this and shot at me. Luckily, they did not hit me.

It didn't last long and the Germans left and the Russians entered. We were overjoyed. Jews became big "machers". They made arrests, they jailed anyone they felt like jailing. The spree didn't last long. After the big celebration came the sorrow. All at once, we heard that the Russians were leaving and the Germans were coming back. Things became tense and panicky. The young people began to organize themselves to escape, heading toward Lemberg. There were many in town who had to flee.

This was after Succot. The nights were already cold and the rains began. I decided that I would have to go. With me came Yenkel Miller, his brother, Shmuel, Piniele Reis, and many others. We left our homes at 4:00 pm heading for Zamosc.

Before we left, we heard that the last train from S would be leaving for Ludmir (Wlodzimierz Wolinski) at midnight. We had no hope of getting on this train because it was coming from Zwierziniec and was already half-full. In S., whole families with children who had to leave were getting ready because it was their last opportunity. Among these families were my sister Chaye and her husband Yenkel Becher who was in the militia that the Communists had organized in the time of the Russian occupation. With no hope of going along, we left on foot.

When my father returned from Minche-Maariv, he was told that I had left without saying good-bye to him. So he declared that I must be made to return. He was not against my leaving, but how do you go away without a "Go in good health?"

We were already quite far. Suddenly, I saw my little brother, Shaye, running after me and crying. I stood stock still, waiting to see what had happened. "Father orders you to come straight back home," said my brother. Understandably, I did not want to do so. So he fell at my feet and did not let me go any further. At that moment, a goyepassed by and said, "Your voyage will not meet with good luck, if you do not return home." I didn't spend any more time thinking about it, and said good-bye to my friends and went back.

Back at home, my father was overjoyed to see me, but he knew I had to leave. We decided that I would leave on the last train at midnight with my sister, brother-in-law and their daughter Sheindele. The train left, however, when it was already daylight.

I made my farewells to my mother, my sister and brother at the house. My father decided to accompany me. Along the way, he stopped, clutched me to his chest and began to cry loudly. Today, after so many years, my ears still ring with the sound of my father's weeping. I believe he felt that we would never see each other again. The last train separated us forever.

*

My brother Shaye, soon after, became the first martyr. He was shot by the Germans. He was not yet sixteen years old.

———

[Page 306]

The Last Evening in My Home

by Sarah Fuks (Ingber)

Translated by Moses Milstein

It was a time of changes. New information came daily. Yesterday, we had the Germans, later, the Russians. The joy when the Russians came to S. is indescribable, because we were free of the Hitler-murderers, even if only for one day.

Suddenly more news: we have to get ourselves ready to leave, because the Russians are retreating, and the Germans are coming back. Rather than fall into German -Polish hands, it would be better to fall on the road. Mother prepares a pack for each child-bread and a little salt.

We are going to the train. In the dark, we see many people-women, men, children-everyone on foot. The question on everyone's mind-where to? Meanwhile, everyone is going in the same direction-to the train. People snake along led by the same desire to live. We are accompanied by a sea of tears. Only the young are going, the old are too exhausted from hunger and the bombings and the hiding. They have no strength to flee. At the train there is a din and a racket. Where do we go, is the question. All carry only as little as possible, something to cover themselves with. Suddenly, a new commotion: There are only a couple of cars along the long platform. There is not enough room for everybody. People crowded together. There are a large number of Jews from Zwierzyniec. The wailing reaches up to the sky.

Parents came to say good-bye to their children. My mother and father and mother-in-law also came, and took off their last little shmate and threw it on us. We looked at our loved ones for the last time, and the train pulled out of the Shebreshin station.

Our closest and dearest ones disappeared, and we lost the hope of growing up together with the rest in our shtetl where everything was so near and dear.

The singing of the Chasidim in the shtiblach is only a memory. Who can forget Moishe Kliske Farber's hammering Friday night, "Kinder, shabes, close up, close up." The tumult of the young people on the new promenade Friday evening when everyone went to their organization-to the Chalutz, to the Bund, everyone with the desire to learn something there.

Early Saturday morning Isak Shmoiger Germanovitch would wake people for morning prayers. A little later we would hear, "To shul, to shul!" And our mothers and fathers, with their deep piety, went to pray.

Our big beautiful shul has been consumed by fire along with our families, and our hope that here, where we were born, we will grow and flourish in the company of our own.

Montreal, Canada

———

[Page 309]

My Ruined Town

by Abraham Weinrib

Translated by Moses Milstein and Yocheved Klausner

A friend of mine
sent me a letter,
On paper he wrote it all
down.
Fear runs through and
hurries...
There are no Jews left
in this town–

The town that was
once full of Jews,
Chasidim, Mitnagdim,
and secular–
Now empty streets, and
a vacant market
Give it a funeral air.

A silent cemetery,
houses–tombstones

stare at the emptiness
around–
The dead, without
graves, lie about,
after the days of
slaughter, that one, the
big one...

The stones, where
Jews once tread
to business, to work, to
prayer–
Lie soaked in tears,
splattered with blood,
in sadness, hidden,
silent as the dead...

They are ashamed
to face the Heavens,
Give testimony of what
they have seen –
As the Germans
slaughtered a town,
From grandfathers to
suckling babies...

The holy houses–
synagogues and
houses of prayer
where Jews poured out
their hearts,
lie in ruins, defiled,
obliterated by the
murderers, bare...

Gone is the Bet
Hamidrash, the books,
the Gemaras,
Gone is the sound of
study through the
night,
the songs

of Abayey and Raba the
Sages
sung by the boys
learning Torah.

Gone is the
the cheder, the rabbi,
the Chumash,
The happy urchins–the
children–
Like an offering of
cattle
Burned on the altar of
the Teutonic Moloch...

And the youth from
libraries, and unions,
with books, theatre,
and songs. –
Gone are the Jewish
sons and daughters,
who marched with
flags along,

They marched,
convinced of their
ideals,
Not just for their
personal welfare,
but fought for the
Jewish people, and
suffered
for humanity, for the
common wheal...

There are no
Jewish youth left in my
town,
from the Bet Midrash,
the clubs, and the
union–
Together with mothers

and fathers...
all went to their death
as one...

    And houses, where
Jews once lived
for hundreds, and
hundreds of years
speaking Yiddish,
dreaming, striving,
are houses where
others now live.

    And the wealth of
Jews: stores and
goods,
workshops with tools
and toil
turned over to the
hands of Polish
enemies
who helped the Nazis
despoil...

    Once neighbors,
now foes,
they have become the
heirs–
of my town, that is
ruined.
Of this, my friend
wrote.

Santos, Brazil, 1947

———

[Page 311]

A night of terror[1]

by Balche Milstein (Langburd)

Translated by Moses Milstein

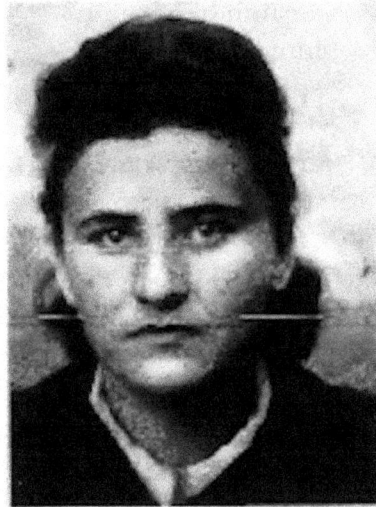

Very early on, the burdens of family fell on me. After a lengthy illness, my mother died. At the age of 9, I had to manage the household. I was forced to go give up my girlhood and become an adult.

My father, Feivel Langburd, like many other Jews who lived in town, carried out his business in the surrounding villages. We saw him only on weekends, because the rest of the week he was busy working among the farmers. Early on Monday morning, he would kiss us good bye, and go back to the villages. On Friday, covered in dust from the roads, he would return. When my little sister, Shaindel, and I would see him, our joy would know no bounds.

There were no modern communication methods then; trains or passenger cars did not travel to the distant small villages. Mostly you traveled on foot. If we were lucky, we could get a ride on a horse and wagon, driven by a farmer we might know, to take us part of the way. Even though we were young, we knew how hard our father worked so that we could be well fed. I took the place of mother and father to my sister.

As the Nazi plague descended on Polish Jewry, the persecution of the Shebreshiner Jews began.

I remember hearing wild cries in the middle of the night. Everyone was awakened. I ran to the window and looked out. and I saw fire. I could see the fire's reflection on the walls of the church, and the windows of the hospital. The sky was flaming red.

People were running and screaming. My little sister and I became frightened. She fainted. Our father was not at home. The Germans banged on the door, and yelled at us to get out. I wanted to save some house-hold things, as well as clothing for my father and sister. I remembered that he had hidden some jewelry under the kitchen floor. But I couldn't find the exact spot where he had hidden it. So I quickly packed a few things, and we got out of the house.

I flew across the street, hoping to get help from the hospital doctor there who knew us as neighbors. While I was standing near the hospital, our house caught fire. The Germans were running around claiming that the Jews themselves had set the shul on fire, and that they would be held accountable. This was a tried and true method of the Germans: pin every crime on the innocent.

The Germans herded the Jewish residents into a garden, near the well, not far from Groisse Shloime's budke. The fire in our house was vigorously being fought, because the priests were afraid that the church near our house would catch on fire next.

I struggled to drag around all the things I had stuffed into a large sheet. My little sister couldn't stop trembling. I calmed her down a little. Not knowing what to do, I decided to go get help from my fiancé's family, so that they could help with the baggage.

A hand grenade was thrown into the courtyard of the shtrickendriers, meant for the Rav. They wanted to punish him. The Germans looked for various measures to frighten the Jews.

While looking for help, I came across the shtrickendrier's daughter, a mother of four children, who had lost track of one of them. I found the child, and brought it back to the desperate mother.

As I walked further along, a German stopped me, and forced me to go where the rest of the people were being assembled. My sister was still with our belongings, back near the hospital. Separated from her, I began to worry about her safety. Suddenly, I saw the Germans leading her and our packs to the gathering place, where I was waiting. My relief knew no bounds.

I saw how Jews were driven from their houses, half naked, in their underwear, some carrying small bags that they snatched in their panic.

Halfway through the night, the Germans ordered everyone to leave their bags behind at the gathering place, and they led us all to the Halle, the market hall. You could only bring along a small pack. So we decided, as before, that my sister should stay behind and guard our things. When I tried to get back to her, a German stopped me, and refused to let me go on. I told him that I had left behind a child, but he didn't believe me, and said that he would shoot me if I were lying. So he accompanied me back. When he saw my sister sitting on the packs, he believed me. To give the impression of "gentlemanliness" he helped us carry our things to the Halle.

The threats of shooting, as well as the minute displays of decency, were one way the Germans played with our nerves.

The majority of Jews were concentrated in the Halle. The stalls were empty, the merchandise had all been stolen. Our pleas to be allowed to bring our things into the Halle with us were ignored. Everything was left lying outside. The Germans assured us they would not allow the Poles to steal anything. They posted guards, and prevented the farmers from the villages from coming into the city.

As we sat in the Halle, we could hear its tin roof cracking from the heat of the houses burning around us. The Germans searched for the Rav, but could not find him. This enraged their beastly instincts. To revenge themselves, they threw an incendiary bomb into the shul. Flames escaped from the windows, and lit up the shul courtyard and the Halle.

The Jews held in the Halle, aware that the shul was on fire, began to bewail the devastation. The flames in the shul consumed its innermost walls, and licked away the prayers of hundreds of years that had been absorbed within. Outside, black crows circled the burning shul, and their cawing was dispersed in the dark night. The Shebreshiner beit hamikdash was no more.

When day came, the Germans accused the Jews of setting fire to the shul, and stated that they would be punished for this. They detained ten Jews, and demanded a large ransom. The rest were let go. The money, of course, was acquired, and the hostages were freed.

After the fire, not a day passed without some new evil decrees inflicted on the Shebreshiner Jews.

———

Translator's Footnote

1. The date of the fire was November 15, 1939 according to the diary of Dr. Zygmunt Klukowski

———

[Page 314]

Wandering

by Shaindl Knabl (Stern)

Translated by Moses Milstein

My seventeen year long journey, counting from the time I left my home, my birthplace, until I came to Israel, was one of hard struggle for life and existence, a fight against starvation and destruction. I can still hear my mother as she came to my workplace at Pesach Berger's, and telling me in tears, "Shaindele, leave your work and come and get ready to leave your home, because the danger is great. All the young people are fleeing, and you and Brochele, will also go."

This was in 1939, when the Red Army was in Shebreshin, and people were saying that they were leaving and ceding the territory to the Germans who had already been here. I obeyed her, settled with my employers who rewarded me generously, and went home to prepare to leave. The following morning-it was Chol Hamoed Succot-my sister and I left on foot on the long journey, following the wagons filled with Jewish refugees from Shebreshin.

We parted from our parents, and my sister Raizele, with broken hearts and hot tears. They accompanied us until the sugar factory, and then they turned back. They kept looking back at us, and we at them, until we were out of sight. My sister and I kept going, resting often, and sorrow kept us from exchanging a single word. Russian soldiers gave us rides on their trucks, and we reached Ludmir by nightfall.

We spent the night in a shul with many others like us, and in the morning we met our relatives who took us to their place which was in barracks on the outskirts of the city. I want to point out that the family were also refugees from Tishvits, and had been here several days, and had secured a room in the barracks. Aside from them, two other families lived in the same room. We slept on the floor. Some had a pillow, others did not. The streets in Ludmir were full of "Biezhentses[1]". To buy bread or other food in the stores was very difficult-the lines stretched far, far.

In a Siberian labor colony

Having no way to provide for ourselves in Ludmir, we signed up to go to the Russian interior for work. We were now three people, because in Ludmir I married my present husband. We arrived in the Siberian labor colony with the registered echelon. Most of the population consisted of exiled Kulaks from the time of the revolution, and criminals. They allotted us a room in the barracks, a plank bed, a blanket, and sent us to work in a textile factory.

The winters were freezing. Snow and frost came in through the wide cracks in our room. Water froze. We had to slice the bread with an axe. (A lot of work with the bread wasn't necessary, because we didn't always have bread.) Both my husband and I worked in the factory. My sister, Brochele, had her own place and earned money to buy the small piece of black bread and watery soup in the "Stolovke" where you had to wait in long lines. There were another twenty Jewish families with us in the "Pasholek." With the coming of summer, the Jewish families set out for the Ukraine, because they did not want to perish of hunger and cold in the Taiga. We were also among the wanderers. We gathered our meager belongings, and with a young child in hand, we set out in a "parachad" (a cargo ship) looking for better fortune. We got to Krukov, a small town in the Ukraine on the Dnieper river. There we met Yankele and Leah Shtible from S. They helped us get a room with a Ukrainian family. My husband had trouble finding work. But finally he found a job which paid very little, but we managed somehow to live.

But we were not to enjoy the Ukrainian Garden of Eden for long. Soon the Russian-German war began. The town was unexpectedly quickly captured by the Germans, and we had barely enough time to cross the Dnieper on a raft and save ourselves. My aunt Iteh-Riva Weinrib and her two daughters Ettele, and Surele, and her sisters Shaindl-Gitl, and Rivka Boim were also in that area. Unfortunately, they could not save themselves. From that time on, we kept running and the Germans kept destroying our home.

In a stone quarry in Uzbekistan

We would stay for several weeks in one place, and then be forced to run further and further until fate drove us to Middle Asia, to Uzbekistan. There we encountered a heartless population. We were in a kolkhoz where we were fed a "lepiashke" (a kind of flat bread). There, our child died of starvation, and we nearly succumbed as well.

At that time, they recruited young people for work in Ural. We registered ourselves, and were taken to a stone quarry. We were given quilted pants, undershirts, and straw shoes with leggings, and we dug out the rocks from mountains that had been blown up with dynamite. We had to break up the rock, load it into wheel barrows, and carry the load onto a barge in the water. The quota was very high. Whoever made the quota received soup and a side dish, and whoever didn't, got soup alone. Thus we lived until repatriation, sundered from the world, from human existence, seeing only rocks and water.

When we registered to go back home to Poland, we had no idea that the devastation was so great. In everyone there had glimmered a spark of hope that, coming back to Poland, we would find someone, that the Poles had saved even one child from families that had remained in Poland. When we crossed the Polish border, we were shocked and depressed by the tragedy that had befallen our people. Many left the train stations to look at the gas ovens, the barrels of ashes, and brought back the tragic news.

Repatriates in Lower-Silesia

Most of the repatriated were settled in Lower-Silesia where Germans had lived. We received good houses with nice furniture, clothes and dishes that had belonged to

Germans. But all this frightened us. I couldn't use any of the German things. I felt they were covered in Jewish blood. Feelings of fear and pain accompanied our stay in the house. I found a lot of anti-Semitic material in the house, illustrated magazines that mocked Jews, and several pieces of soap with the initials RJF. (Pure Jewish fat.) I sent it all to the Jewish historical institute.

The Kielce pogrom completed the bitterness and fear. The Poles believed that there were no more Jews left in the world. At the end, they realized that a few Jews had survived, so they wanted to complete what Hitler had been unable to. Many Jews left Poland illegally at that time, but they soon stopped that, and we remained where we were.

Life became a little more normal. The various gangs were subdued, and it became a little quieter. The government declared that they would support emigration of Jews to other countries, and we lived in hope. A lot of time passed before that became a reality. We underwent many difficulties in that time, both materially and spiritually.

The atmosphere was tense in Jewish circles during the doctors trials in the Soviet Union, and the Slonski murder in Czechoslovakia. We feared that the same thing was imminent in Poland. We were also shocked when we heard about the activities of the NKVD against Jewish authors and artists.

Happy in Israel

Later, the 20th conference of the Communist party proclaimed freedom of speech and democracy. Anti-Semites in Poland used this to spread anti-Semitism in Poland. What was previously hidden was now revealed. But the change also had its good side. It allowed the Jewish masses who had been registered six years before, to leave Poland.

My family and I received permission to make Aliyah to Israel. On November 20, 1957, we crossed the border to Israel, and thereby put an end to the dark wandering episodes of our lives, and thus a new, bright, productive life for me and my family began. I feel fortunate that my children will be raised in their own land, and if they will love and sacrifice for it, they will not meet with disappointment and deception.

Herzliya

Translator's Footnote

1. Homeless people

[Page 318]

In Armed Battle

by Ephraim Farber

Translated by Moses Milstein

Shebreshiner Jews who served in the ranks of the 27th artillery regiment stationed at Ludmir Wolinsk and surroundings were: Yosef Tsoler, Leibish Leibhaber, Ephraim Farber, and others. In far away Danzig, at the famous fortress near the Baltic Sea, Westerplatte, where the German army faced a determined defense from the Polish army, one of the heroic defenders was Moishe Hilf. Shebreshiners fought on every front against the bloodiest enemy of the Jews, the Nazis.

In distant Pomerania, at the slaughter in the Tuchol forest, Yosef Tsoler fell.

After three, four days of fighting the Polish army was completely broken. The military officers took to the air, and fled the field of slaughter leaving the soldiers to their own destiny. The fighting spirit was paralyzed and mass desertions began.

Yosef Tsoler and other Jewish soldiers dug fox holes and mounted a resistance against the bloody enemy with the full conviction that they were defending thousands of Jewish mothers and children. He fought until a bullet put an end to his young life.

His grave is found not far from Tuchol shtetl near a lonely forest path. There are no wreaths or flowers to decorate his grave, just withered leaves that fall in autumn.

*

Berl Koil languished in Stalag A-1 in East Prussia as a prisoner-of-war. I met him at Luba Gall's after I was released from the Lipowa 7 transit camp in Lublin.

I was seized with bitter pity when I saw this person known to the whole working class of S. His belly was swollen from the inhuman conditions suffered by the Jews in Stalag A-1.

I can picture Berl on his shoemaker's stool, his thoughts carrying him far away, over the Alps, where in deep snow the last freedom fighters of the Austrian "Schutzbund" plodded. And, animated, he removes his glue-covered apron. His lion's roar thunders through the Bund hall describing the lost Viennese "Schutzbund" battle. With his mighty voice he recounts the last days of the Austrian "Schutzbund." His listeners are carried along and raise their fists against the oppressors.

He inspired us with his great persuasive voice.

This dreamer of human happiness endured the entire Hitler nightmare until death released him.

Kiryat Yam

September 1940, a bank report from the help committee of the Judenrat

[Page 320]

Do Not Forget the Dead!

by Mordechi Elboim

Translated by Moses Milstein and Yocheved Klausner

I visited the dead last night,
listened to their complaining:
—So what if we wander around lost,
do you not still have to say kaddish?

And if you did not see our death throes,
did not hear our last will,
are you allowed to dance, to tread on us
on the cemetery paths, bloodied, dusty and gray?

Are you allowed to shut our eyes
seal them with mud
and believe that you can redeem a sin
with a moment's tears of regret?

From every bit of soil, stone and flower,
we peer out like tombstones:
and you, laughing,
you don't even bother to look around,
sunken in lies and lust.

And still more their woe reaches me,
their strange, lonely distress

and a cry cuts through like a knife
and subsides in a lonely moan.

    We wander forever in a wild gyre
in winds, in blizzards.
Perhaps you will hide us
so that we can find respite...?

    Bodies sundered, burned, crushed to ash
only a wick remains.
So light the wick even if it's weak
so a memory of life remains.
Bury somewhere deep, in a corner of your heart
a yorzeit to bind us
so that in the union
sorrow will wane
and a flame will ignite.

    Because if not?—
You are naked in our flame,
hollow, empty, and frozen.
You are deader then we
Having lost the spark of holiness.

    Thus did I wander and visit the dead
until the sun's red rays appeared...
From damp ruins the cry arose:
Do not forget, do not forget, the martyrs, the dead!

The Yartzeit of those murdered-23.10.47 in Haifa

[Page 322]

Oh, My Little Shtetl

by Pinchas Bibel

Translated by Moses Milstein

I remember that, years and years ago, when our hopes were still young, when the world was still whole, that in a magical town, Carmel, by the sea, near my San Francisco, the writer Peretz Hirshbein came for a rest after a long world tour.

At the Pacific shore, always stormy yet peaceful, where the Sierra Nevada mountains descend in giant, broken steps, there is a quiet town in the forest. The sand is white as snow, and the waves, calmer now, wash the feet of those who have found this place, and have come to live here in unruly nature.

And I remember a night when the clever Hirshbein had invited me to a dinner that he and his beloved wife, the poet Esther Shumiacher, had so ritually prepared, and we sat by an open fire–the woods were cool and foggy, the ocean rhythmically chased the foamy waves–and we read and talked.

Hirshbein said that he was working on a big novel and a new play. Esther read her lyrical songs, and I–my modest prose.

Late at night, Peretz exclaimed, "Bibel, Tell me something about your shtetl. Tell me about your early years." I laughed, "About my shtetl? What is there to tell? A small dot in Poland, a little yawn, one out of hundreds. It is not important!"

Hirshbein looked at me with warm, sad eyes, "Describe and write, Bibel! Remember and write. Who knows what will happen to our warm homes."

I did not understand it then. It appears that Hirshbein sensed the beginning of the storm. He foretold the future.

I described but I didn't write.

*

Now it is too late. Now every memory hurts. Now we can't touch those events that have formed us. Now we can't write "poetically," sing of our loss. Now we can only look back, and silently remember–and grieve–and regret.

And yet, opportunity demands that we wipe off the dust of the years, to revive and retrieve, if just for a minute, our town that once was. To reconstruct the destroyed houses, put back the streets, the budkes, the fences, the people, to reduce oneself and become a young, dreamy boy again in a small Polish shtetl.

The poets say that as long as we remember someone, that person lives among us, but if we forget, then they return to dust and ashes.

So let us remember for ourselves, for our children, for the deceased, for the Jewish life in Poland that disappeared.

I remember our home–an open door for Jews and goyim. A simple home. My grandfather, my five uncles–simple, good Jews.

My father came from elsewhere, from Chelm, from the Brisker yeshiva, from the Warsaw Bet Hamidrash, and brought with him the impetus of the big city.

The shtetl is calm, sleeping in an old dream. Nothing changes. It is a fortunate shtetl. Although a paved road links to Zamosc, to Lublin and stretches away to Bilgoraj, and far, far away even to Lemberg, the quiet is seldom disturbed.

*

The old, nine hundred year old shul dominates and influences life. It is deeply rooted. It is baked into the good Polish earth. Even when Chmielnicki entered the towns, he left Shebreshin in peace. In 1863, the Polish people revolted (my grandfather told me that many Jews assisted) and when the revolt was suppressed, the Russians came in from the Toplice forests, and determined to wipe S from the map for helping the revolutionaries, but by a miracle the city was saved.

Even in our times we were lucky. During World War I, we were not expelled, not bombed. Even Petlura respected us. Yes, S was a lucky city. It was, until the Germans.

We lived quietly. We accommodated with the Poles. We survived the Russians.

We had our "shtot gvir,[1]" (Mordechai Fleischer in our time) who always ruled over a generous home. It was the dream of poor Jews. The businessmen who worked for a living, and supported a working class in Poland. The workers who accepted their fate–the woodchoppers, water– carriers. The city deaf–mute, even a Jewish thief.

*

The days, the years, passed with quiet, slow rhythms from our river Wiepsz that lovingly divided and encircled our town on three sides. Quiet and rhythmic, deeply rooted in the past, and dreamy, waiting for the Messiah.

I remember the small group that my father belonged to, that met, late in the evening, in our house; the promenading every Shabes morning; the fields on the other side of the cement works; the reading of the first newspapers; the forbidden books.

And the "revolution," the revolution in clothing. Until then everyone (with the exception of Nathan Sheiner and the Bronsteins) wore the traditional clothing: black caftans to the ankles, flat black caps with a tiny brim. Only at night, in the dark, when respectable people were sleeping, would the youth–my father the first–gather near the hospital, put on a European hat and a short jacket, and promenade.

I remember that during an epidemic of typhus, a market woman yelled at my father that children were dying because they were becoming goyim and wearing fedoras.

*

But the wheel was turning faster and surer. We left the kloiz.[2] We sought the light. A library was founded. A Zionist organization was founded in an attic. A little later, a Bund association.

New people arrived. The young children organized into a scout group with green shirts and long staffs. I hold membership card number four.

The shtetl gave itself a shake. The door to the world opened a little. Lecturers came. The workers made demands of the bosses, even dared to strike. Mass meetings took place even in the Bet Hamidrash. A tall ascetic man came to live in our house. Lazar he was called. He had travelled the world, had been to Eretz–Israel where he contracted malaria, and he founded the first Hebrew school in our house. Later, others came and brought worldliness, knowledge and unrest.

We sensed that Shebreshin would not continue in its long sleep. We wanted to learn about equality and justice. We wanted a little tolerance. We rushed to the world. The Polish schools filled with Jewish children, even though I was inflamed by the words of my teachers, like Pan Hartlieb, who expressed often the sentiment that it was regrettable that Poland must support the parasites, the Jews who suck Polish blood.

We got older. We founded the Hechalutz organization. We readied ourselves for a free socialist life, to physical work, to culture, to the Hebrew language. Some of us left for the greater world, others stayed and prepared.

Others acknowledged their place in the life of Poland, with their connection to their roots, to their home Shebreshin. They developed the town, cleaned it, made it European, dried up the mud, paved the streets with cobblestones, straightened the old houses, built a systematic life, hoped for a better, honest tomorrow.

*

Tomorrow came, however, on the wings of German airplanes, came black as the uniforms of the SS–absolute devastation, with true German precision. None of the inheritors of the past still walks upon the earth.

I think often, I think quietly. I want to immerse myself in the last minutes in the cemetery when the mass graves were already dug.

——The quiet, wise rabbi has spoken his last words. ——It is certain that his eyes were turned to the sky, to the far horizon. Did he see all the generations, the long, long rows of ordinary people that lived in the shtetl for 900 years, who lived and came to rest in the earth. Did he see–not just the catastrophe of reality–but did he also feel the pain and shame that a band of barbarians could so demonically annihilate the historic chain that stretched from Kazimierz the Great to the first persecuted Jews who found a haven here?

I think. Only sorrow, and grief, and mute hopelessness remain.

San Francisco

Translator's Notes

1. The wealthy man in town.
2. Small synagogue whose members were often from the same profession/social group.

[Page 326]

My Ruined Home

by Shlomo Reiter
Translated by Moses Milstein

The nigunim of Torah study are no longer heard from the Shebreshiner kloizlach.[1]The folk songs are no longer sung, the beat accompanied by machine, saw or hammer of the tailors, shoemakers, shtepers[2], and carpenters. The storekeepers, Jewish men and women, no longer look out their stores. The Jewish children at play, with their sweet, noisy little voices are silent. The symbol of Jewish Shebreshin–the beautiful old shul–has been wiped from the earth's surface...Only the soil is left, soaked with Jewish blood and tears.

There remain only, floating in the air, the painful groans of the innocent, and the last tears of the children before their death. What remains is the echo–why?!

*

And you, accomplices to murder and indifferent bystanders, you have appropriated their property and goods. You live in their houses, your children play with the toys of the little children who were killed in the middle of their play. Are you not frightened of the blood which is reflected in your windows? Do you not see that the green that grows on the earth is mixed with red blood? Are your eyes not afflicted by the roses and flowers that grow on the holy blood? Those are roses and flowers of prematurely cut down fathers, mothers, brothers, sisters, of brides who did not live to go to the chupa!

Empty are your hearts, you active and passive collaborators to their demise! Now you dress yourselves in lamb's fur and claim to be creators of a new world! May you feel the curses hurled at you by my father, mother, my brothers, sister, my old grandfather in the last convulsive breath of their lives.

You, German culture–murderers, showed my 90–year–old grandfather, Shmuel Zishe, how you murdered his daughter Sarah Libe, and her husband Berish, their children Malkah, Itzik, Abraham, Fradl, Velvelle. You sadistically strangled him in front of his daughter Mantshe and her husband and children, and then took their lives.

In this wild murderous bacchanal, a large part of the Polish population took part. The Poles waited like hyenas for the plunder, the quicker to inherit Jewish possessions. The Poles have forgotten how, before the wheat sprouted and the orchards blossomed, they took money for their future harvests from Jewish merchants. Now they live, the active and passive collaborators in Jewish houses and sleep in Jewish beds.

*

I see before me my holy, dear–ones. I see my father, a simple and honest folks–mensch, who worked with the sweat of his brow to support the family. And if the weight of the wagon he pulled to make his living was too hard, you, my heroic mother, came to meet him, and together you struggled to pull the wagon.

You worried and provided for everyone, my beloved mother. Better to feed everyone first, and whatever was left, you took. Although thin and weary, you took the welfare of the home under your broad wings, like an eagle. Always anxious, you strove to meet the needs of your husband and children. You looked on with joy when they got a new piece of clothing, a new pair of shoes, which you wrested with great hardship from your meager earnings.

You allowed your children to study in cheder and school. May they grow up to be educated people, you said. I see your forehead prematurely wrinkled by worry. Your clever, blue eyes that always looked on with joy at your growing children, will always shine for me. I see the Shabes table, people sitting around it, father making Kiddush, your motherly face shining with joy, and your lips whispering a prayer quietly. "God, may it not be spoiled!" you prayed. One demand you had of God–to live to see naches from your children, and this gave you strength and courage to undergo every difficulty.

But you did not live to see any naches. The German murderers did not permit it. With wild sadism and beastly satisfaction they threw themselves on your innocent and blameless lives. You struggled against your bitter fate: Until the last minute you tried to hide from death. You stuck yourselves in bunkers and holes. In the darkness of night, you stole out, like moles from their burrows, not to be seen by the murderers, to bring a bit of meager food and water for sustenance.

In the most trying times, you, my mother with your motherly wings, strove to lessen the pain of your family, keep them warm and watch over them. You hoped that God, in whose ways you walked, would bring a miracle and save you from the murderers' hands. But God did not bring a miracle...

Instead of the tones of the klezmer you hoped to hear when your daughter was brought to the chupa, you heard the jungle sounds of wild demons as you were all brought to the cemetery. Your eyes must have looked on with horror when they brought your youngest son and daughters to their death. A mother's wings had no power anymore. Death swallowed them along with my father's life, with the lives of my brothers and sisters, my old zeide, and my dear, beloved Shebreshin.

*

Only the echo of their last cries for help remains. Only their holy blood, calling for judgment of the murderers remains, blood from fathers, mothers, from brides and grooms, from babies in their cradles, blood and broken lives, disappeared worlds. Only the big question mark remains–why?

Why were we slaughtered and murdered? Why was the world indifferent to our blood bath? Where were the so called "leagues for human rights", and the Red Cross? Where was the Jewish God when his people, who served him so faithfully, were slaughtered?

Heaven was closed to the final cries of a people taken to the killing fields. The ears of the world were stopped to the great cries of woe. No, the world cannot proceed to everyday life until it has answered, why!

And you, wild vandals, who shed innocent blood, destroyed entire worlds! It is not important where you find yourselves now–in Poland, in West Germany, or even in East Germany. Take the masks off your faces! You want to represent yourselves as creators of a better world. You laugh at the world, which bedecks you again with medals for your great gallantry. Your punishment will yet come! You will drown in your blood and tears! Hatred will consume your filthy bodies! You will not be able to redeem yourselves with money for our blood. Blood for blood, must you give!

*

My Jewish Shebreshin is no more. Gone are my father, mother, my sisters and brothers. Only their cries of agony remain. Only an unhealing, deep wound in my heart remains. Only sweet dreams remain of the home that once was.

We will erect an everlasting memorial to you. We will always remember you, my dear ones! With my last breath, I will remember my beloved shtetl, Shebreshin!

Netanya, October, 1955

———

Translator's Notes

1. Small house of worship
2. Tradesman making the leather forms for shoes

———

[Page 329]

Night of Pogroms
by Batya Bibel

Pale faces,
frightened eyes,
sunken bodies
stretched
through the night.

A tug at the heart
in everyone's step,
a blow to the head
at every turn.

With bated
breath,
eyes full of sorrow
the unfortunate
slowly walked
in the dark night.

Parched lips
murmured a prayer
and bony hands
to the heavens
stretched.

With bloody
hearts,

and heads deeply
bowed,
the shamed
walked with fear
in the dark night.

My Friend's Town

All the lights are
out,
just the candle
gutters,
like a yorzeit candle
which illuminates
and throws shadows
on the wall.

And my friend
tells me
with longing in his
voice
of a town, where he
was born,
long, long ago.

The oldest town
in Poland,
the thousand–year–
old shul,
hundreds of Torah
scrolls
in his town of old.

Of tombstones in
the cemetery,
ghosts that dance in
the night,
of a sleepy young
man,
who jumps from roof
to roof.

In the old
cemetery–
seven graves, hand
in hand
seven sons and a
mother
threw themselves off
a high wall.

By the light of
the burning candle
my friend pages
through a journal
from his old town in
Poland
from his past, long
ago.

New martyrs–
new wonders,
new Jewish strength
and beliefs,
that the accursed
Nazi,
could not steal from
the Jews.

Hundreds
of sefer–Torahs are
burning
and Jews in prayer
shawls praising
God.
Throw themselves
into the fires
and die dancing
a karahod.

Gone are
the sefer–Torahs
gone is the ancient
shul,

gone are the
thousands of Jews
in my friend's town
of long ago.

   All the candles
are extinguished,
everything is deep in
sleep.
But I lie with open
eyes
thinking: why the
punishment on
Shebreshin?

[Page 331]

In the Whirl of War
by Simah Berger (Elbaum)
Translated by Moses Milstein

Our family was not rich, but our upbringing was. There were seven of us children. A grandmother and her son, Shloime Dales, whose father had died, also lived with us.

Life was not easy. We treated the grandmother with respect. This I can't forget. Now I understand it better, being alone in my old age. In general, everyone behaved with respect and love in this small house, where everyone had a place. On Saturdays, my father, z"l, could not sit at table unless we had a guest. There were plenty of poor people coming from other towns. That was the custom.

My father was a scholar. Everyone knew R' David Elbaum from the Radziner shtibl. He would conduct "din-torahs" which were received with great honor but no money, even though he could have used it.

My mother, Bashe, and grandmother, Hinde Beile, did much on behalf of the poor and sick. On Thursday evening, they would bake bread and chales for the needy on Shabes even though we ourselves had very little. Friday morning, my grandmother would run around distributing the chales, although no one was to know who received them, not even we children.

Salvation in Israel

My travel to Israel did not come easily. For my religious father, it was as if I had converted. All of a sudden, here comes a girl from such a Chasidic family, and announces that she is going to a kibbutz for hachshara[1], because she wants to go to Eretz-Israel! It was a difficult fight. I succeeded only thanks to my uncle, Moishe Hersh Berger, who later became my father-in-law. He was in the leadership of the Zionist organizations in S. He also helped me out materially.

While in Israel, I received heartfelt letters full of woe. My father, mother, and the rest of the family envied me because the earth in Europe was burning, although no one was anticipating such devastation as occurred. Later, my relatives began to plead with me to help them come to Israel. However, I did not know how to help them while the British were in charge.

Self sacrifice

My oldest brother, Abraham, z"l, graduated from the Lublin yeshiva with the title of Rav.

At the time of the German occupation, he was selected to be a member of the judenrat. I arrived in Israel in 1936, bur according to the survivors of S. who had been there during the occupation, he often put his own life in danger. At the end, when he was ordered to assemble all the Jews, including his wife and four children, in the center of town on a certain date, he went to the German commander, and out of overwhelming grief, he begged them-"Shoot me!"

To shoot a Jew was an easy thing for the Nazis. In full view of the whole community and his family, he was shot on the spot.

My other brother, Mordechai, baruch hashem, lives in Belgium. He was saved from Hitler's hand and survived the war in Russia.

One of my younger brothers, Moishele, conducted himself-as some children do in times of trouble-like an adult. Much was relayed to me about him.

Prior to being transported to the crematoria, in order to punish someone, they would be confined in jail-they called it the Kozeh-where they experienced pain, hunger and cold. Moishele wanted to help everybody. Fearlessly, he clambered over the high fences to bring food to the prisoners.

He was successful for a short time, until he was shot by the murderers during one such attempt.

Haifa, 1980

Translator's Footnote

1. Agricultural training of prospective emigrants to Israel

[Page 333]

Memories

by Feige Roitman
Translated by Moses Milstein and Yocheved Klausner

Where are you,
brother, sister?
There is no memory,
nothing remains...
My limbs stiffen
with my wailing and
weeping.

Beards pulled
out, burned in fire,
whoever was a Jew
was persecuted.
Everything that was
dear to us cut away
so beastly, so
perverse.

Where are the
blooming, beautiful,

young
with their rousing
songs,
the shul, the holy
prayers, pure,
with the ring of
Jewish devotion?

Burned are the
magnificent shul,
and the books,
our good fortune
ripped away.
Now we search for
the graves,
Longing for just one
glimpse.

Why are you
silent, black night,
with your angry
stormy winds?
You see how I sit
and think,
Bring me the
memories now!

When your moon
was shining
and lit our way
in the nights of great
danger,
that ended with
darker days,
remind me of
memories of our
little town,
the Jewish mothers
in their need,
remind me of the
songs of the
beautiful Sabbath,

the mitzvoth of
giving bread to the
poor.

   Remind me of
Fridays and mother
in the kitchen,
her cheeks flushed,
working quickly.
preparing for
Sabbath for her
household,
The Jewish mother–
where is she now?...

   Appear in my
dreams, beloved
face,
stretch out your
hands, I won't be
afraid.
Embrace me, you
are still young.
I don't want the
earth to cover your
body.

   Where are you,
my father, my
constant friend,
Worried about
tomorrow, and our
daily bread.
Now you do not see
the sun as it shines
anymore.
Ah, my father, why
are you dead?

   Here I write the
words, as well as I
can.

My heart dictates
what my pen should
write.
I see the houses of
the shtetl along,
the streets, the
orchards, the
wooden houses,
there where my
friend spent his
youth,
playing, working,
laughing, in song.
I see the artistic,
beautiful shul
Where Jews
streamed in
numbers
on Shabes.
In the end, the
beauty perished in
flames
and with thousands
of Jews, went to the
grave.

New York

―――――

[Page 335]

Why are the Survivors Silent?[1]

by Shimon Kantz

Translated by Moses Milstein

Help bring the murderers to justice

On May 3, 1942, several gestapo arrived in Torobin, near Shebreshin, and, together with their driver, killed 107 Jews. Five days later, the same slaughter occurred in Shebreshin. On the 8th of May, at 3:00 pm, three gestapo arrived in an automobile, and shot over a hundred Jews. Terrible panic ensued among the Jewish population. The wounded ran to the hospital. The police, however, refused to let anyone enter. A little later, two gestapo, with their rifles still smoking, came to the hospital. They warned the Polish doctors that they too would be shot, if they provided any medical help to the wounded.

After carrying out the mass murders, the gestapo required the Judenrat to pay one kilo of coffee and 2,000 Zl for the cost of the bullets that were used in the massacre of Shebreshiner Jews.

In the nearby shtetl of Josefow, three gestapo murdered over 100 Jews. There occurred such scenes that even German officials who were hard–core antisemites, were upset. Even they were shaken when they saw their ideology become reality.

In Torkowice, the Germans established a labor camp for the Jews of Bilgoraj. Moishe Shuldiner, a Jew from Bilgoraj, escaped. He was caught, and beaten, and led to the camp. He was forced to run between bicycles ridden by Germans. If he paused to rest, the dogs were set on him, and tore at his flesh. Barely alive, he was taken to the camp and tied to a tree. Twelve hours later, he was untied, swollen and unconscious. He was barely revived and set free, because he was of no use for work. He did not, however, get very far. He died in great agony.

The city of Tarnogrod is far from Bilgoraj. The first Aktion took place there in August, 1942. Friday evening, the Germans surrounded the Jewish houses and dragged out the occupants, half–dressed, onto the street, and drove them on the road to Bilgoraj. In a nearby forest they forced the Jews to dig a large grave. When the grave was ready, the German gendarme announced that this would be the grave in which they would soon be buried. Tevl Herbsman stepped out of the ranks and shouted, "Others will come who will avenge the innocent Jewish blood you are shedding. You will not avoid the day of judgment!" Then he turned to the Jews and shouted, "We will not fall at their feet and beg for our lives. Let us die together as martyrs for Kiddush Hashem." A volley of machine gun fire cut short his words, and together with all the kidoshim, he fell into the grave.

Among those shot was the young boy, Shalom Hochman, who was only slightly wounded. After the Germans left, he dug himself out of the lightly covered grave, and covered in blood, he dragged himself to the city, and for a whole twenty–four hours, he hid under a garbage container, and after the second night, he came home to his relatives. His wounds were bandaged, and he repeated, word for word, the heroic address, which the pious Jew, Tevl, gave at the edge of the grave.

In Lublin proper, the SS sent their dogs, and every day they caught a number of Jewish victims at the train station. They brought them to Greier's restaurant where they murdered them. There they also killed the Shper family who had founded the Jewish high school in Lublin. The youngest daughter, Maniah Lewkowich, and her seven year old son, were killed with one bullet.

רעכטם זייטע

שמעון קאַץ

העלפט דערפירן די מערדער צום משפט (4)

„פֿאַרוואָס שווײַגן
די לעבנגעבליבענע?"

דעם ג׳טן מאי 1942 זענען קײן
סוּראָני׳, נעבן טשערנעצין, אַנגעקו־
מען אין טשעסל עסלאבנע גטסטאַפּאַ־
לײַט, וועלכע האָבן צוזאַמען מיט
זייער טאטער אייסנעברנגט 107
יידן. מיט מין מער שוטטטלײ האָט
זיך אזא שהייה איבערנעחורס אויף
אין טענערלשין. דעם ג׳טן מאי
אַזוינער רַדי ג. ס. זענען אַנגעקו־
מען אין אן אויסא דריי גטסטאַפּאַ
לײַט און דערשאָסן איבער הונדערטע
יידן. צווישן דער יידישער באַמעל־
קרונג און אויסגעבראַכן א טרעק
לעכע מאַגיק. יידישע פֿאַרוווגלעטע
זענען אויך געקומען צוליים אין
שפיטאל. די פאַליצי האָט אבער
ניטא דערלויבט קיינעם אַריינצר
לאָזן. אביסל שפעטער זענען אַנגע
קומען אין שפיטאל צוויי געסטאַ
פּאַ־לײם מיס ביקסּן. וועלכע האָבן
זיך נאָך געריכטירבעט. זיי האָבן גע׳
דראסט די פויליישע דאָקטוירים. אז
אויב זיי וועלן דערטיילן פֿאַרחונ־
רעסע יידן מעדיציניישע הילף. וועלן
זיי אויך דערשאָסן ווערן.

גאַנצן דורכפירן די מאַסן־שהיטה
האָט די געסטאַפּא אויפגעפאַדערם
דעם יידן־ראָט אין טשערנעצין. זיי
זאָלן צושטעלן א קילע קאַליל און
צוויי פודינגט זאלעטן אויף צו רענק
די אויסגנאַכל פֿאַר די קוילן. וואָס
זענען באַנוצט געווארן אין דער
שהיטה איבער די שעברעשינער
יידן.

אין דערבייאריקן שטעטל זאמעטין
האָבן דריי געסטאַפּאַודוצע אויסגע
שאַסן הונדערטרם און צעלצבע זענר
דליק יידן. צם האָבן זיך דערבי
אַנגעשפּילט סצענעס. וואָס האָבן
אויפגעשריסלס אפילו דיישסע בא־
אמטע. וו

דעם ג׳טן מאי 1942 זענען קײן

פֿאַר די יידן אין בילעאַי׳ האָבן
די דיישסן געשאַסן און ארגעסם־
לאַנגער איך טורקאַלילע. איינמאל אין
פון דארט אנטלאפן דער בילנאַי
רייוער יד משה שולדיינער. אויסן
וועג. וואָס האָט אים געבראַכט א צ׳
מסיתהאן געבראכס אין לאַנגער אריין.
די דיישסן זענען געטטאָרן אויף ראָי
וטרן און דער יד האָם געמוהט
לויסן צוטיס צווישן די מערגודיקע.
שאָמער אין דער יד א לייל גע׳
בליבן עסין אָנטבלאָאַ וואַם אטהם.
האָבן זיך גליין געטנארן אויף אים
די הינט. געצוסן און נזרוסן פון
אים שטיקער לייב. קוים א לעבע׳
דיקן האָט מען אים געבראַכס אין
לאַנגער און צוגעבונדן צו א בוים.
וועץ מען האָס נאָך צמהלּף שעה
אים אַפֿגעוונל אין אר געסווען
נעשאַעזעל און זאָ באַוויסטמיין. מען
האָם אים קוים אַפֿעסמינטערס און
באַאָריעס. ווייל צר איז שוין נישט
פעהיק געווהן צו קיין שום אַרבעט.
צר אַז אבער לויים נישט נישם דער
גאַנצן. אין גרויס יסורים און צר
געשטאַרבן.

ריינגלם די יידיישע היידער אין
האַלב נאָקטע אַרויסגעשלעפט די
מעטגסטן אויף דער נאס און זי
געשריבן אויסן וועל וואָם שירט
קין בילנאַרי. און נאָצטן וואלד
געצורנגען די יידן אויסצונראָבּן
א טרוים גרוב. ווען דער גרוב
אין שוין געווען פאַרטיק. האָס דער
ווייסטער שאַנדער נעשאָלן. און
דאַס איז זיער קבר. און וועלם.
זיי וועלן באַלד באַראַכן ווערן.
מטהוב תערבסטמאן האָם זיך דעטאַלס
אַרויסגעדרוקט פֿון דער די אין
אייסּנגעלאָפן: ,,מערדער. סילאָטן קר
מען אגדערע. וואָס וועל: קמה
געמען מאַרן אומשולדיקע יידישן
בלום. וואָס איך פֿאַרלויסס. דער
סאָן פֿון משפט וועס אייך גיישע
אויסמיידן!י׳ דערבראָן האָם צר זיך
אייסנצדרלייס צו די יידן און איס׳
געטארון: ,,מיר וועלן זיך גליין גי׳ט
שאַלן צו די מיס אין בעסן פֿאַר אונדוער
לעבן. לאַמיד אינצאיינגעם שטאַרבן
אויף קדוש השם!׳׳ א סעריל פֿון
מאַשין־גטוודער האָס איבערגעריסן
זיינע ריד און אין צוזאַמען מיס אלע
קלסים. איז אן אַריינגעפאַלן אין
דעם אייסגענראַאבנעם קבר.

צוזישן די געשאַסּע איז אויך
געווּאָרן דאָם יינגל שלום טהבמאן.
וועלכער איז אַנגעקומען בלויז מיס
וואונדן און נאָבן אלעוינגעין פֿן די
לדיישן האָם צר זיך אַרויסבאָקר
מעל פֿון צווישן די פוייסע אין דעם
לייכע־מאַרשאַטועמען גרוב. צל אַם
גײנצדיק. אין בלום רמאורשלעטם זיך
צו דער שטאַט. און א גאַבגן מח׳
לעת זיך אויסבאַהאַלסן אונטער א
מיסט־קאַסטן. און ערסס אויף דער

רות. יעדער געבאסטער ייד האט
מסתמא צרגעט באהאלטן אן ארצר
און הייסט זיכער חען באהעלפער
ניצן פון אנדערע ייד. דערפאר
ווערט ער נצפרינוקט מיט אלערלי
צניויים. ער זאל דערציילן, אויס
געבן.

איצט נאך 20 יאר האט דער
דייטשער פראקוראר ה' צויג. ודעל
כער פירט די אויספארשען קעגן
יענע סדרוד אין גריים צו וייערע
פראצעסן, אנומלט נעזוגם צום פא
סטיעד פון דער ישראלדיקער
מישרה, ה' פאליישצשוסקי:

"...כ'בין באואגרנם פון דעם מאאנגל
אין עדות... ודאם וייניטער ודערט
אלץ קלעגער די צאל פון די. יואם
נעדולקען עם. מיט יעדן יאר ודערם
אלך גרעטער די צאל פון די. ודאם
קענען שוין נישט נעדולקען. ודעו
אידך מאר אין אייסשבים. אין דער
באן ציטער אידך פונצם נעדראים. א
מיין זוכן אין. מעגלעך. נטייען
איינער פון יעגע סדרדער. אבער
פייגע קינדער. מאריוסיון שוין
נישם די דעזיקע זרעק. וימיל אין
די שולן לערנט מען זיי נישם ודעגן
יענער שאנד. אין די צייטונגען
שרייבם מען אויך נישם. פאריואס
שוויינם איד ? פאריואס שטורמטצן
נישם די לעבנגעבליבצנע ייד?
מי קעגטן זיי זיצן רוא'יק אין די
פארשידענע שקן העלם און העלם
נישם אויסזוכן אין באהולדיקן יי-
ערע מערדער די"

דער זאויקער דייטשער פראקו-
רער אין שוין איינוקע מאל אויס
נעמאטערם געוארדן צו פאלעצמצן
א חייכן אמם אין יוססיק־סינ־ססטער
ים. ער האם זיד זיך ספעצואנס מים
מאסשוז. אז ער קצן נישם איבער
לאזן זיין ארבעט מען פארדן די
היסלעריסישע פאריברעכער ודלי
כע אין גאך נישם פאראדיקס. ער
האם דערקלערם: "די מאסדיאל.
ודאם איך האב אנגעואמלם. ניבן
םיר נישם קיין רו. מצן אך נאמם
זוכט ער און מארים די פארברע-
כער און רוסם די קרבנות. זיי זאלן
אים העלםן זיי דעמאסקירן.

<hr>

אריג.נם. 1942. ודען דער אויף
באן־סטאנצ'ע האבן זיך באוויזן ליי-
דיקע חאגאנען. ודאס זענען צונגע-
גריים געוארן אויף אוועקצומירן
אלע שעבערשינער ייד. וחודין ?
אסיוע'ל האם עם נעהיטן. צרגעט
אין אוקראינע". חו מצן מצט פון
ייד באזעצן אויף דער ברייט פון
דער סלומה. א גאנצן סאן זענען
ארומגעגאנגען איבער דער שטאם
דייטשע דשאנדאמען און צוואמען
מים צוילינע פאליצ'אנטן נעבאטס
ייד. די ייד זענען נעטריבן ארידער
נעטירם פון ווערט באהאלצעניש
און אויטקעטערים אין די העלדר
סירוב ייד זענען נעוואן אנגעסה
אין שטאטם און די ס'נימער האבן
אויסגעדרקם דישעניתולומיקים
שאטעניגפלאנילקיקין
און פאראוויידתירלוג. פריילן זענען
נעואאגען מים קינדער אויף די
הענם און מצן האם נישם נצהרוים
קיין וויינען. קיין יאמתרן. אך די
יידיטטע הייגער זענען אלע טירך
נעטיוד געטתאנם און דער ודאטנע
פון מאניטעראם האם פון דאום
ארויםנעטערגאגן זאכן און סחירית
און פאראוואלוענ אויף די ודענע
גאט, הצעלכע זי דיסטן האבן א'
נאט. הצעלכע זי דיסטן האבן אל
נעקנעטפטירם אין אן אויסבאקאנגער
רליקסונג.

<hr>

דעם 8'סן אקטאבער 1942 האם
מען אין דאמאנאט אייסגענדיקם
די ייד. בלויז א צצו זאנסוטערקער
האם מען איבערגעלאזען. די צלעט'
רע ייד זענען רערטרטן געווארן
אויא ארם און די אנדערע האם
מען ארוזוקנעפירם קיין אוזוביצצ.
דאריו האם זיך נעטפעגן דער טויסך
לאגער.

אין עם שוין נעצנעדיקט ? וויים
אום, אז נישם. ודיל די דירים
קאטמאצנדריק פינגם ספזדיצ'עלן בא
מאליאן צו ליין די ייד פראנע אין
ליבלינער ראיאן אין וזצך אלו
ביי דער ארבעם. עם ניים אן א נע
ריב נאך די ייד. ודאם זענען נער
בליבן אך די בונקערס. אין די
וחעלדיער. די דאז'וקע ייד דארף
מען אויסזוכן. מען דארף אויך
אויטזוכן באהולסטענע יידישע או'

<hr>

צורייטער גאבט נעקומען אהיים צו
זיינע קרובים. מען האם אים פאר-
באנדאושירם די וחונד און ער
האם איבערגעגעבן וואס בי וחעל-
די טראנאישע רערע. וואס דער
ברומער ייד ר' סצוול האם נע-
האלטן אויפן ראנד פונעם מאמן'
קבר.

אין לובנין גופא האם די עפ'עס
לייט ארויסגעצוקם ודייערע הינם.
וואם האבן יעדן מאג אויף דער
באן'סטאנצ'ע געבאסם די יידי'
שע קרבנות. העלכע מ'האם גע'
ברענגט אין גריוסערם רעססמאראן
אות די דאם דערמאראדסם. דאים
האם מען אמאל דערהרגם די מ'
מחה שטצר. נרינדער פון דער יידי'
שער נימנאניע אין ליבלין. זיין
יוננטרע טאכטער. מאגיע לעהוי'קע
וורים מים אוו וזביצ'אריק קיגד זע'
נען דערשאסן געוארדן מים אוין
קויל.

אין יעגער צייט האב מצן גע'
כאסט יידן אין דער גאם. געהאלטן
זיי צולטבעל טעג ארעסטירם אין
דער שול. בין די קרובים האבן
נעברתגם אין דער נעסטאפא די
באשטימטע סומע אייסלייי'געלם.

שפעטער זענען די דייטשן געקומען
אויף א סייוולאניעטע המצאה: אום
שאטי פון לובלין קיין פירשק האם
זיך נעפונען דער קליינער ישוב
מיידשאן־מצשנאַרסקי. דארים אין בא'
שטים געוארדן אוברצוברירט א
סרויל לובלינער יידן. נאך דער אויף
פון איבערפירן אין בצלד נעקומען
א צחרייטער קלצם. א סיעלצקציע
מים אלע יסחרים. ודאם האבן נער
ודיינלעך באנליים אדעלבצ אקטוצצ.
שפעטער האם חצרומתאף נעהולטן
א רעדע. פארוויקצרנדיק. אז מער
וחעם זיך שוין ענלעקעם נישם אן
בערהרלן. ודיל די אקצ'ע אין
שוין פארענדיקס. פונקם אזוי האם
ער נעורדבם אוך שפעטער. דעם
9'טן נאתרעמבער 1942. ודען מצן
האם ליקוחדירט דאם נעטמא אין
פיירשצן'מצשצ'ארסקי.

די אלע מחיטמות זענען נעותזען
נישם מער ודי א פארשפיל צום
גרויסן חורבן. וחלכמער האם אין
שעבערשין זיך אנגעהויבן דעם 8'טן

At the time, they would capture Jews and hold them in the shul, until the families paid to ransom them. Later, the Germans hit on a devilish scheme: On the road from Lublin to Piosk, there was a small settlement Maidan–Tatarsky. It was decided to transfer a number of Lublin Jews there. After the suffering of being brought there, they received another blow–a selection with all the torture that usually accompanied such actions. Later, Warthoff held a speech assuring them that such things would not be repeated, because the Aktion had ended. He said exactly the same thing later, when they liquidated the ghetto of Maidan–Tatarsky.

These massacres were merely a foreplay for the great devastation that began in Shebreshin on August 8, 1942, when there appeared at the train station empty train cars that were readied to take away all the Jews of Shebreshin. Whereto? Officially it was said, "Somewhere in the Ukraine," where the Jews would be settled for the duration of the war. For an entire day, the German gendarmes and the Polish police went around town capturing Jews. Jews were taken from their hiding places and driven to the market place. Most of the Jews were clothed in rags, and their faces showed hopelessness and despair. Women carried children in their arms but no crying or wailing was heard. The doors to all the Jewish homes were open, and the representative of the magistrat[2] carried away goods and merchandise, and loaded them onto the cars for transfer to an unknown destination.

On October 18, 1942, the Jews of Zamosc were annihilated. Only about ten workers were left. The older Jews were shot on the spot, and the remainder were taken to Izbice, to a death camp.

Was it all over? Apparently not, because the third campaign of the special battalion to settle the Jewish question in the Lublin area was still underway. The hunt for Jews hiding in bunkers and the forest got underway. These Jews had to be found. They also had to find hidden Jewish treasure. Every captured Jew had probably hidden some jewelry, and knew where others had done the same. Therefore, he was threatened with all sorts of things to force him to divulge the information.

Now, after twenty years, the German prosecutor, H' Zwig, who is leading the investigation into the murders, and preparing for their trial, recently said to the representative of the Israeli government, H' Polishewsky, "I am worried about the lack of witnesses...as time passes there are fewer who remember it. With every passing year, the number of those who cannot remember anymore becomes greater. When I travel by bus or train, I tremble at the thought that the person next to me could possibly have been one of the murderers. But my children do not understand this fear, because they are taught nothing about this shameful period in school. The newspapers also do not write about this. Why are you silent? Why do the survivors not cry out? How can they sit quietly in the various corners of the world and not help the search and prosecution of their murderers?"

This prosecutor had been offered a high position in the justice ministry several times. He declined saying that he could not abandon his work of finding the Nazi criminals, a task that is far from finished. He explained, "The material I have gathered gives me no peace." He searches day and night for the criminals, and calls on the victims to help uncover them.

_____

Translator's Footnote

1. Article from "Letzte Neies."

2. City hall

_____

[Page 337]

My Little Town of Shebreshin

by Brochele Stern

Translated by Moses Milstein and Yocheved Klausner

My little town
of Shebreshin
the place of joy
and youth!
Where endlessly
the fields of green
around the city
spread.

Surrounded
by mountains
a river snaking
through
with flowers and
orchards
endowed with
richness, grew.

My little town
of Shebreshin
where my youth
was passed
where my
girlfriends and I

gaily sang and
laughed.

The sun
shone down so
gently
And lit us with
her rays.
We dared to
dream with high
ideals
of fuller, better
days.

I did not know
it at the timev
that the sun
would be lost to
us
that from a
pretty, clear blue
day
the darkness
could arrive.

The night
came down
dark, without any
stars
and covered the
town
with Jewish blood
and tears.

Innocent
fathers, and
mothers
sisters and
brothers
shot in the
cemetery
and, still alive,

with earth were
covered.

    The neighbors
told us,
they knew us
well,
that hand in hand
they walked
going into that
hell.

    Our mothers
quietly asked
God! Why does
this come to pass
that for us Jews
the right to live
has been taken.

    Can one even
express
the grief and the
pain
where mothers
and fathers
go to their death?

    Yes, this
happened in
Shebreshin
where fields and
forests were so
green
the sun that once
so brightly
shone,
shines no more,
the town is gone.

————

[Page 339]

Hallucinations in the Siberian Taiga

by Velvel Ingber

Translated by Moses Milstein

Little streets, little streets,
little streets and walls.
Forever will I
grieve for you

Forever...forever, until my last day, I will be followed, wherever I walk, on any road, by great pain and sorrow for you, my shteteleh. I will be followed by the never–stilled yearning, the sorrow, and consolation, of my shtetele for the joy of my youth, for all your Jews–tailors, shoemakers, storekeepers, carriage drivers, warm–hearted mothers and fathers, bent under the hard yoke of labor.

I yearn for you, my young generation, the flower of our people, dreamers and believers, with a vision of a just world, and the Jewish people redeemed in it. My shtetl is no more, my home destroyed, my generation cut away, and the silence of the cemetery lies over your streets.

But you live on in my imagination. And on the wings of great yearning, I fly back to you and see you as before–with all your poverty, and yet so precious; with all your modesty, and yet so brave; with your stillness, and yet seething with activity and enthusiasm; stuck in the ghetto, and yet with such broad horizons. Surrounded by a sea of hate, and ignorance, of savage, bloody fury, you stood as an island of love, and faith in mankind, and dreamed your dreams–and perished.

*

It is night. I peer, with sleepless eyes through the barrack windows. The Siberian Taiga is unwelcoming and frightening. Sky, forest, and earth run together in darkness. Only the sandy road reflects the light. It tempts me and promises me, "Come, I will take you back."

Like a lunatic, drawn by unseen powers, it pulls me from my bed. I am outside in a single leap. I am covered by the darkness and no one sees me. I am on the road. My heart beats quickly. The road disappears beneath my feet... Faster, faster.

I reach the water. A little farther–and I hear the first whistle from the train. How dear it is to me now, how homey is its call! I look at the gleaming steel of the tracks. They are, after all, one way or another, connected to my tracks far away, and waiting for me to cross them.

I am traveling. The wheels clack with the rhythm of my heart.

Faster...faster...back...home!!! I come to the station. Everything around me is sleepy and as if drunk from the fresh winds coming from the forest, and the fields, and newly chopped wood. From the sandy path, I pass to the pavement. Here, I am on the road. My footsteps quicken: Not far.

From a distance, I see the homey panorama, the roofs and houses thrown together by a careless hand. I am enveloped by the smell of freshly mown hay lying spread out on the fields on both sides of the road.

Here is the sawmill. Here, in the avenue of the tall poplars, we used to walk hand in hand. Our flushed faces were caressed by a light wind, and the night received our youthful dreams. Here, in the still of the night, huddled in a circle, the legendary images of Gershoni, and Vera Figner passed.

Here is the first house, huddled near the road, unafraid of being swept away by the waters that flood the fields in the spring. The river Wiepz flows quietly, and reflects the willows that stand at its banks, bent and thoughtful, as if at tashlich.

I get up on the hill. I know every rock, every hollow here. I have measured every inch of it with my feet. The shul, with its three cornered roof stands like a giant among the little houses, as a memorial to the generations of Jews that arrived and left, stands like a witness and ponders. Kol Nidrei night——shoulders covered by talissim, in repentance, bending before the Creator of the world——Ashamnu.

My father stands at the tailor's table, bent and weeping. How did you sin? Maybe by getting up at dawn for prayers, by providing wood in the winter for poor Jews? How?

And when the shul was set on fire by abominable hands, burned and gutted like a yorzeit candle, Moishe, the shames, stood on the hill of the ruined orchard, dressed in white, and looked with deadened eyes at the burning shul, the names in the attic, the holy books of records where the yorzeits were inscribed. When is it now yorzeit?

The market paved with stones, the little green garden with the budkes[1] standing like guards at the sides–here our martyrs went on their last road, and gave a last look at the cobblestoned pavement, at the familiar roofs–the mute witnesses of their tragic pain and destruction...   Montreal, Canada, 11.3.1956

Translator's Footnote

1. Market stalls

[Page 342]

Posing as Aryans in Belgium
by Ephraim Farber
Translated by Moses Milstein

A brother brought his eleven year old sister, Rivkah Bashe Messinger, (Kuten) to Belgium. At the time, Jews were looking for ways, legitimate or otherwise, to leave Poland, a country saturated with anti-Semitism. Bashe, had to abandon her life-long dream of going to Eretz Israel. It was not to be.

She had to work, from her earliest childhood, helping her brother in his store. With the passage of time, Belgium became her home. She assimilated into Belgian culture and enjoyed the same standard of living as the local population.

Growing up, she studied painting at the Brussels Art Academy, and was distinguished with the Levi-Smitt prize at an exhibition of French painters. She was also honored with an international prize.

She lived happily with her husband, Albert, but a cloud darkened her life. She had no children.

On the "Aryan side"

In summer, 1940, the Nazi army occupied Belgium and immediately began persecuting the Jewish population. Bashe went over to the Aryan side, and declared herself to be Christian. Her husband, Albert, a Turkish citizen, was imprisoned with other Jews of non-Belgian origin. As a Christian, she had some limited opportunity to help her brother, Moishe, and his family, as well as her interned husband.

But living as a hidden fugitive with Christians under an assumed name kept her in a continual state of anxiety and had a fatal effect on her health. In order to pass as a "kosher" Christian, she took work as a domestic servant with a Christian family. She didn't complain at having to do all the hard work, and to have to cater to the whims of her employers, or her servile conditions.

That was the price a Jewish woman had to pay to survive the bloody enemy of the Jewish people. At night, in her room, she wept quiet tears into her pillow. She knew she had to maintain control of herself and not reveal her Jewish suffering.

Results of abnormal conditions.

The months of mortal fear stretched on slowly. The grating songs of the marching German soldiers that could congeal the blood in your veins, entered the house. There were days of disappointment, of hopelessness and feelings of loss without a ray of hope signaling the end of the Hitler nightmare. She heard her Christian neighbors say on numerous occasions, "They deserve this for killing our Holy Jesus."

Her face was painted-like a piece of art-with a picture of good humor, but her heart was aching with pain. The slightest change of her facial expression could betray her Jewish origins and put her life in danger.

Fortunately, only a small part of the Belgian population behaved like this. On the contrary, others distinguished themselves in condemning the Nazi persecutions. The progressive part of the population helped Jews to slip away from the murderer's axe and fought against the occupiers.

After Belgium was liberated by the Allied armies, Bashe put her ruined life together again with her husband who had returned from the camp. But the suffering of the war years took a toll on her health. She died after a long illness in Brussels.

Kiryat Yam, 1982

[Page 344]

Disappointed by the Socialist Regime in Poland
by Bella Rosenblum (Sher)
Translated by Yocheved Klausner

After the beginning of the war between Poland and Germany, we left the country and crossed to the Ukraine, which was occupied by the Soviet Union. We arrived in Wlodzimierz–Wolynski, where we lived in terrible hygienic conditions. Together with more than ten other Polish families, we lived in a building that lacked any sanitary installation. This tragic situation lasted several months.

The only consolation in this situation was the knowledge that, in spite of everything we were free and were not threatened by the German army, which had already occupied most of Poland and spread death over the Jewish towns and villages.

After several months we were forced to leave and go to the Soviet Union. We lived in the area of Vologda and gradually we became accustomed to the new conditions. My father and my brothers found work and I went to school.

Then the German–Russian war broke out, and our situation worsened, as was the fate of all citizens. It was difficult, in particular, to obtain vital products.

When, in 1943, the "Association of Polish Patriots– was established, our situation improved remarkably. From the Polish newspapers that appeared in the Soviet Union we learned about the Shoah that befell the Polish Jews, but we couldn't believe it.

Only when we returned to Poland in 1946, did we realize the hell that the Jews went through. It was a nightmare.

After six years of wandering, we had to build our house anew, and the first period was not an easy one. We made great efforts to help recover our homeland, almost totally destroyed by the Germans. We were partners in rebuilding Poland, this time a socialist Poland. We believed with all our hearts that only in Poland, where the working class would rule, aiming to establish the conditions that would assure social and cultural life and development – only in such a country every citizen, of any nationality, race or religion, would enjoy full and equal rights.

However, after 11 years of living in the new Poland, which had been our homeland, and that we had truly loved, we were forced to leave. Anti–Semitic outbreaks became frequent, and we were clearly given the feeling that we were not welcome in Poland.

Our only aim became then, to leave the country and make Aliya to Eretz Israel, where, as Jews in our own State, we could enjoy full freedom.

Haifa, 25.3.1957

[Page 345]

Returning from the Red Army

by Yehuda Weinstock

Translated by Moses Milstein

In 1944, after leaving the Red Army, I came to Lublin looking for surviving Shebreshiner landsleit. On the road from Kovel to Lublin, I did not encounter any Jews.

Lublin resembled a camp. Bombs were aimed at the Nazi side. The streets were deserted. I met a few Jews and they told me of the terrible fate of the Jews of Poland.

As a soldier of the Red Army, I was invited to Peretz [1] House where there were several hundred Jews-men and women, mostly partisans of the forests, many of them from other countries who had been sent by the Germans to their camps located in Poland in order to be murdered.

It was Hoshana Raba. The Jews erected a lectern of stone for prayers, and a Polish priest who had secreted six sefer torahs, brought them to Peretz House. All of the couple of hundred Jews began to daven and to celebrate the yom tov. I had not come to daven, and I ran around to all the rooms looking for Shebresiner.

In room number one, I saw Jews lying on the floor. A young couple who had spent the whole war hidden by a farmer lay there with injured legs, exhausted, unable to move. There were many such couples.

In the second room, I heard Jews davening and wailing. I am not frum, but it affected me. I joined them in Hoshanes. Women and men together were weeping. Tears were shed, and I was so affected, I began to weep too.

I stood a little apart and observed the group of Jews. I wondered if they were thanking God for having survived, or whether they were asking God for vengeance. I stood there thinking about my parents. If they would still have been alive, and seen me davening and crying, they would have been overjoyed that I had survived the hard battle against fascism. I thought about my beloved wife and my only son who were murdered. I felt that I would be cursed for the rest of my life.

Suddenly, I saw a familiar person who was staring at me. He had been fervently praying and weeping. I could not place him. He could not bare it any longer, and he approached me, and asked, "Are you not Yehuda Weinstock?" And I to him, "Are you not Mendl Moishe Sternfeld?"

I received no answer. Our arms reached out and we embraced. Not a word was exchanged, but we covered each other in tears. Our hearts understood that we were brothers in suffering, the suffering of the Jewish people.

Moishe Sternfeld was sent back from Russia to the Polish army. The second Shebresiner I met, Yosef Shpul, was a partisan in the forests and survived that way.

Haifa

Translator's Footnote

1. Named after Y.L. Peretz, Yiddish writer

[Page 347]

In Shebreshin After the War
by Chanoch Becher
Translated by Moses Milstein

You enter the rooms where you lived with your wife and children. Every corner speaks to you of bygone happiness. But at the same time you are reminded of the suffering and the enormous, inhuman pain, that they endured before death released them. You walk on the earth saturated with the blood of your nearest and dearest, and it sears your feet like burning coal.

I am one of those who sought out our shtetl after the devastation. I would not wish even my worst enemies to undergo what I experienced.

*

Arriving from the Zamosc side nothing has changed, except for the stillness reminiscent of a cemetery. Walking through the back streets, the enormous devastation revealed itself. Everything was destroyed, as if the trees themselves had been torn out by the roots_

I did not recognize the place where my parents had lived. There was nothing to remember of our old beit hamidrash. The large shul, hundreds of years old, a piece of Jewish history, visited by thousands of tourists, Jewish and Christian alike, stood desolate and destroyed.

*

There were about 3,000 Jews Jews in S. as well as those fleeing from other shtetlach, at the time of the aktions. In August, 1942, the tragedy began. The Nazis sent the first 400 Jews, packed into freight cars, to Belzec, near Tomaszew-Lubelski. There they were burned. At the same time, they took 200 old and weak Jews to the pastures, shot them and buried them in a mass grave. Afterwards, they captured 700 Jews, transported them to a camp near Chelm, and then killed them in an inhuman fashion.

Towards the end, the Nazis gathered together all the hidden Jews, brought them to the cemetery, shot them and buried them there. I was told by Christians who were involved in burying them, that some were still alive when the earth was shoveled over them.

I stood by the five mass graves, and my heart turned to stone. My wife and children lay there. My lips whispered curses on all those who murdered and helped destroy our loved ones. In their name, I swore to take vengeance.

*

On the way back from the cemetery, I determined to seek out the house I had lived in. My heart beat wildly as I approached the door. I knocked on the door.

The door was opened by a woman, Christian of course, a former resident of Broida. After saying hello, I said, "I lived here before you." She quickly interrupted me, and hastened to say, "But there is nothing left of yours here."

Looking around, I saw that my house was exactly as I had left it, with small changes only. The bedroom furniture was exactly the same and even stood in the same place.

My head was spinning. I was afraid that I would pass out. I sat down on my own stool, and asked for a glass of water. I rested for a few minutes and said, "Don't be afraid. I did not own this house, and the furniture is of no use to me since I am going away to Israel, to our own land, where such horrible, murderous things can't happen. I want nothing from you."

I left the house, and S., and the blood-soaked earth of Poland, and my heart was full of pain.

*

Once in Israel, I joined the survivors of my family: five brothers, and a sister. In spite of the difficult conditions in the immigrant camp, in a tent, I recovered my strength and the will to go on living.

I was especially moved when I took part for the first time, and had the honor of opening, the Shebreshiner yorzeit in memory of the fallen.

I felt conflicting emotions at the ceremony. Should I cry from sorrow, or should I force the tears inwardly, deep into my heart and acknowledge a more profound happiness? Because, no matter how great the pain is – the loss of our loved ones, mothers, fathers, brothers, sisters, children – my own wife and two children – there is yet a spiritual satisfaction, a deep joy in meeting the small remnant of survivors. We not only managed to remain alive, but we survived the Nazis and their collaborators.

Greater is the joy after so much suffering and pain – the partisans in the forests, those saved from the bunkers in which they hid, or from German camps, or from the wild, wasteland of Siberia where we had to work in minus 40 degree weather for 600 grams of bread as black as earth, and some watery soup. We meet in a liberated Israel, in our hard won country, as free Jewish citizens.

The joy is also greater because we see among us religious Jews, Communists, Bundists, and members of various Zionist groups. We are all gathered here united in observing the holy Yizkor event, to remember our holy, unforgettable brethren from S.

We are determined to erect a monument which will reflect for the coming generations what our landsleit have accomplished, without regard to party or affiliation, up to the war, and the suffering endured by those who died, and what the few survivors, scattered all over the world have endured.

Wrozlaw 1946 – Kiryat Bialik 1982

[Page 352 - Yiddish] [Page 352 - Hebrew]

The Belzec Camp
Translated from Polish by Ephraim Farber
Translated by Moses Milstein

The description of the Belzec camp is the last chapter of the section, "Suffering and Devastation."

At first, in 1940, it was a work camp. Later, from the beginning of November, 1941, until the end of June, 1943, it was an extermination camp where 600,000 victims were killed, among them, most of the Jews of Shebreshin.

Belzec is located in the Zamosc region, south east of Tomaszow Lubelski. The camp was established in a forested area, and occupied an area of six hectares. The trees were cut down, and the area was encircled by three rows of barbed wire. The center of the camp was connected to the Belzec train station through a railroad siding with a ramp for the prisoners.

The building of the camp was begun in November, 1941, and ended in February, 1942. The extermination camp existed until the end of June, 1943.

The camp was divided in two sections–economic and administrative. The economic section held the barracks for personnel, other barracks for the prisoners who worked temporarily, store houses and other installations. In the center, there was an execution building with gas chambers, and graves for the victims. At the beginning, there were three gas chambers active, driven by exhaust fumes from diesel engines. Later, another couple of gas chambers was added.

The Sonderkommando Belzec, or the Dienststelle Belzec of the Waffen SS ruled over the camp. The personnel consisted of thirty SS, and 200 "strazniks", (supervisors), under the command of the commandant. The name of the first commandant has not been established. The second, until September, 1942, was Christian Wirth. The last one was, Hauptsturmbannfuhrer Gottlieb Herring. (The first commandant, Dolf, was personally known to me as a prisoner; mentioned in the description, "In the Hell of Belzec", p.232, E.F). The extermination program was under the leadership of A. Globocnik[1], chief of the SS, and the police in the Lublin district.

The "strazniks" carried out the functions of guards, and sorting the stolen goods. About 1000 prisoners detailed by the camp authorities to collect the clothing from the victims, and to burn the bodies helped them. These workers changed from time to time as new prisoners arrived, and the first ones were murdered.

The prisoners were brought to the camp mostly by train, and from nearer locations, by automobile. The limitations of the size of the ramp at the siding required that larger transports be divided at the train station into sections of 20 cars which continued on into the camp.

It is difficult to establish the number of transports to Belzec, because the documents could not be obtained. As well, the train documents were not saved. Sources of information include: the declarations of the train workers working at the train station; statements of the local population; documents concerning the deportations from the ghettos of the districts Kracow, Lublin, and Radom.

The first hundred people from Lubic Krolewski who built the camp were murdered in February, 1942. The train transports of prisoners continued, with some breaks, from the 15th of March until the end of November, 1942. In March and November, there were 15 transports. In the other months (with some exceptions), about 20. Each transport consisted of 40 to 60 freight cars containing from 100 to 130 people.

The prisoners were driven to the area connected to the off–loading ramp. The men were detained there. The women and children were taken to the "shatniyeh" (cloakroom where they left their clothing, money, jewelry, and so on. Then to the barber where their hair was shorn. Then the prisoners were driven to a small courtyard separated from the camp by a tall wooden fence, and from there, to the gas chambers. When the gas chambers were full, the doors were hermetically sealed. The motors were started and after fifteen to twenty minutes, the dead bodies were dragged out through special sliding doors to the small tram that led to the mass graves.

All the bodies were subjected to a "dental examination" in order to extract any gold dental work.

From among the men left at the arrival place, they chose the young and strong for work in the camp. The remaining men were driven to the barracks where the women and children had been undressed previously. The clothing and monetary possessions from the victims were later taken out of the camp, near the station, and there they were sorted and prepared for shipment. The children were used to tie the shoes together in pairs. Sick and crippled prisoners were forced to walk into the gas chambers on their own.

The bodies of the victims were buried in long graves that were prepared as anti–tank barriers when the war with Russia began.

In October, 1942, they began to burn the piles of bodies from the arriving transports, as well as those previously buried. The incineration of the bodies continued without cease until spring, 1943.

With time, they dismantled certain installations and destroyed the gas chambers. The area was cleared and reforested. The last prisoners who were used to liquidate the camp were sent to the Sobibor extermination camp.

Over 550,000 Polish citizens of Jewish origin were sent to the Belzec extermination camp, of whom around 300,000 were from Galicia, and from Jewish populations in Soviet Russia, Austria, Holland, Germany, Norway, Romania, and Hungary.

Christian Poles were brought from nearby areas and from Lemberg, mostly for helping Jews, or for belonging to opposition organizations.

*

About 600,000 people were annihilated in Belzec. Those who carried out the crimes were not punished. For example, seven criminals–onetime members of the camp personnel–were not punished by West Germany, which, in 1965, recognized that they acted "at the command of Germany's greater needs."

At the site of the camp, a monument has been erected upon which it is written, "The memorial to the 600,000 victims of Hitler's extermination camp Belzec, murdered in the years 1942–1943."

Translator's Footnote

1. Odilo Globocnik

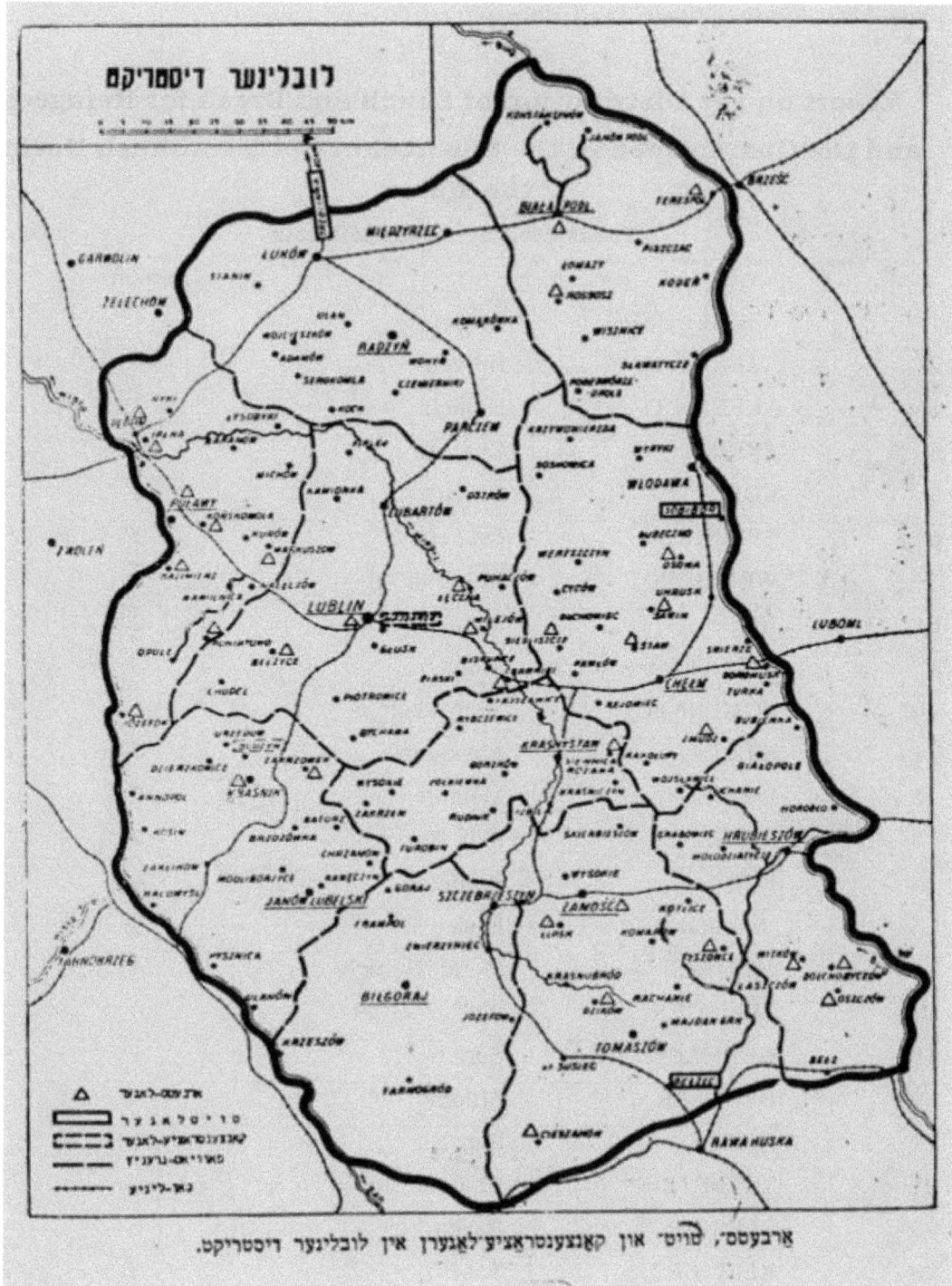

Map of Lublin district work and concentration camps

[Page 356 - Yiddish] [Page 352 - Hebrew]

Report on the Distribution of Lunch and Bread for Refugees and the Quarantined in the Shebreshin Bet Hamidrash During the War

Translated by Moses Milstein

			Persons
1	ASCHENBERG	Sarah	4
2	AKERFLUG	Hersch	4
3	AKERFLUG	Goldeh	3
4	AKERAT	Chanah	1
5	KOIL	Bineh	2
6	SPRINGER	Pesheh	1
7	WEINBERG	Deborah	5
8	NUS	Moishe Naftali	2
9	KALBFELB	Aideleh	5
10	POMERANC	Yechezkel	4
11	ZILBER	Abraham	8
12	INGBER	Moshke	6
13	INGBER	Itzik Ber	2
14	FUKS	Fradeleh	4
15	INGBER	Fesleh	3
16	MONTAG	Mendl Hersch	4
17	ZELINGER	Wolf	4
18	GERMANOVICH	Serleh	1
19	BENDLER	Shlomo	4
20	KEITEL	Sarah	1
21	TRENSTEIN	Shlomo Shia	3
22	KLEINER	Berko	6
23	KLEINER	Yosef	4
24	MANDKER	Tcharneh	6

25	SHER	Sarah	1
26	MEHL	Shmuel Zisheh	5
27	HOLTZ	Sarah Perleh	4
28	KAHAN	Mordechai	5
29	KAUFMAN	Chamia	2
30	KOIL	Chana Dobreh	1
31	MESSINGER	Esther	1
32	MESSINGER	Feige	5
33	TAUBENBLATT	Yehuda Tuvieh	4
34	GROSSBARD	Pinchas	5
35	STEINBERG	Chana	3
36	STEINBERG	Shia	5
37	FEIRER	Berko David	8
38	HAUFLER	Israel	3
39	KRAMER	Leah	2
40	BORENSTEIN	Yosef Leizer	2
41	PECH	Shia	4
42	SPRINGER	David	4
43	FEIRER	Etla	5
44	ZUCKERSTEIN	Zviah	1
45	PORTER	Aharon	6
46	DREIR	Devorah	3
47	LIEBL	Perla	5
48	BERGER	Leah	1
49	RICHTER	Yankel	5
50	BLEIWEISS	Sarah	2
51	ROSENBLATT	Itzko	7
52	ROITMAN	Feige	4
53	LERMAN	Itzko	7
54	FROST	Abraham	5
55	FALICK	David	4

56	HALPERN	Mordko Wolf	2
57	KNEIDEL	David	1
58	GOLDGROBER	Gitl	3
59	SHPER	Mirl	3
60	SHER	Sholom	8
61	HALPERN	Chana	5
62	GREBER	Zalman	8
63	GAIER	Hersch	7
64	LANDAU	Elikim	7
65	FEDER	Yoel	8
66	FLEISCHER	Moshke David	2
67	HALPERN	Moshko	5
68	KALMANOVITCH	Fishl	6
69	ZEGERMAN	Mordko	3
70	ROSENEIL	Hadass	2
71	BERGER	Abraham Moshko	1
72	FLAKSER	Mordko	4
73	BRIKS	Ephraim	3
74	FRENKEL	Shmuel	5
75	ZUKER	Chava	5
76	STERNFELD	Shia	3
77	BAUMFELD	Mordechai Yosef	3
78	ZIMMERMAN	Yechiel	5
79	KAUFMAN	Itzko	5
80	GRINSPAN	Mala	3
81	HILF	Rivkah	3
82	KLIEGER	Menashe	2
83	KAUFMAN	Shimon	3
84	KORN	Rashe	6
85	LERNER	Shlomo	2
86	MINTZ	Israel Mendel	7

87	SCHWARTZ	Benjamin	5
88	WACHS	Aharon Leib	3
89	ZISSHONIG	Nachum	7
90	BEITCHER	Yosef	5
91	STEMMER	Itsko Hersh	3
92	ZISSER	Matis	5
93	BRUNER	Kyla	4
94	BEITCHER	Yosef David	2
95	PECH	Blima	2
96	ZAMLER	Raphael	5
97	FEDER	Rivkah	2
98	HALPERN	Hersch	8
99	SHTICH	Perla	3
100	HOFF	Wolf	5
101	SHTEMER	Mindla	1
102	COHEN	Chaim	5
103	FROST	Benjamin	7
104	SCHATSKAMMER	David	6
105	MONTOG	Raizla	4
106	BRONSBERG	Tzviah	6
109[1]	NADEL	Mala	4
110	KOIL	Berko	5
111	HARMELIN	Hinde	4
112	INGBER	Sarah	4
113	KLEINER	Ella	6
114	BRAVERMAN	Devorah	3
115	NICKELSBERG	Moshko	4
116	HILF	Leib	5
117	MAIMON	Aharon	4
118	HOCHMAN	Meyer	5

119	LICHTFELD	Chezkel	1
120	SPRINGER	Leib	8
121	KOTLAGE	Shmuel Itzik	6
122	CHESSNER	Yankel	5
123	RIEDER	Braneh	4
124	ELBOIM	Chana	4
125	LERNER	Ella	3
126	ARBETFELD	Yankel	6
127	ZILBER	Feige Leah	3
128	ROITMAN	Abraham	2
129	SHMIRER	Hadassah	3
130	OBERFERSCHT	Yechezkel	5
131	KOIL	Abraham	5
132	SHISSEL	Gitla	1
133	MITZNER	Rivkah	1
134	MELDINER	Ephraim	5
135	GARFINKLE	Chana	4
136	BLEIWEISS	Raizla	1
137	HALPERN	Nicha	5
138	KINIGSWALD	Chaya	7
139	KINSTLICH	Zanvel	5
140	FRANK	Baile Itte	1
141	WEINSHELBOIM	Frume	3
142	SEIDWEBER	Pinchas	4
143	WALDMAN	Esther	3
144	SOBELMAN	Shmuel	8
145	KAUFMAN	Mendel	5
146	FRISCH	Jakov	3
147	SHTIEBEL	Chaya	3
148	KOVERSTOCK	Itzko	3
149	TENTZER	Shmuel	4

150	MEHLER	Shmuel Ber	7
151	BLEI	Shmuel	4
152	REITER	Berish	7
153	ROSENGARD	Leib	6
154	WEISS	Leah	1
155	LEFLER	Yosef	5
156	BRAFMAN	Leah	5
157	BRAFMAN	Itzhak	5
158	BEGLEIBTER	Yakov	7
159	FASS	Chaim	4
160	WEISSTUCH	Mordechai	4
161	GERMANOVICH	Issar	7
162	SHPIRA	Bina	3
163	ROSENBERG	Shia	6
164	ROTH	Chaim Ber	5
165	HOCHMAN	Yankel	5
166	WALDMAN	Sarah	5
167	WALDMAN	Shmuel	5
168	HOFF	Nachum	5
169	SHIPPER	Abraham	4
170	HOFF	Daniel	6
171	PECH	Shmuel	6
172	FRAMPOLER	Mendel	8
173	MILDINER	Hersch	5
174	EICHENBLATT	Leib	3
175	HOFF	Hinde	4
176	FRAMPOLER	Yosef Aharon	6
177	WALDMAN	Liebe	3
178	ROTH	Tuvieh	2
179	KLEINER	Kayla	3
180	WARTMAN	Abraham Isser	6

181	WEINBERG	Frimet	3
182	WARTMAN	Moshe	4
183	KISLOVICH	Hanoch	4
184	HONIGMAN	Sarah	4
185	WEBER	Yosef	5
186	NOBEL	Yankel	5

[Page 363]

Translators Footnote

.Numbered as per original

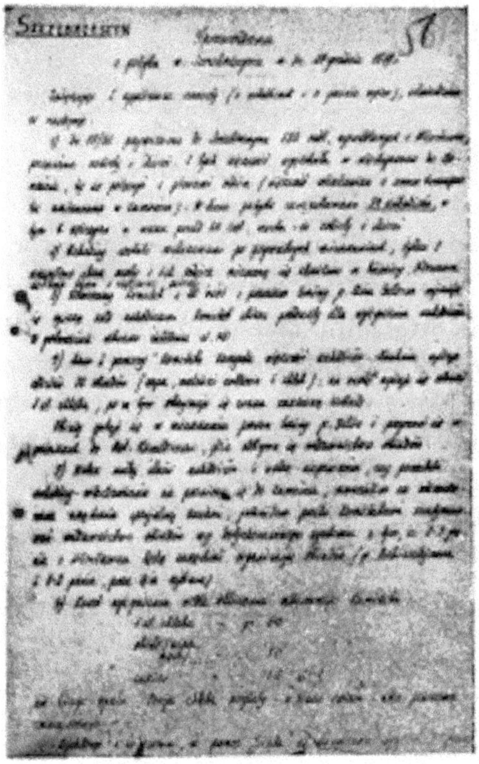

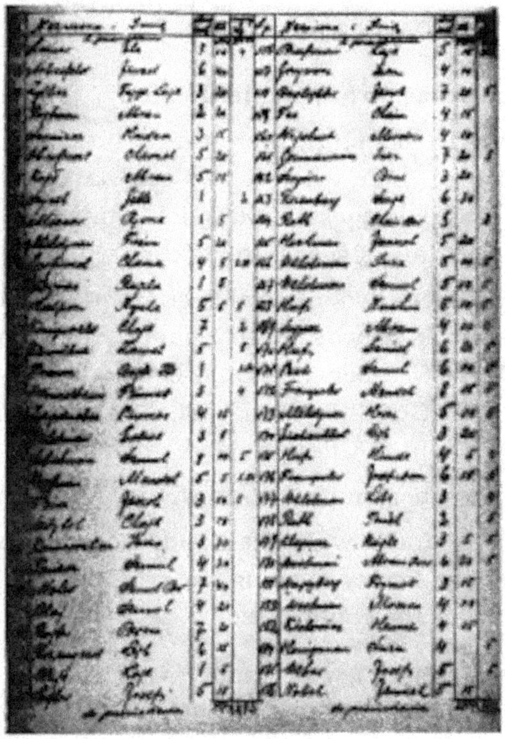

Figures In Our Town

A Gallery of Characters
by Moshe Messinger
Translated by Moses Milstein

Characters from the little shul

Near the big shul, there was a little shul where mostly tradesmen davened. They would come there when it was still dark, in order to recite a few psalms. When dawn began to break, they would quickly finish davening and talking to God before they set out on the daily struggle to make a living.

There were two admirable characters in the little shul. One of them–Chaneh Ba'al Hagula, or as he was called Chaneh Bork, had one task his whole life. Every winter, in the coldest weather, he would be the first to arrive and heat up the stove. Jews must argue with God, not from cold, but from warmth, he used to say. No one began to daven without R' Chaneh's agreement.

I remember that his sons immigrated to America before my time.

The second Jew, Yoske Kandel, or as he was called, "Der Grobe Yoske," had a beer stall. Every Friday evening, he would bring the wine for Kiddush, and he made the Kiddush for the congregation.

Young leader and lecturer

When Zionist thought began to be developed in our home, Shmuel Kliger was among the first of the young who took part in the Poalei Zion movement. He quickly became one of the exceptional leaders and lectures of our shtetl.

He was liked by people of all parties and social classes. He was respected even by political opponents. Because of his weak physiognomy, he seldom made a presentation. But at literary discussions and debates, his participation enriched the knowledge of the young. His words were given respect. There was no social or political question that was considered without his input.

His parents, R' Menashe Kliger, and his wife Feigele, were called, "The Brooks." The name comes from the mother's side. David Brooks, a rich man, married his daughter, Feigele, to Menashe Kliger. In those days, it was known as a "glick shiduch." He was a great scholar, a ba'al menagen, and a well known ba'al tefila. I remember that when he davened on the holidays, people came from far and wide to hear him.

After David Brooks' death, his whole fortune went to his daughter, Feigele. But after, the fortune was ruined, and the family became impoverished.

Shmuel Kliger inherited the character of his mother, and the modesty of his father. He saw how his mother shared her food with others even when she had not enough for herself. At first he was a student, but he had to stop his studies and help his family earn a living.

Active in the American aid committee

I want to give an overview and characterize certain of our social organizations, which operated at a high level, and allowed others to attain a higher level. Especially important were the activities to enable the young to change their standard of living, to bring out a way to achieve better days, to live better.

From his earliest days, Pesach Borek (born in 1911) had to learn a trade in order to help his parents. His parents, Chano and Rivkah, were not wealthy, very honest, hardworking and busy in order to achieve a respectable existence for the family.

Pesach had a strong desire for study and learning. He worked by day, and at night, he sat and studied and read. In the workers circle, he was known as an honorable man. Slowly, he became a leading personality for the workers.

Unsure of his ability to exist in Poland, he immigrated to America at the age of twenty. There, he married his wife who originated from Josefow, and he led a modest worker's life. But even in America, amid the turbulent chaos of business, he did not forget his old traditions, and took part in social works.

After the world learned about the devastation that Hitler brought upon European Jewry, and on our shtetl S., Pesach, without hesitation, established the aid committee for our landsleit. Also involved were many others such as, Hersh (Harry) Tolkop, David Waldman, and Yakov Gerstnblit. Pesach often contributed out of his own pocket, money for social aid.

Whoever examines the archives of the Shebreshiner committee in America, will discover how much effort he put into not only social help, but also in uniting the lost, the scattered in all the corners of the world. Hundreds of request for help, and for help in finding relatives, passed through his hands. The best hours of his free time, he dedicated to his brothers overseas.

*

In this holy work, he was helped by others, as mentioned, founders of the aid committee, who did not forget their old home.

Yakov Gerstnblit was born in 1893. At the age of seventeen, he was delegated to the regional Zionist meeting in Lublin. By day he worked, and at night, by the light of a tallow candle, he studied science. In 1912, he left Poland and came to America, where he completed his university studies in architecture. He received a position of responsibility as architect in a New York hospital. He was married in 1920.

Although involved in establishing himself, he did not forget his Shebreshiner brothers. He was one of the founders of the Shebreshiner committee in 1931, and served as secretary from 1931–1946. He devoted all his energies to the help of his landsleit during the tragic events in Poland.

*

Harsh (Harry) Tolkop was an interesting person. Just as at home he stood for the ideological struggle to develop Jewish youth, also here, he was involved in social struggles. Quiet and modest, he was selflessly dedicated to the aid committee for years.

[Page 366]

Warmhearted characters

by Yehuda Kelner

Translated by Moses Milstein

In writing this article, I cannot help but think that the shtetl characters do not exist anymore, but belong to history. It seems as if I had just seen them, spoken with them.

I have the greatest respect for them, because from them grew all those who built the new progressive life from the old, all the parties, the progress, the youth of the shtetl. I will never forget all these warmhearted characters.

My sorrow is great because they could not live their normal allotted life, but were cut away by savage hands. With my meager talents, I will describe them.

The ben Torah

Moishe Honigman was a fanatic, a ben Torah. He was always in a hurry. He always rushed through the streets, his hat slanted over his eyes so as not to encounter any women.

He was of medium height and thin. He never paid any attention to his attire.

After midnight, he could be seen in his Chasidic shtibl with the Gemora in his hands. He studied until day began. He was there davening with the first minyan. Finished davening, he ate barely enough to sustain the soul, and he spent whole days sitting with the rabbi as a boyrer[1] of Torah law. He had a grudge against the youth who–according to him–were not following the proper way.

The Gretzker

He was called the Gretzker, but no one knew his real name. He was a scholar, a hidden sage. Tall, erect, he walked with measured steps, wrapped in thought and always alone.

If you met him, told him something, he was in no hurry to respond, but would close one eye, smile, and look into your soul. Then he would answer your question, and give his opinion, which was profound, considered, and logical. He was not a great religious fanatic.

He made his living as a Gemora teacher. With a student, he would interpret, and translate and look deeply into his soul, and simply force him to give his opinion on certain interpretations of ancient sages. More than one student received a slap for not knowing what to answer.

He used to bang on the table and yell, "Rambam said so and so, and R' Papa said so and so, and what do you say, you complete goy?"

His students thought him hard, but they loved him.

The watchmaker

He was called Moishe David Zeigermacher[2], and no one knew his family name. He was held in great respect by everyone in the shtetl. He was knowledgeable, an Ilui[3], and had a rabbinical license, but for various reasons he did not want to be a rabbi.

He was not a religious fanatic. His views were modern, although he never showed this. He was a good person, and it was a pleasure to talk with him.

He made a living through his own hands. He repaired watches.

The rich man

The richest man in town was Mordechai Fleischer. He ran a princely home with maids and servants. A hungry person coming to his house left sated.

He was a great philanthropist. As the owner of a sawmill, he would donate wood in the winter for the poor to heat their homes. Passover, he would distribute potatoes to the needy families. He also had a mill.

He reached his status thanks to Graf Zamoysky, the construction of whose sugar factory he supervised, and earned a fortune thereby. In the process, he also built his own home. When Graf Zamoisky learned about this, he forbade Mordechai Fleischer from ever crossing his threshold.

Being a rich man, he bought himself yiches. He got good matches for his children and had sons–in–law like Yankele Mintzberg, and Yermiyahu Rabinovitch.

Teacher waiters

In those days, there were no modern schools, just cheders and melamdim. Among them, R' Motyeh Shpitz was the "top of the heap." When a student finished cheder with R' Yankel Shlomele, or with R' Shlomele Itche Shalom, he went to study with R' Motyeh Shpitz.

Aside from these there were dardekei melamdim[4]; in our language they would be called "folks shulen." They taught the aleph–bet to young children and a bit of chumash. These were: Shlomo Gal (Belfer), Itche Belfer, and Yakov Belfer. Chol HaMo'ed they would visit parents and sign up children for the coming term.

The work did not provide enough money for them, and so the dardekei melamdim also used to serve as waiters at Jewish weddings. The waiters had their own cooks who would prepare food for the wedding guests. There were three cooks: Chava Etl, Iteh Ketzele, Feige, Itchele Beder's wife. They were deathly afraid of the waiters.

I want to note, in several sentences, a few other warmhearted characters in our shtetl.

Velvele Broche–Zoger used to repeat one word several times while davening, until he was certain he had not made a mistake.

Eltshe Weiss never had enough to eat and lived in the greatest need. But he never lost his sense of humor, and was always joking.

Nechamia Anbren divorced and remarried his wife several times.

Buenos Aires

Translator's Notes

1. arbitrator
2. Watchmaker
3. child prodigy
4. Teachers of young children

[Page 369]

Praiseworthy Doers

by Yankel Lam

Translated by Moses Milstein

Three people were particularly praiseworthy in the raising and education of the youth in shtetl.

Yosel Springer, by trade a teacher, really influenced the process of drawing youth out of darkness and ignorance. He spread knowledge and culture among the students. He helped found the General Zionist organization, –HaTehiya." In 1917, along with the teacher, Lazar, and Abraham Itche Becher, he founded the library.

Later, in 1918, he founded the Bund, which included almost all the working-class youth of the shtetl. He was also elected to the city council, and as a Jewish representative, he devoted himself to the general good. He was particularly dedicated to the needy, poor, and the sick. He defended Jewish interests against the antisemitism of the Poles. But thanks to his honesty, he was respected by the better among the Christian population.

*

Particularly influential in the development of the youth was the Hebrew teacher, known as Lazar.

As religious people themselves, they knew how to draw the boys of the Bet HaMidrash to their organizations like HaTehiya and the General Zionists and to the city library.

Moishe Hersh Berger also took part in organizing Zionist endeavors. He and Hersh Getzl Hochbaum and others helped to form HeTehiya. He was elected to city council by the small businessmen and merchants. He founded the Folks Bank. Later he helped organize, unofficially, Betar.

Yankele Honigman took part in Zionist activity from the very beginning. Later he worked for the Bund, principally for the Tsisha.[1] Later, he was active in the underground organization. In 1939, he escaped from S to Vilna, where he was one of the first to fall at the hands of the German murderers in 1941.

Yerachmiel Ginsberg was the director and bookkeeper of the Folks Bank. He held the position from the beginning to its end. As an old bank director he knew well his poor clients: merchants and tradesmen. He did whatever he could to help them. The bank was held in high esteem and was recognized by the authorities.

Brooklyn, New York

Translator's Footnote

1. Zionistishe Yiddishe Shule

[Page 370]

In Appearance, Military–In Spirit, Pioneer
by Emanuel Chmielash
Translated by Moses Milstein

Leibel Licht was the leader of the Brit Hatzahar (the revisionist organization) in Shebreshin. His political talks, and his political views were sincere and evident. In a word, a brilliant speaker and organizer.

I return to the years when I was 16–17 years old. Two organizations were located opposite our house. Leibel moved the library there. It seems that the old library fell apart because of the rivalries of the various parties, and the books were distributed among them.

At the beginning, the Betar library had few books, and Leibel Licht enriched the library. I was a member then, and twice a week, I went to exchange books. As a result, I had the opportunity to engage in discussions with other young people, and became an active member in Brit HaTzahar.

Leibel Licht was interested in everyone's abilities. One evening, he asked me to go to a meeting to be held in a few day's time. When I arrived, they sat me next to Mordechai Yorpest and Berish Macharowski who was the secretary, and wrote the agenda. They asked me and M. Yorpest to join in writing the agenda. A few days later, they asked me to become the secretary of the Brit HaTzahar. It made me proud.

A short time later, the revisionist party split, and I became one of the first members–along with Givertz and Ch. B. Bok–in the "Yudenshtat Partei."

I can still see the imposing entrance of the then commissioner of Betar in Poland, Aharon Propes. The Betar organizations around S. took part in welcoming him. I remember the Betar guards in the carriage he was riding in, the finest boys dressed as high–ranking military men. They marched from the train station like a battalion of army officers.

I know that some of those reading this will say that I have forgotten, or have intentionally omitted, the words to "Die Broine Mundiren."[1] That was then, and nowadays, brown and red are inappropriate. I just want to bring out that Leibl Licht had the audacity to bring, to our small shtetl, the head of Betar in Poland, and to organize such an exemplary march of ordinary Jewish boys who had no prior military training, but who nevertheless looked like "Pulkovnikes."[2]

Leibel Licht created idealistic Zionists among the young. Two of these, from well to do homes, travelled to Israel: Neshe Hochgelernter, and Perl Mabe. They were formed politically in Betar not in HeChalutz, and still were pioneers, worked hard in Israel, suffered hunger, but they passed the test.

He also founded a school for woodworking for prospective immigrants in Binyamin Hersh's woodworking shop. Thanks to that, Biyamin Hersh's whole family went to Israel, as well as others who worked there. That was the result of Leibel Licht's education: in appearance–military, in spirit–pioneer.

Montreal, Canada

Translator's Notes

1.   The Brown Uniforms
2.   Colonels

[Page 372]

The Leader and Teacher of the Bund
by David Fuchs
Translated by Moses Milstein

Yosel Springer dedicated his whole life to the general welfare of society, and the activities of the Bund. He was elected to city council in S from the first elections, and for each election thereafter.

His social work brought him full recognition from the whole Jewish population. Even religious Jews voted for the Bund, arguing that they were not voting for the Bund, but for Yosel Springer.

He did indeed help the poor. People would seek him out at all times of the day. If the matter were urgent, he would forgo his meal, and immediately go to resolve the issue, usually successfully. He was active in every aspect of Jewish social life: City council, Jewish community, Jewish Folks Shule, "Folk's Zeitung," etc. Even the Christian community respected him.

When the Germans entered our shtetl, we were in the Bund office, and we burned all the party documents so they would not fall into the hands of the murderers. Shia Blei was also with us. He buried the party seals. They are probably still lying buried there.

Yosel Springer served our shtetl until the last minutes of his life. Everything changed with the outbreak of the war. Hitler brought an end to all the youthful dreams of the Bund and HeChalutz.

I see, as in a foggy, grey dream, my shtetl, the streets, the blue skies. My heart bleeds; we have lost the melodies of mothers bending over their children's cradles.

I see my brothers, my heimische Jews, worried, hurried, yet always happy. I see you, the young, united as one, the builders, the seekers, the eternal dreamers.

Now ruins stand in our scorched shtetl, and the shadows of desecrated lives weep.

Montreal, Canada, 24.12.52

[Page 371]

Two Activists for the People

by Zanvel Aschenberg

Translated by Moses Milstein

The talented public speaker

My friendship with Berl Koil began in childhood. We played together. I saw how the son of Abraham Hersch Treger–the future public speaker, the best declaimer of modern poetry, lover of music, talented interpreter of L. Kobrin's ",Dorf's Yung,"– brought out awe in everyone.

He devoted himself zealously to reading, and steeped himself in Jewish literary works. He told me with such joy that we would now understand the intent of Peretz Markish in his " Kupeh," because the beloved poet, Melech Ravitch was coming to our shtetl. Along the way from the train station to town we accompanied him, and he really "opened our eyes."

Berel Koil

No one was more fascinated with his virtues than I was. I never stopped wondering how such a flower could develop from such humble soil. Hunger, dampness, smoke from the fallen chimney–this was the air breathed in the house in which he was raised, and yet, how much lust for life, and joy, and gentility he possessed.

From what I know, Berl Koil was one of the first to be taken for slave labor, from which he returned in ruined health and beaten spirit. I heard no living words of him after. In a nightmarish document, I found his name among the martyred. My dear friend, with his warm hearted love that radiated from him to everyone, who gave all his energies to his ideals, to his fellow man, to striving for a better tomorrow, fell in his youth.

The protector of the poor classes

Yosel Springer was born to poor parents. But no one in the family, not the parents, not the sons–Yosele, Leibele, and Avremele–no one complained. On the contrary, the parents shepped naches from their children.

Yosele was the pride and joy of the family. From an early age, he demonstrated intelligence in studies. In cheder, he surpassed his friend, the rabbi's son, in his studies, and helped him out.

The city bestowed honor and love on the shoemaker's son, Yosele, because of his wisdom, which he obtained through self–study, his talents, and his physical energies.

He bequeathed to his children one goal: to help the poor with knowledge and learning, with a will to fight for a better world.

Our great teacher, Y. L. Peretz, taught us about the greatness of the Nemirow rabbi who said that keeping the house of a sick woman warm, is greater than reaching heaven. Yosel Springer, in his day–to–day work for the poor of S., was a Nemirover. His greatest pleasure was when, with his mandate as alderman, he could provide a load of wood for a poor family, a free visit to the doctor for a destitute sick person, get them a bed in the hospital, or send them to a larger city for treatment. He battled with the N.D[1]. majority in city hall to allow more opportunities for Jewish workers. He identified with all the miseries of the poor.

Only one truly needy home was off–limits for him–his own. This he got from his father. He received a greater reward than his father. He was enriched by his work with the Bund that he helped found, the trade union, the school that took its toll on him.

Here, with the school, which should have been the pride of the movement, his true personality was revealed. He battled with all kinds of hardships, and infected others with his boundless enthusiasm in getting a branch of the Tzishah[2] in S.

His stature grew with every branch of the Bund movement in S. : the youth wing, "Zukumft," the doubling of the number of city council seats, winning a Bund seat. That was the greatest victory of his life. He did everything with joy, and dedicated his life to it.

Chasidic Jews openly campaigned for him, because he had the courage to confront the authorities, and stand for office. "In the Kehila, we will send religious Jews; to city hall we will send the bold."

I had the opportunity to get to know him better when we were arrested when the Warsaw Citadel was blown up. Many prisoners were interned in a small cell. We had to sleep in shifts of two hours. He was always one of the last. But when it came to sharing a last cigarette, or a piece of bread, he was always the first. He gave us courage to laugh at "them," the investigators, and their idiotic evidence to force us to confess we took part in a conspiracy.

As the youngest of the group, I was beaten during the investigation. How much pain it caused him! "Why didn't you cry out? We would have broken down the door of the cell!" He yelled at me like a father with a foolish child. Seeing the pain I caused him, I forgot the blows I received, and regretted having told him.

For his entire life, he was ready to sacrifice himself for others, for the community. And with the community, he was led to his death.

Buenos Aires

Translator's Notes

1. Narodowo–Demokratyczne, Polish nationalist party
2. Zionistishe Yiddishe Shule

[Page 376]

The Good–Hearted Doctor

by Berl Entberg

Translated by Moses Milstein

At the end of the First World War, the need was great in Shebreshin, and included broad segments of the city. A group of social activists, however, did not fold their hands helplessly, but tried to do whatever they could to reduce the need.

The first activities took place on Passover, when the poor had no opportunity to obtain matzah. They established a matzah bakery which not only provided matzah for free, but also some earnings for the poor, so they could celebrate Passover.

The spirit of the activity was personified by Simchele Roife, who devoted all his energies to the task.

But aside from this, Simchele Roife (actually a feldsher)[1] was the angel Raphael for the poor of S. Whenever someone fell sick, Simchele was at his bedside. He not only received no fee, but he provided medicines from his homemade laboratory. When he couldn't provide the required drugs, he bought them from the apothecary himself with his own money. In the case where he could be of no help, he sent for the doctors and paid them himself.

I remember that, in 1915, when the Germans occupied our city, an epidemic of cholera and typhus broke out. A hospital for the epidemic was created, and Simchele became the director, because it was full of the poor.

The attitude of the people to Simchele was seen when he finally passed away. All the Jewish poor, the tradesmen and working people, mourned the death of this true friend of the poor. His coffin was followed by his son, and his wife, Chialeh, who was a true partner in life, and as midwife, delivered many children of the poor without payment.

Translator's Footnote

1. A feldsher was a folk doctor

[Page 377]

Mohel and "Doctor"

by Mendl Farber

Translated by Moses Milstein

R' Yankel Nickelsberg, who was called R' Yankel Shimon's, was a Ben Torah, and a good mohel. He did not miss one bris in town, especially not for the poor who had no money for a celebration.

He himself was a pauper. He would somehow obtain the needed money and provide a simche with whiskey and cake. He had modest needs, but at a poor family's bris, he would celebrate along with everyone else.

For a time he was Rosh Kahal, but not like others; he didn't profit from it.

When I studied in the Belzer shtibl with three of my friends, he would sit alone near the stove, and poor women would come and bring their sick children to him to be examined.

He would take the baby from its mother's arms, take its clothes off, and lay it on the shulchan where we studied Torah, and tapping with his fingers on the small body, he would reach a diagnosis. He would then take out a small pencil, and on a scrap of used cigarette paper, he would write out a prescription. He would announce that it would cost "a sixer."

When the poor woman complained that she did not have the money to buy the prescription, he would bang on the wall on the other side of which, his grandfather, R' Eliezer Papieroshnik, was teaching Gemora to children, and call to his grandmother, "Ruchel Leahleh, Ruchel Leahleh! Send me over a sixer! Quickly, it's pikuach nefesh!"

Grandmother, upon hearing it was pikuach nefesh, would run out of the house, open the door of the shtibl, and throw in the "sixer."

In this manner, R' Yankele Shimon's healed the poor children of the shtetl.

[Page 378]

Exaggerated Fanatics
by Mendl Farber
Translated by Moses Milstein

The shtetl was frum.

Frum, frum, but isn't there a limit?...

We must carry out mitzvoth. But it can be taken to extremes...

In this, there were various characters.

A hero for punishing

R' Moishe Honigman was a great scholar, very pious, and strict. As soon as he saw a Jew doing something forbidden, he reacted with his mouth. If that did not help, he laid hands on him, even though he was a weakling. But in such cases, he was a big hero.

It is interesting that he had a son who was far from religious. But, in his son, he saw no evil.

Not speaking during prayers

Shabes, during prayers, R' Yankel Getzl's used to walk around the shul to make sure no one uttered a word during prayers. And, in truth, no one dared to say a word. Prior to his appearance, people would be busily engaged in conversation during davening.

Ready to throw a knife

R' Shmuel, the shoichet, was in his seventies, and full of energy. He was still able to slaughter the strongest ox.

In the Days of Awe, he would daven Musaf for the congregation. He had a voice like a lion. His voice could be heard, even in a congregation of 1000, as if he were standing by your side. He davened heartily and no one was tired of hearing him.

He was very fastidious about kashrut. There was a story that he went once to the matzah bakery on Passover when his matzot were being baked. He instructed one of the women kneading the dough to scrape off the table. She did not do as he wished, so he grabbed a knife, one used to cut the dough, and threw it at her. Thankfully, it missed her eye, striking her just beside it.

It was much talked about in town, and everyone regretted that a person should show such rage. However, he was forgiven, because he did not do it for himself, but for Heaven's sake.

He lived to be over eighty.

A Dybbuk in the kasha

There were two old brothers. They were hardworking shoemakers, and did not partake of the pleasures of life.

In the morning, they would study a page of Gemora and Talmud, after which they would work until minche–maariv, and then they would go again to the shtibl to daven and study, and then, back to work.

When donations were being sought for a public cause, their house was omitted, because it was known they did not have much money. But they would find out, and give the nicest contribution.

One of them was childless. The other had children, and he contributed to their weddings with generosity. One was a Kuzmirer Chasid, the other a Radziner. But that did not prevent them from living together with love.

They were very superstitious. Once, one of them was cooking buckwheat kasha. The kasha began to emit noises like groans. So the brothers gathered together several religious people in order to give the soul, which had entered the kasha, a tikun.[1]

The people told them that these noises were commonly heard in cooking kasha. But they were not persuaded. They argued that a human soul came to them for tikun, because the groaning was exactly like a person's.

With holy mikvah water

The "meshugener of the shtetl" was not always crazy. He had normal periods and behaved quite normally.

When he was seized by his madness, he would wrap himself in his talis and tefillin and begin to daven all kinds of prayers, mostly from Yom Kippur and Rosh Hashana. On any given day, he would recite Kol Nidrei and it was astonishing to hear such a pure, clear, pleasant voice. People would stop and listen. He would daven off by heart, without a siddur. He would daven like this for three days, and include books of the Kabbalah.

He used to say that he was Meshiach ben Yosef, and he was preparing the way for Meshiach ben David. He used to go to the river at night, even in winter and take a dip. It did not bother him. He was always in good health.

He liked to go to the Bet Hamidrash and help out the scholars. He would bring them water, take out the water. His help was not wanted, because he was a gentle person, and a learned man. But to no avail. He did everything he could for them.

It is told that, once, motzi shabes kodesh, when the Chasidim were celebrating a feast for melave malka, he grabbed a pitcher and went to get water. He filled the pitcher in the mikvah, and cooked a borscht with it.

After it was heartily consumed, before the prayers, he said, "Today, we had a good borscht from holy mikvah water!"

What ensued there is hard to describe. Everyone who had eaten the holy borscht, brought it back up again.

From that time on, the Chasidim vowed never to use his services again.

Kiryat Yam

Translator's Footnote

1. Kaballah, salvation of a soul in torment by the prayers of the living

[Page 380]

The Tzadeket (saintly woman)

by Chava Sapian

Translated by Moses Milstein

In the Bet Hamidrash, near the courtyard, the young students used to study Torah, day and night. Religious women used to bring them food.

Among these women was Ruchel Leahle, the tzadeket, Laizer Papieroshnik's wife, who used to fast every Monday and Thursday and slichot days. Everyday, she would bring hot beans to the students. She would also care for those who had nothing to eat, so that they would not, God forbid, go hungry.

Especially Erev Shabes, she would go house to house, mostly to the well–to–do families. People would wait impatiently for her, and give her of the best.

She also had assistants, her neighbors. One of them was Keile Moishe Yosef's, Abraham Burstein's mother, a very honest woman, and a koshere neshome.

[Page 381]

Zenik the Partisan

by Yankel Lam

Translated by Moses Milstein

In 1946, in Ulm, Germany, I meet Zindl Reiber, known among the partisans as Zenik. He was the youngest son of Yosel and Feige Reiber, Yuske Kandel's daughter. With deep sadness, he revealed to me only a few drops of the well of tears filled with suffering and death that he was drowning in.

Hundreds of Jews fled to the forests, mostly to the Kasabader forest, with the frail hope of saving their lives. Among these were Zenik and his family.

He told me, "After days of hunger and thirst, we were forced to look for food in the nearest village. When we returned bringing food, we found all of our dearest ones, almost my entire family slaughtered, together with many other Jews. "

"My brother and I, and some other young people, fled deeper into the woods. We acquired weapons–rifles and bullets, and began attacks against the murderers knowing full well that the game could not be won...We joined with other partisans and kept on attacking but our numbers kept diminishing. "

"My brother and I avenged our parents.... After Mandza, Zeftl Reiber's daughter, fell in battle, my brother was wounded in the arm. Not wanting to fall into the hands of the murderers, he took his own life with his last bullet. "

"I wandered in the never ending forests until Izbice, my only friend the rifle on my shoulders, under my coat. I got into the Izbice ghetto, and looked up the Pelz family. I encouraged them to leave, and guided them out, one by one, to the forest. As a result, twelve of them survived to the liberation."

I spoke to him at length, trying to reawaken some hope in him. My gaze was concentrated on his characteristically good-natured face in which only some outlines of the blossoming youth that once was remained. I saw no trace of happiness anymore, no sign of a future.

The abnormal conditions of his life–nights without sleep, days without food– created medical complications in this, not yet mature, boy. In 1948, he underwent an operation, and at the age of twenty-two, he breathed his last.

Brooklyn, New York

The Great Scholar, Rav Yechiel Blankman

May God avenge his blood

by Rav R'Avraham Golshmid

Translated by Yocheved Klausner

When R'Yechiel Blankman was appointed rabbi in Szczebrzeszyn, the community received a letter from the ADMOR, the Tzadik from Sokolow, saying that a great light was beginning to shine in Szczebrzeszyn, and, paraphrasing a verse from Isaiah 12:6 he added: Cry out and be joyful, inhabitants of Szczebrzeszyn, for a great man is sitting amongst you.

My father z"l told me, that when rabbi Blankman would come to Zamosc to take care of community matters, his lodging would be in our house. He enjoyed discussing verses of the Torah and debating the fine points of the Law. My father would stress the fact that he had a very sharp mind, and in addition, he was an excellent speaker, a genius in rhetoric, explaining and arguing the Scriptures and the Midrash in a modern way.

His articles and commentaries were printed in the book Sefer Habe'er [The Book of the Well] by the Rav R'Zvi Hirsh Frueling z"l (the rabbi of Biscovice) and in monthly magazines. With all his heart he was devoted to educating the young in the spirit of Torah and Judaism.

His son, Meir'l, may God avenge his blood, was already well known at the age of 15, and a great future was predicted for him. He studied at the Yeshiva Chachmei

Lublin [The Sholars of Lublin], under the guidance of the Head of the Yeshiva, our teacher and rabbi R'Meir Shapira z"l. At the funeral of Rav Shapira, R'Blankman's son gave the main eulogy.

When the Nazis besieged Szczebrzeszyn, before the occupation in 1939, Rav Blankman said in his sermon, among others: "The lions are hunting for prey and asking for their food. They gather at sunrise and are hungry. They are seeking out their food and when the sun is shining high in the sky, they are hiding with their finds. But the Nazis are doing their evil deeds, without any shame, at high noon."

Rav Yechiel Blankman perished with all the Szczebrzeszyn, martyrs. May God avenge his blood.

The Rav R'Avraham Golshmid

Son of Rav R'Chaim z"l

Head of the religious court in Zamosc

Author of the book Zecher Chaim

[Page 384]

The Cheerful Grandfather

by Ephraim Farber

Translated by Moses Milstein

Shebreshin gave rise to many interesting personalities. One of these was my grandfather, Moishe Farber (Kliske), z"l. Neither the winds of Haskala, nor modernity had any effect on these stubborn Jews. For hundreds of years, religious ideas, which did not diminish with time, were deeply rooted in them.

My grandfather was a simple man. Imbued with common sense, he followed in the footsteps of our great–grandfathers. He bubbled with folk wisdom, with folk humor. He had a clear mind and was capable of scholarly study. In the fallen, in the oppressed, he saw his fellow man. Quietly, without clamor or advertisement, he helped the needy. It hurt him to see injustice, and the deeds of the bloodsuckers which were not unknown in the Jewish community. His personal philosophy about the daily problems of life was a wonder to behold.

During Sukkot, as a child, I used to eat with my grandfather in the sukkah.[1] There, his approach to life was revealed to me. Like a bubbling well, his knowledge about religion poured from his lips. He did not hold with the rabbis and their leadership. In his opinion, a true rabbi should travel on foot, and eat black bread with garlic! He believed that the pidyon of rich Chasidim should be immediately distributed to the poor. And if such a rabbi did not exist, he was no Chasid.

Elul, when even the fish in the river were trembling, was the season of cheshbon-hanefesh.[2] Erev Yom Kippur, he would take a dip in the river Wieprz. It could be a rainy, foggy day, with strong winds, the kind of day common during autumn in Poland, but it did not bother him. Bathing Erev Yom Kippur was an ancient custom for him.

I keep remembering his witticisms, his aphorisms, and jokes. For example, a Shebreshiner came to him with a question: "R' Moishe, what use do you have of your swamps? (He had a few hectares of marshy fields)". He answered, "When Meshiach comes, the mud will be transformed into sugar cakes, and the water into Baczewski whiskey. And all Shebrishiner Jews, regardless of rich or poor, will enjoy it."

*

One winter morning at dawn, going to open the shul, which was closed by two massive wooden doors reinforced with iron, he beheld a strange sight: A figure, with a talis over his head, davening before the oren kodesh...

My grandfather used to say that he was not afraid of the dead, only of the living. So he called to the one from the other world to return to his rest. It turned out that this was a Shebreshiner Jew who had stayed behind after ma'ariv and spent the night in the shul. My grandfather's "ani ma'amin was not a primitive fanaticism, but a heartfelt belief.

*

As a young man, he studied in the Bet Hamidrash and was an expert in halachah. He knew Yiddish, Hebrew, Polish and Russian perfectly. According to my father, he wrote rhyming verses in Hebrew. Unfortunately, they were lost along with his prose works. My father remembered a few lines.

He became the only shames in the shul. The rabbi would consult him on various laws and matters relating to burials. He was a shining ba'al koreh and had a beautiful bass voice. What a pleasure it was to hear his haftorah!

He was loved and praised in the whole shtetl, both by Jews and Christians, by rich and poor. He was afforded the greatest respect, because a Jew like him was exceptional. He was always happy, merry, content with all that God has created.

I dedicate these words to my grandfather, in place of the tombstone in the Shebreshiner cemetery desecrated by the Nazi vandals.

Kiryat Yam, 1958

Translator's Notes

1. Gift to a Chasidic rabbi after a meeting

2. Examination of one's soul

[Page 386]

Hard work, beautiful manners

by Ephraim Farber

Translated by Moses Milstein

Everybody in the shtetl loved the Dreier family. The grandfather, Moishe Chaim, made a living as a carpenter. The grandmother, Machle, also worked, and brought help to the needy.

*

While it is still dark outside, and the only sounds are the crowing of the black crows on the church steeples, and a fine autumn rain is falling, Moishe Chaim hurries along with a talis and tefillin in hand to the first minyan. After davening, he can't afford the luxury of sitting around until late in the day like the batlonim. The need to make a living makes him hurry his davening.

He's also a member of the Chevrah Kedusha. He receives no money for this holy work. He does it "l'shem shamayim." Someone, after all, has to look after graves going back 120 years. He will have something to complain about when he gets to the Bet din shel male and gives an accounting of his deeds in this sinful world.

*

Babe Machle wore a bonnet over her wig from which fringes appear giving her a coquettish appearance.

Hidden in the creases of her old face are the hard bygone days, the mother's care for her children, the sleepless nights.

Most of the time, she is occupied with her small stall in the large market hall. The stall contains: buttons, thread, needles, combs–in brief, a "haberdashery." Most days of the week, she looks for customers, who rarely show themselves. The big "pidyon" is market day which takes place on Tuesdays.

On cold winter days, she warms herself with a pan of glowing coals which she keeps at her feet covered with her long petticoat. The pennies earned are an important contribution to the household.

Aside from her "big haberdashery business," she is busy with her twelve children.

In her free time, she helps needy families and sick widows of which there are many in the shtetl.

*

Machle's daughter, Mattl, followed in her mother's footsteps. She was "goodness itself," compassionate towards her fellow man and his suffering.

She would discreetly gather chales, and fish and other dishes from the better-off families. Quiet as an angel, she would slip into a house whose poverty glared from every corner, and with a mild, warm smile spread on her face she would put down the basket of goods. She was careful to do this so no one would see, in order not to shame those in need.

Her reward was the happiness in knowing that Shabes would not be spoiled here, and a family would enjoy the Oneg Shabbat.

*

One of Babe Machle's sons, David, dealt in fruits, which added a bit to their income.

Right after Purim, matzoh baking began. It was a supplement to carpentry. The kneading was done mostly by women and girls. It was hard, exhausting work. Also employed were a redler[1]. a baker, and a water-carrier. The work began at dawn and carried on until the middle of the night.

From the hard-earned money, they saved enough for a dress for someone, or a coat for the husband for yom-tov.

*

Only a small part of this extensive family survived the Hitler plague. Some immigrated to Eretz Israel before the war. Some fled the deluge for the Soviet Union. The rest were dispersed over the whole world: Austria, Canada, Argentina, and Israel.

May these simple words serve instead of a tombstone in the ruined cemetery in Shebreshin.

Kiryat Yam

Translator's Footnote

1. Worker who perforates matzohs.

[Page 388]

Taking Care of the Needy

by Rachel Greenspan

Translated by Moses Milstein

My father's, Hershel (Zvi) Ingber's, lineage stemmed from a generation of rabbis. He had his rabbinical diploma, but he did not make his living from it. He worked as a shipping clerk for the railway. When his job required him to work on Shabes, he quit, and opened a food store, in order not to desecrate the Sabbath.

He was a man of faith and Torah, and strongly believed in God's providence, the protector of the people of Israel. He had a profound, but not a fanatical belief, tempered with modernity, which was already beginning to be felt in the Jewish street. He also mastered foreign languages.

He was not unacquainted with Zionist thought. He sensed the storm that was approaching Polish Jewry, seeing the signs in local antisemitism, and the persecutions that were becoming more evident every day. His conclusion was that there was no future for Jews in Poland, especially for the young.

After Hitler came to power in Germany in 1934, he counseled his children, Rachel, Moishe, and Devorah, to make aliyah to Israel. After I met my husband, a refugee from Berlin, we received a certificate from Germany, and, Erev Pesach, 1935, we came to Israel.

*

My mother, Faige Weissfeld, was a tsadeket[1]. She had a compassionate heart, and helped the sick, orphans, and widows seeing it as her responsibility.

When Shabes approached, she began to worry that, God forbid, Jews should not have every opportunity to celebrate Shabes properly, as God had ordered–with meat and fish, and wine for Kiddush. She went around in the shtetl, and gathered whatever she could. She also urged the fortunate not to forget the hungry. She wanted her little reward in the world to come, like the woman in Y.L. Peretz's story who was satisfied to be the footstool of her husband, the scholar, in the Garden of Eden.

My grandfather, Zalman, was a community representative. He was elected as alderman in city hall, where he zealously pursued the agendas that the Jews expected of him.

After World War I, when there was great need in Jewish homes, he strove, through various means, to get help from American Jews. His goal in life was to ameliorate the needs of the suffering. Help consisted of food and clothing and words of encouragement. He kept the American aid locked in his store, and he guarded the key.

He was afraid that his wife, Feige, might take a little flour, sugar, or a garment for her children. He took care that his hands would be "clean."

There was also a communal kitchen run by volunteers, and the food was distributed for free to the needy. The Bubbe, Feige, contributed much to the management of the kitchen.

*

When a rabbi was being chosen, among the many candidates was R' Yecheiel Blankman, z"l. There was bribery during the elections; voters were paid for their votes. My father wanted a progressive rabbi, one who could speak Polish well, and could represent the Jewish population honorably before the state authorities. To that end, he supported R' Blankman, and brought him to the big shul to give a droshe[2].

An opponent to his candidacy gave my father a shove, and his glasses and siddur fell to the floor. A few days later, the guilty one–Chaim Einbren–walked through the market in his socks, and begged his pardon and forgiveness. In the end, my father's candidate, R' Yechiel Blankman, was elected. It later turned out to be a fortunate decision.

Hershel Ingber was one of the ten prominent Jews murdered by the Nazis on September 1, 1939 in the center of Shebreshin.

Jerusalem

Translator's Notes

1. A saintly woman
2. sermon

מנחם מסינגר — הנאיבי בן ה־80

מאת אריאלה ראובני

הצייר הנאיבי מנחם מסינגר
מחיפה, שהגיע בימים אלה ל־
גבורות, בחר לציין את יום הו־
לדתו בשתי תערוכות: בגאלריה
של גילדמן בחיפה ובגאלריה 19/4
בתל־אביב. הנושא המרכזי בשתי
התערוכות הוא השלום, שמסליו
בעיני מסינגר הם חיות הנצורה
ומים צוהר עם כנפים, על רקע
נופה של ירושלים (אגב, הגב־
עים השולטים בציוריו המרכזי־
נים של מסינגר הם כחול־תכול,
צהוב, כסף וזהב).

מנחם מסינגר נולד בעיר קטן
בגליל, למשפחת חוסידי מתבג
שעסקו במשך דורות רבים בע
צוב השמימי קדושה ופוחחו ל־
בתי־הכנסת ולמבנסים, בכל הנראה,
מכאן נגזר גם שם משפחתו.
מסינגר — חרט גויסת, בילדותו
לספד ב "חדרי ונובד בגיל 11 בני־
לך לסייע לפרנסת המשפחה. הוא
עשה זאת על־ידי גילוף מקלות
הליכה.

ידידו מספרים כי בעודו נער
גילה עניין רב במוסיקה ובשירה
יהיה רגיל מאד למרצת טוף, בי־
שנת 1992 עלה לארץ והתארגם
בעיקר מצבותות בניית, לצייר התחל
רק בגיל 70, לאחר שהחלים מי
יתקף לב, ציוריו הראשונים,
שבהם הקסד לרשים את התאי־
שים הדקים ביותר, המניעו ל־
מירה רבת את הציור הנורט. הוא
הורבה לצייר בעלי כנף, פרחים,
מלאכים ובתי כני. כן צייר
את סיפורי התניך וסיפורי אגדות
ומעשית עם ארמונות מלכים,
שירות ובצלות אב.

חדשים אחרים לאחר שאחז
מסינגר במכחיל נערכה לו תע־
רוכת־יחיד בחיפה, שהוקנ אר
תה למענני בתו חנה שהוקנע
קולנוע לשעבר, שנוספמה לאמור־
נית שלו ולוא הסכה מאמצים ל־
יחסי־ציבור כדי לעשות שם ל־
יצירות אביה. בצקמת התערוכה
הראשונה בא צייר תערוכות, בי־
ארין ופמחזו לה, ובנאירגונו החלו
מסייעים גם מוסדים תקלעדים
ליחתי צימור. כיום מצירות יצי־
רותיו של מסינגר באוסים פר־
סים בארץ ובחוץ־לארץ ובמוזיאו־
נים בישראל. באחיו־ב, בגרמ
ובנראסל. לפנו חדשים אחרים
זה הצייד בגרם ראשון בתחי־
רות ארצית של ציור על נושא
הים.

כאשר מבקשים מהאמן הקשיש
להסביר את ציוריו־המיצרתיל ואת
סמליו הוא נוטה ברצון. חלק מי
ניסאוו הוא שואב, לדבריו, מי
ניסמרית חנה, למשל, בטנת הי
90 לפדינת ישראל הוא רואה
רמוס מבטיחים לבוא השלום הי
נכסם והוא נותן לכך בישרי ב־
ציוליו האחראינוס.

"אם מוסיסים עשר שנים
ומנין", שהם בנ׳סטריות, לעשרים
שנה, שתן כי בגיטסריה, מתבלים
את הסלום כי, שבה פיתח הפסיק
בתפילה "כי לעולמ", מפביר
מסינגר. "האות ל — הראששונה
במהה, לשולם — מבטאאת את ה־
נפט ותרדוהיות של והם היהורי,
ל נשול י הו שין, כיימרי 300.
אגי חוזה אישמית, כי בשנת הי
90 למדינת ישראל יבוא השלום
שיימשך לפחות 300 שנה".

דמותו של הפלאן, המופיעה
ברכים מציריו של מסינגר, מד־
פלת — לדבריו — את רוח של
אליהו הנביא, שהוא נביא הי
ישלום, הסם הטאתר הוא סימו של
אליהו, "שיביא אלינו, אם ירצה
השם, בלומדית המשיח".

כמה מבקרי אמנות, ישראלים
ורים, משבים את עבודותו של
מסינגר ויש אף הפטומדים אותו
לפבתא מום באירציב ולרוסל ב־
צרפת, עם זאת זם מודיישים, כי
אין הוא נוסמאלני. אורבא, הוא
רואה בציור כלי העשי לסטר ל־
ישת את העולם סמו אמו חיים,
"מסינגר משתמש בשפה ויסואלית,
המבסאאת אידיאות שבדרך כלל
מוצאים רק במתוימ. ובמה ייחוי
חי", סתוב מבקר ברחילצי, מבקרה

ישראלית מצויינת כי מסינגר שו־
אב את הישראל מן התנין, מ
התיסטוריה, היהודית ומהגאו־
גרסיה של הארץ, אך גם מאיידינ׳
מולין, צייר הנוף של מכתירים.
לדעתה, תמונות עתיקות של עד
לי רגל מטיילי בארץ הקודם.
התמונות המבוגנות בתערוכה
"גנבאית, שהנושא העיצרי שלתן,
באמרה, הוא השלום. שיזות מ
יצירותית הקדמות של מסינגר.
איטית, נראה לי כאילו אבד משהו
מן האותנטיטית לגברביתה שלו, מכן
הילרות ומהרמיטז המובלב שאאי־
ינני את הפושמה בנבני המוב, ה־
תמול, הבסף והזהב סנגו, לדאי
תי, באיזיתם של הצירים ונסלו
מהם את חוש האנדריהחיוי שׁ
כ"צין את צירו הראשונים, ו־
חבל.

דבר

יום רביעי, א' באדר א' תשל"ת.
8 בפברואר 1978

[Page 390]

Menachem Messinger – the Naïve 80–Year–Old
by Ariela Reuveni
Translated by Yocheved Klausner

Messinger with his paintings: Peace in bright colors

The naïve painter Menachem Messinger from Haifa, who reached these days the age of eighty, chose to mark his birthday by two exhibitions: at the Goldman Gallery in Haifa and the 131/2 Gallery in Tel Aviv. The main topic of the two exhibitions is Peace, whose symbols in Messinger's eyes are the clear–white dove and a white, winged horse, on the background of Jerusalem. The dominant colors in Messinger's later paintings are light blue, yellow, silver and gold.

Menachem Messinger was born in a small town in Poland, to a family of blacksmiths, who, for many generations made ritual objects for synagogues and churches. This was probably the source of his name Messinger – blacksmith. In his childhood he went to the heder, and at the age of 11 he had to help with earning a living for his family. He did that by carving walking sticks.

His friends relate that as a young boy he showed interest in music and poetry and was very observant, and sensitive to various landscapes. In 1932, he made Aliya and made a living mostly by working in the building and construction business. Only at the age of 70 did he begin to paint, after recovering from a heart attack. His first paintings, in which he paid meticulous attention to the minutest detail, are reminiscent of Persian art. He painted birds, flowers, angels and prayer–houses. He also painted bible stories and legends, with palaces, kings, castles and witches.

Only several months after he began using brush and palette, his daughter Hannah arranged an exhibition in Haifa. Hannah, a former movie actress, became his manager and made every effort to publicize his work. Hannah was helped by professional public relations firms, and more exhibitions followed in Israel and abroad. Today, Messinger's works are found in private collections and in museums in Israel, USA, France and Brazil. Several months ago, the artist won first prize in a competition on the topic "the sea."

The elderly artist willingly consents when asked to explain his paintings and symbols. Some of his themes are drawn from the Gimatria [the numerical values of the Hebrew letters]. For example, in the 30th year of the State of Israel he finds hints to the much awaited peace, and reflects that in his paintings. Patiently and carefully, he explains his calculations, with examples.

The angel that appears in many of his paintings symbolizes the spirit of the prophet Eliyahu [Elijah], the prophet of peace. The white horse is the horse of Eliyahu, who will come to us, God willing, together with the Messiah.

Some of the art critics, in Israel and abroad, praise Messinger's works and some even compare him to Grandma Moses in the United States and Rousseau in France. However, he is not nostalgic; in painting he sees a tool that may improve and beautify the world in which we live. "Messinger is unique in that he uses visual language to express ideas that we can usually find only in written text" – writes a critic in Brazil. A critic in Israel observes that Messinger draws his inspiration from the Bible, Jewish history and the geography of Israel, as well as from secular events. His landscapes remind one, she said, of antique paintings by pilgrims in the Holy Land.

The paintings in the present exhibition, whose topic is, as mentioned above, peace, differ from Messinger's earlier works. Personally, I think that they lack some of the naïve authenticity, childhood charm and extended imagination that characterized his earlier paintings. The exaggerated use of the colors yellow, blue, gold and silver impaired, in my opinion, the quality of the paintings and removed some of the legend–like beauty that characterized his earlier paintings.

Davar
Wednesday, 1 I Adar5738
8 February 1978

[Page 393]

Old Szczebreszyn

Shebreshin of Long Ago
by Dr. Zygmunt Klukowski
Translated from Polish by Abraham Wolfson
Translated by Moses Milstein

The Polish physician, Dr. Zygmunt Klukowski, who lived in S. for 22 years, occupied himself greatly with the old and new history of S. We present here, with some abridgements, a chapter of his work that is distinguished by objective and scientific observations.

Various Polish archives, particularly those of the Zamoyski's in Warsaw, in Zwierzyniec, and in state archives in Lublin, and the oldest Shebreshiner city books, exist barely untouched. Researching this material is beyond my capabilities. But I used to take note of every bit of information about S. that would come my way. In this way, I was able to collect a little historical information and to acquaint myself with S's history better than most.

I used to give lectures about S. and her history. I had to prepare myself well for them. Others, who were interested in history, profited from my material.

Early history

S. is a very old city. Her first recorded date is 1352. In that year, king Kazimierz Wielki, stayed here. But the community of S. existed several hundred years prior.

The so–called zamchisk was once a fortified city, evidence for which are the remains of fortified walls and moats, and shards of pottery. Names of neighboring villages from the eleven hundreds are encountered in Nestor's Russian Chronicle. One can deduce from that that S already existed then, lying on a trade route that stretched from south to north.

In the time of Ludwik Wegierski, a large part of the Belz and Chelm district, with the spacious Shebreshiner and Torobiner estates, belonged to Dimiter of Goraj, upon whom the king, Wladislaw Jagiello, bestowed extraordinary privileges. He installed him at the head of the nobility that lived around S., creating a form of independent duchy. The "Shebreshiner Herr" had much power. At times of war, he was at the head of the entire noble class in the region. In times of peace, he was the judge, hosting the aristocracy at his Shebreshiner residence. There he was accorded great respect, and he bestowed lands with generosity. This was practically the only time that an independent duchy existed in Poland.

Dimiter of Goraj, in 1393, financed the construction of the first parish church. His heir, Jan Amor Tornowski, was very preoccupied with his properties and his subjects. He established markets, and in order to encourage merchants, he freed them of taxation. He founded various guilds, bestowing special privileges on the shoemakers guild.

Industry and trade developed to such an extent that, in 1492, king Jan Olbracht, in a special act, established which routes the Shebreshiners merchants had to travel through in Greater Poland. Many merchants travelled through S. from south to north, paying the required toll, eg, for a wagon with merchandise–2 groschen, for an ox–1 groschen, for a wagonload of salt–a measure of salt, and so on. This brought much revenue to the city.

After the death of J. A. Tarnowski in 1500, S belonged to the Tarnowskis for another 20 years. Later, it was given as a dowry to the Kmitas. Quarrels about the inheritance began between the two families, which lasted for a long time, and other magnate families made claims to S as well. In 1555, king Zygmunt August adjudged the dispute and gave the rights to S. to the family of Greater Poland.

The names of the Gorki sons, Andrzej and Stanislaw, are still remembered in the legends told by the oldest S. residents. The Gorkis confirmed the many privileges given to the city earlier. They renovated the "defence keep ," of which there are traces remaining on the "zamchisk." Their permanent residence was in Greater Poland, and while they were entertaining in S., the keep was tumultuous and cheerful, in the magnate custom. It was extraordinarily lively as the Gorkis were social people.

The Gorkis were greatly interested in religious matters. They bestowed freedom on all religious sects. They built a Greek Orthodox church, and they converted the parish Roman Catholic church into a Calvinist one, and opened a synagogue nearby. The well–known fighters of the Reformation, Stanker and Felix Kreutziger, who came from S., sought the protection and trusteeship of the local magnates. S. reached the highest level of development at the time.

Rise and fall

Various reasons led to the halt in development and later–a gradual decline. The terrible fire of 1583, which broke out at night in the keep, created much damage. The keep was destroyed, as well as the documents detailing the privileges from the king. The fire broke out so suddenly, that the inhabitants of the keep barely escaped with their lives.

In the same year, king Batory, as a result of the efforts of Andrzej Gorki, renewed the privileges. The Gorkis, for the good of S., confirmed and even broadened the Magdeburg laws that reigned in S. for a long time, and brought in changes that benefited all of the citizens.

The Gorkis did not rule for very long. In 1592, the last of the Gorkis, Stanislaw, died, and the Czarnkowski family took over the estates. In 1593, Jan Zamoyski, bought the city and the surrounding 35 villages, and incorporated them into his Ordinat, which was created in 1589. Subsequently, he founded a magnificent city, Zamosc, in the territory of his estates, and he was especially devoted to its development. From that time on, S lost its importance, its special character, and its decline began.

S. took on the same position as all other shtetls in the Ordinat, about which Zamoyski cared less than about his beloved Zamosc. Then he founded the Franciscan monastery, and nearby, the cloister of the Holy Trinity, today's cloister of the Holy

Katarzyna near the hospital. Aside from this, he liquidated the Catholic Temple and returned to them the parish cloister.

In the 17th century, religious warfare was widespread. The Arians [1] were treated with great hatred, and excesses were committed, for example, during the funerals of the Arians. This forced Tomasz Zamoyski, in 1637, to issue a decree expelling the Arians from S., "where Arians and disciples of New–Christian sects have settled."

The city suffered greatly from attacks by Tatars, Turks, and Cossacks. In 1672, the Tatars set fire to the city and plundered it. Masses of people suffering from various epidemics used to arrive. The dead from the plague were carried to a separate cemetery outside of town.

S. was sometimes the arena for historical events. In 1672, the so–called Shebreshiner Confederation was organized with the goal of defending the power of the Hetmans. The meetings took place in the cloister of the Holy Katarzyna, and Jan Sobiewski took part when he was still "Hetman Wielki Koronny."

In spite of everything, many new guilds arose in the 17 century, and reached the highest level of development: bakers, barrel–makers, shoemakers, furriers, linen workers, textile workers, smiths, wheelwrights, locksmiths, sword makers, harness makers, coppersmiths, goldsmiths, brush makers, rope makers, weavers, and butchers. The names and numbers of the guilds give testimony to the high development of trade and industry in S.

The 18th century was not particularly noteworthy. The city gradually declined. S became part of Austria during the breakup of Poland. Austrian coins can still be found buried in the ground today.

New development

S. began to develop anew at the beginning of the 19th century when Zamosc was no longer the possession of the Zamoyskis, and their attention was diverted to S. which was nearer their home. In 1811, they transferred the Provincial school that had been closed in 1809. In 1812, they transferred the hospital of Holy Mercy from Zamosc to the building of the previous monastery.

The city was revitalized. New people arrived: teachers, students, and visitors. New schools and houses were built.

The health service of the Ordinat decreed that the head doctor should be located here. A hospital for venereal diseases for peasants was established since the monks opposed their admission to the general hospital. Lady Teophila Reder opened a private high school for girls offering three grades. A Sunday trade school was organized. Trade flourished. More and more people arrived. But the main role was played by the Provincial school which attracted talented teachers and students.

The Provincial school was under the direction of the influential Stanislaw Zamoyski, senator and Voivod, and it, and the hospital owe their existence to him. The numerous members of the Zamoyski family, who mostly lived in Klemensow, had a positive effect on the region. Andrzej Zamoyski organized well–attended conferences of landowners. Before the January uprising, the most important landowners of almost all Poland convened, creating an impact on the nearby shtetl.

Because of the authority of Stanislaw Zamoyski, Shebreshin and the Provincial school suffered less than other places from the Russification policy that followed the November Uprising. Nevertheless the school was closed in 1852 as inimical to the Russification policies. It was a severe blow to S.

The city markedly declined. It did not recover from this, even after liberation, and in spite of the establishment of a teacher's seminary and a high school. It never returned to its former prominence.

During the revolution

The quiet way of life was disrupted in 1831 during the November Revolution. I found a short description of the events in the memoirs of the well–known pedagogue, Vincenti David, written in 1887. The following is a short excerpt from his memoirs.

"Finally, our quiet and work–a–day lives, and our well established order in the Shebreshiner schools, were disrupted for a time. The news that a revolt had broken out in Warsaw, and that the Russians had abandoned the capital and the borders of the kingdom, elicited great joy among the population. The quiet shtetl, which knew no other politics other than the rule of the stewards, felt called upon to step out on the political arena along with the rest of the country.

In a matter of an hour, the black eagles of the city hall and other institutions were pulled down. Old swords and guns were brought out, cleaned and readied. In the smithies, the smiths worked even on holidays. Agricultural tools were modified into pikes. Scythes were mounted on poles.

The intelligentsia and even the rector called upon the students to arm themselves. They celebrated the unfurling of the flag with prayers in the school. The rector, Zenkowski, addressed the ranks of students and citizens arrayed with home–made weapons. They concluded with the singing of "Jeszcze Polska nie zginela." This occurred in mid–December. Professor Zenkowski and a number of older students went off to the Polish military. Only the younger students remained behind.

After Christmas, the Russian military began reacting. The first to enter S. were the dragoons, with wild beards that made a frightening impression on us. We regarded with fear the giant men who camped in the same place that the students had earlier mustered.

We soon heard news of the decisive battles of the polish army and their heroic leaders on the fields of Grachow, outside Wawer. Every scrap of newspaper was passed fervently from hand to hand, and was commented on, and plans were made for the future as is common in a small shtetl. The joy was greater in the spring when our army entered Lithuania with Dembinski and Gieldung in command, when Chrzanowski and Dwernicki entered the Lublin region, marching on Wolhyn, on the other side of the Bug, while fighting along the way outside Czaczki, and Old–Zamosc.

On that great Thursday, camped in the same schoolyard, Dwernicki's Ulans [2] and the Krakusi [3] with several cannon arrayed, which, I believe, were taken at Czaczki. We dared to approach the cavalry and played with their weaponry. We brought them food and drink from the city for several days. We received them like brothers.

In the heat of spring and summer, cholera broke out in the city for the first time. Horse manure was burned in the market and streets to combat the cholera. But it was of no help. Many families left the city for the neighboring forests. Prayers were conducted in the churches to halt the epidemic, and prayers of thanks were given for any successes. The young priest, Nowokowski, a passionate speaker, after the prayers, told the congregation about the heroic deeds of the leaders. He punished and accused the youth who had not joined the army, identifying them by their names.

Zamosc, the closest fortress, and other points, were in danger of being surrounded. Many clashes occurred in Shebreshin. Cossacks entered the town, and robbed, and beat the Jews, and the townspeople. They were quickly followed by the Ulans or the Krakusi. Once, the Cossacks, as a response to the attacks, determined to take revenge on the town, and on the youth who took part in the skirmishes between the Polish army and the Cossacks. The Cossacks approached the town at night in order to set it on fire, and kill the inhabitants. Panic ensued in the town. Half the city fled to the forests. The shooting could be head in Janow.

But despair turned to wonder. The daring armed themselves. The city policeman, an old army man, and the sexton of the church, raised the alarm. Drumming on the church drum, they gave loud orders, giving the impression that they were a large military contingent. The Cossacks and the Dragoons, who were already on the outskirts, decided to withdraw. Later commands prevented them from taking their revenge."

*

The national liberation movement after the January uprising reverberated more in S. than elsewhere in the Zamosc Powiat (which today encompasses 4 Powiats). S. played a special role in it.

We have very scant details about the revolution itself. Many people enrolled in the party. There was a civil organization. In 1865, the local pharmacist, Antony Topolski was arrested under the charge of leading the revolt.

The first skirmish in the planned attack on the Cossacks on the 30th of January, organized by the party of Lesznice, from the Ordinat of Henrik Gronowski, ended in failure. Many wounded rebels found themselves in the local hospital. Some were buried in the Shebreshiner parish.

Russification efforts

After the failure of the revolution, the Russian powers began to apply a strict Russification policy, trying artfully to implant everything Russian.

I tried to get the elders to write down their memories of that time, but they were mostly illiterate. Some described them to their children who, following my instructions, recorded fragments with dates and names. I had hoped by that to gather important material, but the war interrupted the work.

Those difficult times, when the weak slowly gave up, and the strong tried with all their might to resist the Orthodox priests, gendarmes, and the border police, are being slowly forgotten. Women were, in this case, stronger than the men.

Persecution of the Uniates took on dramatic forms. I will never forget my talks with an old farmer from Zurawice, who told me about the frightful scene that occurred when one of his neighbors, a Uniate, agreed to convert to the Orthodox religion in spite of his wife's objections. When all the formalities were observed, and the communion was underway, his wife went mad with despair, and fell on the priest. This had a frightful effect on her husband, and he refused to continue with the ceremony.

Fascinated by these stories, I tried to gather details about the Uniates in Shebreshin. An 1863 document points out that the Uniate parish was very poor because it had " a very small number of adherents in Shebreshin." In December 1877, the priest, Alexander Gorski, who, it seemed, did not belong to the resistance fighters, signed his letters as "Rector of the Shebreshiner Ortodox parish." Then the Uniates were abolished and the Greek Catholic church was turned into an Orthodox church.

Later, the priest, Timofey Tracz, arrived as rector, and a sad chapter for the Polish Catholics, and especially for the Uniates, began. The priest was himself once a Uniate priest who freely converted to the Orthodox belief and became an ideological Russifier and disseminator of his new beliefs. He led an ascetic life, and his activities took on a fanatical character. With time he became recognized by the highest authorities and became very influential.

He instilled fear in everyone in the Zamosc area. No one opposed him. It must be said that he made great strides in spreading Orthodox beliefs. He carried out his mission without too many reservations: with promises, harassment, threats, and force.

Data from the Zwierzyniec archives show that there were no Orthodox in Shebreshin other than the officials who came to visit occasionally. Aside from the Orthodox church, which was, as mentioned, formerly a Greek Catholic church, the Catholic church near the hospital also became an Orthodox church. The number of adherents to the Orthodox parish grew relatively quickly and consisted of 486 souls at the time.

In 1905, in the first two months after the declaration of the Tolerance Manifesto, the Shebreshiner parish saw 4195 people convert from the Orthodox to the Roman Catholic religion, of which 402 were from Shebreshin and Zamosc environs. The Tolerance Manifesto was a sever setback to the priest, Tracz. All his work was undone with one blow. He could not tolerate this, and struggled with all his might to counter the desertions, but with little effect. These developments profoundly affected his health and hastened his death. He died in 1909.

During World War I, when the Russians left Shebreshin, both churches were closed. The entire Orthodox parish disappeared instantly. In order to wipe out any trace of their former beliefs, families changed the inscriptions of their kin on their tombstones from Russian to Polish. On the instructions of the mayor, someone vandalized Tracz's memorial. His coffin was transferred from near the church, and reburied in the public cemetery.

The preacher of the Roman Catholic parish was then the priest, Grabarski. He was very popular and known for his philanthropic work, even towards Jews. He was very beloved by the Jews. An elderly Jew told me that prayers were said for him for many years in the synagogue.

The era of Russian rule in Shebreshin was grey and sad. The oppression of Russian authority was deeply felt. Social and spiritual activity was minimal. Nevertheless, there was a certain measure of underground activity, such as illegal study. There were various organizations: Macierz Szkolna, N.D., P.P.S.

The external character of Shebreshin was set by the army, a Cossack battalion that was stationed here. The world war broke out, and masses of armies passed through: Russian, Austrian, then again Russian, and later, a longer period of Austrian occupation. Various orientations existed; pro–Moscow, Pro–Austrian, independence movements. Part of the youth went away to the legions.

I heard many stories about the earlier way of life, about the cholera epidemic, about the rapid organization of the Polish school system, about the first months of existence of the Polish state. I asked many people to write about their memories of the pre–war years, and the occupation. I found no one who could, or would, do this. I managed only to get a few fragments of an autobiographical nature.

_____

Translator's Footnotes

1. A Protestant sect

2. Polish light cavalry

3. Polish light cavalry

_____

[Page 402]

Geographic, Ethnic, and Historic Shebreshin

Translated by Moses Milstein

Szczebrzeszyn, in documents, Scebresinum–a city on the left bank of the river Wieprz, Zamosc district, latitude 50° 41' North, and longitude 40° 37' East, on the Zawichost–Uszczilug highway, in the plain of the river, abutted on the west by the so called Shebreshiner mountains, with a sloping cliff, and the ragged valleys of the flat peaks of the Lublin mountains which reach a height of 1000 to 1500 feet above sea level between Goraj and Szczebrzeszyn. The valley of the Wieprz rises to 700 feet. At Krasnistaw, the river is navigable by ships. Outside S., the river reaches 7 fathoms. During flood periods, it covers the fields for half its width.

Two bridges connect S. with the village, Brody. In the south–west, S. is 20 verst [1]from Zamosc, from Janow–Ordinacki–42.75, Bilgoraj–32.50, Krasnistaw–40, the train station Rejowiec–59.50, Lublin–105, Zwierzyniec–12 verst.

There is a walled Catholic church, two Orthodox churches, a synagogue, and two guest houses, a hospital, Saint Katarzyna, with a resident doctor, an asylum, a preschool with two classes, a city hall, a post office, and as of 1887, a notary, a pharmacist and 38 shops.

Industrial facilities include a water mill, eight stoned; a factory of black and grey cloth for peasants. The peasants primarily occupy themselves with working the land, the Jews with trade and brokering. There are 18 shoemakers, 8 smiths, 2 dairymen, 2 furniture makers, 1 harness maker and several tailors, locksmiths, weavers, barrel makers, potters, tanners, whose output barely meets local demands.

Szczebrzeszyn lies in a picturesque verdant environment, with wooden one–story houses, some walled dwellings, with small gardens, a market, narrow streets, (Skolna, Turobinska, Klasztorna, Tserkiewna, Parkowa, Zatylna, and Bilgorajska), unpaved streets, except for Zamosc street on which the highway that connects Szczebrzeszyn with Zamosc and Zwierzyniec runs.

A tall, walled, multistoried building stands near the courthouse called Oberza. Until 1876, part of the building housed the Zamosc district court. Only ruins are left of the keep which burned down in 1840, and the city walls. The remains of the city walls were used in 1840 to build the new courthouse. Only the tower remains of the keep. The city was surrounded by ramparts. Szczebrzeszyn had the suburbs: Blonie, Zamoyski which stretched along the length of the Wieprz until the Bodaczow farm.

Szczebrzeszyn belonged to the Zamosc peace court from 1876. The city extended over 4,565 acres, of which 3,319 were farmed, fields–588 acres, unusable land–104 acres, for building–548 acres, and water–5 acres. The soil was lime over stone and chalk. There were many fields, but no forests.

In 1827, there were 499 dwellings, 3,233 residents: in 1832–5,433 residents; in 1860–4,018 residents (2162 Roman Catholics, 1683 Jews); in 1875–4,743 residents; in 1878–433 houses (66 walled) and 4750 residents.. In 1881–463 houses and 5,064 residents (2677 Jews); in 1885–433 houses (39 walled) and 5,129 residents (2,381 Jews); in 1888–488 houses (54 walled) and 5,264 residents (2,398 Jews); in 1890–5,418 residents (912 Orthodox, 2,429 Jews).

Szczebrzeszyn is one of the oldest settlements in the Chelm region. It belonged to the chain of keeps that defended the settlements along the Wieprz valley. It most probably stemmed from the time of Casimir the Great. Szczebrzeszyn is not mentioned in the act of 1377. Wladislaw Jagiello, confirming the old privileges in Krakow in 1388,bestowed by Dimitri of Goraj, decreed them eternal for Szczebrzeszyn and all its inhabitants. Paprocki stated that he saw documents, issued by the same Dimitri, which began "Nos Demetrius de Goraj et in Szczebrzeszyn haeres." On the basis of this act, he bestowed the villages Gruszka and Zaparoze on a certain Tsedzikow Prochanski, "ratione servitii in terra Chelmensi." (Both villages in the neighborhood of Szczebrzeszyn). After the heirs of Dimitri passed, the wealth was given to the families Leliwit of Tornow, and Rozits of Kzepic, and Toporsztik of Tenczyn, as a dowry. The city rights were probably passed to the duke, Wladislaw Opolski, during his reign in Russia.

Jagiello, confirming the edicts of Dimitri, gave the city certain freedoms. Jan Tornowski, in 1492, established a fair, freeing the merchants from paying taxes. The rights were confirmed in 1520 by the landholders of Szczebrzeszyn, Piotr and Stanislaw Kmit, Count of Szreniawa.

After them, the rulers of S. were the Gorkis. They built the Orthodox church probably on the place of the previous one. They converted the Catholic church into a Calvinist church, and established a school. Andrzej Gorki, privileged from 1560, assured the suburbs, Blonia, and Zazecze their use with the Magdeburg rights as an example for the city which had since long ago been in place, as well as the city's revenues. Andrzej of Gorki was the feudal baron of the whole area. The keep was the site where courts were held for local and city matters for the whole population and for the Powiat. The nobility, who had their estates here, were his vassals.

Feudalism was in full force until the end of the 17th century. When Jan Zamoyski received a certain village from Anna Niedzwiedzka, Countess of Gorki, she freed him from her jurisdiction, assuming the influence that Zamoyski had in the land.

In the first days of September 1583, a fire broke out at night in the keep. The fire was so intense that the Starosta [2] barely escaped with his family. All the acts and documents were destroyed. Gorki begged the king, Stefan, to reinstate his privileges, and his jurisdiction over the vassals, and supported his claims with court documents. The king was convinced of the righteousness of the claims, and on December 12, 1583, he renewed the privileges, in perpetuity, in Lublin for Andrzej Gorki, and his desendants as the owners of the keep, the city and the whole Powiat, with his jurisdiction, excluding S. from all kinds of rules, even from tribunals.

From the acts of the magistrate, we have the following privileges:

Rights of Andrzej Gorki, landowner of S., declared in 1586, which renewed the Magdeburg rights of S., in place of the original document destroyed in the keep in 1583. At the same time, the residents were freed of repairing the dams and providing wheat. On the other hand, taxes were raised and the peasants were required to plow for 6 days, and to remit to nobility half of every sheaf, "in natura." At the same time, Jews were forbidden from buying goods in the villages, and the city councilman was empowered to prosecute Jews for not participating in putting out fires, or paying debts. The elder councilmen were required to keep a record of mill production, of measures, weights and stores. The city notables were exempted from paying, "in natura."

Stanislaw Gorki, the son of Andrzej, with his privileges of January 9, 1595, confirmed the earlier privileges with a pledge to pay money.

Zygmunt III forbade Jews from collecting taxes and from owning leases of liquor taxes, on March 25, 1597.

The rights of Jan Zamoyski, Hetman and Chancellor, confirmed the previous privileges of the city of S., as of August 27, 1598, as well as permitting the harvesting of wood from the Shebreshiner landowners for building and heating, and repealed the levy on cooking honey and other taxes.

The privileges of Tomasz Zamoyski of August 26, 1629, confirmed the earlier privileges of the city of S.

In June 26, 1643, the privileges of the same Tomasz Zamoyski, permitted the residents to build on empty lots.

In august 25, 1673, king Michal Korybut permitted the residents to distill and sell spirits for a small levy, and confirmed the earlier rights of the city of S.

The privileges of Jan Zamoyski of May 21, 1700, permitted the residents to have businesses in private houses and to distill spirits for a levy of 3 Zl a barrel.

The privilege of king August II of July, 1729 established 3 new fairs: in the name of John the Baptist, the Ascension of the Virgin Mary, and of Saint Michael.

The guilds in S. possessed prior privileges, bestowed by Jan Zamoyski in 1661 and 1694 for tailors, shoemakers and barrel makers, and detailed standards for students, apprentices and masters, and determined the procedures for acquiring master status, the fees involved, and providing penalties for non compliance and corruption. It was also permitted to collect fees during the fairs from foreign tradesmen with similar wares, and for substandard work. It was also forbidden to bring in outside products and handiwork a mile from S.

The city of S., which followed German jurisprudence, had its own courts, which consisted of appointed justices–of–the–peace, aldermen and "jos gladiyi" (sword laws). The acts of the courts have been lost.

From the Gorkis, S passed to the ownership of Jan Zamoyski, (in the years 1595 and 1598), who incorporated S. into his Ordinat.

S. and the plain which lies at its feet, and is constrained by mountains in the south west and which surround it, is mentioned in the following historical fact. When the Commonwealth was established at the Lublin pact, and the consultations carried forward to Warsaw on January 4, 1673, the victorious army of Hetman Sobieski (against the Tatars) with the king at the head, the Shebreshiner confederation was tied to the defense of the wavering Hetman reign and freedom. The act was signed by the Field–Hetman, and the son–in–law of the king, and the royal military company.

*

During the first partition of Poland (1772), S. came under the rule of Austria, and then the privileges of S. were repealed and carried over to Lemberg. The Orthodox church and the Roman Catholic parish were probably established by Dimitri of Goraj in 1397. The Catholic parish included the city of S. and the suburbs, Blonie, Zamoyski, and Zaszec, and the villages: Brody, Czarnystok, Deszkawice, Kaweczyn, Kulikow, Lipowiec, Michalow, Obrocz, Rudka, Sulow, Sulowiec, Topolcza, Czenszynie, Wielacza, Zwierzyniec, Zurawnica, Bodaczow, altogether 9,307 people.

The Orthodox church, Uspenya, was renovated by the government in 1868, and later in 1876. The second Orthodox church was rebuilt from the Catholic church with the name of Holy Trinity, with donations from Jan Zamoyski, who also donated a large field and a garden, and was enclosed by a high wall stretching to the river Wieprz. After the dissolution of the Franciscans, the cloister and the Orthodox church were given to the Franciscans of Zamosc, and the magnificent temple was turned into barracks during the Austrian reign.

The cloister existed for a short time, and in 1793 was abandoned. The building was near collapse, and in 1812, it and the church were given to the Sisters of Mercy, who arrived from Zamosc in 1784. (Now a city club).

The hospital named after St. Katarzyna, was small at first, in 1812, having 30 beds. In 1845, Count Andrzej Zamoyski, enlarged it, creating spacious hallrooms, one on the ground floor, and two upstairs. In 1870, the hospital was placed under the supervisory board of Zamosc, and an attendant was engaged. As of May 10, 1883, the sick were looked after by the Elizabethan Sisters. In 1879, an ambulatory service was started, and the sick were given medicine without charge. While enlarging the hospital, Count Zamoyski founded a school in two of the rooms, and allocated a room for the steward.

The existing shul–home for the old and disabled was also a gift from Andrzej Zamoyski. Poor Jews had a small commissary, run in 1880, by Itzhak and Berek Feldman, who paid a yearly fee. The well–known schools in that time were, to a certain extent, an extension of the Zamosc academy.

In 1809, Zamosc was transformed into a fortress, and the buildings of the academy, and the lyceum, were taken over for military use. Count Stanislaw Zamoyski founded a school in S. that underwent a number of phases and name changes: lyceum, school of higher learning, provincial, and finally, gymnasium named after Zamoyski, which existed until 1852. The building and the garden were the property of the government and were used as barracks. Professors at the school who achieved renown were: Francziszek Kowlaski–poet and author, Adolf Kodasziewic–grammatician, Basili Kokolnik, Ignace Richter–bibliographer, Teodozi Szieroczinski–grammatician and pedagogue, Jan Zenkowski–agronomist, Josef Zochowski–naturalist.

Thanks to the low fees and the cheap living conditions, the school was always overflowing with students. The gymnasium published, in Warsaw, between the years 1834 and 1844, " A ceremonial act for closing the school year." At the same time, there was a private girls school of four classes run by Teofila Reder. The closing of these institutions diminished the welfare of the city.

*

S. is the birthplace of many scholars. Among the famous are: Wojcech Baseus–Latin grammatician of the 17th century. Josef Brand–painter, Isachar Ber Cohen–a

Talmudist of the 17th century, and Jan Szieszczinski–doctor, philanthropist, pedagogue, and one of the first Polish lithographers.

Translator's Footnotes

1. Measure of distance in Tsarist Russia, equal to 1.06 km
2. Village elder

[Page 408]

The Surroundings

by Moshe Messinger

Translated by Moses Milstein

The shtetl of Shebreshin was surrounded by beautiful villages, fields and forests. There were Jews in practically every village. Most of the buildings in the suburbs belonged to Count Zamoyski, who leased the fields to tenants. Every village had its tenant who managed the wealth of the Count. In every "court" there were several Jewish families who inherited their positions from their grandfathers.

Little by little, the number of Jews in the surrounding villages increased until there was a minyan or two of Jewish families whose only occupation was agriculture. The largest village where the largest number of Jews was concentrated, up to three minyans, was Gorajec. Jews lived there freely and independently, together with the Christian population, working their land. With the natural increase of Jewish families in the villages, the allotment of available land, which served as their livelihood, decreased. Some of them, unable to make a living from their allotment, migrated to the city.

Among the Jewish families in Gorajec was a fine family called Met, or as the head of the house was called, R' Yankel Greiyetser. He was no illiterate. He had a good knowledge of scholarly Jewish works, and served as an example for all the Jewish families in the village.

In the village of Radecznica there were about 30 Jewish families. But these were of another sort, more progressive, almost urban.

Jews also lived in the village of Zaklodzie. One of them, known as R" Dudl Zaklodzer, kept his doors open for Jewish travelers and merchants by day and by night. He was renowned for his tsedaka, not only to individuals, but also for social institutions–religious ones, it is understood. He was rich not only in fields and forests, but also in good intentions. His wealth passed to Hersh Zelig Weinblat.

I visited R' Hersh Zelig Weinblat several times. He was distinguished by his generosity just like other Jewish village families. His wife also knew no boundaries to her generosity. Their house contained not only teachers for the children, but also teachers of foreign languages. One of the children studied in Paris.

In later years, when antisemitism increased in Poland, Graf Zamoyski confiscated the wealth of all these Jews. Many of the families left for other cities. R' Hersh Zelig Weinblat wandered to Lublin, where he remained until World War II.

It is also worthwhile mentioning other villages where Jews lived, such as, Radziecin, Sulowiec, Deszkowice, Sulow, and Sanczask.

*

All of the aforementioned village people took part in the social life of the time. After the First World War, when the chapter of revival and political formations began in Shebreshin, the village youth joined in with the city youth.

The library, named after Mendele Mocher Sforim, served as the general meeting place for young people seeking to slake their thirst for knowledge.

The Zionist movement served as a more narrow link. Here the "pintele Yid" surfaced. The youth zealously affiliated with Zionist ideology, especially with proletarian Zionism. The rise of antisemitism between the years 1932–1935 was associated with a worsening of the economic situation. In spite of the loss of their economic positions, Jewish youth helped shoulder the burden of cultural development, and the rise of progressivism.

[Page 410]

Shebreshin in the Register [Pinkas] of the "Council of the Four Lands"
Translated by Yocheved Klausner

The Council of the Four Lands – Greater Poland, Little Poland, Reissen (Belarus) and Lithuania – was an autonomous authority of the Jewish communities in Poland and Lithuania from the 16th to the 18th centuries. The Council was responsible for taxation, cultural and social life, and religion. Each "Land" elected 2 –3 delegates to the Council, in addition to the delegates of 3 large communities. The number of members of the Council was 25. In 1764, the Polish Sejm dissolved this organization.

The collection of documents connected with the Council of the Four Lands was published by the name " The Pinkas [register] of the Council of the Four Lands, a Collection of Regulations, Writings and Records, Arranged and Explained by Israel Halperin," Jerusalem, Mossad Byalik, Jerusalem 1945 (Acta Congressum Generalis Iudeorum Regni Poloniae, 1580–1764).

Shebreshin is mentioned 23 times in the Pinkas (Zamosc – 34 times). It is clear that Shebreshin occupied an important place in the organization. The town is mentioned in particular in the context of approbations to publish books (obviously, in the spirit of the times, mostly religious books and various commentaries).

The Rabbi, R'Chaim Rogovin, resident of San–Francisco, was asked by R'Baruch Bibel to "help save from historical oblivion the scholars and illustrious people of this hometown, Shebreshin." Rabbi Rogovin prepared a comprehensive work based on the work by Israel Halperin (mentioned above), and other sources. We present here a short summary, written in the style of the author, R'Chaim Rogovin.

An Important Community

The first official document of the Council of the Four Lands that we received was from 1579. However, according to some sources the Council was established in 1570. The documents, recorded in the Pinkas of the Council, are reliable sources of the history of our people in Poland in those days. They reflect the problems of the times concerning the relationship with Christians, as well as internal Jewish affairs; they also echo the reaction of the Jewish leaders to the persecutions, accusations and violent incidents. The specifically Jewish social and spiritual problems facing the leaders, scholars and rabbis of Polish Jewry can also be found in the documents.

The positive indication, that the Shebreshin Jews sent their delegates to the Council at the beginning of the 17th century, points to the fact that it was already an important community at that time. In about 25 documents, we found the signatures of Shebreshin delegates.

The first such document is from 1617 – an approbation of a book. Writing approbations posed not only intellectual problems, but also economical questions, which arose in connection with the spiritual ones,

[Page 411]

in particular problems of plagiarism. A person, who has not worked and has made no effort, would print and sell the fruit of the pen and spirit of a scholar who worked for many years without reward, and sometimes lost the sums that he had invested in paper and printing. The Council of the Four Lands made great efforts to correct this situation.

The swindlers also appropriated books that were public property, such as prayer books, although the author had spent time and energy to make corrections of language and version, and had added explanations and commentaries. The prohibition of use was for a limited time, to enable the author to enjoy the fruit of his work.

Three types of books were given approbations: 1. Popular books, such as siddurim[prayer books], and mahzorim [High Holiday prayer books], where explanations and commentaries were added. 2. Original works, written mostly for the average learner, such as Bible commentaries, Midrash, Ethics and religious books. 3. Original works – innovations and commentaries on the Talmud and its Commentators, on the Shulchan Aruch [codex of law] and its Commentators – written for scholars knowledgeable in "Talmud and Codifiers" and authorized to teach the Law, and for professional ordained rabbis.

Approbations of Popular Books

One of the four signatures of the approbation mentioned earlier is that of the Shebreshin representative, our master and teacher Yosef ben Matityahu Delakrot, z"l, who wrote a book about the Tractate, Eiruvin. In the year the approbation was signed, 5377 (1617), the book, Yesh Nochalin, was printed in Prague, with an approbation by Yosef ben Matityahu Delakrot, head of the religious court and head of the Yeshiva in the holy community of Shebreshin. Since, obviously, the community had a functioning court and a Yeshiva – we can safely assume that it was an important community.

The father of the author, R'Matityahu, was well-known among Polish Jews. He was one of the first Kabbalists, who spread the Sephardic Kabbala in Poland. In 1550 he went to Italy to study, visited the University of Bologna and studied natural sciences, mathematics and astronomy. In Italy he met the Spanish exiles or their descendants, and from them, he learned the Sephardic Kabala. Among his pupils was R'Mordechai Yoffe, well known as the author of the Levushim. Yoffe mentions his teacher R'Matityahu in his book Levush Even Yekara as "a man of faith, one of the greatest of the later Kabbalists."

In a document from 1618, an approbation of a prayer book, the 9th signature is: Efraim, son of my master, and father of our master and teacher, R'Naftali, z"l, who is called Zalman.

[Page 412]

He was head of the religious court in the community of Lublin, and earlier, was rabbi in Brisk, Horodna and Shebreshin. He was the son–in–law of the legendary Jewish king, R'Shaul Wahl (the "King for a Day" in Poland). When he was Rav in Shebreshin, he wrote an approbation to the book Etz Shatul [A Planted Tree], a commentary on the book Sefer Ha'ikarim by R'Yosef Albo from Spain, who lived about one hundred years before. R'Efraim wrote a book titled Tevuat Shor.

In 1642 the book, Ein Yaakov, by Shlomo Even Haviv, was published. It contains legends from Talmud Bavli and Talmud Yerushalmi. It was first printed in 1516, and the approbation is signed, by, among others, "Yakov, son of my master, and father of

Avraham, the monthly Gabay of the synagogue" [the gabay was replaced every month]. The brother of R'Yacov from Shebreshin was R'Yeshaya, son of R'Avraham Halevi Horowitz, known by the acronym The Holy SHELAH, after the title of his book Shnei Luchot Habrit [The Two Tablets of the Covenant].

Approbations of Books for Scholars

The rabbis and other respected personalities in Shebreshin have signed approbations for another type of book – books that were written for scholars, learned in Talmud and Midrash. These were mostly summaries of famous books which had been printed before, but for which buyers were few, as well as books of ethics and faith, and sermons. There was no fear of plagiarism concerning these books, and the approbations served mostly as moral support.

The following signed approbations of books of this type:

R' David ben R'Yakov from Shebreshin – approbation of a summary of the book by the famous minister in the government of Portugal, Don Yitzhak ben R'Yehuda Abarbanel, who was born in Lisbon in 1437. The summary was published in 1603 by R'Yakov ben R'Elyakim Halperin, and was titled "A Summary of Abarbanel's Commentary on The Sayings of the Fathers [Pirkei Avot] and the book of Haggadah."

Yosef, son of our master and teacher R'Matityahu Delakrot, z"l, head of the religious court and head of the Yeshiva in Shebreshin (mentioned above). He signed the book Yesh Nochalin, by Avraham Sheftils Segal, z"l, with additions by his son, R'Yakov: "Several Matters, Halachic Decisions and Laws, and Moral Lessons." Giants in the study of Torah are signed on this approbation, such as R'Yehoshua Falk, author of the book Me'irat Einayim, and the famous MAHARSHA [Rabbi Shmuel Eidels] – which is an indication that the Shebreshin R'Matityahu was an important scholar as well.

R'Yehuda – "the young Yehuda who lives in the holy community of Shebreshin" in 1664 signed the book, Amudeha Shiv'a [the seven columns], about the seven fathers of our nation (from Abraham to King Solomon) by "our respected teacher and rabbi, Betzalel ben of Rabbi Shelomo of Kabrin." It is clear from the context that the undersigned was a deputy of nine communities, with Shebreshin as the main city.

"The young Yoel, son to my master, and father of the great rabbi, our teacher R'Gad, z"l, lived in the community of Shebreshin" and was one of the undersigned of the approbation of the book, Ketonet Passim [A Coat of Many Colors], by Yosef of Przemyslow.

[Page 413]

R'Yoel, rabbi in Shebreshin, authored the book, Meginei Zahav [Golden Shields], to defend his grandfather, R'David ben R'Shmuel Halevi (author of Turei Zahav –

commentary on the Shulchan Aruch) against the criticism of R'Shabtai ben R'Meir HaKohen (the SHACH, author of the book Siftei Kohen).

"I Aharon Shmuel, son of the great scholar and rabbi, the late Azriel Lemel Kahana Shapira, z"l, who lived in Shebreshin," signed a book published in 1713 by the rabbi R'Pinchas, z"l, who had been Dayan [judge] in Pozna, and later, head of the religious court, and head of the Yeshiva in Vladova. He left manuscripts of discussions and commentaries on several Tractates, in particular the Tractate, Chulin. R'Aharon Shmuel was obviously a great Torah scholar, since the approbation ended with the words "Thus said the great luminaries, the eminent rabbis."

Approbations of Original Works

Following are approbations of the third type of book – books written not for regular scholars, but for outstanding students and scholars, and for renowned rabbis. Two of them were from Shebreshin; their names were already mentioned above, but their signatures here emphasize their greatness and erudition in Torah, Talmud, and Codifiers.

Our teacher and Rabbi, R'Yakov from Shebreshin, signed the book, "Commentary on the Prohibition Commandments in SAMAG" [Sefer Mitzvot Gadol = the Great Book of Commandments], published probably in 1605. The author is R'Moshe ben R'Yakov from Coucy, of the French Tosafists in the 13th century.

R'Yoel, author of Meginei Zahav [Golden Shields], which he wrote in order to defend his grandfather, R'David ben R'Shmuel Halevi, who has become world–famous as the TAZ, an acronym of the title of his book Turei Zahav [Golden Columns], a commentary on the Shulchan Aruch.

In the introduction to his work, the author explains why he had chosen the title Turei Zahav: "In this work I shall comment on the Tur and the Shulchan Aruch, and the gimatria [numerical values of letters] of my name equals the gimatria of the word Zahav," meaning that he chose this title for his work, because in addition to the commentary of the Shulchan Aruch, by Yosef Karo, he explains issues in the Tur by R'Yakov Ben Asher, and the gimatria of the second word of the title, Zahav, is 14, as is the gimatria of his name, David.

R'Shabtai ben R'Meir the Kohen, who has written a book titled Siftei Kohen (was known by the acronym of the title, the SHACH), disagreed with the TAZ, and wrote a book in which he enumerated his criticisms. The book was completed in 1848, the year of the Khmelnitsky's pogroms, and was printed 14 years after the death of the author (who died in 1667) by his son, R'Moshe, thus carrying out the will of his father.

The controversy between the two great men was an important factor in publicizing the Shulchan Aruch, which penetrated the study rooms of the Yeshivot in Poland and Lithuania, and the scholars of all generations, to this day, wrote commentaries on it.

[Page 417]

The History of R' Yakov Reifman

A Great Jew and a Genial Person
by Itzhak Warshawski
Translated by Moses Milstein

ר' יעקב רייפמאן

People who receive their education in a normal fashion, in a school, cannot appreciate the many difficulties a young, religious, Jewish person, who had a desire for education, had in those days. All avenues were closed to them.

First, such a young man only knew Yiddish and Hebrew, and there were hardly any books in those languages that dealt with worldly knowledge. Second, in the Jewish shtetls and cities in Poland, Galicia, and Lithuania, there was bitter opposition to studying anything other than Torah. Such a young man was expelled from the Bet Hamidrash, beaten, and often sent away to the army. About marriage, there was no question: which Jew would take as a son–in–law, an apikores [1].

Nevertheless, there were many boys who risked their lives in order to obtain an education. It was their ideal. When such a young man learned, for example, a law of logic, or mathematics, or physics or geography, it was, for him, a joyous occasion.

One such, who later became a renowned scholar, was Yakov Reifman. Only a few decades after his death, legends and stories about him began to circulate.

A sharp mind

Yakov Reifman was born in 1817, in the village of Lugow., near Opatow, Radom Gubernia. His father, R' Hirsh, was a "writer", albeit a writer in a forest.

In his short autobiography, he describes how, at the age of three, he was already awakened at dawn by his mother Rachel, and taken to a teacher to study.

When he was four, his father's house burned down. He also, it seems, gave up his occupation as a writer. He moved to Opatow, and became a teacher.

Yakov studied first with his father, and then with others, and quickly demonstrated a sharp mind. In those days, young boys were taught simple things. Before a boy was properly able to study a page of Gemora, he was expected to be skilled at asking questions, solving them, and building castles in the air around the laws of the Talmud. But even though he had an extraordinary mind, and could run rings around the other boys, he had no interest in these things, and wanted to study formally and with order. At the age of fifteen, he ended his studies with teachers and took to studying on his own.

What's written in those books?

While studying in the Bet Hamidrash, Yakov learned that there were "other ways of knowing." He heard that, somewhere, in the big cities, there were learned people, universities, and libraries. Yakov was an inquisitive boy. He immediately acquired a strong desire to know: What are they writing about in those books? What do they teach, the professors? But in Opatow (or Opta, as the Jews called it), he could find nothing about the subject. The only thing he did hear was that the great minds are great apikoreses.

Aside from hearing these things, he also occasionally found books about those knowledgeable in worldly things. He learned, for example, that some were versed in mathematics, and could predict when eclipses would happen. It was sometime mentioned in books that some rabbi had had a debate with an apikores. This awakened a great curiosity in him, but there was no way for him to satisfy it.

He was married at seventeen. He had, of course, never seen his bride–to–be. His father–in–law, R' Yosef Maimon, lived in Shebreshin, quite a distance from Opatow.

But matchmakers often made matches in far away cities. Yakov had a reputation as a scholar: the father–in–law was a rich man. He promised his son–in–law that he would support him while he sat and studied. In 1836, Yakov settled in Shebreshin.

New opportunities in Shebreshin

About the conjugal life of the newly–weds, little is known. But it is known that in his father–in–law's house, he found a "treasure." The treasure consisted of a number of books that he had heard about but did not exist in Opatow. One book was "Moreh Nevochim", by Rambam, a philosophical work written in Arabic, and later translated into Hebrew. A second book was "Hachuzri", also philosophical, written by the great philosopher and poet, R' Yehuda Halevi.

From these books, Yakov began to study worldly knowledge. He read them with such passion that after a few months, he knew them by heart. But his hunger for learning was not yet sated. On the contrary, these books whetted his appetite for more spiritual matters.

In those days, all the maskilim [2] had one way to haskala: learning German. First, all sorts of books were available in German, but were not available in Russian or Polish. Second, learning German was easier, because of its similarity to Yiddish. But there was a third reason why it was the language of the maskilim. The renowned Jewish philosopher, Moses Mendelssohn, had translated the Tanach into German (with a commentary). It was published with one side in Hebrew, and on the other, in German with Yiddish letters. From this translation, most of the maskilim learned to read and understand German, which, next to Hebrew, became the language of the maskilim.

S had an advantage, which Opatow did not. It was near Zamosc, which had long been a city of maskilim, of enlightened people. How Yakov acquired Mendelssohn's translation in S is hard to say. It was no easy thing. It had to be kept a strict secret. When a young man was found to be studying Mendelssohn's Tanach he was beaten, thrown out of the Bet Hamidrash, and forced to divorce his wife, because which father–in–law would continue to support an apikores?

But there is nothing one can't achieve if one desires it strongly. Yakov Reifman acquired Mendelssohn's Tanach, quickly learned German, and soon acquired more German books. He also taught himself how to write Hebrew in the old–fashioned way.

Caught up in the revolution

Sooner or later, it was discovered in Shebreshin that Yakov was caught up in the progressive movement, but it was too late for his father–in–law to drive him away. He already had a child. Aside from that, he did not behave like other maskilim, who wore modern clothing, and became apikoreses. Yakov remained, although exceptional, a pious Jew. He davened, observed all the mitzvoth, and sat and studied.

Chasidim say that Yakov's wife went to see the Belzer rabbi, R' Shalom, to ask him whether she should divorce her husband, the apikores. R' Shalom Belzer asked her if her husband washed his hands before bed. She answered that he did. "If so, the rabbi replied, live with him, you will have a good son with him."

Chasidim point out that the rabbi's prediction was accurate. R' Yakov Reifman's only son, R' Nathan, became a properly religious young man, and later, a rabbi in Lublin. Like other religious Jews, he held his father to be a bit of an apikores. Nevertheless, he accorded him respect because, firstly, a father is a father, and, secondly, his father was a great scholar, one of the greatest in Poland.

Yakov Reifman was, by nature, a rationalist, a person who does not believe in secrets and mysteries. More than anything he revered clarity. But that did not prevent him from writing poetry in Hebrew and Aramaic. How did he know Aramiac? In every Chumash there is a "Targum" in Aramaic, a language that was spoken in Babylonia and in Israel where not everyone knew Hebrew. For their benefit, the Tanach was translated into Aramaic. As he had learned German from Mendelssohn's translation, he learned Aramaic from the "Targum." He had a strong affinity for languages.

It did not take long for him to acquire a reputation among learned Jews as a philologue. He wrote many books and published many articles in German and Hebrew journals. Among his well–known works are, "Bet Yakov"–a book about the Tanach. "Pesher Davar" , a book about the history of the Talmud and Midrash; "Moadi Erev", a book about the logic of the Talmud; "Sanhedrin", a book describing the sofrim circle in Israel. He wrote a book about the great, extended family Rapaport, "Avi Mishpachat Rapaport" which was published in Vienna in 1872.

A Golden Cup from Montefiore

How did Yakov Reifman live in later years, after his father–in–law died? We do not have a clear answer to the question. His writings brought him some income. Maskilim the world over helped him out a little. And, he probably received some money from the articles he published from time to time. Also, it did not take much money to live in S. in those days; one could live on a few rubles a week.

In 1881, the well–known Jewish–English philanthropist, Sir Moses Montefiore, sent Reifman a golden goblet on which was inscribed a Hebrew poem written by Montefiore himself. In his short autobiography, Reifman wrote that he was never more gladdened than by this gift. If the Jews of S. did not yet believe that the "apikores," Yakov Reifman was held in great esteem by the world, this convinced them.

Another happy event was receiving a chest full of rare books from an admirer of his in Amsterdam, R' Abraham Chaim Wagna. Reifman corresponded with many scholars of his time, including the Jewish–German scientist Abraham Geiger, and Itzhak Mordechai Jost. In his later years, he taught himself Latin, Greek and Arabic. His books were published in Berlin, Vienna, Warsaw, Vilna, and St. Petersburg.

The Hebrew poet, Y.L. Gordon, thought the world of Reifman, and wrote a Hebrew poem about him, where he says, "Wherever I go, I see your ghost, which searches for the hidden in the Torah with the light of a flame...I have not forgotten you, my brother, and who can forget you? How many Yakov Reifmans are there in the Jewish streets?"

Y.L. Gordon was not one prone to idle flattery.

Not copying others

In 1888, during the celebration of Reifman's 70th jubilee, a short autobiography was published in the Hebrew anthology, "Knesset Israel." He described certain of his character traits. First, he preferred that everything be original–he said of himself. He did not like to copy others. Second, he detested dishonesty, flattery, and politics. More than anything he loved sincerity, and for this reason, he mostly befriended young people who had not yet learned to be false, and were freer thinkers. Third, he loved company, only occasionally preferring solitude. Fourth, he was a very loyal friend, and if he didn't like someone, he did not keep it secret.

R' Yakov Reifman died on Octber 13, 1895, at the age of 78.

*

He was very popular in the Lublin region. He was especially esteemed in Zamosc, which was, as already mentioned, an enlightened city.

Without a doubt he was a role model for Y.L. Peretz, when he was still a young maskil in Zamosc. He probably knew Reifman personally.

Chasidim considered him an apikores, but held him in greater respect than other maskilim. He conducted himself as a religious Jew, and raised a religious son, a rabbi; this was an exception among the maskilim. Most likely, he truly was a pious Jew, and therefore, he kept on living in the small and pious Shebreshin, where he could remain religious, and carry on his scientific work.

Translator's Footnotes

1. Heretic, free thinker
2. Followers of Haskala, Jewish enlightenment movement

[Page 423]

A Great Shebreshiner, Pious Man, and Scholar

by Yakov Shatzki

Translated by Moses Milstein

Yakov Reifman, 1818-1894, was an important figure in Zamosc. He lived in Shebreshin in poor economic conditions. His father-in-law, Yosef Maimon, was a well-known maskil. Reifman's name appeared often in books of that era. He wanted to be active in the field of Jewish education. This apikores and Jewish scholar, who Peretz alluded to with respect, had to endure great distress from Chasidim. They wanted to excommunicate him. This was because, in his younger years, he was associated with the founding of Jewish elementary schools in Lublin (1833), and later, in Chelm (1862). Strong Chasidic opposition led to the closing of the schools.

As mentioned, he was held in great esteem in Zamosc. The maskilim there liked his approach to Jewish education. He believed in a balance between religious education and other forms. Reifman dreamed of a modern yeshiva, and in 1862, thanks to the help of Yehoshua Margolis, a near relation of Peretz, he succeeded in establishing such an institution. It only lasted for one year, but it became renowned in maskilimcircles in Poland.

Every Saturday evening, he gathered together a group of young people, and delivered a series of well thought out lectures on scientific matters. He gave them good instruction in all things relating to chachmat-Israel[1], and acquainted them with the newest developments in the field. He strongly criticized the Warsaw rabbinical school for their negative attitude to Jewish history. He was bitter that the rabbinical school had not kept its word. It had invited him in 1854 to teach Talmud. But to the Warsaw educators he was the face of piety, and in the eyes of the Chasidim he was a terrible apikores.

He believed that Polish youth had a stronger Jewish intellectual potential than the Jews of Western Europe. One just had to find a middle way between the chaotic, old-fashioned method of learning, and the modern one. The role of a rabbinical school—he declared to his Zamosc students—was not merely to increase the number of teachers, or bookkeepers and secretaries of commercial houses, but to develop a scholarly, intelligent mind.

A strong circle formed around Reifman in Zamosc. Thanks to him, the local Talmudists had a good library. The fact that he was able to give such serious courses was proof of the existence of a scholarly maskil youth in Zamosc.

Yehoshua Margolis, Reifman's patron and friend, died in 1877. His later years were spent in terrible poverty, living in a "chicken coop," as he complained in a letter, living on donations, which were solicited on his behalf in the Hebrew papers. The older maskilim of Zamosc died off, and no new ones with fresh energy came to take their place.

Reifman's scholarly works (he was very productive) were truly only meant for scholars, because he was not a writer, but rather a researcher. His works impressed the world of scholars. The world around him helped him little, although they were proud of him. Of his students, the Hebrew writer, David Shifman, (1828-1903), who was a private Hebrew tutor and bookseller, was the only one who helped out the old rebbe. Shifman was Peretz's secretary at one time. He was the local correspondent for "Hamelitz", put out unpublished songs of Yakov Eichenbaum, and did all that he could to keep the haskala movement alive in Zamosc.

Y. L. Peretz**Error! Bookmark not defined.** writes about rabbi R' Moshe Wohl, that this "small, sweet Jew, with a silver-white beard" and with eyes "like doves" was the gentlest rabbinical authority in a congregation where maskilim played a very important role. He was a close friend of Reifman, the apikores, and defended him strongly. When they wanted to excommunicate the great Shebreshiner scholar and pious man, R'Moshe Wohl said, "He who performs an excommunication without the approval of the local Rabbi and his Religious Court, shall himself be excommunicated."

Copied from "YIVO Bleter", Vol. XXXVI
Researched and submitted by Abraham Wolfson

Translator's Footnote

1. Science of Judaism, schools of thought among Jewish intellectuals in Germany beginning in the first half of the 19th century

[Page 425]

It is not Permitted to Hold it in One's Hand

by Abraham Bernstein

Translated by Moses Milstein

The Kuzmer shtibl in which my father davened, was in Yosele Reifman's house. Sometimes, we youngsters managed to climb into the attic where we found boxes of writings and letters written by Yakov Reifman. At the time, he was well known for his wide–ranging correspondence with Jewish philosophers and thinkers.

We did not understand the writings, but we were fascinated by the beautiful, rounded handwriting, and especially the hand–printed words.

Our parents discovered some of the papers in our possession, and asked us how we came to acquire them. They told us to immediately get rid of them, because, "it is not permitted to hold them in one's hand."

That was their attitude to the boxes of writings that were treasures of important thoughts and ideas. They remained in the attic for many years, and no one was interested in them. That is an example of how our shtetele, with its mud and poverty, remained trapped in fanaticism for many years.

[Page 425]

"How Many Yakov Reifmanns are there in the Market?"

by Zvi Kramer

Translated by Yocheved Klausner

The researcher and critic Yakov Reifmann, of excellent common sense, wise and scholarly, was a very fruitful author. He devoted much of his efforts to correcting contradictory versions and made small changes and remarks – but his small notes are often very important. He was one of the first to include scientific clarifications in the reviews of our modern literature. Aided by his scholarly skills, he could refer to ancient sources, following our early Sages.

Among his many books:

"Tavnit Habayit" [The Structure of the House], which includes 6 questions and answers on Talmudic subjects. This is part of his larger book "Beit Yaakov" [The House of Jacob] (Zholkava, 1843);

"Pesher Davar" [Explanation] – 22 articles containing reviews (Warsaw, 1845);

"The life of Rabenu Zerachia, author of "Hamaor" [The Light] (Prague, 1853).

He published about 20 books.

The poet, Y. L. Gordon, wrote about Yakov Reifmann in the section of his book, "Occasional Poems:"

> Why should you say, Yakov, that Yehuda has forgotten you?
> I, with all the strength of my heart, am seeking you.
> Wherever I turn, I see your power
> Dwelling in the rooms of Torah at the light of the burning torch.
>
> Your song is pleasant to my ears,
> Your voice, the voice of Yakov,
> Is superior to the sound of pure gold,

Or the sound of layers of silver.
If, for many days I have not written to you
It was because of my own impatience, hard work, and trouble.

  I have not in me the wise study of Torah
With which to welcome you,
And my soul detests a letter of emptiness and void...
But I have not forgotten you, my brother –
Who can forget you?
How many Yakov Reifmann are there in the market?

Rechovot,
November 1980

[Page 426]

In a Room like a Cage

by Solomon Lastik

Translated from Polish by Ephraim Farber

Translated by Moses Milstein

While living in Shebreshin after his marriage, Yakov Reifman developed strong ties to Zamosc with its significant effect on the cultural milieu of S. The winds of haskala found fertile soil in S.

Yakov Reifman occupied himself with modern philosophy and conducted research. At the age of 24, he published his first Talmudic research in the eminent organ of Jewish history, "Zion." In time, he became an authority in the realm of knowledge. But this did not prevent him from living a life of need.

An excerpt from his letter to Zalman Chaim Halberstam, a scholar of Chachmat-Israel, [1] gives testimony to this.

"Alas, I must live in a room, which is no bigger than a cage, together with all of my family, and the poultry who cackle day and night disrupt my research, and don't allow me to sleep."

He learned mathematics, physics, natural history, and astronomy from the works of Chaim Zelig Slonimski. Reifman, an expert on ancient scriptures, taught a rational analytical approach to the ancient literature, how to recognize hidden meanings, to appreciate the worth of translating commentaries, and identifying false and twisted texts in certain midrashim of the Talmud.

The world of Talmudic study bowed its head at the death of this giant, the modest priest of pedagogy, the self taught man of Shebreshin.

———

Translator's Footnote

1. Science of Judaism, schools of thought among Jewish intellectuals in Germany beginning in the first half of the 19th century

[Page 429]

עברי טיטשע שפראך דינקמעלר
DEUTSCHE SPRACHDENKMÄLER
IN HEBRAISCHEN SCHRIFTCHARAKTEREN
I.

LIEDER
DES VENEZIANISCHEN LEHRERS
GUMPRECHT VON SZCZEBRSZYN
(UM 1555)

HERAUSGEGEBEN
VON
MORITZ STERN

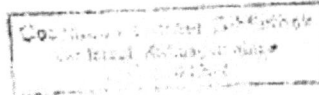

BERLIN 1922
VERLAG HAUSFREUND

German Translation of Chanukah and Purim Piyutim [religious poems]
Translated by Moses Milstein

A manuscript by Gumprecht of Shebreshin, written in octavo format, [1] was discovered, in 1892, in the anthology, "Hebraica," of the Trieste brothers in Padua, Italy. With the mediation of the rabbi of Padua, Dr. Albert Zamatko, the discoverer was able to copy the original handwriting from 1555, written in the German–Gothic style, and publish it in 1895.

After that, the Trieste collection passed to Rosa Gompertz, and professor David Kaufman in Budapest. After his death, the collection, as well as other books, passed to the Hungarian Academy of Science in Budapest.

In the catalogue of Hebrew handwriting and books in professor Kaufman's library, described by Dr. Max Weisss of Frankfurt–Am–Main in 1906, the work is listed under number 397.

The German translation of "Chanukah and Purim piyutim" is, in reality, a poetic reworking of the Chanukah and Purim stories. The source of the Chanukah poem was the "yoytser" [2] of Chanukah. The events of Chanukah are described in 49 stanzas taken from the yoytsers of Shabbat–Chanukah: the edicts of King Antiochus, (stanzas 2–4), the death of the martyr, Eliezer (stanzas 5–7), the death of the martyr Hanna and her 7 sons (stanzas 8–15), the wedding of Judah Maccabee, and the death of the city ruler (stanzas 16–25), the story of Holofernes and Judith (stanzas 26–34), and at the end–the miracle of the oil (stanzas 44–46).

The same format was used to tell the story of Megilla Esther in 78 stanzas. To complement the historical tale, he used the Targum Sheini, and the Gemora, Maskat Megilla, and the Midrash, Esther Raba.

Gumprecht was a teacher in Venice in the years, 1570–1571. (A contemporary was Abraham Hasofer ben Itzhak of Shebreshin, who completed a copy of "Esis Rimonim" (catalogue Neubauer no. 1808).

The flames of the Inquisition began to burn on October 19, 1553, and destroyed the entire rabbinical literature of the Venetian Republic. Publication of Jewish works was banned for a decade. It was not until 1563 that publications resumed.

Gumprecht found it necessary to compose the two poems for pious women in order to explain why Purim and Chanukah are celebrated. He dedicated the poems to the daughter, Sarah, (Zoorlein) of the rich and esteemed Simcha of Venice. The melody was taken from an old German song, "Die Schpinerin." The second poem was sung to the melody of an old German song, "Leid von kalb und landsknecht."

The entire manuscript is written in one hand but for several words that are struck out and changed by another hand. The name, Zoorlein, was changed to Mestlein, and Simcha to Kalman Azolei. On the last page of the manuscript there is a note with the date 1579–80, with the name, Isaac. One can conclude that this Isaac was either the owner of the manuscript, or the one who changed the names in order to give the manuscript to Mestlein, the daughter of Kalman Azolei of Venice.

Translator's Footnotes

1. An octavo is a book or pamphlet made up of one or more full sheets of paper on which 16 pages of text were printed, which were then folded three times to produce eight leaves. Wikipedia.

2. Part of the morning service where special hymns are interpolated on certain holidays

[Page 431]

"History of the Persecutions of the Jewish People"

Translated by Yocheved Klausner

In the booklet, "History of the Persecutions of the Jewish People," [Letoldot Hagezerot al Israel], which appeared in 1889 in Krakow, booklets No. 2 and 3 by Chaim Yona Gurland, we find several passages about Shebreshin personalities. Below are the quotes, as they were written, in the style of those days.

Stress of the Times

This is a long story in rhymes and flowery language about the pogroms in the years 1648 and 1649, by R'Meir son of R'Shmuel of Shebreshin z"l. Even though this book saw the light of day 238 years ago (Krakow 1650), it is dearer than pearls [rare, difficult to find – YK] and is considered a true manuscript; and the book "Stress of the Times" by R'Yehoshua son of R'David of Lwow (Venice 1656) is a forgery from beginning to end. This man has taken all that R'Meir had written and used it as if it were his own – he wore a stolen prayer–shawl and cried Shema Israel. For fear that he may be caught, he dared to blind the eyes of his readers in the Introduction, and without shame, instead of the letters at the beginning of the lines [the acrostic – YK] of the true author Meir ben Shmuel Zecher Tzadik Livracha he deceitfully wrote Yehoshua, son of the great scholar our teacher and rabbi David Zecher Tzadik Livracha etc., as I shall demonstrate in my introduction to the book, soon to be published as Booklet No. 4, God willing.

I shall repeat here my humble request from the wise and learned rabbis in our country and abroad, to send me copies of the registers of their communities, memories from the life in the communities and inscriptions on tombstones in the cemeteries – anything that relates to the above–mentioned persecutions, and I shall be forever thankful from the bottom of my heart and bless them by the "triple blessing" [the blessing of the Kohanim – YK] mentioned in our holy and pure Torah; may you be blessed.

Ch. Y. Gurland

Odessa

Tears are flowing from my eyes as I think of the dear members of the Holy Community of Boska, the honest members of the Holy Community of Brehin, the pure members of the Holy Community of Zalkawa, the righteous members of the Holy

Community of Shebreshin, our friends the members of the Holy Community of Yavdov, the respected members of the Holy Community of Turbin and the outstanding members of the Holy Community of Tamishov, when from all sides came the oppressors, and murdered more than thirty thousand women and men, learned and shining with the brilliance of Heaven – – – –

*

Shebreshin. A town of scholars and praiseworthy people – see the remarks to Ohel Yissachar by the wonderful critic R'Yakov Reifmann (Bet Otzar Hasifrut, note 3), and the supplements by Rabbi R'Nachum Brill (p. 18). And the reader in the coming generations shall add: Rejoice, Shebreshin, for you are the place where our rabbi Rabenu Yakov Ish Tam, whom we can truly call by the honored name "the Second Ibn Ezra", has chosen to pitch his tent, the tent of Torah and wisdom.

[Page 432]

Cover Pages of Old Books, Documents and Certificates
Translated by Jerrold Landau
Donated by Anita Frishman Gabbay

שערי ספרים עתיקים, מסמכים ותעודות

טיטל־בלעטער פון אלטע ספרים,
אקטן און דאקומענטן

לקורות

הגזרות על ישׂראל

מחברת שניה

מאת

ה"י גורלאנד.

קראקא

נדפס של ר'זה יוסף פישער

שנת תרמ"ט לפ"ק

BEITRAGE
zur
GESCHICHTE der JUDENVERFOLGUNGEN.
ZWEITES HEFT
von
JONAS GURLAND.

[Page 433]

צוק העתים

The Tribulations of the Times

This is a memorial to the difficulties and tribulations that we endured year by year from the years Tach and Tat[1]. For the two tails of the firebrands[2], with sharp swords. Had we not had some survivors, we might have all be destroyed, Heaven forbid. Therefore, so that the last generation will not forget, someone unique in his community arose and ??? of the thousands of victims, whose souls were for pillage.

The author is the exalted Torah scholar, Rabbi Meir the son of Rabbi Shmuel of Szczebrzeszyn[3].

[Page 434]

Two compositions included in this book in photocopy. These are:

Tzuk Haittim [the Tribulations of the Times], by Reb Meir the son of Reb Shmuel of Szczebrzeszyn, first printing, the year Krakow, 5410.

Yaven Metzula [Deep Mud], by Rabbi Natan Nota Hanover, first printing, Venice, 5413.

Tzuk Haittim was reprinted in Salonika in 5412; in Venice in 5416 in the name of Yehoshua the son of Rav David of Lwów, omitting the name of the actual author; in the book of Ch. Y. Gurland, The Decrees against the Jews, fourth notebook, Krakow 5649. A. Yaari (Kiryat Sefer, 5698 – 1938, 375–377) he compares the Salonika edition to the Krakow edition (from Gurland), and the Venice edition, and comes to the following conclusions: 1) The Salonika edition is more precise than the Krakow edition (transcribed by Gurland). Whomever from now on comes to prepare a scholarly edition of Tzuk Haittim must rely on the Salonika edition, which is more precise. 2) The Venice edition was not transcribed from the Krakow edition, but rather from the second edition that was printed in Salonika. On the other hand, Y. Heilprin is of the opinion (Tzion Koh, 5720 – 1960, page 17) that 3) Gurland's Krakow edition is not sufficiently precise, and there is room to go back and test the conclusions arrived to by A. Yaari — — regarding the quality of the later editions and their common qualities — — the prefaces of the author and the "lawgiver" and several "fine versions" that Yaari notes in two later editions, and are not noted by Gurland. Therefore, he concluded that which he concluded. Both are found in the Krakow edition itself.

Yaven Metzula again appeared in its original, as well as in translation into several languages and in several editions. A popular edition appeared in the year 5705 (1945) with vowel marks and commentary by Y. Heilprin. It includes a literary introduction by Y. Pichman, and was published by Hakibutz Hameuchad.

[Page 435]

Translator's note: The photocopy on this page is uncaptioned. The top line is "In old Szczebrzeszyn." The text is written in "Rashi script" and is seemingly meant as an illustration of a page of one of the two aforementioned books.

[Page 436]

קול־מבשר

(במקום הקדמה)

אמר חיונ:

הנני מציע היום לפניכ, קורא נבבד, את החברת השלישית מסדרי
רגהיל: לקורות הגזרות על ישראל, הכוללת אספת כל הספרים
והמאמרים והמזרונות וגם כל הקינות והסליחות ודבקשות וכו', אשר מצאתי
ואשר עוד אשגא — בגשרה אל חי — בספריותנו היבתהיורים, הן בדשש והן
בדריהם, בעיני אל העורות של היה ותים ביםי בענראן הכיל יבשי יבשי אידזן
נויבא '?) בשנת הקבלת.

היברת הראשונה מדירת: א) שבחי־ראובן ביםי גאונא בשנת הקבלה
(1656); נ) וב לגוירות בלדשי חביל בשנת חיה ות שֿ (49—1648); ג) שתי
קינות ורטפיה על נוהת הָ ל; ד) לקט ישבהה, אז ענוֹנים שנֿים השנעים
הגויית השרה ').

היברת השנּיה כוללת: ז) מי צער בת רבים מאת ר' אברהם ביר
שנּיאל אַשכנזּי ויל, בן דודו שר הגיורות תקן, עם ראֿיות והערות ובאור הענן:
ו) נסבהים הברברים על בֿ' שם ההיים. מאת ר' אברהם אשּנזֿי אסישיֿק
בֿר ל ווארבּר בברינה וואקן (פראַנ שֿ'ן); על בֿ' שבחי להוה מאת הגאן
ר' יהאֿל סינב ב ר אֿלּיעֿר שנהֿרג בֿקֿק נעשֿיב הקורה (לובלין הים); ועֿל
בֿ' יַן בדֿילה בל־א מאֿת ר' מֿשה ביֿר אבֿרהם (אֿמֿסטֿֿרים תֿמֿ ').

היברת השלישית היא היא לפנֿיֿך, הֿך בֿה ודֿפֿך בֿה, שֿם עֿינֿך
הפֿקוהה על בֿל עֿנֿיֿה ופֿיֿקֿיֿה בֿבלֿ ועל הֿמֿאֿמֿר הֿראֿשֿון — בֿקֿשֿת ר' מֿשֿה
גֿיֿאֿל וֿד בֿפֿרֿיֿ — וֿתֿשֿמֿֿ הֿרֿשֿות אֿף נֿצֿורֿות לֿא שֿיֿנֿֿו הֿחֿֿוֿקֿרֿים הֿקֿֿוֿדֿמֿים.')
והֿֿת הֿקֿֿרֿא, אֿם אֿֿהֿב בֿֿפֿֿרֿֿיֿֿתֿֿנֿו אֿֿתֿֿה וֿֿחֿֿוֿֿבֿֿב קֿֿורֿֿה עֿֿֿֿֿֿֿֿֿֿֿ יֿֿֿעֿֿֿטֿֿֿ הֿֿֿגֿֿֿר אֿֿֿבֿֿֿשֿֿֿרֿֿֿך בֿֿֿשֿֿֿורֿֿֿה

'(עֿֿיֿן הֿֿמֿֿֿנֿֿֿחֿֿֿ הֿֿרֿֿֿֿֿֿֿֿֿֿ (דֿֿֿף 5—4). ²(וֿֿֿֿבֿֿֿר בֿֿֿֿֿֿ : כֿֿֿֿ לֿֿֿֿֿים פֿֿֿֿ רֿֿֿֿֿה
וֿֿֿֿֿ '(וֿֿֿֿֿֿֿֿֿֿ : זֿֿֿֿ וֿֿֿֿֿֿֿ. ⁴(וֿֿֿֿֿֿ פֿֿֿֿֿ בֿֿֿֿֿֿֿ פֿֿֿ סֿֿֿֿ.

Kol Mevaser (In place of the introduction)

Ch. Y. G. (Gurland) says:

Today I present before you, erudite reader, the third booklet of my large book: History of the Decrees Against the Jews, including a collection of all the books, articles, and memories, as well as all the dirges, penitential prayers, petitions, etc. that I have found and that I will still find – with the help of the Living G–d – in our vast literature, whether in print or in manuscript, relating to the decrees of Tach ve Tat during the days of Bogdan Chmiel and Ivan Gonta[4] in the year 5525 (1654)[5].

The first booklet includes: a) Slaughter in Uman during the time of Gonta in the year 5525; 2) for the decree during the time of Chmiel in the years Tach ve Tat (1648–1649); 3) Two dirges and a prayer for the aforementioned decrees; d) Leket VeShichecha, or various matters relating to those decrees[6].

The second booklet includes: a) Tzaar Bat Rabim [Agony of the Many] by Reb Avraham the son of Reb Shmuel Ashkenazi of blessed memory, who lived during the times of those decrees, with notes and commentary; b) appendixes dealing with Sam Hachayim [Potion of Life] by Reb Avraham Ashkenazi Opitiker from the community of Wolodimir in the State of Wolhyn (Prague, 5350); on the book Shivrei Luchot by the Gaon Rabbi Yechiel Michel the son of Rabbi Eliezer who was killed in the large, holy community of Nemirov (Lublin 5560); and on the book Yaven Metzula by Rabbi Moshe the son of Rabbi Avraham (Amsterdam, 5516)[7].

The third booklet, the one before you, delve into it, direct your wise eyes onto all its matters and chapters in general, and on the first article – the petition of Rabbi Moshe Nalel of blessed memory in particular – and you will hear new things, even hidden things that the ancient researches did not imagine[7]. And behold, oh reader, if you like the book and value the history of our people, I will tell you pleasant news, for after a search and great effort, I succeeded in dredging up a very precious stone from the sea of forgetfulness, I aroused myself to obtain and understand the pages properly, and the ideas in the precious book, one of a kind, that is not well known in our literature and among our people, called A long book in poetic style about the decrees of the years Tach veTat by Re Meir the son of Reb Shmuel. Even though this book was published 238 years ago (Krakow...) it is more precious than pearls, literally like a ... And the book Tzuk Haittim that is still in circulation and has very little essence, by Reb Yehoshua the son of Reb David of Lvov (Venice, 5416), is a complete forgery. For this man took all the words of Reb Meir and reworked it on his own accord. He is enwrapped in a stolen tallis, while calling out loud Shema Yisrael. So that people will not discover his travesty, he calls out before his readers and in his introduction Hamechokek, so that no one can change the headings at the beginning of the book. Instead of the true author, Meir the son of Shmuel, may the memory of the holy be blessed, he writes Yehoshua the son of the Gaon Rabbi David, may the memory of the holy be blessed. Thus, I will expose his forgery at length in my introduction to the book that will be printed in the fourth booklet, G–d willing[10].

[Page 437]

— 7 —

נצים ה' כי אחרי חפש בחפש ויגיעה רבה עלתה בידי להמ"ם שהם י"ם ישבחה אבן ------ מאיר, יזל התעוררתי ויתעוררתי להשיג ולרהב לרסיס בתקן והצגת וכרירת והאיר"מ את הספר היקר, האחד בכינו, אשר יזינו איננו נ דין בספ"יתני ומשמיו למנה בשם:

צוק העתים‏ *)

ספור ארוך בפלומה הרותיא ליד הגבות בשנות ת"ח ות"ם נאת ▬▬▬ גיל שמואל ▬▬▬▬▬ ואם נם לפני רלות שנים יאר רספר רזה את אני הטבש וקומני חיי, בב'י יד פשנעים בטרו ונאמת נכו נ ת ביר פ בש רשב: ויספר יעק רשא"תב' אשר עלהני בחילק באין ונם ישמו בנם מועד במעשיות, ראת ר' יהושיע בד ריר מלבינ וויניבלת יב' א', הוא ם ז"ו"ע בירזל ועד כלה כי ראיש הזה לקח את נר דבר ד' מאצ"ד ישם בכלת' מאיש העישה בסלו יהבית' במעלית' נעובה קרא בקילה ישבינ ישראל, ולזען לא ינבא במהבותי צרב ליני יכ"ע עיני הקריעים בהקרבתו ובהקרבסת, ובסיוקתי וזם רעלה לא ידע לשבות את ראשי התוזוים נראש הספר, ובמקום שם ומיזבי האאסת"ה באיר בן שמיאל וב"ר צדיק לברנה ובו הפרים וכתבו: יהושיע בן הגאון סוהריר דוד זב"ר עדיק לברמה יב', כאשר אגלה זיום באויבה בהרבמת לספר, אשר יצא יאור במה"ית הר ב'י'ע'י ת, אם ירצה הישם ‏[8]‏.

לשוף אביות היום ליטנה ולשלש את בקשתי הגדולה והנבאלת אשר כבר הבינתי ‏[9]‏ לפני הרבנם והחכבים היושבים ויורשים באויגו ובהון בי ישבכו וראיניק לי פשובם, הלא הן העתקת נאשמת מבנקסי עדתם, מזכרוגות חיי קהלתם וכסצבות כתי יה קברים בערי כושביתם, הגוונעית ברכן אל בקשתן אל הגוות הבדבר בהן, ואוזה להם סקיב לבי אף אבינם בגבוה ובסללשת כתוזתנו הקדושה והמהורה ונרוגים יהיו! ‏—‏

אורבסמא זאת ועגב לפיק.

חיי נורלאנד.

*) כהנם זה: :זיעבניזד טורוטו בימבוט בי הבטר טיק, ‏‏‏ לאג נם בנשיוק כאת הע זני לטאו יינ אברנם רחשו בידי רתו ני סיבל סידם, מרים נסראלו, אם ורבטן לפ' לא שלבם נדי לטבש בטוב חינם וחיבי שלו' אננ ש יתוקנים ותיו ותחרי רבי בכל בזיר תחוגי יסבוברים‏—‏ בל שבל ועיני ובגו פשל, וסי יק בי מזבלו אף הבוגו בבונלי ונבן קבול ‏—‏ ועד הבוכר ‏(95, XIX)‏. ‏—‏

‏‏) כהוזבקו פסוב הקוגבים כמאו נבלמות ועיר הכבצרה (נבשליב) טמכ ‏+)‏ בקטו וכהאגוטי פי פהעוטק כוהבפ סרא בשירה בם‏——‏ושגיוחי ג.

‏‏) ט' נבקבישי הקומה לבחבית כלהווגום‏——‏והמבת.

Tzuk Haittim [The Tribulations of the Times][8][9]

Finally, I state today, to repeat my request multiple time that I already presented[11] to the rabbis and scholars who live and preach in our country and abroad, that they would do good to grant me of their munificence, that is the faithful transcriptions of the ledgers of their communities, of the memories of the life of their communities, and of the gravestones in the cemeteries of their cities, for the most part or a smaller part, regarding the decrees discussed in them – and I will thank them from the depths of my heart, and bless them with the threefold blessing from our pure, holy Torah. May they be blessed.

Odessa, the last day of Chanukah.

Ch. Y. Gurland

[Page 438]

קול־מבשר

(במקום הקדמה)

אמר חוזע:

הנני מציע היום לפניך, קורא נבון, את החברת השלישית מספרי
הגדול: לקורות הגזרות על ישראל, השכוללת אספת כל הספרים
והמאמרים והזכרונות וגם כל הקינות והסליחות ובקשות וכו', אשר מצאתי
ואשר שיר אשמא — בנשה אל חי — במפרזותי יתבח־יהודים, הן בדפוס והן
בכתובים, בנוגע אל הגזרות של זמן היה ותלש ביבי בענאן חביל ובימי איואן
גרונא ( ) בשנת תקכ־ה.

החברת הראשונה מליאה: א) שבח־ האגם ביבי נאונא בשנת תקבה
(שס1); ב) לקורות בלבי חביל בשנת תיה וח ש (1648—49), ג) שתי
קינות ותפיה על נוות הנ ל, ( ) לקם וישבנה, או שנעים שנה הנועים
הנויית הראה ( ).

החברת השניה מליאה: א) שי צער בת רבים מאת ר' אברהם ביר
שניאל אשכנזו וז"ל, בן דוד שר הגזרות תקן, עם ראזית והעדות ובאור הענין:
ב) נספהים הדברים על כ' שם החיים, מאת ר' אברהם אשכנזו אפישקי
בק ק וילאדיר במדינת חאין ופראנ שון; על כ' שבע־ לוחות מאת הגאן
ר' ישראל טיט ב ר אלינער שכרח בקק נעשיב העזולה (לובלין היוס); ועל
כ' ין בגיית בלא מאת ר' משה ביר אברהם (אמשטרדם תש י).

החברת השלישית והא היא לפניך, הך בה ורפך בה, שם עינך
הפקוחה על כל ענינה ושיקיה בכלל ועל הבאטי ראשון — בקשת ר' משה
ניאל ד ר בפרט — ותשמן הרשות אף נצורה יא שינוי הואקיים הקודמים.
והנה הקורא, אם אוהב בפרינתו אתה וחובב קורוה עמנו הנך אבשרך בשורה

---

¹) עבך החברת הראשונה (וף 5—4). ²) גדסבר במאכן: כיה תחיים מוה ואשוה
(ית') וכקנטרם נזר ומשיח. ³) ודפפו מזוץ בכלודים מוה מניל.

Kol Mevaser (In place of the introduction)

Ch. Y. G. (Gurland) says:

Today I present before you, erudite reader, the third booklet of my large book: History of the Decrees Against the Jews, including a collection of all the books, articles, and memories, as well as all the dirges, penitential prayers, petitions, etc.

that I have found and that I will still find – with the help of the Living G–d – in our vast literature, whether in print or in manuscript, relating to the decrees of Tach ve Tat during the days of Bogdan Chmiel and Ivan Gonta[4] in the year 5525 (1654)[5].

The first booklet includes: a) Slaughter in Uman during the time of Gonta in the year 5525; 2) for the decree during the time of Chmiel in the years Tach ve Tat (1648–1649); 3) Two dirges and a prayer for the aforementioned decrees; d) Leket VeShichecha, or various matters relating to those decrees[6].

The second booklet includes: a) Tzaar Bat Rabim [Agony of the Many] by Reb Avraham the son of Reb Shmuel Ashkenazi of blessed memory, who lived during the times of those decrees, with notes and commentary; b) appendixes dealing with Sam Hachayim [Potion of Life] by Reb Avraham Ashkenazi Opitiker from the community of Wolodimir in the State of Wolhyn (Prague, 5350); on the book Shivrei Luchot by the Gaon Rabbi Yechiel Michel the son of Rabbi Eliezer who was killed in the large, holy community of Nemirov (Lublin 5560); and on the book Yaven Metzula by Rabbi Moshe the son of Rabbi Avraham (Amsterdam, 5516)[7].

The third booklet, the one before you, delve into it, direct your wise eyes onto all its matters and chapters in general, and on the first article – the petition of Rabbi Moshe Nalel of blessed memory in particular – and you will hear new things, even hidden things that the ancient researches did not imagine[7]. And behold, oh reader, if you like the book and value the history of our people, I will tell you pleasant news, for after a search and great effort, I succeeded in dredging up a very precious stone from the sea of forgetfulness, I aroused myself to obtain and understand the pages properly, and the ideas in the precious book, one of a kind, that is not well known in our literature and among our people, called A long book in poetic style about the decrees of the years Tach veTat by Re Meir the son of Reb Shmuel. Even though this book was published 238 years ago (Krakow...) it is more precious than pearls, literally like a ... And the book Tzuk Haittim that is still in circulation and has very little essence, by Reb Yehoshua the son of Reb David of Lvov (Venice, 5416), is a complete forgery. For this man took all the words of Reb Meir and reworked it on his own accord. He is enwrapped in a stolen tallis, while calling out loud Shema Yisrael. So that people will not discover his travesty, he calls out before his readers and in his introduction Hamechokek, so that no one can change the headings at the beginning of the book. Instead of the true author, Meir the son of Shmuel, may the memory of the holy be blessed, he writes Yehoshua the son of the Gaon Rabbi David, may the memory of the holy be blessed. Thus, I will expose his forgery at length in my introduction to the book that will be printed in the fourth booklet, G–d willing[10].

[Page 437]

— 7 —

נשיפה, כי אחוי חפש בחפש וינגעה ונה עלתה בידי לרפט פתחם ים השמחה
אבן יקר, באה, יהל התעוררתי יתעוררתי להשג ולהבך לרפים בחקן והגהת
וברירית והאיץ, את הספר היקר, האחד בביעב, אשר חזנו איננו נסין בפפריתנו
ובמגנות הכנגה ביאה:

עמק הענתים [1].

בסוד ארוך בפלומה הרוסית קד הנגרות בשבות ת ח ותש באר ים געשר
ביד שמואל ... ואם נם לפני ולית שנם יאך רבפר רזה
את אוי הושפים וקוהקי ליי, בנו יקר מפנינים בטנו ונאמת נמו בת ביר בפש
ישב ויכפר עמק רעתים אשר עדני בתהלך באריו ונם ישני הנם פוני בשמואית
באת ר יהושיע ביד דיר מלנינב ועוניולת רני [4], הוא פוויית בידהל ועד בלה,
כי ראש הוה לקח את כר דביי ר מאץ ושם בפליו פאיש הועישה בשלו,
יתנבה בטלית נטובה יקרא בקילו ישבנע ישראל, ולשען לא יבוא בפתתיתו ציב
יבו ר י יעני הקריאש בהקרמתו ובהקרבת, ובמתוקק ונם רפלה לא ידע לשכות
את ראשי והרוום בראש הספר, ובמקם שם ובהני האמתי באיר בן שמיאל
ובר צדיק לברבה ועד הערים וכתב: יהושיע בן הגאון שההריר דוד וכה
ציקר לברבה יכר כאשר אגלה דופו באדובך ברקרמתי לספר, אשר יצא
לאור נהבות הרביעית, אם ירצה היום [5].

לסוף אמרתי היום לישנה ולשלש את בקשתי רכפולה והנכפלת אשר כבר
רעשתי [6] לפני הרבנים והחכבים היושבים וריושדים בארצנו ובחון לארין כי ישמכו
רדענך לי פשונם, הלא הן השתקות נאמנות בפנקסי ערתם, מזכרונות חיי
קהילתם ובקצבות בתייהקברים בערי כושבותם, הגונפות כרנן אל בקצתן
אל רגנות הובדבר נהכן, ואודה להם סקיב לבי אף אבינם בכרנה הסשלפת
בתוהתנו הקרושה ורמטורה ונרובים יהוו! —

אורקספא ואת תענה לפיק.

חיי נורלאנד.

[1] כהנם רך, בשיעניידר כותימו במכותו כי הפפר טיה צ"ל לאור נם בפלוניק כמה
היא וני לשי ייל שנה נם רלתו בירי פוי סינך פורם, מרים בטרחים, אך ורתבן לני לא שלתה
ניר לבותנו בטום חוק ואחרי פתלי אך צי ריתוקרים וחום ותחרי ורני בבל ביהיחוער יספפריום —
כל שמתי פניני נכתלו פעלן: ומי יחך כי פמתלו אף אביענו בשמים וכאם קריל — ותר
הפתר (XIX, 93). —

[2] כהעתקה פפום הקטיפדם כמוחא בטלפות נעיר אבפמרד (נפפליט) טמפר יש
בקשיר וקובזולתי כי התטחיק כומט פרי פפורה פם—רשורת לי. —

[3] עי' נהקדפתי הקטות להרבנית קלהבינס—ונהכה.

Tzuk Haittim [The Tribulations of the Times][8][9]

Finally, I state today, to repeat my request multiple time that I already presented[11] to the rabbis and scholars who live and preach in our country and abroad, that they would do good to grant me of their munificence, that is the faithful transcriptions of the ledgers of their communities, of the memories of the life of their communities, and of the gravestones in the cemeteries of their cities, for the most part or a smaller part, regarding the decrees discussed in them – and I will thank them from the depths of my heart, and bless them with the threefold blessing from our pure, holy Torah. May they be blessed.

Odessa, the last day of Chanukah.

Ch. Y. Gurland

[Page 438]

{Uncaptioned: The introduction.}

[Page 439]

האוניברסיטה העברית – החוג להיסטוריה של עם ישראל
קונטרסים לתלמידים – מקורות ומחקרים

ר' מאיר משעברעשין   ר' נתן נטע הנובר:

סיפורי הגזירות בשנות ת״ח ות״ט

ירושלים תשכ״ה

Hebrew University – the Department of the History of the People of Israel
Booklets for Students – Sources and Research
Rabbi Meir of Szczebrzeszyn   Rabbi Natan Nota Hanover:
Stories of the Decrees of the years Tach ve Tat

Jerusalem, 5725 (1965)

[Page 440]

פנינים

דברים נעימים, מדבש מתוקים, לזקנים ויונקים, פשטים,
רמזים, דרשות, פרישות, אזהרות נוראות, שיש בהם טוב
וטעם, ויתרון הכשר חכמה ודעת, והמה לכל נפש שוים.
(לשון רבינו המחבר בהקדמתו)

שדלה והעלה מספר הזהר הק' כולו
החכם השלם המקובל

מוהד"ר ישֹשכֹר בֹעֹר ב"ר נֹפֹתֹלֹי כ"ץ זללה"ה

בעל „מתנות כהונה" על מדרש רבה
תלמיד הרמ"א זללה"ה
והוא חלקם לי"ז שערים כמנין טו"ב
וקרא החיבור בשם

מראה־כהן

(יקר המציאות מאד לא נדפס כשלש מאות שנה)

ועתה נדפס בסידור חדש ומועיל
עם ביאור מלים קשות

הוצאת „פנינים"

עיה"ק ירושלים   תובב"א   ה'תש"כ

Pninim

Pleasant words, sweeter than honey for the old and young, simple explanations, innuendoes, explanations, investigations, strong warnings, which are beneficial and in good taste, and have an abundance of properness, wisdom, and understanding, equal to every person.

(In the words of our rabbi, the author, in his introduction)

Drawn and taken wholly from the holy book of the Zohar

By the wholesome scholar and kabbalist

Rabbi Yissachar Ber the son of Rabbi Naftali Katz, may the memory of the holy be blessed.

Author of Matanat Kehuna on the Midrash Rabba

The student of the Rema, may the memory of the holy be blessed

Divided into seventeen sections

And he called this composition by the name

Mareh Kohen

(The find is very precious, as it has not been published for 300 years)

And now we print it in a new, beneficial, arrangement

With an explanation of difficult words

Published by Pninim

The Holy City of Jerusalem, may it be built up 5720 (1960)

[Page 441]

שער הספר במהדורות הקודמות

ספר מראה כהן

הכינו ונם חקרו החכם השלם המקובל מהר"ר יששכר
בן נפתלי כ"ץ אשר גם הוא לרבו"ת אתא ועשה לו פירוש
מפורש נודע שמו בישראל, מת"נות כה"ונה והמעיין
בהקדמתו לזה החיבו' יראה יבין תועלת חיבורו כי רב
הוא כאשר עשה אזנים לספר הזוהר והראה לעמים עם
ה' אלה תוקף גבורת בקיאותו וסידור חכמתי

━━━━━

במהדורת הראשונה
והיתה התחלתו ביום השלישי ז"ך ימים לחדש הרביעי
שנת אשמ"ח לפ"ק
פה ק"ק קראקא
תחת ממשלת אדונינו המלך זיגמונד שלישי
על ידי יצחק בן הר"ר אהרן ז"ל המחוקק
מפרוסטין

━━━━━

במהדורה השנית
והיתה התחלת המלאכה הזאת ביום שני י"א לחדש מנחם
תל"ג לפ"ק
במצות הגביר האלוף כהר"ר נח בלא"א כמוהר"ר חיים פרץ
זצ"ל הי"ה פרנס ומנהיג בק"ק פוזנא
נדפס באמשטילרדם
בדפום הגביר והנעלה
אורי וייבש בלא"א כהר"ר
אהרן הלוי זצלה"ה

The title page of the book in an earlier edition

Mareh Kohen

The wholesome, scholarly Kabbalist Rabbi Yissachar the son of Naftali Katz, who came and made a commentary and became renown in Israel.

Anyone who delves into his introduction to this composition will see and understand the benefit of it, for it is great. He elucidated the book of the Zohar, and demonstrated to the Nation of G–d the strength of his expertise and the organization of his wisdom.

First edition

Beginning on Tuesday, 27 of Tammuz, 5359 (1589).

Here in the holy community of Krakow

Under the rule of our master, King Zygmunt III

By Yitzchak the son of Rabbi Aharon of blessed memory of Paraystis

In the second edition

This work began on Monday 11 Av, 5433 (1673)

At the behest of the wealthy benefactor Noach the son of Rabbi Chaim Peretz

Of holy blessed memory who was a Parnas and leader of the community of Poznań

Printed in Amstilerdam[12]

Published by the exalted wealthy man

Uri Weibsh the son of Aharon HaLevi, may the memory of the holy be blessed

[Page 442]

Introduction by the Rabbi, author, may the memory of the holy be blessed[13]

Yissachar the son of Naftali Hakohen, called Ber, from the community of Szczebrzeszyn, who lives in the country of Russia, may G–d raise it up; imbued with a wise spirit, the spirit of the holy G–d, the spirit of knowledge and fear of G–d, with pure, bright, clear words, as a clear day, with splendid language, bright and shining as the splendor of the firmament, sevenfold like the light of the sevenths, are these not the words of words, the matters of matters. These are matters which cannot be measured, pure water emanating from the sanctuary, here in the Holy of Holies, the supreme angel, the holy candle, the faithful servant, that is the bright, praiseworthy, renowned light, Rabbi Shimon bar Yochai, may the memory of the holy be a blessing – who in his great purity and supreme holiness, called it the Book of the Zohar. As is explained for everyone, with reasons and explanations, at the beginning of the Portion of Nasso. And behold even this, as is seen before our eyes with good view, with the words of our ancient ones of blessed memory, that if we have someone of renown with us today in this generation, he would be small, and merely just a small replica of him, a tiny portion of the great value, and he would also be speckled and spotted, lacking and not with anything extra. Nevertheless, if we had two mouths filled with song as the great sea, we would describe the righteousness of G–d, as a full day, with darkness and light – it would be insufficient to give thanks and praise to the L–rd of Hosts, Blessed be He, who left us some small remnant. One spoonful of satisfaction from him, with thousands of thousands and myriads and myriads of logical, spiritual notes standing above, high above the high, wonderful, powerful secrets streaming from his mouth, from true Kabbala, from the Merkava (chariot) mysticism, from the mystical emanations – are in this wonderful, sublime book, floating atop the waves, open and publicized to the eye of all hearts of wisdom, to those of clear vision, with a good eye, as the sun in its power. Blessed is he who gave of his wisdom to those who fear him.

[Page 443]

He did this as well, he grasped every prior thing with great brevity, in the Holy Tongue, for the community of those who do not understand the vernacular, with clarity, the holy words, shining as the sun. And I, in my paucity, who has no Torah, and not one of the traits that our sages of blessed memory have enumerated. I did not merit to see the countenance of the face of my grandfather, I saw only the back, and it is the fault of the Mareh. Only at the time when I studied Torah from my rabbis, may their light shine, Rabbi Yitzchak of the holy community of Poznań, did I hear from the peddlers who made the rounds in the Sanhedrins, that there is still an isolated branch from my great–grandfather. I searched and found it, to my heart's satisfaction. I delved into the honorable book by reading it with the quick quill of the scribe, in order to reprint it anew. Then my soul rested, as I said that this time, it is a bone of my bones and flesh of my flesh, and this should be called[114] the fire of G–d, the offering of a pure priest on the fire. I spoke to the heart of my father–in–law, may is name be mentioned positively, the Torah giant Noach the son of a fruitful tree, the fruit of the tree of life such as Rabbi Chaim of holy blessed memory, who upholds the Torah of G–d, in order to establish it in a second printing, in the eyes of all living and speaking people in the field of the holy apples, to impart a good thing from the lips of those who slumber. In this merit, let songs ascend, in thousands of pathways, from great strength to He who neither slumbers or sleeps, the guardian of secrets, and let him send a banner of notations.

These are the words of the lowly, priest, of meager worth,

Avraham the son of Rabbi Eliezer Katz.

[Page 444]

ל ע ל ו י נ ש מ ת

הרה"ח ר' יוסף יעקב נ"ע ב"ר ישראל איסר ז"ל
ורעיתו הצדקנית מרת שרה מרים ע"ה
בת ר' שמשון ז"ל

סייע להוצאת ספר זה בנם הדגול הרה"ג רב הפעלים
לתורה וחסד מוה"ר חיים שמשון גולדשטיין שליט"א
רב בקהלת מערב ניו-יורק

In Elevation of the Soul

Of Rabbi Yosef Yaakov the son of Rabbi Yisrael Isser of blessed memory

And his righteous wife Sara Miriam of blessed memory

The daughter of Reb Shimshon of blessed memory.

Their illustrious son the rabbi, Gaon of great works in Torah and benevolence, Rabbi Chaim Shimshon Goldstein, may he live well, the rabbi of Kehilat Maarav in New York, assisted in the publication of this book.

[Page 445]

מדרש רבה

על

חמשה חומשי תורה וחמש מגלות

ועליו

הרבה פירושים ממבחרי המפרשים הקדמונים והאחרונים . רבים מאלה שכבר נדפסו
על המדרשים או בספרים לבדם . ורבים אשר היו בכתובים עד כה ולא זכינו עוד לאורם .

ואלה המה :

א) פירוש רש"י על בראשית רבה , לרבינו שלמה יצחקי ז"ל . תותר מטעו וחבטושטם והטגיאות שרבו בו בדפוסים הקודמים :

ב) מתנות כהונה (והשׁל) לחרב החסיד שבכהנים חו' המפורסם טו' מהר"ר יששכר בער בהר"ר מהר"ר נפתלי כ"ץ
המכונה בשם בערמן אשכנזי ז"ל מקק שעברשין , נרפס בשלמה כמו שנרפס ברפוס בנבנשתי
טבו"א חדשנו אלה כל הענים שנשטטו ממנו ברפוטים האחרונים , וחשנו אזי חזר יווד גא"ן [ ]:

ווילנא

בשה חמשת אלפים ושש מאות וארבעים וחמש לב"ע

ברפוס יורשה

האלמנה והאחים ראם

Midrash Rabba

On the Five Books of the Torah and the Five Megillot

Including

Many commentaries from the early and latter commentators. Many of these were already printed separately in Midrashim or books. Many were in manuscripts up to this point, and we did not merit to see their light.

And these are:

The commentary of Rashi on Bereishit Rabba, by Rabbi Shlomo Yitzchaki of blessed memory. We have corrected the man distortions and errors that existed in the earlier printings.

Matnot Kehuna(complete) by the pious rabbi and Kohen, Rabbi Yissachar Ber the son of Rabbi Naftali Katz, who is nicknamed Berman the Ashkenazi of blessed memory, from the community of Szczebrzeszyn. Printed in its entirety as it was printed in Novoneshti and Padua, and we have resolved all the matters that were omitted from the most recent publications.

Vilna   5645 (1885), Published by the Romm widow and brothers.

[Page 446]

Szczebrzeszyn

The city of Szczebrzeszyn near Chełm is one of the oldest cities in Poland. Already in the 1300s, it was "a city full of scholars and scribes," a center of Torah. Famous Torah sages lived there, in good merit. Even the regular householders were scholars, some of whom were authors of books who earned a name in Torah literature, which was disseminated throughout the entire Diaspora. As an example, we will present here the names of several authors of the city of Szczebrzeszyn, along with the titles of their books. A Kohen reads first[15] – he is the Gaon Rabbi Yissachar HaKohen Berman, one of the great scholars of Szczebrzeszyn, known for his book Matanot Kehuna on the Midrash Rabba. After him, — a Levite, that is the Gaon Rabbi and Hassid Rabbi Yaakov Ish Horowitz, the brother of the Holy Shela[16], who published the book of his father, the Gaon Rabbi Avraham HaLevi with his own notes, on the topic of morality and Jewish law, Yesh Nochalin[17]. He disseminated Torah in public in Szczebrzeszyn, "Torah is sought from his mouth, and he is known in the gates for his deeds"[18].

One of the scholars of Szczebrzeszyn was the Gaon Rabbi Mordechai the son of Rabbi Naftali of Krezmir, the author of the books Ketoret Hamizbeach and Ketoret Hasamim, commentaries on the Targums[19]. The author of the book Korot Haittim, on the tragedies and slaughters endured by the Jews of Poland during the time of Tach ve Tat, was also a native of Szczebrzeszyn[20]; as was the Gaon Rabbi Eliezer the son of the Gaon Rabbi Yehoshua, the author of Damesek Eliezer[21].

The following were the rabbis and heads of the rabbinical court of Szczebrzeszyn that we know of:

Rabbi Yeshaya Menachem the son of Rabbi Yitzchak, known as Reb Mendel Reb Avigdor. In his youth he served as the rabbi and head of the rabbinical court in Szczebrzeszyn[22]. Later, he was appointed as the head of the rabbinical court of Ludmir, and toward the end of his life, as the head of the rabbinical court of Kraków and the district[23]. He died there in the year 5359 (1599).

The Gaon Rabbi David the son of Rabbi Yaakov, who came there as a result of the charter of the year 5347 (1587),[24].

[Page 447]

Shebreshin (Polish: Szczebrzeszyn), a city in central Poland.

There was an organized community from the middle of the 16th century. At the end of the century, a splendid synagogue was built in Renaissance style (it was burnt down in 1939).

Jews engaged in the spice trade, and frequently visited the Lublin fair. The tribulations that afflicted the community during the Decrees of Tach ve Tat (1648–1649), were described by Meir the son of Shmuel in his book Tzuk Haittim (Kraków, 1650).

Over one hundred years later, there were 444 Jews in the city. After Szczebrzeszyn was included in Congress Poland (1815), the restriction on residency were lifted, and the community grew to a population of 2,450 toward the end of the century. Hassidic influence was very strong there.

In the elections to the city council in 1931, the General Zionists received three seats, Poalei Zion – one, Agudas Yisroel – one, and Bund – five. On the eve of the Second World War, there were about 3,200 Jews in Szczebrzeszyn.

The Germans entered on September 13, 1939. They retreated on the 27th, and returned on October

9th on the basis of the demarcation line fixed between Germany and the Soviet Union.

In August 1940, 300 Jews were requisitioned to register for forced labor. Most did not heed the command, and escaped. In May 1942, 100 Jews were killed by the German police.

The rest of the Jews were sent to Belzec in two deportations, in August and October of that year. Hundreds succeeded in escaping to the forests and Jewish fighting brigades, but only a few remained alive until the liberation.

{Translator's note: This is a printout of an Encyclopedia Judaica article on the town from Beit Hatefutzot Museum of Tel Aviv.}

Translator's Footnotes

Tach and Tat refer to 1648–1649, the years of the Chmielnicki uprising. See https://www.jewishhistory.org/tach–vtat/ https://www.jewishgen.org/Yizkor/Szczebrzeszyn/szc432.html - f432-1r

A reference to Isaiah, 7:14 https://www.jewishgen.org/Yizkor/Szczebrzeszyn/szc432.html - f432-2r

Followed by an obscure acronym mnemonic for the year 5410 / 1650. https://www.jewishgen.org/Yizkor/Szczebrzeszyn/szc432.html - f432-3r

See https://en.wikipedia.org/wiki/Ivan_Gonta https://www.jewishgen.org/Yizkor/Szczebrzeszyn/szc432.html - f432-4r

There is a footnote in the text here: See first booklet (pp. 4–5). https://www.jewishgen.org/Yizkor/Szczebrzeszyn/szc432.html - f432-5r

There is a footnote in the text here, as follows: Printed in the anthology: Beit Ohim first year, and in a separate, special booklet. https://www.jewishgen.org/Yizkor/Szczebrzeszyn/szc432.html - f432-6r

There is a footnote in the text in these two places, as follows: Both were published in Bohemia in the second year. https://www.jewishgen.org/Yizkor/Szczebrzeszyn/szc432.html - f432-7r

There is a footnote in the text, as follows: The scholar Dr. Steinschneider informed me in his letter that the book was also published in Salonika in the year 5412, and that he had seen in twelve years previously in the hands of Fischl Hirsch, bookseller in ???, but to my dismay, I was not able to obtain it by any means. After asking researchers and booksellers, and investigating in all the libraries, all my efforts were for not. I would wish to find it and obtain it in the near future! – the council of the secretary (XIX, 95). https://www.jewishgen.org/Yizkor/Szczebrzeszyn/szc432.html - f432-8r

Parts of this photocopy are unclear and smudged, and other parts are obscure. I will put ellipsis [...] on parts that I skip. https://www.jewishgen.org/Yizkor/Szczebrzeszyn/szc432.html - f432-9r

There is a footnote in the text here: A copy from the book can be found in full in the city of ... (Italy) was prepared at my request and through my efforts by the faithful transcriber Reb Y. Shapiro, there, and I thank him. https://www.jewishgen.org/Yizkor/Szczebrzeszyn/szc432.html - f432-10r

There is a footnote in the text here, as follows: See my brief introduction to the first booklet – and you will find it. https://www.jewishgen.org/Yizkor/Szczebrzeszyn/szc432.html - f432-11r

Doing a web search for this book, and then following it to the publisher, it seems that this is a typo, and should be Amsterdam. https://www.jewishgen.org/Yizkor/Szczebrzeszyn/szc432.html - f432-12r

These two pages are written in extremely cryptic form. It is replete with Kabbalistic innuendoes (one such innuendo is the "field of holy apples"). I have translated it somewhat literally. Hopefully the essence will come out, albeit the translation is very convoluted. https://www.jewishgen.org/Yizkor/Szczebrzeszyn/szc432.html - f432-13r

Genesis 2:23. https://www.jewishgen.org/Yizkor/Szczebrzeszyn/szc432.html - f432-14r

A Kohen is called to the Torah reading first, and therefore is honored by being mentioned first. A Levite is called to the Torah second. https://www.jewishgen.org/Yizkor/Szczebrzeszyn/szc432.html - f432-15r

See https://en.wikipedia.org/wiki/Isaiah_Horowitz https://www.jewishgen.org/Yizkor/Szczebrzeszyn/szc432.html - f432-16r

There is a footnote in the text here as follows: Published in Prague, 5377 (1617). https://www.jewishgen.org/Yizkor/Szczebrzeszyn/szc432.html - f432-17r

There is a footnote in the text here as follows: There in the introduction to the book. See the approbations of the book. https://www.jewishgen.org/Yizkor/Szczebrzeszyn/szc432.html - f432-18r

There is a footnote in the text here as follows: Amsterdam 5420 (1660); 5431 (1671). Translator's note: Targum is one of various Aramaic translations of the Bible. https://www.jewishgen.org/Yizkor/Szczebrzeszyn/szc432.html - f432-19r

There is a footnote in the text here as follows: See preface to the book. https://www.jewishgen.org/Yizkor/Szczebrzeszyn/szc432.html - f432-20r

There is a footnote in the text here, as follows: Published in Wilhemsdorf, 5478 (1718). https://www.jewishgen.org/Yizkor/Szczebrzeszyn/szc432.html - f432-21r

There is a footnote in the text here, as follows: Mentioned in the book Matanot Kehuna, Portion of Vayikra, section 2. https://www.jewishgen.org/Yizkor/Szczebrzeszyn/szc432.html - f432-22r

There is a footnote in the text here, as follows: See the book Ir Hatzedek, and the writings of the history of Rabbi Demtibzer, pp. https://www.jewishgen.org/Yizkor/Szczebrzeszyn/szc432.html - f432-23r

The original seems to end here, in the middle of an article, and indeed in the middle of a sentence (as does the previous footnote). https://www.jewishgen.org/Yizkor/Szczebrzeszyn/szc432.html - f432-24r

[Page 448]

From the Literature

Translated by Jerrold Landau

Donated by Anita Frishman Gabbay

From Korot Beitinu (from the eighth volume of his legacy)

Sh. Y. Agnon

Now I will write about the deeds of our ancestor Reb Shmuel the son of our ancestor Reb Asher the son of our ancestor Reb Yosef. Our grandfather Reb Shmuel was of handsome appearance, had a good voice, expert in languages, and splendid in his garments. On weekdays, he would wear clothing in accordance with Italian custom, and on Sabbaths and festivals, he would dress in accordance with the Hassidim of the Land of Israel. He did not have renown among those who were expert in Torah but he was a grammarian, and knew all the texts of the Bible, the divisions, and the notations of the Masoretes. Already in his youth, he occupied himself in his holy work of editing books, a task that required wisdom.

Now I will describe how he married our grandmother from Poland, and how our grandmother arrived in Italy.

Our grandmother Yocheved's father, our ancestor Reb Ephraim of Szczebrzeszyn, was one of the arbitrators

[Page 449]

of the Council of the Four Lands. Once, he went to intercede before the great ministers who sat at the forefront of the Kingdom off Poland. There was one minister there who was the master of several towns and villages in which numerous Jewish lessees and tavern owners earned their livelihoods. The minister realized that Reb Ephraim was wise, wealthy, and expert in business. He said to him, "I appoint you over all my property, and now, expel all the Jews who live in my cities and villages, who banded together in unison to cheat me. Put others in their place in accordance with your wisdom and spirit of understanding."

Reb Ephraim realized the direction in which things were leaning – that is to expel Jews from their livelihoods, heaven forbid. He was afraid to tell the minister to take back his offer, for in those days, the ministers ruled over the people in body and soul, and every minister ruled over his city an did what was right in his own eyes. If someone said something that displeased the minister, it would cost him his life. Reb Ephraim abandoned all his affairs to the hands of his sons and sons–in–law, and took his wife and young daughter Yocheved, the daughter of his old age whom he loved more than all his sons and daughters – for his fortunes had turned great from the day she was born – and traveled to the Land of Israel. Along the way, as he waited in Italy for a ship that was going to the Land of Israel, a letter arrived from his sons and sons–in–law stating that debtors are neglecting to pay their debts, claiming that their father has canceled them prior to his journey. Therefore, all of his sons, daughters, sons–in–law, and daughters–in–law were requesting that their father return to his house to repair the breach, for if not, all of his toil would have been for naught. Furthermore, there is no reason to be afraid of that minister, for out of his great anger toward Reb Ephraim who left him and went away, he severed a nerve and is now ill with paralysis. Combined with that letter was a letter from the leaders and barons of the communities who all agreed unanimously, along with the rabbis, may they be well, that Reb Ephraim must forego the benefit of a burial in the Land of Israel for the benefit of the public.

When Reb Ephraim was in Italy, he saw our grandfather Reb Shmuel, who was still a lad. He liked him, and found him fitting for his young daughter Yocheved, the daughter of his old age whom he had taken along for the journey to the Land of Israel. Our ancestor Reb Asher was already no longer alive.

After his wedding, our grandfather Reb Shmuel drew near to the people of Ashkenaz [Germany], to the point where he began to speak their language and pray in their synagogue. Even though his melodies were different from the melodies of the Germans, they would ask him to lead the prayer services, for his voice was pleasant and his melodies were fine. We have heard that he composed a melody for the piyyut Hakol Yoducha[1], composed with great skill, especially in the transition from Hakol Yomru Ein Kadosh Kashem, the meaning of which is that everything is subordinate and nullified, and there is nothing compared to the holiness of the Blessed One, Who is everything, and Whose holiness is everything. Such things cannot be explained in writing. That melody is beloved by the Ashkenazim, who use it to test cantors who wish to be appointed as prayer leaders.

After our ancestor Reb Ephraim and his wife returned to Poland, our grandmother Yocheved remained in Venice with our grandfather Reb Shmuel, and gave birth to sons and daughters.

[Page 450]

Our grandfather met difficulties due to the apostates, for the owner of the printing house made the enemies more senior than the friends, for the apostates came to the printing house on the Sabbath to do their work, and their masters did not have to forego an entire day on account of the Sabbath observing Jews. Nevertheless, our grandfather was happy, especially on the Holy Sabbath. When our grandfather returned from the synagogue on Sabbath eves dressed in the Sabbath clothes of the style that our ancestor Reb Asher worse when he came to Italy from the Land of Israel, he would sit at his table, with his wife, sons, and daughter around him, his pure soul would be aroused from the love of the Sabbath, as he would sing melodies sweeter than honey. The soul of anyone who heard them would be uplifted from the holiness of the Sabbath. We still have a pleasant tune for the hymn Kol Mekadesh Shevii, that our grandfather would sing on Sabbath eves, which aroused great salvation from G–d, as is described at length in the story LaEved Nimkar Yosef [Joseph was Sold as a Servant], which I transcribed from a copy.

23. The Book of Melodies

Now I will tell what happened to our grandfather Reb Shmuel, the firstborn of our ancestor Reb Asher of blessed memory, during the time he was living in Italy. One night, he was informed in a dream that the book of melodies of the songs of the Levites, that the Levites used to sing in the Holy Temple, was hidden in the archives of the pope. Our grandfather girded himself with strength, and went to Rome. The priests did not recognize that he was a Jew, for he was wearing the garb of the Land of Israel that our ancestor Reb Asher had worn when he came to Italy from the Land of Israel. As he arrived at the outskirts of Rome, both the Jews and gentiles inquired who this prince was, and from what country had he come, for his appearance was that of a prince and his garb exuded splendor and honor. The priests opened their archives to him, and he could go into every place he wanted. After he transcribed the book of melodies, he returned to his home and his Beis Midrash.

One night after midnight, at the time of Tikkun Chatzot[2], as we sat and lamented the memory of Zion, his longing for the Temple and the city overtook him. He rose from the ground, and stood up to take out the book of melodies. He read the psalm according to the musical notes that our ancestors the Levities would sing in the Holy Temple. When he reached the verse "May my tongue cleave to my palate if I do not remember thee"[3], his power of speech was removed from him and left him for several days. His wife found out about this, and hid the book away. After she hid it, he never found it again.

24. I Will Open my Doors to a Guest

We do not know the reason why our grandfather Reb Shmuel left Italy and went to Poland. Some say that our ancestor Reb Yosef left a chest of letters in Poland, and our grandfather Reb Shmuel went because of that chest. Other said that he was called with a summons of love to establish[4]

[Page 451]

printing houses in Poland. His name is mentioned in the communal ledgers regarding the etrogim he imported from Italy. It seems to me that the first reason is the main one, that our ancestor Reb Yosef uncovered some hidden matter in the Zohar regarding the end [of days], and our grandfather Reb Shmuel went there to search for the letters.

And so our grandfather Reb Shmuel left Italy and travelled throughout Poland, Podolia, and Wolhyn. He went to the community of Ostraha and met our relative Rabbi Shmuel, who wrote novella on most of the tractates of the Talmud – he is the Mahar'sha of blessed memory. The entire land quaked from his Torah.

When he entered to him, and saw the light of his countenance, he was confounded, for his facial appearance was similar to that of our ancestor Reb Asher of blessed memory, the father of our grandfather Reb Shmuel, although his beard was black and well–kempt, and his peyos did not reach his beard, as was the custom of our ancestor Reb Yosef, may the memory of the holy be blessed, wo conducted himself like his rabbi the Ar'i [Rabbi Isaac Luria] of blessed memory. The Gaon's peyosextended to below his ears, his beard was full, and his eyes were like the eye of the world when it was frozen. There was another difference between them. The light of the eyes of our ancestor Reb Asher was turned inward, whereas the eyes of the Gaon were open, peering with strength and fortitude. There were similar to each other in height and facial contours, an even their fingers were similar.

The Gaon placed a finger on the Gemara in the place where the guest had interrupted him, greeted him, and looked at him with surprise: why did this person come to disturb him from his studies.

Our grandfather responded to him with the language of wisdom, "I have come to see if the external matters are explained inside to the correct degree, or if the explanation is forced." Some people said that he told him as follows, "If the matters inside are like the external matters, and there is no explanation to the essence of the acquisition, for both this and that are one matter."

The Gaon understood that the guest wanted to see how the head of the house fulfils inside his home that which he writes outside, for the following verse is written atop the lintel of the Mahar'sha's house, "A stranger shall not spend the night outside, for I open my doors to a guest." The Gaon told our grandfather that he did not have to make all this effort, for it is assumed that the descendants of Abraham welcome guests. However, it is somewhat difficult, for sir explains the verse according to its form, and it is said that if one explains a verse according to its form, it is definitive. However, one can answer: with regard to what is this stated? With regard to the verse, "And they saw the G–d of Israel,"[5], for it already had said, "For no person shall see Me and live."[6]. Unkelos in his wisdom translates this as "The precious G–d of Israel," but with regard to the hosting of guests, where it says (Tractate Shabbat 127a), the hosting of guests is greater than greeting the face of the Divine Presence – everyone who translates the verse in its form translates it correctly.

Our grandfather heard this and said, "Had I journeyed to Poland only to hear this, it would have been sufficient. And now I will tell him my name and my connection. My name is Shmuel, the grandson of Rabbi Yosef, the brother of the father of sir."

[Page 452]

Isaac Bashevis Singer

The Mirror

Published by Y. L. Magnes at Hebrew University of Jerusalem 5735 (1975).[7]

An error is no small matter – Levi–Yitzchak would say. And when one invited Kamtza to the feast, and Bar Kamtza came, Jerusalem was destroyed[8]. If one word is incorrect, a Torah scroll can be invalid. About a hundred years ago, and perhaps more, a scribe lived in Szczebrzeszyn named Reb Meshulam. That Reb Meshulam was famous. It would be said of him that he would immerse in a mikveh [ritual bath] every time he wrote the Divine Name. For that reason, it took him a long time to write. It was expensive to purchase the parchments for tefillin or mezuzahs from him. Poor people could not afford them, but wealthy people would come to him from all over, Zamość, Janów, Hrubieszów. He had a script –

[Page 453]

???. He used a gall nut ink and a format that he saw in Leipzig or in other far–off places. He made the rounds every day. On Sabbaths and festivals, he gathered young people around him and preached to them. My grandfather was of them. Usually, a scribe was unemployed, but Reb Meshulam was an accountant, and was invited to other cities to be an arbitrator. It seems that he did not have any children. I never heard that he left behind a generation.

There was a wealthy man, Reb Mottel Wolbromer, in Szczebrzeszyn at that time. He owned a house in the market and did business with grains and forests. One day, news spread in Szczebrzeszyn that Reb Mottel had begun to become unlucky. First, he became ill, and then – his wife. Later, the children became ill. He had a grain storehouse, which was set on fire and burnt down. Reb Mottele sent rafts over the Bug, but the storm winds disrupted them, broke them, and caused damage. It is said that if a person encounters tribulations, he must search his deeds. Reb Mottele was a proper, Torah observant Jew, and he made an accounting of his soul. He identified all kinds of sins, and began to fast for them. He began to arise earlier, and study before praying. He gave more charity. The wealthy people of those days were not like those of today.

Perhaps he did not have enough troubles. A good–for–nothing broke into his house. In the middle of the night, one heard steps and the wanton laughter of women.

Doors opened by themselves. As Reb Mottele was sleeping, an invisible person broke in and pulled him of the bed. One becomes embarrassed from such an encounter and tries to keep it secret. It is not appropriate for business, and certainly not for matchmaking. Aside from this, one things: perhaps it was an illusion, someone who had gotten lost. However, for how long can one hide the truth in such a small town? The household had a maid, and she fled. A demon pulled her by the hair, and he does not forgive it for sullying the bedding. It got more serious day by day. During the night, there was steam from the attic. They rolled barrels, and pushed cabinets and dressers. They whistled in the chimneys. They whispered and giggled. One Thursday, Reb Mottele's eldest daughter was kneading dough. She adorned the trough with a cushion so that ??? could lie down to sleep. She gets up in the middle of the night and lies by her on the straw sack. She made a commotion and ??? woke up. My grandmother, peace be upon her, was their neighbor, and she knew everything. She told me everything. The bandits overturned all the pots, threw the food out of the closets, ate what was prepared, and even hauled out the Passover dishes from the attic. One evening, a bandit started to bang on a window with such a racket that half the city ran away. It was no longer a secret. We stated their name but it did not help. We knew that in Szczebrzeszyn, Meshulam the scribe had amulets that stemmed from the author of a Hassidic book. We went to him, and he asked for a high price. With all his fine traits, he was someone who demanded high prices. He could demand four guilders and even more for a few parchments. One could hang up the amulets in all nooks and crannies. Nevertheless, the klipot[9] were irritated, and they broke all the vessels into shards. A stone fell near Reb Mottele's feet that would have smashed his skull into tiny pieces had it hit him on the head. He fell in the ??? hot as if he was just taken from the fire.

[Page 454]

When a tribulation comes, all ideas fall away. However, it is difficult for the intellect to comprehend. It was specifically on Thursday when the poor people would make the rounds to the houses. Some hobo came around, saw the commotion, and asked, "What is this?" The wife or a daughter explained the misfortune to him. The indigent asked, "Did you check the mezuzah?" Reb Mottele immediately entered the kitchen, washed his hands, and said, "Yes, perhaps the Jew is correct?" The wife claimed, "If a mezuzah is ??? with smoke, one does not inspect it." Nevertheless, the warning hit Reb Mottele in the head. All of his mezuzahs were cut. He ordered that they all be taken down and be repaired. After he took once glance, he let out a bitter cry. The letter daled from Echad looked like a reish[10], and read as "Acher" which is blasphemous. He took the other mezuzahs and did the same thing. It seemed as if a letter was jumping out, however the ink was fresh. There was a tumult in town. What was going on here? Whomever had one of Reb Meshulam's mezuzahs found the same mistake. It was clear that this Meshulam was a follower of Shabtai Zvi. People opened up their tefillin and discovered that they were all invalid. The man must have believed that the Messiah can only come when the people are completely guilty. They tossed sins at Jews. They rendered books invalid. The tossed a bone of a dead body into the house, so it will become impure. In those days, the Council of the Four Lands would excommunicate people in a ceremony with the blowing of the shofar and black candles. They believed that there would not be any survivor, for many had requested this gold coin. Only small change remained, and Meshulam was one of them. I forgot to mention another error that he made in the mezuzahs and the scrolls: Instead of "so that you may remember" [lema'an tizkeru], he wrote "so that you may ???" or "so that you may lie" [lema'an tishkeru]. He wrote the names of ??? and the name of Shabtai Zvi, may his name be blotted out. That Meshulam should be ??? in the city. He should be torn into pieces. However, he had traveled to Lublin for an arbitration. He wife was a coarse Jewess, who did not know her right from her left. Nevertheless, they broke all her windows. The ??? even tried to remove the beams from her house. However, the rabbi came running and stopped them. What could they do, unfortunately?

[Page 455]

It became clear that Reb Meshulam was not alone. There was an entire sect in Szczebrzeszyn. When it became clear that they had uncovered their ill deeds, they sent for a rider from Lublin to warn Meshulam that he should flee. They also left, and left their wives behind abandoned as agunot[11].

"What became of them?" asked Zalman Glezer.

"They all became apostates."

"The wives were not allowed to get married?"

"A wife of an apostate remains a married woman. It seems that none of them were given a get [bill of divorce]."

"An apostate can give a get?"

"According to the law, he remains a Jew."

———

Translator's Footnotes

Portions of the Sabbath morning service. https://www.jewishgen.org/Yizkor/Szczebrzeszyn/szc448.html - f448-1r

See https://en.wikipedia.org/wiki/Tikkun_Chatzot https://www.jewishgen.org/Yizkor/Szczebrzeszyn/szc448.html - f448-2r

Psalms 137:6. https://www.jewishgen.org/Yizkor/Szczebrzeszyn/szc448.html - f448-3r

This ends in mid–sentence here. The next page begins in Yiddish rather than Hebrew, and is apparently a different story – and the page begins in mid–sentence. The continuation is on page 454 (it seems that there was an error in collating the pages of the original book, with 451 and 454 interchanged). I moved the pages to their correct places. https://www.jewishgen.org/Yizkor/Szczebrzeszyn/szc448.html - f448-4r

Exodus 24:10. https://www.jewishgen.org/Yizkor/Szczebrzeszyn/szc448.html - f448-5r

Exodus 33:20. https://www.jewishgen.org/Yizkor/Szczebrzeszyn/szc448.html - f448-6r

On this page and the following pages, the first or last word of many lines is smudged. I put ??? where I could not make it out. https://www.jewishgen.org/Yizkor/Szczebrzeszyn/szc448.html - f448-7r

See https://en.wikipedia.org/wiki/Kamsa_and_Bar_Kamsa https://www.jewishgen.org/Yizkor/Szczebrzeszyn/szc448.html - f448-8r

A Kabbalistic word for husks or shells (i.e. non–holy or impure emanations), that does not translate well into English. See https://kabbalah.com/en/articles/klipot/ https://www.jewishgen.org/Yizkor/Szczebrzeszyn/szc448.html - f448-9r

A mezuzah with errors in the text on the parchment is considered invalid from the point of view of Jewish law, and as a bad omen in Jewish thought. The error here is particularly serious, as the word "Echad" means that G–d is one, whereas the word "Acher" (exchanging the daled for a reish), would imply that G–d is "other"). https://www.jewishgen.org/Yizkor/Szczebrzeszyn/szc448.html - f448-10r

An aguna [plural: agunot] is an abandoned wife, who is not allowed to marry. https://www.jewishgen.org/Yizkor/Szczebrzeszyn/szc448.html - f448-11r

[Page 456]

Personalities from the Past

Translated by Jerrold Landau

Donated by Anita Frishman Gabbay

Yaakov Zipper (1900 –). The adopted name of Yaakov Shtern, born in Szczebrzeszyn, near Zamość, Poland. He lived in the town of Tyszowce, near Lublin, where his father, the author of several Hebrew books, was the shochet and rabbi. He studied in cheder, and then studied Talmud and Jewish law with his father. He studied Polish and German from private tutors. He left Tyszowce in 1919, and lived illegally in Wolhyn. At the time of the Bolshevik attack on Poland (in the summer of 1920), he was sentenced by the Poles to be shot, but he was saved thanks to a guarantee that the Jews from the town of Hrubieszów gave for him. He was an active member of Hechalutz, Young Zion, and the right–leaning Poalei Zion. He worked for the TSYSHO school network in Poland. He was a member of the culture committee of the professional unions in Ludmir, Wolhyn, and later a member of the "Jewish National Workers Farband" in America. Since 1925, he was a Yiddish–Hebrew teacher in Canada, and the principal of the Peretz Schools of Montreal. He was the principal of the Winnipeg Peretz School from 1930–1934, and then again a teacher in Montreal. He made his debut with a brief sketch To Shalosh Seudos in the Palestine Shtima, Brisk, 1923. He then published narratives, poems, articles, and spreads in the Hebrew Hakochav of Warsaw, Undzer Shtime of Chelm, Green Trees, Der Chaver of Vilna, the Brisker Wachenblatt, the Kanader Adler of Montreal, and Dos Yiddishe Vort of Winnipeg, Lid Becher of Los Angeles; Kultur, Shul–Pinkas, Oifbroiz of Chicago; Di Yiddishe Velt of Vancouver; Di Woch, Yiddishe Zukunft, Oifkum, Der Yiddish Kempfer, Kinder Journal, Kinder Zeitung, Veiter, Oifn Tevel, Bitzaron, and others of New York; Haolam, Jerusalem; Hatzofeh of Tel Aviv; Argentiner Beimlech of Buenos Aires; Proletaretariter Gedank of Toronto; Oifgang of Bucharest, and others. He published in book form Geven Iz A Moment, five stories from the life of the Baal Shem Tov, published by Chaverim, Montreal, 1940, 167 pages (published also in Hebrew in Tel Aviv), On the Other Side of the Bug, a novel, published in Montreal 1946, 283 pages (published also in Hebrew in Tel Aviv, 1956, 367 pages). He received a prize from Der Zukunft for his story Mageifa [Plague]. He edited the Kanader Wochenblatt, Montreal 1926–1927 under pseudonyms: Y. Shein, Alef, Yitzchak Sternberg, Y. Nitles, and others. He was a delegate to the second World Jewish Culture Congress in New York, 1959. He lives in Montreal, Canada.

Ch. M. Keiserson, Kanader Adler, Montreal 27th edition, 1940; Sh. Giner, Tog, New York, May 1941; Y. Entin, Yiddisher Kempfer, New York, September 19, 1941; Dr. A Sukrani, from the Journal, New York, October 1941; Y. Y. Tinel, Kanader Adler,

Montreal, February 11, 1945; M. Ravitch, ibid. October 21, 1945; Avraham Reisen, Di Feder, New York, 1949; L. Steinman, History of the Zionist Workers Movement in North America, New York, 1955; Sh. Belkin, The Poalei Zion Movement in Canada, Montreal, 1956, no. 320; Nima, Avigor, Massa, Tel Aviv, September 20, 1957; M. Ungerfeld, Hatzofeh, Tel Aviv, 22 Sivan 5617 (1957); Y. Midrash, Kanader Adler, Montreal, September 25, 1959; Y. Rabinovitch, ibid. November 2, 1959.

An Unknown Commentator

In the Encyclopedia of the History of Torah Greats, page 383, we read about an "unknown commentator" with the following survey. (It is also mention in the article on Szczebrzeszyn in the Ledgers of the Council of the Four Lands.

Reb David the son of Reb Yaakov of Szczebrzeszyn

He was an author in the middle of the middle of the fourth century of the sixth millennium (at the end of the 1500s). He authored a commentary on the Targum Yonatan[1] and the second Targum on the Book of Esther, first printed in Prague, 5369 (1609), and later several more times, and it even was included in Chumashim. We do not know anything on the events of his life.

Lexicon of the New Yiddish Literature, New York, 1960

Meir Ben Samuel of Szczebrzeszyn[2]: Hebrew author of the seventeenth century. In the disastrous years of 1648–1649, he lived in Szczebrzeszyn, Russian Poland, an honored member of the community, whence he escaped on its invasion by the Cossacks, to Cracow; there he published his "Zok Haittim" (1650), an account in Hebrew verse of Jewish persecution during the Cossack uprising. This book was afterward published by Joshua B. David of Lemberg under his own name; Steinschneider was the first to discover this plagiarism. Meir wrote also "Mizmor Shir" a Sabbath hymn, in Aramaic and Judeo–German (Venice 1639).

Bibliography:

Gurland, Le–Korot ha–Gezerot, no. 3; Steinschneider, Cat. Bodl. No. G384; ??? A.S. W.

From the Jewish Encyclopedia_____

Translator's Footnotes

See

https://en.wikipedia.org/wiki/Targum_Jonathan https://www.jewishgen.org/Yizkor/Szczebrzeszyn/szc456.html - f456-1r

Spelling transcribed from the

original. https://www.jewishgen.org/Yizkor/Szczebrzeszyn/szc456.html - f456-2r

[Page 457]

Landsmanshaftn

[organizations of former residents]

The Organization of Former Shebreshin Residents in Israel

Translated by Yocheved Klausner

The echoes of the Holocaust in Europe, as millions of Jews were murdered by the Nazis and their helpers, were late in reaching the Jewish settlement in Eretz Israel. Even when the tragic news was brought by authorized and trustworthy people it was hard to believe the extent of the horror. The possibilities to save the remnants and bring them to our land were limited, due to the policy of the British government, who would not issue Aliya certificates and in general constrained the freedom of action of the Jewish settlement. However, despite the German Reich and the British authorities, the "Illegal Aliya Movement" was established in those days, bringing thousands of immigrants to our country.

With the news coming from Europe, a feeling of mourning spread over the Jewish population. At the same time, however, an intense organized activity of help and rescue began. Former residents of the various towns and shtetlach began forming organized groups – "Landsmanshaften" – aiming to extend help to the survivors and erect memorials to the annihilated Jewish settlements. The residents of each town desired to honor their past, their origin and their beloved families that had been burned at the stake, and also to remember the suffering and the heroic efforts to survive. The Shebreshin Residents' organization was among the first to undertake this task.

The first meeting of the organization, under the initiative of Mendel Boim, took place at the home of Rivka Deilis–Becher and her husband Binyamin Hersch, in Haifa. Among the first to engage in this important work were: Rivka Weinstock, Mendel Messinger and Shmuel Reichstein. A small sum of money was collected at the meeting, and it was decided to collect written material and to publish a memorial book about the Jewish community in town. Mendel Boim agreed to start collecting material and donations were received from friends all over the country. Very important help came from former Shebreshin residents living in the United States; among them the most active member was Pesach Borek.

The organization elected a committee, and it was decided to hold new elections every few years. Every year, on 27 Cheshvan, a memorial ceremony took place, to remember the perished martyrs, residents of our town. This was also an appropriate occasion to meet friends from all parts of the country and exchange stories and impressions, in an atmosphere of friendship and nostalgia.

Shebreshin was one of the oldest Jewish settlements in Poland. The Jews in town led a deep–rooted and dynamic Jewish life. However, systematic collection of material on the life in town and the happenings during the Holocaust was not easy. Shebreshin did not have a newspaper, and writers have not devoted time to write about it. The town is mentioned – occasionally and randomly – in old documents: in the reports of the Council of the Four Lands, in government archives, in books. All this had to be researched, collected and prepared for publication. Articles about the way of life in our shtetl and the horrible events that put an end to that life – we had to obtain directly from the people that are living with us today.

Our friend Mendel Boim devoted his time voluntarily to collecting material for the book, and invested great efforts in this endeavor. Material began to arrive from former residents of the town in Israel and abroad – United States, Canada and Argentina. Mendel Boim published part of the material –

Mostly reports from meetings of the committees and from assemblies – in 5 booklets (in Yiddish and Hebrew). These booklets became the basis of the book about to appear.

[Page 458]

The work gained momentum with the arrival of Devora Fleischer, who also compiled a list of Shebreshin martyrs and sent it to Yad Vashem in Jerusalem.

When Efraim Farber and Avraham Wolfson made Aliya, they too joined the effort to promote the publication of the memorial book. They undertook the task to acquire the means and to complete the collection of the material, and the enterprise moved a considerable step forward. An editorial board was elected, headed by a professional editor, who, unfortunately, found the material not organized at all. The authors had not been given guidelines and so every participant wrote on the subject that was close to his heart. The job of editing and completing the missing subjects was not easy, and it is worth mentioning that some of the important articles, quantitatively and qualitatively, were added when the book was in its last stages of preparation. Printing the material also took more time than expected, but we think that the result speaks for itself.

It is not by chance that the book appeared in the State of Israel: not only because here is the center of the Jewish people, but also because most of the former residents of the shtetl live here: they are the people who decided to complete the project, which demanded hard work, faith, perseverance and the ability to overcome obstacles.

[Pages 460-464]

The Landsmanschaft in Montreal

by Emanuel Chmielash

Translated by Moses Milstein

In 1949[1], Jews from the DP camps in Austria and Germany, the Sh'erit Ha'Pletah, among them Shebreshiner Jews, began arriving in Montreal, Canada. In 1951, there were about twenty of us. Others arrived from Israel having spent a short time there.

In the fifties, we settled in the Jewish neighborhood of the time, around the commercial center of St. Lawrence Street. We lived close to each other and saw each other practically every day. On Sundays, we all used to meet on Esplanade Street in front of the Jewish Public Library.

In 1949, the secretary of the New York Shebreshiner society, Pesach Borek, a"h, came to visit us. The meeting took place at Ephraim and Balche Milstein's house. For newcomers, it was a great pleasure to meet with old residents in a new land.

At the Milstein's house, together with P. Borek, we decided that the Shebreshiners in Montreal should organize themselves. We should get together and discuss ongoing problems. The committee was then formed of David Fuks, Wolf Ingber, and Ephraim Milstein. At the end of 1949, we called a meeting of all the Shebreshiner at Laizer Borek's house. We then elected a committee consisting of David Fuks, Wolf Ingber, Laizer Borek, Emanuel Chmielash, Azriel Drayer, and Chaim Unger, a"h. We decided that everyone should pay dues of fifty cents a month.

We then established ties with the new Shebreshiner olim in Israel. We began to send the few dollars from the dues collected to the needy landsleit, the olim chadashim, in Israel. When we discovered that there was a Shebreshiner committee organized in Israel, headed by our respected landsman, Mendl Boim, we began corresponding with him. We sent the aid money to the Shebereshiner committee care of Mendl Boim.

Our activities also consisted of honoring the yorzeit of our fallen brethren. We hired a room at the Jewish Public Library and engaged a chazzan. All the Shebreshiner in Montreal, without exception, attended. After the memorial, we dealt with various issues.

When M. Boim wrote that they were gathering material about the destruction of our people in S. in order to publish a journal describing Jewish life in S., we sent them some documents: Dr. Klukowski's book, works by the poet Sholem Stern, (a descendant of S. and Tiszewic, living now in Montreal.) Others sent along certain descriptions of organizations and living conditions in S.

Although the collections were first published in journal form, the goal of the Israeli society was to publish a yizkor book. We in Montreal began collecting funds and transferring them to the committee in Israel. However, with the arrival of new olim in Israel, the committee found itself having to use the money to help the needy.

The task of producing a yizkor book stalled. Much documentation was already in the hands of Mendel Boim. We in Montreal wrote to him often. His answers were always full of hope, but little action was forthcoming. After a while, we gave up hope, but not without disappointment. We frequently asked each other why so many other shtetlach, some smaller than S., had already produced yizkor books, but we could not seem to manage it. We went over it so often and for so long that we finally gave up on it. We all felt a certain disappointment and regret.

Then the survivors of Lublin approached us: They were going to erect a monument in the Jewish cemetery to the memory of the Jews of Lublin and surrounding area. They asked if we also wanted to commemorate the S. victims. We convened a general meeting of our landsleit. I, personally, was against a monument of stone. A tombstone, no matter how tall and wide, no matter how beautiful, is simply an "idol". On the other hand, a yizkor book is a living, movable, monument that everyone of us can embrace like a holy book, and pass along to future generations, to our children and grandchildren and great grandchildren that tells them about their origins.

We learned from the Lubliner representatives that they had sent emissaries to Poland and had brought back a small box of ashes from Belzec. According to what we know, there were also Jews from S. in Belzec. The monument was erected over the grave where the ashes were buried. It was engraved also with the name of the Shebreshiner community. Every year, during the days of repentance, we convene a yizkor at the monument.

In time, Montreal grew larger, new suburbs were built. Shebreshiners also spread out. we no longer live in compact neighborhoods near each other. But we are still close. Telephone conversations are frequent and prolonged. To every simcha celebrated by one of us, every Shebreshiner is invited. And whenever we met, we always asked, "Is there any news from Israel", meaning the yizkor book. Until...

Until several years ago, we received a letter from the Shebreshiner committee written by Ephraim Farber. Upon reading the letter resignation disappeared and hope shone on everyone's face. I myself did not remember Ephraim Farber. (He was youger than me, and before the war, he was in Warsaw). I just heard that he was Moishe "Kliske's" grandson and Mendele "Kliske's" son, and I was filled with hope that he would achieve the goal and bring out the book. Just as every Friday evening Ephraim's grandfather knocked on the doors of the stores with his hammer reminding Jews that the holy Shabbos was coming, so did his grandson with his letter hammer an "awakening".

He awakened us from our lethargy. His letter called out to us: a new committee has been established among the Shebreshiner in Israel young people who will make the yizkor book a reality.

The Israelis remember the phrase, "M'Zion tetzeh torah" to which they added three words, "M'America tetzeh mamon". We had faith in the new endeavors. They woke us up and asked of us, "Send money!" We have many feelings for our old Shebreshiner home, our spiritual home is there. We raised several thousand dollars from the barely twenty Shebreshiner families here. Some of us were vacationing in Miami, Florida for the winter and there, in the home of a Shebreshiner, Hersh Fruchter, and thanks to our dynamic president, David Fuks, we had a meeting and raised money receiving contributions as well from people who were not actually from S but from nearby shtetlach.

Thanks to David Fuks, we also managed to raise money in Toronto. There is a small, not organized, group of Shebreshiner there. David Fuks traveled to Toronto, knocked on doors, and raised funds.

We are also allied with the Shebreshiner immigrants in New York. We were visited by Freida and David Blatt of New York.

At the request of the committee in Israel regarding expenses, we organized a standing committee. along with the emissaries who had recently been in Israel, at Leibl and Gitl Akerfkug's home. Freidele Blatt was also present. We Montrealers, and Freidele Blatt speaking for the New Yorkers, undertook to raise the necessary funds.

We have to recognize our honored landsman Mendl Boim who had amassed a larger amount and speeded up the work.

We Montrealers continue our correspondence with landsleit in various cities in Canada and the U.S. Some families live in Detroit Yankel Miller; in Winnipeg Itschak and Lube Gal; in Vancouver Raizel Berger; in Nova Scotia Sapian.

We see it as our duty to hold onto our connection with every Shebreshiner. Rather than extolling the virtues of individuals or groups I will end by saying, **"Am Israel chai,b'chol tfutzot ha'olam."**

Emanuel Chmielash In the name of the Shebreshiner committee:

President: David Fuks

Secretary: Emanuel Chmielash

Montreal, September, 1982

Chairman: David Fuks, Secretary: Emanuel Chmielach

Canadian committee for Shebreshin, Montreal, September 1982

S. Landsleit in Montreal-20.5.1954

Translator's Footnote

1. Some arrived in 1948. MM

[Page 465]

The Landsmanschaft in New York
by Freide Blatt
Translated by Moses Milstein

The immigrants who came to America at the beginning of the twentieth century were not rabbis, or doctors, or professors, but they brought with them their religiosity and humanism. Not wanting to break their ties with the past, they immediately set to creating a landsmanscaft that was a model of solidarity and self–help.

The "Independent Shebreshiner Congregation" was founded on October 1, 1911. These simple people, without diplomas or rabbinical certificates, composed a constitution of 19 articles and subparagraphs. I want to note the more important paragraphs in order to bring out the noble and humanitarian approach to the problems that preoccupied them at the time: to maintain the Shebreshiner identity, and to help the members with their economic and social problems, so they would not feel alone. In other words: to give them the courage not to be overcome by demoralization and disappointment.

As I found out from others, the society sent help not only to individual people, but also to the community, to be distributed on Pesach for the needy.

The constitution was written in German–Yiddish.

****

Article 18: Executives

Abraham Begleiter–Ex–president

Chaim Weinblatt–Ex–president

Yehuda Diener–President

Leibush Neider–Vice–president

David Kave–Protocol secretary

Nachum Borenstein–Finance secretary

Chaim Mordechai Waldman–Cashier

Moshe Aharon Tolkop–gabai rishon

Mendl Bak–gabai sheiniv Zindl Messinger–Trustee

Itzhak Shafir—Trustee

Laizer Borek–Trustee

Chaim Bronfenbrener–Syangogue secretary

Leibush Waldman–Shamash

Legislative Committee

Moshe Mel–Chairman

David Eisen

Cahim Weinblatt

Yehuda Diener

Abraham Begleibter

David Kave

Moshe Aharon Tolkop

Mendl Hoff

Leizer Borek

Zindl Messinger

Yakov Shlomo Berger

Moshe Diener

Cahim Mordechai Waldman

Maier Dinerstein

Seeing the abovementioned names, we can say with pride: Ashrei, it is fortunate that the surviving Shebreshiners had such predecessors.

Unfortunately, the situation changed drastically. The few members passed away, and the direction passed to their children who were more Americanized, and the Shebreshin name held less nostalgia for them. Added to that, the great devastation tore away the tree and the roots of our origin. No more letters came from the other side to remind us who is who. Everything disappeared as smoke.

But it must be said that there remained certain individuals, such as the good and noble Pesach Borek, z"l, who came to America shortly before the outbreak of the war. He organized a committee to help the survivors. It was difficult to convince the middle-aged, and harder still, the younger generation, to walk in the footsteps of their parents. He gave a lot of his time, energy, and strength to the society. He never tired of it. He helped all the arrivals in any way he could. He was also president of the society for a short time.

Unfortunately, he became a martyr of the times, where human life is not valued. He was killed by a murderer's hand while coming back from a hospital visit to a sick Shebreshiner.

Pesach personified the most noble, the best, the most beautiful that our shtetl could produce. Whoever knew him, as I did, will never forget him. His death contributed greatly to the weakening of the landsmanschaft. One must also add that the new arrivals did not contribute as much to the wavering existence of the previous organization.

As the names of our parents, brothers and sisters were inscribed in our heart with fire and blood, so may the abovementioned names, who wrote a golden page in the history of Shebreshin, also be inscribed in this book which should serve as a monument of our martyrs.

Secretary of the Shebreshiner Society in New York

S. Relief committee New York

לזכרם

אל מלא רחמים, דיין אלמנות ואבי יתומים, אל נא
תחשה ותתאפק לדם ישראל, שנשפך כמים. המצא מנוחה
נכונה על כנפי השכינה, במעלות קדושים וטהורים, כזוהר
הרקיע מזהירים, לנשמותיהם של שש מאות רבבות בני
ישראל ובתוכם בני הקהילה הקדושה שברשין, גברים
ונשים, ילדים וילדות, שנהרגו, נשחטו, נשרפו, נחנקו ונקברו
חיים בידי מפלצות הצוררים הגרמנים ומשרתיהם הרשעים
— פולנים, אוקראינים ואחרים בגולת אירופה (במחנות
הריכוז בלז׳ץ, מיידאנק, אושוויינצ׳ים, טרבלינקה).

כולם קדושים וטהורים, בגן־עדן תהא מנוחתם. לכן
בעל הרחמים יצרור בצרור החיים את נשמתם, ה׳ הוא
נחלתם ויזכור לנו עקדתם ותעמוד לנו ולכל ישראל זכותם.
יבואו שלום וינוחו על משכבותם ונאמר אמן.

ארץ, אל תכסי דמם, ואל יהי מקום, שבו לא תישמע
זעקתם !

[Page 472]

In Their Memory

Exalted compassionate God, Judge of widows, and Father of orphans, please do not be silent or restrain Yourself for the blood of Yisrael that was spilled like water. Grant infinite rest, in Your sheltering Presence, among the holy and the pure, for the souls of the 6,000,000 children of Israel, and among them, the holy community of Shebreshin, men, women, boys and girls who were murdered, slaughtered, burned, suffocated, and buried alive by the hands of the deadly German monsters and their evil legions—Polish, Ukrainian, and others throughout Europe (in the concentration camps in Belzec, Majdanek, Auschwitz, Treblinka).

May all of them, holy and pure, find peace in Gan Eden. Therefore Master of Mercy, may their souls be bound in the bond of life, the Lord is their inheritance, and may we remember their sacrifice, and stand with us and all Israel for their merit, and let us say, amen.

NECROLOGY

Please note that the page numbers below refer to the page numbers in the original Yizkor Book and not this translation

Land, do not cover their blood, nor become a place in which their cries are not heard!

[Pages 473- 518]

Necrology - Szczebrzeszyn, Poland

Last Name	First Name	Page no.
ADLER	Alia	473
ADLER	Brane	473
ADLER	Hersch	473
AKERFLUG	Feige	474
AKERFLUG	Hersch	474
AKERFLUG	Khana	474
AKERFLUG	Rishe	474
AKERFLUG	Shamai	474
ALDER	Yitzkhak	473
ANKER	Elkana	474
ANKER	Khana	474
ANKER	Tzipe	473
ANKER	Yaakov	474
ANKER	Yisrael Pinkhas	473
ANKER	Yitzkhak Gershon	473
APELBAUM	Moshe	474
ARKES	Menakhem	485
BABAT	Shlomo	474
BAK	Khaim -	474
BARIK	Khona	474
BARIK	Leibish	474
BARIK	Moshe	474
BARIK	Pinkhas	474

BEGLEIBTER	Machle	475
BEGLEIBTER	Meir	475
BEGLEIBTER	Meni	476
BEGLEIBTER	Moshe	476,503
BEGLEIBTER	Moshe -	476
BEGLEIBTER	Natan	475
BEGLEIBTER	Perl	475
BEGLEIBTER	Pesakh	476
BEGLEIBTER	Pinkhas	475,502
BEGLEIBTER	Pinkhas	476
BEGLEIBTER	Pinkhas	476
BEGLEIBTER	Rakhel Beile	475
BEGLEIBTER	Reizl	476
BEGLEIBTER	Rivka	476
BEGLEIBTER	Roise	476
BEGLEIBTER	Sara	475,502
BEGLEIBTER	Sheindl	476
BEGLEIBTER	Shlomo	475
BEGLEIBTER	Shmuel	475
BEGLEIBTER	Simkha	475,502
BEGLEIBTER	Tova	475
BEGLEIBTER	Tscherne	476
BEGLEIBTER	Yaakov	475
BEGLEIBTER	Yaakov	475
BEGLEIBTER	Yaakov	476
BEGLEIBTER	Yekhezkel	476
BEGLEIBTER	Yeshayahu	475
BEGLEIBTER	Yisrael	476
BEGLEIBTER	Yisrael	476
BEGLEIBTER	Yosef	476
BEGLEIBTER	Yudel	476
BEGLEIBTER	Zisha	475
BEGLEITER	Yitzkhak	475
BEHAGEN	Mendl	475
BEHAGEN	Mordekhai	475
BEHAGEN	Shakhna	475

BEITSCHER	Avner	474
BEITSCHER	Avner	496
BEITSCHER	Ber	475
BEITSCHER	David	474
BEITSCHER	David	475
BEITSCHER	Eliezer	474
BEITSCHER	Ester	474
BEITSCHER	Hadas	474
BEITSCHER	Ite	474
BEITSCHER	Ite	475
BEITSCHER	Khaia Beile	474
BEITSCHER	Khana	475
BEITSCHER	Lazar	474
BEITSCHER	Leib	475
BEITSCHER	Libe	474
BEITSCHER	Male	475
BEITSCHER	Malka	474
BEITSCHER	Miriam	474
BEITSCHER	Mordekhai	474
BEITSCHER	Mordekhai	474
BEITSCHER	Moshe	474,499
BEITSCHER	Sara	474
BEITSCHER	Yaakov	474
BEITSCHER	Yehudit	499
BEITSCHER	Yitzkhak	474
BEITSCHER	Yosef	474
BEITSCHER	Yosef	474
BEITSCHER	Yosef	474
BEITSCHER	Yosef David	475
BEITSCHER	Yoseph	475
BEITSCHER	Yossel	474
BEITSCHER	Zelig	475
BERLAND	Yekhezkel	476
BERNSTEIN	Feige	476
BERNSTEIN	Feige -	476
BERNSTEIN	Perl	476
BIBERMAN	Khaia	475

BIBERMAN	Khaim	475
BIBERMAN	Leizer	475
BLANKMAN	Yekhiel (Rabbi)	475
BLAT	Motel	475
BLAT	Yaakov Moshe	475,500
BLEI	Ite Lea	475
BLEI	Mintsche	475
BLEI	Shmuel	475
BLEI	Yente	475
BLEI	Yossel	475
BLEI	Zalman	475
BLEIVEIS	Getzel	475
BLEIVEIS	Leibke	475
BLEIVEIS	Sara	475
BLEIVEIS	Shaul	475
BLEIWEISS	Bentzion	501
BLEIWEISS	Sheindl	501
BLEIWEISS	Unknown	501
BLESER	Shimon	475
BLUMBERG	Batia	475
BLUMBERG	Beile Gitel	475
BLUMBERG	Feige	475
BLUMBERG	Frida	475
BLUMBERG	Gitel	475
BLUMBERG	Sara	475
BLUMBERG	Sheindl	475
BLUMBERG	Yitzkhak	475
BLUMBERG	Yosef	475
BLUMBERG	Yosef	475
BOIM	Barukh -	474,499
BOIM	Feige	474
BOIM	Feige Beile	474
BOIM	Golde	474
BOIM	Khaia	474
BOIM	Khaim Shmuel	474

BRONSHTEIN	Aharon	476
BRONSHTEIN	Avraham	476
BRONSHTEIN	Beni	476
BRONSHTEIN	Dvora	476
BRONSHTEIN	Natan	476
BRONSHTEIN	Rostsche	476
BUKOVITZ	Yossel	474
BURSHTEIN	Gitel	474
BURSHTEIN	Leibel	474,500
BURSHTEIN	Rivka Rakhel	474
BURSHTEIN	Sara	500
BURSHTEIN	Yehoshua Yaakov	474
BURSHTEIN	Yosele	500
CHESNER	Avraham	510
CHESNER	Bat Tziona	510
CHESNER	Mordekhai	510
DANZIGER	Barukh	478
DIAMANT	Ester	478
DIAMANT	Feige	478
DIAMANT	Khana	478
DIAMANT	Libe	478
DIAMANT	Menakhem	478
DIAMANT	Shimon	478
DIAMANT	Shlomo	478
DIAMANT	Volf	478
DIAMANT	Yosef	478
DILES	- Beile	478
DILES	- Meir	478
DILES	Ester	478
DILES	Feitsche	478
DILES	Henekh	478
DILES	Shlomo	478
DILES	Yehudit	478
DIM	Dina	479
DIM	Dovsche	479

ELBAUM	Efraim	486
ELBAUM	Khana	486
ELBAUM	Moshe	486
ELBAUM	Pinkhas	486
ELBAUM	Reizl	487
ELBAUM	Sime	487
ELBAUM	Yaakov	487
ELBAUM	Yossel	487
ENGELSBERG	Unknown	487
EPPEN	Efraim	474
ERENSHTEIN	Shlomo -	474
ERLIKH	David	487
ERLIKH	Lea	487
ERLIKH	Rive	487
ERLIKH	Rukhama	487
ERLIKH	Tscherne	487
ERLIKH	Yekhezkel	487
ERLIKH	Yisraelke	487
FARBER return	Zalman	487
FAS	Chanatsche	487
FAS	Khaim	487
FEILER	Feivele	487,510
FEILER	Rivka	487
FEILER	Shaul Yosef	487
FELHENDLER	Etel	506
FELHENDLER	Rachle	509
FELHENDLER	Shmuel -	509
FERBER	Avraham	487
FERBER	Barukh	487
FERBER	Mendl	487
FERHENDLER	Barukh	496
FERSHT	Moshe	487
FERSHT	Moshe	487
FERSHT	Yitzkhak	487
FINK	Barukh	487
FINK	Lea	487

FINK	Malka	487
FINK	Tzvi	487
FINKEL	Avraham	487
FINKEL	Barukh	487
FINKEL	Frida	487
FIRER	Elke	487
FIRER	Etel	487
FIRER	Hene Brakha	487
FIRER	Khaim	487
FIRER	Khava	487
FIRER	Mordekhai -	487
FIRER	Nekhemia	487
FIRER	Perl	487
FIRER	Rakhel	487
FIRER	Shmuel	487
FIRER	Tuvia	487
FISHER	Khana Brakha	487
FLEISHER	Aharon	488
FLEISHER	Avraham	488
FLEISHER	Barukh	488
FLEISHER	Dan	488
FLEISHER	David	488
FLEISHER	Dvora	488
FLEISHER	Dvora	488
FLEISHER	Ester	488
FLEISHER	Etel	488
FLEISHER	Kopel	488
FLEISHER	Lea	488
FLEISHER	Mashe	488
FLEISHER	Meitsche	488
FLEISHER	Miriam	488
FLEISHER	Mordekhai	488
FLEISHER	Motel	488
FLEISHER	Nicha	488
FLEISHER	Reuven	488
FLEISHER	Rivka	488

FLEISHER	Sara	488
FLEISHER	Sara	488
FLEISHER	Sender	488
FLEISHER	Shalom	488
FLEISHER	Shlomo	488
FLEISHER	Somek	488
FLEISHER	Yaakov -	488
FLEISHER	Yaakov Leib	488
FLEISHER	Yitzkhak	488
FLEISHER	Yoel	488
FLEISHER	Yoseph	488
FLIGELTOIB	Binis	488
FLIGELTOIB	Nakhum	488
FLINDER	Nicha	488
FRENKEL	Barukh	488
FRENKEL	Mordekhai	488
FRIDMAN	Miriam	488
FRIDWALD	Eliahu	488
FRIDWALD	Hadasa	488
FRIDWALD	Nekhama	488
FRIDWALD	Pinkhas	488
FRIDWALD	Rivka	488
FRIDWALD	Sara	488
FRIDWALD	Yehudit	488
FRIMER	Motel	488
FRIMSON	Simkha	488
FROST	Arie	488
FROST	Avigdor	488
FROST	Avraham	488
FROST	Beniamin	488
FROST	Brakha	488
FROST	Bronia	488
FROST	Dvora	488
FROST	Dvora	488
FROST	Ester	488
FROST	Khava	488

FROST	Leibel	488
FROST	Moshe	488
FROST	Rakhel	488
FROST	Rivka	488
FROST	Sara	488
FROST	Shamai	488
FROST	Shlomo	488
FROST	Tova	488
FROST	Yona	488
FROST	Zalman	488
FROST	Zeev	488
FUKS	Blime	487
FUKS	Efraim	487
FUKS	Fishel	487
FUKS	Fradel	487
FUKS	Lea	487
FUKS	Male	487
FUKS	Roise	487
FUKS	Sheindl	487
FUTER	Berisch	487
FUTER	Sara Khana	487
GARTLER	Pinkhas	476
GEDOCHT	Bentzion	477
GELD return	Avraham	477
GELD	Khana	477
GELD	Lea	477
GELD	Rakhel	477
GELD	Sara	477
GELD	Sheindl	477
GELD	Yokheved	477
GELERNTER	Drezil	477,504
GELERNTER	Khava Sara	477
GELERNTER	Moshe Arie	477
GELERNTER	Yitzkhak	477
GELIE	Yehoshua	477
GERENREICH	Shaulke	478

GERENREICH	Yehoshua	478
GERENREICH	Yente	478
GERENREICH	Yitzkhak	478
GERENSTEIN	- Ester	478
GERENSTEIN	Hinde	478
GERENSTEIN	Khaim	478
GERENSTEIN	Shmuel	478
GERENSTEIN	Zelig	478
GERMANOWITZ	Isser	478
GERMANOWITZ	Meno	478
GERMANOWITZ	Shlomo	478
GERMANOWITZ	Yisrael	478
GERSHTENBLAT	Rakhel	478
GERTNER	Rakhel	477
GESHICHTER	Yosef	478
GEVERTZ	Avraham	477
GEVERTZ	Mordekhai	477
GEVERTZ	Peshe	477
GEVERTZ	Pinkhas	477
GEVERTZ	Sara	477
GILIS	Reizl	477
GINTZBURG	Perl	477
GINTZBURG	Yerakhmiel	477
GLATMAN	David	477
GLATMAN	Hoshea	477
GLATMAN	Lea	477
GLATMAN	Rukhama	477
GLATMAN	Shia	477
GLATMAN	Yehoshua	477
GLATMAN	Yehudit	477
GLAZER	Leibke	477
GOLD	Avraham	477
GOLDBERG	Rafael	477
GOLDBERG	Sara	477
GOLDBERG	Yente	477
GOLDGOBER	Avraham -	477
GOLDGOBER	Mendl	477

GOLDGRUBER	- Meir	477
GOLDGRUBER	Avraham	477
GOLDGRUBER	Ester	477
GOLDGRUBER	Feiga	477
GOLDGRUBER	Gitel	477
GOLDGRUBER	Hersch	477
GOLDGRUBER	Itsche Hirsch	477
GOLDGRUBER	Khaia	477
GOLDGRUBER	Khana	477
GOLDGRUBER	Mendl	477
GOLDGRUBER	Miriam	477
GOLDGRUBER	Miriam Lea	477
GOLDGRUBER	Mordekhai	477
GOLDGRUBER	Moshe	477
GOLDGRUBER	Naftali	477
GOLDGRUBER	Serl	477
GOLDGRUBER	Yaakov Leib	477
GOLDGRUBER	Yeshayahu	477
GOLDGRUBER	Yosef	477
GOLDMAN	Grine	477
GOLDMAN	Shimon	477
GRAD	Shmuel Yankel	478
GRAF	Shakhna	478
GRAND	Berisch	478
GRAND	Leibish	478
GREIBER	Tova	478
GREIBER	Zalman	478
GRIN	Eidel	478
GRIN	Moshe Shmuel	478
GRINFELD	Hinde	478
GROISBARD	Moshe David	478
GROISBARD	Pinkhas	478
GROISBARD	Riva	478
GROISBARD	Rivka	478

KAVERSHTOK	Berisch	489
KAVERSHTOK	Brone	490
KAVERSHTOK	Getzel	490
KAVERSHTOK	Khaim	490
KAVERSHTOK	Rivka	489
KAVERSHTOK	Yaakov	490
KEITEL	Mechl	490
KEITEL	Sara	490
KELACH	Bentzion	491
KELACH	Lane	491
KELACH	Shlomo	491
KELNER	Khaia	491
KELNER	Pese	491
KESEL	- Elimelekh	491
KESEL	Yehoshua	491
KHMELASH	Avraham	483
KHMELASH	Beniamin	483
KHMELASH	Berisch	483
KHMELASH	Elkana	483
KHMELASH	Feige	483,508
KHMELASH	Khana	483
KHMELASH	Lea	483
KHMELASH	Miriam	483
KHMELASH	Renele	483
KHMELASH	Reni	483
KHMELASH	Rivka	483
KHMELASH	Rivtsche	483
KHMELASH	Shabtai -	483
KHMELASH	Sheindl	483
KHMELASH	Shmuel	483
KHMELASH	Tzipora	483
KHMELASH	Yaakov	483
KHMELASH	Yehoshua	483

KLEINER	Berele	491
KLEINER	Lea	491
KLEINER	Yaakov	491
KLIGER	Etel	491
KLIGER	Feige	490
KLIGER	Menashe	490
KLIGER	Moshe	491
KLIGER	Moshe	491
KLIGER	Shalom David	491
KLIGER	Shmuel	490
KLIGER	Shmuel -	491
KLIGER	Shmuel David	491
KLINGER	Shmuel	491
KNEIDEL	Dovidsche	491
KNEIDEL	Feivel	491
KOHEN	Dvora	489
KOHEN	Khaim	489
KOHEN	Yehoshua	489
KOHEN	Yehoshua	489
KOHEN	Yente	489
KOHEN	Yosef	489
KOIFMAN	Avraham	490
KOIFMAN	Gitel	490
KOIFMAN	Guta	490
KOIFMAN	Khaia	490
KOIFMAN	Khana	490
KOIFMAN	Male	490
KOIFMAN	Mendl	490
KOIFMAN	Mendl	490
KOIFMAN	Sara	490
KOIFMAN	Shimon	490
KOIFMAN	Shimon	490

KOIFMAN	Shucher	490
KOIFMAN	Shucher	490
KOIFMAN	Yaakov	490
KOIFMAN	Yitzkhak	490
KOIL	Aharon	490
KOIL	Avraham	490
KOIL	Avraham	490
KOIL	Avraham -	490
KOIL	Berl	490
KOIL	Berl	490
KOIL	Dov	490
KOIL	Dvora	490
KOIL	Dvora	490
KOIL	Eliezer	490
KOIL	Gitel	490
KOIL	Hinde	490
KOIL	Khaim	490
KOIL	Khaim	490
KOIL	Rakhel Lea	490
KOIL	Riva	490
KOIL	Shimon	490
KOIL	Shmuel	490
KOIL	Shmuel	490
KOIL	Shmuel	490
KOIL	Tscherne	490
KOIL	Tuvia	490
KOIL	Yehoshua	490
KOIL	Yehuda	490
KOIL	Yosef	490
KOPACH	Etel	490
KOPACH	Rakhel	490
KOPACH	Yosef	490

KOPF	Yosef	512
KORN	Mendl	490
KORN	Rosche	490
KORNSTEIN	Efraim	490
KORNSTEIN	Leibel	490
KOTLOSCH	Shmuel -	490
KRAMF	Shia Grishke	491
KUCHER	Leib	490
KUCHER	Simkha	490
LANDAU	Eliakim	483
LAS	Berisch	483
LAS	David	483,508
LAS	Lea	483
LAS	Lipman	483
LAS	Mordekhai	483
LAS	Rakhel	483
LAS	Sara Ite	483
LAS	Yente	483
LAS	Zlate	483
LAZAR	Yitzkhak	483
LEDERICH	Frida	484
LEDERICH	Moshe	484, 508
LEMER	Leibish	484
LEMER	Mordekhai	484
LEMER	Yitzkhak	484
LERMAN	Moshe	484
LERNER	Gitul	484
LERNER	Khaia	484
LERNER	Mosheke	484
LERNER	Shlomo -	484
LERNER	Yekhiel	484,512
LERNZON	Yitzkhak -	484

LIBEL	Perl	483
LIBEL	Pinkhas	483
LIBEL	Sara	483
LIBHABER	Volf	483
LIBLE	Yaakov	483
LIKHT	- Alia	483
LIKHT	Rivka	483
LIKHT	Yitzkhak Eli	483
LIKHTENBERG	Yente	484
LIKHTFELD	Blime	484
LIKHTFELD	David	484
LIKHTFELD	Dvora	484
LIKHTFELD	Khaia	483
LIKHTFELD	Menashe	484
LIKHTFELD	Mordekhai	483
LIKHTFELD	Sara	483
LIKHTFELD	Yekhezkel	484
LIKHTFELD	Yossel	484
LOHS	Khaia	483
LOHS	Yosef	483
LONGBARD	Faivel	483
LONGBARD	Sheindl	483
LOTVOK	Shmuel	483
LUSTENBERG	Menakhem	483
LUSTENBERG	Pinkhas	483
LUSTENBERG	Yosef	483
LUSTMAN	David	483
LUSTMAN	Feige	483
LUSTMAN	Khaim	483
LUSTMAN	Khana	483
LUSTMAN	Moshe	483

MEIMAN	Fradel	485
MEIMAN	Gitel	485
MEIMAN	Hersch	485
MEIMAN	Ite	485
MEIMAN	Khaim	485
MEIMAN	Khaim	485
MEIMAN	Khana	485
MEIMAN	Leib	485
MEIMAN	Reizl	485
MEIMAN	Rochtsche	485
MEIMAN	Shlomo	485
MEIMAN	Yaakov	485
MEIMAN	Yosef	485
MEIMAN	Yosef	485
MEL	Avraham	485
MEL	Ite	485
MEL	Libe	485
MEL	Malka	485
MEL	Miriam	485
MEL	Sara	485
MEL	Shemaia	485
MEL	Shmuel	485
MEL	Shmuel -	485
MEL	Tzipe	485
MEL	Yitzkhak	485
MELER	- Feige	485
MELER	Brone	485
MELER	David	485
MELER	Shmuel -	486
MELER	Tzadok	485
MELER	Tzipora	485
MELER	Tzvi	485

MILSHTEIN	Yisrael	485
MINCBERG	Reuven	485
MINCBERG	Yitzkhak	485
MINTZ	Beile	485
MINTZ	Fania	485
MINTZ	Mikhal	485
MINTZ	Motel	485
MINTZ	Sara -	485
MINTZ	Shlomo	485
MINTZ	Yaakov	485
MINTZ	Yisrael -	485
MINTZ	Yisrael Menakhem	485
MITAG	Yudel	484
MITLER	Barukh	484
MITLER	Barukh	484
MITLER	Chanatsche	484
MITLER	Leib	484
MITLER	Rakhel Lea	484
MITLER	Rivka	484
MITLER	Yitzkhak	484
MITZNER	Aizik	485
MITZNER	Khana Rakhel	485
MOBE	Feige	484
MOBE	Heschel	484
MOBE	Motel	484
MOBE	Pesel	484
MOBE	Pesel	484
MOBE	Rivka	484
MOBE	Shmuel	484
MOBE	Tova	484
MOCHEROVSKY	Berisch	484

ROITMAN	Khaia Ite	491
ROITMAN	Khaim	491
ROITMAN	Nakhum	491
ROITMAN	Nakhum	491
ROITMAN	Roise	491
ROITMAN	Yaakov Moshe	491
ROITMAN	Yehoshua	491
ROITMAN	Yisrael	491
ROSENAIL	Yisraelke	491
ROSENFELD	Binis	491
ROSENFELD	Erisch	491
ROSENFELD	Feige	491
ROTENTELER	Berl	491
ROTENTELER	Feivel	491
ROTENTELER	Khaia	491
ROTENTELER	Mintsche	491
ROTENTELER	Roise	491
ROTMAN	Moshe	491
ROZENBERG	Yehoshua	491
ROZENBLAT	Yitzkhak	491
_SACHAWOLSKI	Avraham Yitzkhak	486
SACHAWOLSKI	Bentzion	486
SACHAWOLSKI	Nekhemia	486
SAFIR	David	486
SHAFIR	Roise	492
SHAK	Henekh	492, 515
SHAPIRA	Asher	494
SHAPIRA	Bina	494
SHAPIRA	Lea	494
SHAPIRA	Rivka	494
SHAPIRA	Yitzkhak	494
SHAPIRA	Yosele	494

SHER	Mordekhai	494
SHER	Mordekhai	494
SHER	Moshe	494
SHER	Moshe	494
SHER	Neche	494
SHER	Noakh	494
SHER	Rafael -	494
SHER	Sara -	494
SHER	Shimon	494
SHER	Shlomo Yisrael	494
SHER	Shmuel	494
SHER	Shprintza	494
SHER	Yaakov	494, 518
SHER	Yaakov	494
SHER	Yeshiyah	494
SHER	Yisrael	494
SHFER	Avraham	495
SHFER	Beniamin	495
SHFER	Daniel	495
SHFER	Itsche	495
SHFER	Leibel	495
SHFER	Moshe	495
SHFER	Moshe	495
SHFER	Sheindl	495
SHFER	Yankel	495
SHFER	Yosef	495
SHIEWITZ	Eidel	493
SHIEWITZ	Eliahu	493
SHIEWITZ	Lea	493
SHIEWITZ	Leibish	493
SHIEWITZ	Malka	493
SHIEWITZ	Yeshayahu	493

SHIEWITZ	Zinvel	493
SHISEL	Aharon	494
SHISEL	Avraham	494
SHISEL	Berisch	494
SHISEL	Bina	493
SHISEL	Brone	493
SHISEL	Matatiahu	493
SHISEL	Sara	493
SHISEL	Shmuel	493
SHISEL	Shprintza	493
SHITZ	Bashe	494
SHITZ	Bentzion	494
SHITZ	David	517
SHITZ	Khana	494, 517
SHITZ	Leibel	494
SHITZ	Moshe	494
SHITZ	Rivka	517
SHITZ	Shmuel	494, 517
SHITZ	Yankel	494, 517
SHITZ	Yitzkhak	494
SHITZ	Zalman	494
SHLEIFER	Barukh	494
SHLEIFER	Brakha	494
SHLEIFER	Freidel	494
SHLEIFER	Moshe	494
SHLEIFER	Shlomo	494
SHMIRA	Feige	494
SHMIRA	Hadas	494
SHMIRA	Tudrus	494
SHMIRA	Yosef	494
SHMUEL	Khaim	518
SHPEIZINGER	Hersch	494
SHPEIZINGER	Monisch	494

SHPEIZINGER	Yetel	494
SHPER	Beile	515
SHPER	Etke	515
SHPER	Goltsche	515
SHPER	Leon	515
SHPER	Unknown	515
SHPER	Unknown	515
SHPRINGER	Avraham	495
SHPRINGER	Berl	495
SHPRINGER	Betzalel	495
SHPRINGER	Brakha	495
SHPRINGER	David	495
SHPRINGER	Hersch	495
SHPRINGER	Hersch	495
SHPRINGER	Khaia	495, 518
SHPRINGER	Khaia	495
SHPRINGER	Khaia Lea	495
SHPRINGER	Leib	495
SHPRINGER	Leib	495
SHPRINGER	Moshe	495
SHPRINGER	Moshe Aharon	495
SHPRINGER	Perl	495
SHPRINGER	Peshe	495
SHPRINGER	Reizl	495
SHPRINGER	Shimon	495
SHPRINGER	Shimon	495
SHPRINGER	Yeshayahu	495
SHPRINGER	Yeshayahu	495
SHPRINGER	Yosef	495
SHPUL	Barukh	495
SHPUL	Brakha	495
SHPUL	Etel	495
SHPUL	Getzel	495

SHPUL	Hersch	495
SHPUL	Ite	495
SHPUL	Keila	495
SHPUL	Keila	495
SHPUL	Khaia -	495
SHPUL	Khana	495
SHPUL	Khana	495
SHPUL	Malka	495
SHPUL	Miriam	495
SHPUL	Miriam	495
SHPUL	Moshe	495
SHPUL	Pinkhas	495
SHPUL	Rakhel	495
SHPUL	Shimshon	495
SHPUL	Shmuel	495
SHPUL	Sonia	495
SHPUL	Yosef	495
SHPUL	Yosef	495
SHREIER	Reizl	495
SHRIFT	Beile	495
SHRIFT	Berl	495
SHRIFT	Dina	495
SHRIFT	Itzik	495
SHRIFT	Khaia	495
SHRIFT	Mashe	495
SHRIFT	Race	495
SHRIFT	Reuven	495
SHRIFT	Sara	495
SHRIFT	Shlomo	495
SHRIFT	Yeshayahu	495
SHRIFT	Yosef	495
SHTADFELD	Gershon	492
SHTAHL	Efraim	492

SHTAHL	Getzel	492
SHTAHL	Hersch	492
SHTAHL	Sara	492
SHTAHL	Yona	492
SHTARKER	Motel	492
SHTEIKELER	Pesakh	515
SHTEINBERG	Eidel	492
SHTEINBERG	Etel	492
SHTEINBERG	Frida	492
SHTEINBERG	Hersch	492
SHTEINBERG	Khaia	492
SHTEINBERG	Khana	492
SHTEINBERG	Riva	492
SHTEINBERG	Shimon	492
SHTEINBERG	Yehoshua	492
SHTEINBERG	Yosef	492
SHTEINKLOPER	Khana	493
SHTEM	Simkha	493
SHTEMER	Mintsche	493
SHTERN	Dovidsche	493
SHTERN	Efraim -	493
SHTERN	Frida	493
SHTERN	Khanan	493
SHTERN	Reisele	493
SHTERN	Sara	493
SHTERN	Sara	493
SHTERN	Simkha	493
SHTERN	Yaakov -	493
SHTERN	Yisraelka	493
SHTERN	Zalman	493
SHTERNFELD	Gedalia	493
SHTERNFELD	Yosef	483,510
SHTERNFELD	Zelig	493

SHTREIKHER	Yentsche	493
SHTROUZER	Aharon David	493
SHTROUZER	Fradel	493
SHTROUZER	Peshe	493
SHTROUZER	Rakhel	493
SHTROUZER	Sara Gitel	493
SHTROUZER	Tova	493
SHTUB	Motel	492
SHTUB	Perl	492
SHTURMAN	Avraham	492
SHUR	Khaia	492
SHUR	Moshe	492
SHUR	Rakhel	492
SHVARTZ	Beniamin	492
SHVARTZ	Efraim -	492
SHVARTZBERG	Daniel	492
SHVARTZBERG	Yehoshua	492
SHVITZER	- Zaidel	492
SHVITZER	Alter	492
SHVITZER	David	492
SHVITZER	Frida	492
SHVITZER	Henie	492
SHVITZER	Khana	492
SHVITZER	Khava	492
SHVITZER	Lea	492
SHVITZER	Mordekhai	492
SHVITZER	Moshe	492
SHVITZER	Reuven	492
SHVITZER	Yaakov	492
SHVITZER	Yankel	492
SHVITZER	Yitzkhak	492
SHVITZER	Yosef -	492
SHVITZER	Zalman	492

Shebreshin Memorial Book

TENENBAUM	Hersch	482
TENENBAUM	Meml	506
TENENBAUM	Mordekhai	482
TENENBAUM	Rechl	506
TENENBAUM	Yisrael	482
TENTZER	- Moshe	482
TENTZER	Avraham	482
TENTZER	Avraham	482
TENTZER	Barukh	482
TENTZER	Bat Tziona	482
TENTZER	Beile	482
TENTZER	Beile	482
TENTZER	Bentzion	482
TENTZER	Eidel	482
TENTZER	Khaia	482
TENTZER	Khaim	482
TENTZER	Khana	482
TENTZER	Leibish	482
TENTZER	Mordekhai	482
TENTZER	Mordekhai	482
TENTZER	Motel	482
TENTZER	Motele	482
TENTZER	Roschke	482
TENTZER	Shmuel	482
TENTZER	Yaakov	482
TENTZER	Yehoshua	482
TENTZER	Yehoshua	482
TENTZER	Yekhiel	482
TENTZER	Yerakhmiel	482
TSHOPKOVSKY	Alter	482
TSHOPKOVSKY	Eli	482
TSHOPKOVSKY	Yekhezkel	482
TUKHSHNEIDER	Azriel	482

TUKHSHNEIDER	Dvora	482
TUKHSHNEIDER	Etel	482
TUKHSHNEIDER	Itsche	482
TUKHSHNEIDER	Khana	482
TUKHSHNEIDER	Leibish	482
TUKHSHNEIDER	Motel	482
TUKHSHNEIDER	Sheindl	482
TUKHSHNEIDER	Yitzkhak	482
TUKHSHNEIDER	Yoseph	482
TULKOP	Tscherne	482
TUPEL	Mendl	482
TUPEL	Rakhel	482
TUPEL	Yisrael	482
TZALER	Berl	489
TZALER	Khana	489
TZALER	Mordekhai	489
TZALER	Yosef	489
TZALTER	Itke	489
TZIMERMAN	Yehoshua	489
TZITRIN	Chanatsche	489
TZITRIN	David -	489
TZITRIN	Dnuch	489
TZITRIN	Ester Gitel	489
TZITRIN	Khaim	489
TZITRIN	Monik	489
TZITRIN	Note	489
TZITRIN	Note	489
TZITRIN	Perl	489
TZITRIN	Shmuel Leib	489
TZITRIN	Yaakov	489
TZITRIN	Yaakov -	489
TZITRIN	Yaakov -	489
TZITRIN	Yankel	489

TZITRIN	Yehoshua	489
TZITRIN	Yente	489
TZUKER	- Meir	489
TZUKER	Avraham	489
TZUKER	Elke	489
TZUKER	Hersch	489
TZUKER	Hersch	489
TZUKER	Hersch	489
TZUKER	Hinde	489
TZUKER	Khaia	489
TZUKER	Lea	489
TZUKER	Male	489
TZUKER	Meir	489
TZUKER	Mordekhai	489
TZUKER	Moshe	489
TZUKER	Moshe	489,510
TZUKER	Pnina -	489
TZUKER	Rakhel	489
TZUKER	Reuven	489
TZUKER	Riva	489
TZUKER	Yaakov	489
TZUKER	Yehoshua	489
TZUKER	Yehoshua	489
TZUKER	Yitzkhak	489
TZUKER	Yitzkhak	489
TZUKER	Yitzkhak Meir	489
TZUKER	Yosef	489
TZUKER	Yosef	489
TZUKERSTEIN	Herschel	489
TZUKERSTEIN	Sheindl	489
TZUKERSTEIN	Sheindl	489
TZUKERSTEIN	Tzvia	489
TZUKERSTEIN	Yankel	489

TZUKERSTEIN	Yisrael	489
TZUKERSTEIN	Yudel	489
UNGER	- Leib	473
UNTZUG	Rivka Rakhel	473
VAGNER	Avraham	480
VAGNER	Eliezer	480
VAGNER	Leizer	480
VAGNER	Ozer	480
VAGNER	Shmuel	480
VAGNER	Tzila	480
VAKS	Aharon Leib	480
VAKS	Avraham Yitzkhak	480
VAKS	Feige	480
VAKS	Gitel	480
VAKS	Khaim	480
VAKS	Khaim Zalman	480
VAKS	Khana Ite	480
VAKS	Mikhael	480
VAKS	Moshe	480
VAKS	Neche	480
VAKS	Perl	480
VAKS	Rakhel	480
VAKS	Sara	480
VAKS	Shia	480,506
VAKS	Yaakov	480
VAKS	Yehuda	480
VALDMAN	Avraham	480
VALDMAN	Tova	480
VARTMAN	Nekhama	481
VASER	Khaim Moshe	480
VASER	Shlomoke	480
VEGMEISTER	Ester	480

VEGMEISTER	Yekhezkel	480
VEINBERG	Barukh Leib	480
VEINBERG	Dvora	480
VEINBERG	Dvora	480
VEINBERG	Hersch	480
VEINBERG	Nicha	480
VEINBERG	Reizl	480
VEINBERG	Shalom	480
VEINBERG	Volf	480
VEINBERG	Yaakov	480
VEINBERG	Yermiyahu	480
VEINBLAT	Arie	506
VEINBLAT	Getzel	480
VEINBLAT	Lea	480
VEINBLAT	Leibel	480
VEINBLAT	Mendl	480
VEINBLAT	Perl	480,504
VEINBLAT	Yosef	480
VEINBLAT	Zelig	480
VEINSHTOK	Shaul	481
VEINSHTOK	Zelde	481
VEIS	David	481
VEIS	Eliahu	481
VEIS	Etel	481
VEISSFELD	Aizik	481
VEISSFELD	Sheindl	481
VEITZ	Feige	481
VERCER	Shmariahu	481
VERCER	Yisrael	481
VILDMAN	Perl	481
VILDMAN	Rakhel	481
VILDMAN	Yokheved	481
VINMAN	Khaia	480

VINMAN	Mordekhai	480
VOLF	Brakha	480
VOLF	Male	480
VOLF	Moshe	480
VOLF	Yehoshua	480
VOLFSON	Dvora	480,505
VOLFSON	Elke	480
VOLFSON	Henekh	480
VOLFSON	Yosef	480
WARMAN	Lea	480
WARMAN	Rivka	480
WARMAN	Yisrael	480
WARMAN	Yosef	480
WEINREB	Avraham -	481
WEINREB	Ite -	480
WEINREB	Shakhna	480
YAHR	Fradel	482
YAHR	Lea	482
YAHR	Yankel	482
YAHR	Yoel	482
YURPEST	Avraham	482
YURPEST	Henie	482
ZEIDEL	Aharon	481
ZEIDEL	Gershon	481
ZEIDEL	Mirl	481
ZEIDEL	Moshe	481
ZEIDEL	Sheindl	481,508
ZEIDEL	Shifra	481
ZEIDEL	Yaakov	481
ZEIDMAN	Mendl	481
ZELTZER	Shalom	482
ZHIRO	Keiltsche	482
ZHIRO	Leizer	482

[Page 496]

They Fell in Battle with the Nazis

Yosel Bokovitch

Avner Beitcher

Aharon Dreier

Abraham Hochboim

Abraham Waldman

Abraham Farber

Baruch Feldhendler

Yosef Tzoler

Ephraim Itzhak Schwartz

Motl Shtarker

Hersh Schpilzinger

[Page 497]

Fallen in Battle, in the Israel Wars

Translated by Yocheved Klausner

Yitzhak Lechfeld

Yitzhak Lechfeld fell in the battle of Jenin on Tuesday, 27 Iyar 5727 (6 June 1967).

"Yitzhak, z"l, was on his way to rescue wounded soldiers when he was hit by enemy gunfire. He was loyal to his task and his friends. Yitzhak's holy memory will be kept proudly in our hearts. May his memory be blessed."

(From the announcement of General Moshe Dayan, Minister of Defense).

Yitzhak Lechfeld

Yitzhak Meir Messinger

On Yom Kippur 1973, Yitzhak Messinger and three other IDF officers fought with their tank against 30 Syrian tanks. They were hit and burned with their tank. He was 26 years old.

He left a wife and two little children, who are mourning their father to this day.

Yitzhak Meir is the son of Hersh Messinger (son of Yitzhak Meir) from Shebreshin. He survived the Russian concentration camps, helped many friends in their need, but unfortunately lost his wife Chaia Kelner. Returning to Poland, he built a new life with his wife, Sheindl, who had experienced the difficult road of war and suffering. They had two children, one of them Yitzhak Meir, who fell heroically in battle.

Yitzhak Meir Messinger

Moshe Sher

Moshe Sher was three years old when he made Aliya with his parents in 1950. He was born on 14 Tevet 5708 (27 December, 1947) in Reichenbach, Germany.

He attended Moriah elementary school in Haifa. After that, he studied at an evening school for a year, and became a locksmith specializing in welding. He was a member of Hano'ar Ha'oved movement, and became an instructor. He was very active in public issues.

In July 1965 he enlisted in the IDF and volunteered for the Nahal brigade. He was killed during active duty as the car he was driving had an accident on the way to Eilat. It happened on 4 Sivan, 5728 (31 May, 1968), he was buried in the Military Cemetery in Haifa.

משה זיסברגר

(נהרג: בחיפה בפ' תשרי תרצ"ט — 4.10.38)

א.

שוטר עברי היה, ועל משמרתו נפל.
בערב יום הכפורים, כשהוא עומד במש־
מר הדרכים בחיפה, פגע הכדור מן
המארב בלבו והוא נפל בפקטים. איננו
עוד אתנו. החבר הטוב עם ארשת הח־
נים העליזה תמיד כאומרת: יש טעם
לחיים, כדאי לחיות.
בן 24 במותו. משברשין, ליד לוב־
לין בפולין, עיירה הקטנה, אשר בערב
קונגרסים ציונים גדולה ההתלהבות בה
ומלאו הוצאותיה ויכוחים ומריבות ומ־
את שקלים נפוצים, למעלה מהמשוער.
והגא, משה, בראש הפעולה. עשה עבר־
דתו בערנות ובמסירות בה רבה, כאשר
ידע רק האדם, שהעבודה הזאת היא
עיקר חייו. שנים רבות היה מקומו
בשרות "החלוץ", וגם כאן נילח כרך
ויכולת, וחיה הרוח החיה בסניף.

1932. תנועת הכבוש הגדול של החלוץ
בהכשרה, תנועת המרד המפועיר של
נוער. חברים בורחים מהבית עם תרמי־
לים על השכם, מי ברגל ומי ברכב,
ונודדים בהמונים ברחבי פולין, כובשים
ערים ועיירות נדחות — לעבודה, לחי־
שותוף, ושירת חיים עוה בנפשם: ארץ
ישראל. ומשה בין הראשונים. מתנלגל
לכפר נידח, בורקוב ליד קילץ. שם נע־
שה "כיבוש" חרש — פלונת הכשרת
"אגרודת ישע במסתרה, בתנאים גרו־
ים, קם המפעל הודש, קבוץ התכשרה
"נש בורוכוב.

ב־1933 אנשר לעבר יוצא הבוהת
לתכניות. העליה סונבית. הפצב בציונות

עורד, קשה. הוא נאלץ ל־הכות. נפטר־
תי אתו בעיירתי ושברשין כבר אינה
סוערת. פנה ההתלהבות ואת הכל נשא
הרגז. התיאש. והוא מסתובב יחידי,
אין פניות, אין חברים. והגא כאן —
נשינו עורות לארץ, גורלו רק בארץ יש־
ראל. חבריו לועגים לנ, "מסתדרים".
ומגא מאט בזה. "צריך לשוב להכשרה
— להתחיל מחרש, לאסוף כוח".

כעבור שבוע בא לקיבוץ ההכשרה
בקילין. ואמר: "גמרתי את התשבון
שם, מכאן אין דרך, אלא לארץ ישר־
אל". ב־1935 הוא מתכונן לעליה. קור־
נים פני: מאווי שנים מתמלאים. הנא
עולה! בינתיים חלה בדלקת הריאות.
חברים רואים ;ו במסירות רבה, הוא
קם מחטיטה, ולמחרתו הגא ב.ארשה,
מוכן לעליה.

קרוב לשלוש שנים עשה בארץ, כב־
בישים ובמקומות עבודה שינים. קור־
אים לניום למשטרה, והוא נענה.
לפני זמן נשיגד אתו חטוים מהתכשרת
והגא ישמח לקראתם, הנכנס לביתו, אל
חברתי. ודבריו הראשונים ' "אני חי,
אני נארץ ישראל, בהגנגם הפולדת, יש
טעם לחיים",

יצחק שפיס

ב.

עם משה אשל זיסברגר, בן עירי, לא
וכיתי להפגש באדן. הוא בא כמה
חדשים אחרי ושמחתי לבואו. לא בני
מפלגן אחת היינו ולא פעם נפלו בי־
נינו סכסוכים מפלגתיים. שם בעיירה.
אבל אני ידעתי היטב את סבלו טרם
שזכה לעלות לארץ. ידעתי היטב את
חייו בקבוצי ההכשרה, ה"גורד" הת־
מידי מכרך לכרך, ומתבוני לקבוץ וי־
רעתי את הפעגלות שלו אחרי שובו
מהקיבוץ — היה מן היחידים בין חב־
ריו שלא התיאש ולא הזניח את תפקידו
הציוני החלוצי. על כן שמחתי לבואו.
אך הנה הגיע ערב יום הכפורים
תרצ"ט ושם קץ לשמחתי. וכשנודע לי,
שחברי ובן־עירי נפל על משמרתו, או
התפללתי בלבי: אם הוטל עלי ליפול,
אפול'נ'א גם אני על משמרתי, כחבר.

י. ב.

נוטר במשמר הירדן.

Moshe Zisberger

(Killed in Haifa 9th of Tishrei, 5699 – October 4th, 1938)

A.

He was a Jewish policeman and fell while on duty on Yom Kippur eve 1938. He was guarding a check-point in Haifa when he was ambushed and hit by a bullet that killed him instantly. The good and happy friend is no longer with us. His happy face always beamed with optimism: "Life is good, it is worth it".

He was a native of Shebreshin, near Lublin in Polalnd and was 24 when he was killed. Shebreshin was a small town, but just prior to Zionist Congresses was enthusiastic, full of debates, vocal arguments and in spite of its small size raised much funds for the cause. Moshe was always in the center of activity, with dedication knowing that this work is his life purpose. He was among the "HeHalutz" member and here too he showed much enthusiasm and energy and was among the leaders of the local branch.

1932. The big youth rebellion. Kids were leaving their homes with only a backpack, wandering in Poland to convince other youth to join the movement. One song in their heart: Eretz Israel. And Moshe was always among the first ones. Eventually he ended in a tiny the village of Borków near Kielce. A "training company" was established there "Gush Borochow" (Borochow Bloc).

In 1933 he was approved to immigrate and he left Borków to get ready. But there were limitations on immigration and the whole Zionist situation was unclear. He had to wait. Shebreshin changed. The enthusiasm was gone. People were disappointed. He was the only one who did not give-up. His friends mocked him: "We get by" they said. But his soul longed for Eretz Israel. And he decided: "I need to go back to the training camp. I need to start again".

After a week he arrived at the training kibbutz in Kielce and said: "I am done there. From here there is only one way – to Eretz Israel". In 1935 he was finally getting ready to immigrate. His happiness had no bounds. The yearnings of many years would be finally fulfilled. Just prior to leaving he contracted pneumonia. His friends tended to him and immediately upon recovery he boarded a train to Warsaw.

He spent close to three years in Israel working hard – on roads, construction and other odd jobs. When there was a call to join the police – he responded. He worked at the police station in Haifa. A while ago, he met with some friends from the training kibbutz. They visited him in his home and he was so elated: "I am alive. I am in Eretz Israel, protecting the homeland. Life has a meaning".

Yitzhak   **Shefayim**

B.

Moshe Zisberger, was a native of my town of Shebreshin. He arrived in Israel a few months after me. Unfortunately, I was not able to meet him here. We were not of the same ideology and we had some heated arguments back home. But I knew his suffering before he immigrated to Eretz Israel. His wanderings from town to town, and from one training kibbutz to the next. He was the only one from his group who did not give up and did not abandon the Zionist pioneering ideas. Therefore I was happy to hear he arrived.

And then came Yom Kippur eve 1938 when he fell while on duty. I mourn him. And then I pray: "If I have to die, I want to die while on duty protecting my homeland just like Moshe"

I. G. a guard in Mishmar Hayrden.

Photos of Shebreshin Holocaust Victims

Eisen Ahraham

Ingber Hershel

Beitsher Moishe and daughter Yehudit

Baruch Boim

Burstin Yosele Burstin

Leibel and wife Sara(Blatt)

Blatt Yacov Mosh

Sheindel Lerner-his wife

Bleiweiss Ben-Zion

their son

Becher Simcha and Sara-children of Hanoch Becher.   *Pinchas Becher and wife*

Becher and Limuni (Cytrun) families

Berger Moshe and family

Beker Eliezer and family

Hochboim Mangze-Hersh Getzl's daughter

Gelerente Dreizel

Weinblatt Perel

The children of Berish Dreier

Wolfson family

Weinblatt Arieh

Wax Shia

Tenenboim family

Tenenboim Memel, Kulpes Rechel, Felhendler Etel

Weinstock family

Treger family

Chmielash Feigele

Zeidel Sheindel

Moishe Ledereich

David Lass

Milstein Moishe and family

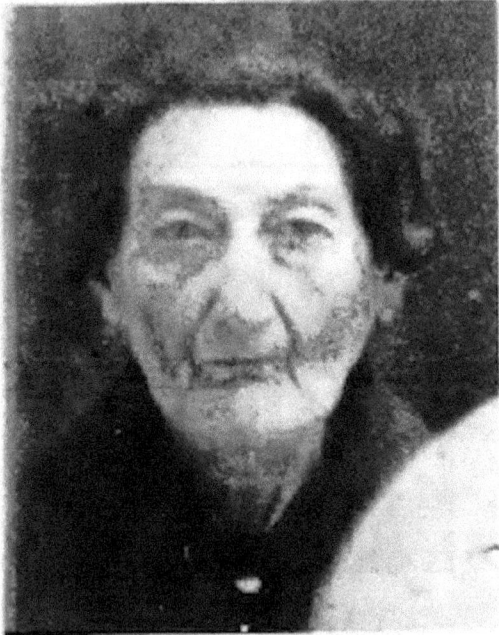

Rochel Tzimmerman

Mel Shmuel Ziche

Tzuker Moishe and Sterenfeld Yosef.

Feiler Faivel and Borik Yochnan

Zisner Bet-Ziona, with her children:

Ahraham, Mordechai, Yosef Boim

Lass family

Makrofski family

Fruchter family

Kopf Yosef.

Lerner Yechiel

Kondel Rivk

Reitman family

Kaverstock family

Reiber Feiga and her partisan children

Reiber family

Beile Sper's 2 children

Schuk Henech and family

Streicher Chaim Leizer

Steinkeler Pesach

Streicher Mirka and Muniak

Stibel Chaia Ita

Shper Gultze, Leon and Etke.

Shper Beile

Shitz Chana with her sons David and Shmuel

Shitz Rivka-the grandmother.

Shitz Yacov and David

Scher Yacov

Shmuel Chaim

Springer Chaia

Scher Hesia

English Summary

[Page I]

Book of Memory
To the Jewish Community Of Shebreshin

Published by the Association of Former Inhabitants of Shebreshin in Israel and the Diaspora

[Page II]

Members of the Editorial Board

Moshe Weinstock, Efraim Farber, Abraham Wolfson, Shimon Scher,

Zwi Traeger (Tal), Hanoch Becher, Chaya Schissel

Editor: Dov Shuval

Address: Efraim Farber, 8a Jabotinski Street, 2900 Kiriat Yam

[Page III]

Preface

This book was written in commemoration of the Community of Shebreshin, one of more than a thousand Jewish communities annihilated in cities and town–lets of Poland, and it appears on the 42th anniversary of the massacre perpetrated there, 39 years after the fall of the Nazi rule and the end of World War II. Is this not somewhat late? Has not its day passed and its importance diminished? Has not all been told yet of the destruction of Polish Jewry? Was the subject not yet fully exhausted?

And yet, this dark period in the history of the people is not forgotten and all that was written until now does not exhaust the magnitude of the loss: the tragic end of the deep–rooted Jewry of Poland, the Jewry of a thousand years.

Many are the books of "Yiskor", the memorial prayer, published in memory of annihilated communities, but it does not fill the need. Every one of the survivors of the Holocaust abreacts in memories of his past; everyone wants to see himself reflected in his book, his town and wants to perpetuate what is closest to him personally.

Each city and town–let was in a way a small world until itself; a Jewish world with all its signs and symbols, with its public institutions, political parties, organizations, synagogues and academies – a collective tradition are remembered and demand expression.

And such was Shebreshin, a township in the province of Zamosc, in the district of Lublin, counting 8000 inhabitants with about 3000 Jews among them before World War II.

Not only did many years pass since then, but revolutionary changes took place in many spheres: in social life, policies, conceptions varied, outlook altered, new values were created and the State of Israel was founded.

[Page IV]

And yet, there is to a certain extent, a yearning for just the very period that knew full and perfect Jewish life, community life, that feeling of "togetherness", to be one in sorrow and one in hope.

*

Much is to be told, therefore, of the problems involved in editing the book.

Most of the material was written by survivors of the Holocaust: part of the incidents were yet noted down abroad, close to the time of their occurrence. Of course, therein lies an advantage as memories were still fresh. Most of these records were, therefore, made in Yiddish, either before or shortly after the arrival of the townsmen in the State of Israel; in other words, before these new immigrants were able to acquire sufficient knowledge of Hebrew to enable them to give expression to the feelings in their hearts in that language. Only a very few records were originally put to paper in Hebrew.

So as to make it possible for the young generation, among them the children of survivors of the Holocaust, those born in Israel who are not conversant with the Yiddish language, to read the book thus not remaining strangers to, but sharing the experiences and feelings of their parents and realizing what this generation who suffered the pangs of hell went through, we translated part of the material into the Hebrew language. In consideration of those townspeople now living in the diaspora, we felt the need to publish a synopsis in the English language as well, in particular for the young generation in the United States of America and in Canada.

No historians nor authors versed in the art of writing composed the book. Those who wrote it, each one from his point of view, described the experiences he went through – restrictions, persecution, degradation, life in days of calm, the vivacious and the many–hued way of life sprouting from deep roots, the will to live, the fight for survival. This again brought various disadvantages, such as partial lack of dates of occurrences. Of course, in the torrent of the nightmarish atrocities, it was neither feasible or did it occur to anyone to keep chronological order; only a very few, those with a feeling for history, thought at the time of committing reminiscences to paper so as to leave the memory of the horrible misdeeds to generations to come.

[Page V]

Not every recording is a work of art and not every song is the perfect lyrical creation. Here, people who are neither writers nor composers, endeavoured to express in their own way their deepest emotions and recount the history of their lives during a period fraught with calamity and under certain conditions. But it is just the authentic description, the personal observation, the direct attempt that have special flavour and give documentary value to the written material.

When collecting the material, no attention was given to division of subjects. T our regret, no guidance was given at the time to the contributors and each wrote at his own discretion, without planning. And so it came to pass that many wrote "about everything"; a few words on the way of life in the town–let, some sentences about the

Holocaust period – on the escape and the wanderings, on the suffering and the destruction, but sometimes also some comments on characters and persons, etc., and all this blended together.

Since each subject was in most cases only lightly touched upon, just a smattering and all in "one package", that written does not, of course, fully exhaust the subject matter; such writing does not lend itself to give expression to any one subject whatsoever. Henceforth, there were repetitions, duplications and lack of coordination of the material submitted. It was, therefore, none too easy to sort the material and select that worthy of publication and to assemble the book.

It should be mentioned, however, that there were also those who, with their own insight and understanding, brought memories and evaluations to paper in a detailed manner and on a suitable level.

In the course of time, there were changes in the editorial staff of the book – a circumstance which made the work difficult and impaired its continuity. On the other hand, irregularity in collecting the material caused considerable time delay in dealing with it.

Those participating in the book are scattered in various places in Israel and abroad. This presented difficulties when it became expedient to clarify one detail or another.

However, in spite of all difficulties and limitations, we did our best to achieve perfection. We managed to overcome all these obstacles by careful selection, precise editing and made efforts to complement the

[Page VI]

missing. We believe that we brought the book to a fitting level of expression.

*

The editorial staff took pains to ensure that the material remains true to its original form without changes being made but as far as possible, adhering to the version of the participants, albeit not in a distorted manner.

The editors had no political approach when assembling the book. If here and there a sympathizing tendency with anyone political ideology emerges, this has its origin in the natural and legitimate inclination of the writer and is, of course, his responsibility.

We endeavoured to correct the style but took care not to beautify and polish unduly; not to impose too literary and flowery a form of expression but also not to present any material in a blemished style. We tried to avoid presenting confusion and disorder, tastelessness and leanness of form, but as far as possible, sifted and arranged clear and precise material.

We also took care to preserve the essence of concepts, the terms and expressions of the local people and the specific environment.

*

As is customary in town–lets, the people, in general, were not called by their surnames. Nearly everybody had a kind of nickname, a given name – whether after that of the father or the mother – sometimes after his profession or occupation, but also after his outer appearance, or in memory of an incident that happened but at times, also derisive and insulting. These nicknames were so popular as to make it difficult to identify the people without them, so that we did not omit them.

It was particularly difficult to "hebrewnize" these given names since in that guise they would not be recognizable. For that reason, some of these names were not translated but brought in their original Yiddish version.

*

Our gratitude is extended to all who assisted us in this sacred task – to those who contributed their writings and to those who donated funds, their generosity making the publication of the book possible.

[Page VII]

Special heartfelt thanks are deserved by our friend Mendel Boim, who, over many years, gave generously of his time and effort in collecting the material from contributors in Israel and abroad. He was the address for contacts with friends in Israel, Poland, U.S.A., Canada and Argentina, and encouraged them to write. He did all this voluntarily. The five brochures he published were the swallows that heralded the appearance of the book and laid the foundation to it.

*

Today, so long a time after the destruction of the town–let, its former inhabitants are prepared to forgive it all its shortcomings and omissions – and are longing for it. As is known, people tend to return to the place of their youth, to search for their roots. But no, Heaven forbid, no – they do not wish to return to the town–let not even for a short visit. There is no one for them to visit. It is there that their loved ones were killed and butchered and the few survivors escaped to wherever their legs could take them. No happiness could be found there, only pain and anguish. There are only a very few of the refugee–survivors who have the wish and courage to visit the place of desolation.

The town–let has certainly changed its appearance with time – no doubt new buildings have been erected on graves and ruins but they, the former townsmen carry its image in their hearts, as it was then, before those dreadful events. The imaginary town let has, therefore, become a symbol around which they gather as one family.

The townsmen, today, scattered and dispersed, live on various continents at great distance from one another. Their hearts are divided. There they are in their new homes, spending their days and nights with their families, at work, at business, but they feel a closer affinity with the friends of their youth with whom they can exchange reminiscences of the past, talk of the present and exchange hopes for the future, discuss many more subjects with them than with their close neighbours. It is the share heritage that creates a bond between them. The man from New York, Montreal, Buenos Aires or from San Paulo, feels closer to his fellow–townsman from Haifa, Tel–Aviv and Jerusalem than to his present–day next door neighbour.

[Page VIII]

It is natural for the book of memories to appear in the State of Israel. Not only because this is the centre of the Jewish people, but also because it is here that the largest number of survivors from our township are living.

May this book be a sign and symbol for shared fate, for shared meditation. Here the contributors gave their thoughts, their hopes, the abundance of their soul and they desire to draw from it the feeling of reciprocity, of "togetherness" beyond geographical boundaries. It would appear that, notwithstanding the contrasts, differences and disputes of the past – here they are once more standing together as one, hand–in–hand, united in feeling and in thought.

The Editorial Board

NAME INDEX

This is the Name Index for this English translation pagination, not the
original Yizkor Book

C

D

L

M

N

O

P

www.ingramcontent.com/pod-product-compliance
Lightning Source LLC
Chambersburg PA
CBHW082007150426
42814CB00005BA/253